Spiritual, Religious, and Faith-Based Practices in Chronicity

This book explores how people draw upon spiritual, religious, or faith-based practices to support their mental wellness amidst forms of chronicity. From diverse global contexts and spiritual perspectives, this volume critically examines several chronic conditions, such as psychosis, diabetes, depression, oppressive forces of colonization and social marginalization, attacks of spirit possession, or other forms of persistent mental duress.

As an inter- and transdisciplinary collection, the chapters include innovative ethnographic observations and over 300 in-depth interviews with care providers and individuals living in chronicity, analyzed primarily from the phenomenological and hermeneutic meaning-making traditions. Overall, this book depicts a modern global era in which spiritualty and religion maintain an important role in many peoples' lives, underscoring a need for increased awareness, intersectoral collaboration, and practical training for varied care providers.

This book will be of interest to scholars of religion and health, the sociology and psychology of religion, medical and psychological anthropology, religious studies, and global health studies, as well as applied health and mental health professionals in psychology, social work, physical and occupational therapy, cultural psychiatry, public health, and medicine.

Andrew R. Hatala, PhD, is an Associate Professor in the Department of Community Health Sciences, Max Rady College of Medicine, Rady Faculty of Health Sciences, University of Manitoba. As a practicing member of the global Bahá'í religious community, and a medical and psychological anthropologist with interest in cultural psychiatry, spirituality, and health psychology, his published works and research focus on qualitative methodologies, culture and spirituality, mental health, Indigenous healing and epistemology, Indigenous nosology of mental illness and disorder, and resilience and wellness among Indigenous youth populations.

Kerstin Roger, PhD, is a Professor in the Department of Community Health Sciences, Max Rady College of Medicine, Rady Faculty of Health Sciences, University of Manitoba. Her current research focusses on chronic illness, aging, caregiving, and the family. Dr Roger has been a Principal Investigator on multi-site, nationally funded research (e.g., PHAC, SSHRC, Movember, federal government), as well as conducting provincial and regionally funded research. She has worked on international collaborations, local not-for-profit community initiatives, and continues to co-author and engage graduate students in her research.

Routledge Studies in Religion

Cosmologies of Pure Realms and the Rhetoric of Pollution
Yohan Yoo and James W. Watts

Former Muslims in Europe
Between Secularity and Belonging
Maria Vliek

Religion and Violence in Western Traditions
Selected Studies
Edited by André Gagné, Jennifer Guyver, and Gerbern S. Oegema

Jewish Approaches to Hinduism
A History of Ideas from Judah Ha-Levi to Jacob Sapir (12th–19th centuries)
Richard G. Marks

Spiritual, Religious, and Faith-Based Practices in Chronicity
An Exploration of Mental Wellness in Global Context
Edited by Andrew R. Hatala and Kerstin Roger

An Anthropology of the Qur'an
Ahmed Achrati

Contrasts in Religion, Community, and Structure at Three Homeless Shelters
Changing Lives
Ines W. Jindra, Michael Jindra and Sarah DeGenero

Enhancement Fit for Humanity
Perspectives on Emerging Technologies
Michael Baggot

For more information about this series, please visit: https://www.routledge.com/religion/series/SE0669

Spiritual, Religious, and Faith-Based Practices in Chronicity

An Exploration of Mental Wellness in Global Context

Edited by
Andrew R. Hatala and Kerstin Roger

LONDON AND NEW YORK

First published 2022
by Routledge
2 Park Square, Milton Park, Abingdon, Oxon OX14 4RN

and by Routledge
605 Third Avenue, New York, NY 10158

Routledge is an imprint of the Taylor & Francis Group, an informa business

© 2022 selection and editorial matter, Andrew R. Hatala and Kerstin Roger; individual chapters, the contributors

The right of Andrew R. Hatala and Kerstin Roger to be identified as the authors of the editorial material, and of the authors for their individual chapters, has been asserted in accordance with sections 77 and 78 of the Copyright, Designs and Patents Act 1988.

Trademark notice: Product or corporate names may be trademarks or registered trademarks, and are used only for identification and explanation without intent to infringe.

With the exception of Chapter 1, 6, 7, 10 and 12 no part of this book may be reprinted or reproduced or utilised in any form or by any electronic, mechanical, or other means, now known or hereafter invented, including photocopying and recording, or in any information storage or retrieval system, without permission in writing from the publishers.

Chapters 1, 6, 7, 10 and 12 of this book are available for free in PDF format as Open Access from the individual product page at www.routledge.com. They have been made available under a Creative Commons Attribution-Non Commercial-No Derivatives 4.0 license.

British Library Cataloguing-in-Publication Data
A catalogue record for this book is available from the British Library

Library of Congress Cataloging-in-Publication Data
A catalog record has been requested for this book

ISBN: 978-0-367-48912-0 (hbk)
ISBN: 978-1-032-07756-7 (pbk)
ISBN: 978-1-003-04350-8 (ebk)

DOI: 10.4324/9781003043508

Typeset in Sabon
by Taylor & Francis Books

For my mother, who has always instilled in me a deeper sense of faith.
Kerstin Roger

For my daughter Tsedal, that your future steps remain grounded in spirit.
Andrew R. Hatala

Contents

List of illustrations ix
List of contributors x
Acknowledgements xiv

1 Chronicity, mental wellness, and spirituality: An introduction 1
  KERSTIN ROGER AND ANDREW R. HATALA

2 Religiosity and spirituality in mental health contexts: Perceptions of psychologists and chaplains 16
  MARTA HELENA DE FREITAS, EVELYN FIGUEIRA LIMA RUAS AND EMMANUEL IFEKA NWORA

3 Responding with Anishinaabek values: Understanding the importance of living as a spiritual being for mental wellness 37
  LESLIE MCGREGOR AND GERALD PATRICK MCKINLEY

4 Tradition and modernity in Somali experiences of spirit possession: An ethnographic exploration 57
  AARON MORATZ

5 Politics and aesthetics of care: Chronic affliction and spiritual healing in Brazilian Kardecism 76
  HELMAR KURZ

6 Nourishing exchanges: Care, love, and chronicity in Lourdes 100
  SARAH GOLDINGAY, PAUL DIEPPE, SARA WARBER AND EMMYLOU RAHTZ

7 Miyo-wîcêhetowin in the city: Indigenous youth spirituality, good ancestors, and mental wellness through healing journeys on the land 124
  DARRIEN MORTON, KELLEY BIRD-NAYTOWHOW AND ANDREW R. HATALA

8 Psychosis, spiritual crisis, and narrative transformation: An ethnography of spiritual peer-support networks in the United Kingdom 148
RAPHAËLLE REMY-FISCHLER

9 Prayer camps, healing, and the management of chronic mental illness in Ghana: A qualitative phenomenological inquiry 173
FRANCIS BENYAH

10 "God takes care of it": Spiritual practices and mental wellness of people living with type 2 diabetes in Belize 195
LINDSAY ALLEN, LUCIA ELLIS AND ANDREW R. HATALA

11 Cultures of wellness and recovery: Exploring religion and chronicity in relation to severe mental illness 221
G. ERIC JARVIS, ROB WHITLEY AND MARIE NATHALIE LEBLANC

12 Global mental wellness and spiritual geographies of care: Concluding remarks 247
ANDREW R. HATALA AND KERSTIN ROGER

Index 271

Illustrations

Figures

2.1	Positive relations between religiosity and spirituality and mental health	26
2.2	Negative relations between religiosity and spirituality and mental health	28
2.3	Ways of handling religiosity or spirituality and mental health	29
8.1	Campbell's Hero's Journey Narrative	156
10.1	Recommendations for coordinated service provision between health care providers and community leaders	214

Tables

6.1	The nexus of beneficial factors	119
7.1	Data collection procedures for CBPR Project 2014–15 and CBPR Project 2017–18	131
11.1	Characteristics of cases (n=41)	230
11.2	Religious/spiritual representations of the presenting clinical problem (n=38)	231

Contributors

Kerstin Roger, PhD, is Professor in the Department of Community Health Sciences (Rady Faculty of Health Sciences), Max Rady College of Medicine, University of Manitoba, Canada. Dr Roger has been a Principal Investigator on multi-site, nationally funded research (e.g., PHAC, SSHRC, Movember, federal government), and has conducted provincially and regionally funded research.

Andrew R. Hatala, PhD, is an Associate Professor in the Department of Community Health Sciences (Rady Faculty of Health Sciences), Max Rady College of Medicine, University of Manitoba, Canada. Dr. Hatala is a practicing member of the global Bahá'í religious community, and a medical and psychological anthropologist with interest in cultural psychiatry, spirituality, and health psychology.

Marta Helena de Freitas, PhD, has been a Professor at the Catholic University of Brasília (UCB) since 1989. Her research includes the psychology of religion, thanatology, gerontology, the Rorschach psychodiagnostics, phenomenology, and training in psychology and mental health. She is currently the Coordinator of the Religion, Mental Health and Culture Laboratory at Psychology Graduation Program at UCB and a member of the International Association for the Psychology of Religion (IAPR).

Evelyn Figueira Lima Ruas, MA, is currently a postgraduate student in Psychoanalysis, Psychopathology, and Psychotherapy in Adolescence and in Brazilian Sign Language (LIBRAS). She teaches Psychology of Religion at the Theological Faculty of the Assembly of God of Brasilia (FATADEB). She is also a psychologist. She is a member of the Religion, Mental Health and Culture Laboratory Research Group.

Emmanuel Ifeka Nwora, PhD, is the chaplain of the Catholic University of Brasília, Brazil and a member of the British Association for the Study of Religions (BASR) and the International Association for the Psychology of Religion (IAPR). He is also a psychologist.

Leslie McGregor is the Family Well-Being Manager for Whitefish River First Nation, Canada. Her work focuses on the development of a strong and healthy community through the incorporation of local, traditional knowledge. She is a passionate advocate for youth in her community and social change. McGregor is a proud Anishinaabekwe Indigenous woman with strong connection to her family, land, water, and community.

Gerald Patrick McKinley, PhD, is an Assistant Professor in the Department of Pathology and Laboratory Medicine and is Core Faculty in the Schulich Interfaculty Program in Public Health at the University of Western Ontario. He is a Medical Anthropologist who trained in the social aetiology of mental illness at the Centre for Addictions and Mental Health in Toronto. His research focuses on community-based mental wellness and adolescent suicide prevention in First Nations communities.

Aaron Moratz, MA, is Dean of Postgraduate Studies and Deputy Coordinator of Research, Development, and Innovations at University of Burao, Togdheer, Somaliland. His particular interest is in Somali Studies and phenomenological approaches to the study of spirit possession.

Helmar Kurz, PhD candidate, a research fellow of Professor Helene Basu within the DFG-granted project *Diversification of Mental Health: Therapeutic Spaces of Brazilian Spiritism*. He is a board member of the Association of Anthropology and Medicine (www.agem.de) and the related journal CURARE (http://agem.de/en/curare/about-curare/), as well as engaged in other notable studies related to the Aesthetics of Healing.

Paul Dieppe, MD, is Emeritus Professor of Health and Wellbeing at the University of Exeter Medical School. His main passion before his retirement was being able, as a doctor, to work on the problems of people with severe arthritis. He has had two main research interests, first in osteoarthritis, and second in the power of caring in health care. He currently does research on caring and healing.

Sarah Goldingay, PhD, is a Senior Lecturer in the Department of Drama and Director of the Centre for Performance, Sciences, and Community at the University of Exeter. An interdisciplinary specialist, her current research interests focus on how healing is facilitated or retarded by the interpretation of context. She is a regular presenter on BBC Radio 4, where she speaks about how her research relates to the big questions of twenty-first-century ethics and spirituality.

Emmylou Rahtz, PhD, is a Research Fellow at the European Centre for Environment and Human Health, University of Exeter, researching healing responses and how caring is understood in society.

Sara L. Warber, MD, is a Clinical Professor Emerita of Family Medicine at the University of Michigan (UM), Ann Arbor, MI. She co-founded the UM Integrative Medicine program. Her research focuses on how holistic health programs and time spent in nature affect human well-being. She is an Honorary Professor at the European Centre for Environment and Human Health,

University of Exeter, where she completed a Fulbright Scholarship. She is currently a Scholar at The Institute for Integrative Health in Baltimore, MD.

Darrien Morton, MSc, received his Bachelor of Arts (Honors) degree in Health Sciences from Simon Fraser University, British Columbia in 2014 and his MSc in Community Health Sciences at the University of Manitoba in 2018. His research interests align at the intersection of participatory action research, Indigenous health and resiliency, and youth engagement and decision-making. His current research centers on supporting Indigenous youth, families, and organizations involved with the Child Welfare System through research, policy, and community-based advocacy.

Kelley Bird-Naytowhow, MA, is a Cree First Nations from Montreal Lake reserve Saskatchewan and is currently pursuing his Master's degree in Social Work at First Nations University of Canada. Kelley is passionately committed to working with Indigenous youth and local organizations serving youth in Saskatoon, Saskatchewan, Canada and has extensive community-based research experience working on several diverse research projects over the last eight years. He is also known in a spiritual or ceremonial context as Black Buffalo Man.

Raphaëlle Remy-Fischler, MSc, holds a BA in social anthropology from the School of Oriental and African Studies in (London, UK), and an MSc in medical anthropology and sociology from the University of Amsterdam. Ongoing work and interests include a focus on mental health and psychiatric care amongst refugees in Paris. She holds an interest in peer-support and community-based care.

Francis Benyah, PhD, is currently a PhD candidate in the Study of Religions, Åbo Akademi University, Turku, Finland. He has also served as a Visiting Research Fellow in the Minority Research Program of the Åbo Akademi University. His research interest focuses on African Pentecostal Christianity with a special interest on how it intersects and interacts with public life in areas such as media, politics, health, and human rights.

Lindsay Allen, MSc, works and studies in the Department of Community Health Sciences at the University of Manitoba. Her research areas include anti-racist education, the Truth and Reconciliation process in Canada, the relationships between biomedicine and Indigenous medicines, psychospiritual aspects of health, models of integrative health care, cultural safety and cultural humility, land-based education, ethnobotany, maternal and child health, diabetes, chronicity, international health, and program evaluation.

Lucia Ellis is currently the coordinator of the Belize Diabetes Self Care Program. She is an advocate of culture as the foundation of the human identity incorporated into her 45-year professional career as a health advocate, teacher, counsellor, and consultant. Ms. Ellis is a writer and recently launched a book "A Rainbow in Her Eye." She retired from teaching, and registered her organization NUMASA Wellness Resource Centre (NWRC). Her work has also included networking with: TRAMIL (Traditional Medicine in the Islands), Martinique, West Indies; Campus Yard, Trinidad & Tobago; Kairi, Trinidad & Tobago; the University of Manitoba, Canada; and The Garifuna Heritage Foundation in St. Vincent & the Grenadines.

G. Eric Jarvis, MD, is an Associate Professor of Psychiatry at McGill University and Director of the Cultural Consultation Service and the Culture and Psychosis Working Group at the Jewish General Hospital. His clinical work involves the assessment of immigrants and refugees with early psychosis. His research interests include the cultural adaptation of interventions in early psychosis, language barriers in mental health care, religion and mental health, and the process of cultural consultation.

Rob Whitley, PhD, is an Associate Professor of Psychiatry at McGill University and a Research Scientist at the Douglas Research Centre. He has published over 100 papers in the field of social psychiatry, and his research interests include recovery, stigma, men's mental health, and religion and mental health.

Marie-Nathalie Leblanc, PhD, is an Anthropologist and Professor in the Département de sociologie at Université du Québec à Montréal (UQAM). Since 2018, she holds a UQAM Research Chair in Contemporary West African Islam (Chaire ICAO, https://chaireicao.uqam.ca). Her publications deal with religious transformations in West Africa, civil society, youth, and women. She is currently leading a research project entitled: "'What have become of the marabouts?' Occult trajectories and social change in West Africa" (SSHRC). Professor LeBlanc acts as a cultural mediator at the McGill University Cultural Consultation Service in the Institute of Community and Family Psychiatry of the Sir Mortimer B. Davis – Jewish General Hospital.

Acknowledgements

We would like to acknowledge the following contributions: Lindsay Allen, for editing the final submission copy; Drs Robert Lorway and Javier Mignone in the Department of Community Health Sciences at the University of Manitoba, who both offered useful comments and critical feedback regarding drafts of our conclusion chapter; and all the participants in all studies who came forward to share sometimes vulnerable stories of chronic illness, workplace realities, and their stories of faith. We would also like to give a special thank you to all the authors who have inspired us to work in this area, as well as to our co-authors. We would like to acknowledge funders who support research in this area, as well as the practitioners around the globe who strive to bring wellness to their communities. We thank our partners at home for supporting the other aspects of this journey.

1 Chronicity, mental wellness, and spirituality

An introduction

Kerstin Roger and Andrew R. Hatala

Introduction

This book came into being by listening to stories of research participants living with chronic illness. Spirituality and religion, and in that context faith, emerged in the lives of many individuals as an enduring and unavoidable narrative. While this thread was evident in the lives of those affected by chronic illness, it also became clear that service provider narratives demonstrated a gap in their training, institutional support, or overall awareness when working professionally with clients' spiritual, religious, or faith-based practices and queries. This recognition led us as co-editors, each independently in our own work, to see that there was a gap in the literature concerning the knowledge and lessons learned about more effectively integrating discussions of spirituality and religion into service provision, in particular on the topic of chronic illness. As a start, our scoping review was published in 2017, exploring intersections between service provision, chronic illness, and spirituality or religion (Roger and Hatala 2017).

This exciting new collection is a robust addition to the current literature in the area, which has been scant in addressing the often-charged issue of spirituality and religion, one that is increasingly relevant for many global communities. Authors describe evidence-based, empirical research investigating participants' experiences of mental wellness in the context of spirituality, religion, and faith, widely defined; they represent dynamic and diverse views and perspectives from around the globe, including research conducted in rural and urban spaces. The chapters explore spirituality and religion in a way that does not presuppose benefits or pitfalls, but rather considers how people explore their own day-to-day practices and clinical work in the context of chronicity. Nor are the chapters designed to place value on any specific type of faith, religion, or spiritual practice; rather, they are included here because they focus on people's lived experiences, attending to both social and individual, structural, and existential contexts (Roger and Hatala 2017).

While the chapters could have been grouped by conceptual themes (e.g., land and space, mind, and wellness), grouping them by region was another consideration (e.g., North America, Africa, Europe), as was grouping them by stated chronic illness or religious affiliation (e.g., Christianity, Islam). In the end, we eliminated grouping the chapters with the agreement that this approach would simplify or reduce the richness of the findings. As such, we argue that the themes of living with chronic illness and working with those who do invite wellness and spirituality to mirror each other regardless of the type of condition, faith base, or region in which the studies have taken place. The unifying principle is that each of the authors explores: the apparent role of spirituality and religion in shaping mental wellness; the practices described by participants associated with unique places, cultures, and contexts; the participants' reflections on health and well-being, alongside their hopes for recovery and healing, all of which endure throughout the collection. The authors' research findings stand on their own, despite these characteristic variations. In an effort to allow the multiplicity of participant experiences to speak for themselves, this collection is grounded in a mandate to uncover in an empirical or evidence-based manner how spirituality and religion emerged, both for those living with chronic conditions and for those who are care professionals and health providers offering services to them.

As these chapters demonstrate, individuals come together at times in formal and organized institutions (e.g., hospitals), and at other times, in less formal community settings and rural spaces, to share in and produce opportunities for strengthening the spirit and mental wellness, and the possibility of physical healing and resilience. Some accounts reveal the tensions that exist between service providers and their training, as they consider their clients within institutions they inhabit and the affiliated professional mandates and policies, and as they undertake the daily work of care and caring. The tensions between service provision, training and skills, institutional policy, and participants' needs are real here. These findings foreground, in detail, the complexity of accepting spirituality and religion as powerful forces in the lives of those depicted, people living with diverse chronic conditions. Other accounts reveal the commitment of professionals living in specific faith-based communities and their efforts to develop pathways to healing and wellness, comforting practices, and new coping strategies that re-direct or re-interpret experiences of illness and pain. In some cases, authors reveal the use of a spirit world or archetypes as a healing strategy. Recovery emerges as part of an important tonal landscape in which the fugal counterpoint between living with mental illness and using religion or spirituality towards wellness is not just a single voice but a choir. Most often, the authors describe how spirituality includes deepening a sense of meaning-making and purpose for their participants despite their suffering with chronic illness or helping those who do towards recovery or new definitions of wellness (i.e., being "well" despite living with chronic illness). Prayer in solitude or together in community, reading from meaningful texts, or learning to be a "good ancestor" are each an example of strategies revealed that aim to move participants towards transformation, healing, and self-defined wellness.

This inter- and transdisciplinary collection includes contributions from health care, the humanities, medical anthropology, and social sciences. We take as our theoretical point of departure the phenomenological and hermeneutic meaning-making traditions and share a concern for the manifold struggles that abound amidst the management of chronic conditions. In so doing, this collection makes a substantive contribution to the role of spirituality and faith in health and wellness, with a focus on the personal lived practices of spirituality and religion in contexts of chronicity. The main themes include an exploration of how spirituality and faith-based practices can support people (or not) as they live with(in) chronic conditions of various kinds.

We include authors from around the globe who explore how specific geographic spaces or unique places, including Indigenous notions of "land" or alternatively religious pilgrimage sites, are central to the practices and meanings associated with religious, spiritual, or faith-based striving amidst chronicity. Sacred spaces become central in some of the chapters, where hope and transformation are linked to healing, practicing, and simply being in those spaces. There, the space itself becomes a focal point for the manifestation of spiritual practice and hope towards some kind of new found wellness. As a result, it offers some form of amelioration amidst chronicity. Community emerges as highly relevant in many of these land-based spaces and indicates an interpersonal site for exploration of the connection between faith-based practices and how these might shape interpersonal domains of social suffering in community. Examples include authors who explore histories of colonization or people who otherwise live with profound stigma due to mental illness in mainstream society but feel valued and accepted in these communities and spaces. The chapters demonstrate a great diversity in existing mental wellness and health concerns and cultural contexts through global problems. The authors explore cultural approaches that shape ideas about spirituality, religion, health, and wellness in new ways, spaces, and contexts that inform coping strategies, forms of resistance, help-seeking practices, ideas for recovery, or self-care more broadly from a global perspective.

Set against the cornerstone of chronicity, the authors expand our understanding of how their participants live out their daily lives to promote wellness through, and sometimes despite, spirituality and religion. At times this involves a focus on spiritual entities and how these intersect with individual experiences of conditions that can shape a "sick" or "marginalized" role in society but also, how individual agency and performative notions of a wellness identity challenge discourses of illness, marginalization, or disability in such contexts. Sustaining a framework of chronicity assists in building a cohesive argument in favor of much needed further research in this area. This collection revitalizes the understanding that we live in a global context in which faith continues to play an important role, and religious and cultural variations exist and are becoming commonplace no matter where we live and work. All of this underscores the need to establish awareness, training, and tools for professionals working within their own communities. In all chapters, the authors strive to highlight how practitioners, either medical, social, or faith-based, are assisting those with various chronic conditions within health care settings, hospitals, and communities, including challenging "what works" within these settings and systems. This includes the exploration of what is most at stake for people who draw on faith or spirituality in their management of chronic conditions and those who support them but particularly also the moral contours of their daily experiences

(Kleinman and Hall-Clifford 2010). The collection brings to mind concerns in modern health care around "quality of care" and how recovery should and can look, including discourses around contradictory faith practices between "clients" and professionals and how such interactions are sometimes managed and negotiated on behalf of others both usefully and to their own detriment. The richness of these chapters invites further reflection and exploration of this evident gap in the literature.

Chronic illness as context

A key health crisis and social issue facing humanity today is the increasing burden of "chronic" conditions. While the context of the "chronic" condition is most well known as medical- and treatment-oriented, this collection reflects on chronicity beyond the diagnosis of chronic medical conditions (Manderson and Smith-Morris, 2010) and brings a critical lens to the exploration of daily experiences of various forms of chronic conditions. The emerging focus is one of mental wellness, although several conditions or contexts are referenced by our authors. As a framework for considering persistent forms of distress, chronicity draws together developed and developing countries, the global North and South, East or West, including all contemporary human populations, "uniting us in desires for improved prevention, treatment, and care" (Kleinman and Hall-Clifford 2010, 247). In this context, this collection explores spirituality and faith-based practices of mental wellness while people are living amidst conditions that might incur struggle and distress for themselves but also for their families, their communities, and those who care for them.

The contemporary emergence of chronic conditions as a dedicated area of international attention arises from multiple intersecting factors and social processes. In many parts of the world, medical science and technological innovations have allowed patients who endure significant health problems to live considerably longer than only a few decades prior. People living with (by way of example) heart disease, diabetes, amyotrophic lateral sclerosis (ALS), multiple sclerosis (MS), Parkinson's disease (PD), tuberculosis (TB), many forms of cancer, and HIV/AIDS all have the potential to live relatively long and fulfilling lives today. The 2020–2021 pandemic, COVID-19, exacted a new narrative related to chronic illness and health and ongoing persistent forms of social or individual distress. From another vantage point, places around the globe mired with insistent poverty, wars, environmental devastation, and various forms of social suffering, precarity, structural violence, or oppression all shape another form of chronic condition or "crisis *as* context" (Vigh 2006). People come to endure and struggle against unjust social forces that can oppose and limit their agency and wellness in significant ways, which can also be heightened when living with chronic conditions considered to be medical. This increase in what we are framing as chronicity, in turn, creates a significant challenge for and places a significant burden on health care systems and helping professions of various kinds, in both professional and popular, home-based sectors (Mattingly, Gron and Meinert 2011). Along these lines, Kleinman and Hall-Clifford (2010, 250) argued that there is inadequate attention on daily lived experiences of wellness among chronicity and that "chronic conditions and quality of care need to be included in our discourse and in our funding allocations in global health programming."

Chronicity theory

The concept of chronicity first gained attention in a special issue of *Social Science and Medicine* in 1990. In his introduction to the issue on medical anthropology and chronic disease, Anselm Strauss (1990) drew attention to the social and cultural complexities of chronic diseases and their distinctiveness in different settings. Following this, Sue Estroff (1993) used chronicity to discuss her research on schizophrenia. Chronicity, according to Estroff, incorporated symbolic and meaning-centered processes, such as inter- and intrapersonal conflicts that stem from a struggle to reinstate and negotiate who "I am" in the face of persistent illness. With a focus on the meaning-centered aspects of illness experiences over time, chronicity here described both the identity-related and social changes that occur in a person's life, particularly with respect to relationships and social roles (Estroff 1993). Manderson and Smith-Morris's (2010) edited volume, *Chronic Conditions and Fluid States*, advanced chronicity theory by including studies from non-Western contexts. From its early use, chronicity was historically linked to Western societies where individualistic identities prevail, but it has more recently been applied cross-culturally to explore both chronic and infectious diseases, and here we refer to mental wellness as a key thread in our work. For instance, Good et al. (2010) reported that culturally specific models of psychosis etiology, spiritual beliefs, and family care in Yogyakarta, Indonesia help schizophrenia sufferers stabilize or recover from their symptoms, rather than experience the illness as a degenerative condition.

Today, chronicity helps draw attention to the fluctuations amidst challenging life circumstances over time. Chronic conditions are thus distinctive because they do not end; rather they become entangled in people's work, families, and life stories. Chronic conditions impact everyday routines, functioning, and capability as people are forced to grapple with mortality and their human limitations as a part of their daily routines. Indeed, by advancing the notion of "chronic homework," Mattingly, Gron, and Meinert (2011) drew our attention to the kind of cultural work that patients and families are expected to carry out in their home or "popular health sector" during the day-to-day management of their chronic conditions. These authors argue that such "low tech" social technologies – day-to-day strategies or the work of coping – have received minimal attention in the academic literature. These issues suggest we focus on the way people cope not through crisis but *in* crisis (Vigh 2006). Doing so will provide valuable insight into this increasingly important, and increasingly common, area of human life. The authors in this collection do this brilliantly, offering much richness and texture to their daily experiences and work in this area.

Spiritual, religious, and faith-based striving

Despite a wealth of concepts and research looking into the day-to-day experiences of people living with various chronic conditions, it is surprising to note that there is minimal research looking into how individuals creatively, and at times subtly, draw on aspects of their spiritual, religious, or faith-based practices to find strength and build meaning amidst their sometimes distressing experiences. This becomes an especially important area of focus in the current context of globally increasing chronic conditions (Roger and Hatala 2017) but also in the more pronounced and often charged conversations surrounding religious, spiritual, and faith-based practices around the globe, evidenced even more so through wider access to social media. Understanding this, it is immeasurably valuable to reference the work of Koenig et al. (2012), who notably found that religion and related beliefs and practices of spirituality can in fact have a protective impact on those living with mental disorders and distress.

Identified in our chapters are themes that deepen and explore these issues, including: the creation and recreation of complex networks of care based on sacred relationships; the immense efforts people make to be well despite local and global challenges; the varied resources they draw upon in creating new communities intertwined with their attempts to carry out wellness (Mattingly, Gron and Meinert 2011, 354). Cutting across many of these themes, we contend and our authors demonstrate that spiritual, religious, and faith-based strivings are approached in meaningful ways but from sometimes quite disparate perspectives present in different forms across diverse cultural contexts. Indeed, individuals living with various chronic conditions continue to seek out and utilize both faith-based, religious, and/or spiritual practices in order to cope with their illnesses and life circumstances and to promote or support a general, more positive view of health and wellness (Hank and Schaan 2008; Roger and Hatala 2017). However, as our authors also illustrate, these practices are embedded in complex interpersonal relations where stigma and ostracization from the mainstream can accompany pre-existing mental health concerns.

Pargament (2002) argued that the efficacy of spiritual variables depends on the kind of religious or spiritual practice, "the criteria of well-being, the person, the situations and social context, and the degree to which the various elements of religious life are well integrated into the person's life" (169). These are all areas that the current collection of chapters, authored from around the globe, explore. Thus, just as chronicity research turns from the clinic to the home environment of patients' day-to-day work, so too, we argue, must the spiritual and faith-based health literature follow to build knowledge of the daily spiritual and faith-based practices of health maintenance, primarily regarding mental wellness within global contexts. Because some research has identified spirituality as a key resource amidst chronic conditions in health care contexts (Ai et al. 2010; Büssing and Koenig 2010; Craig et al. 2006), this book is important for individuals, families, communities, and health care practitioners. Settings include private and public spheres and popular and professional sectors. Another focus is those working closely with individuals to identify how to better utilize spiritual and faith-based resources to build mental wellness while living with and within chronic conditions. In this context, the idea that people living with chronic conditions can experience wellness, and furthermore that spirituality, religious, and faith-based practices may be supports towards wellness, may explore, problematize, and even challenge an increasingly medical approach to mental health and a medicalization of the popular health sector. This is not to ignore or excuse how religion can and has had negative impacts on individuals and communities; however, knowing and respecting this reality, this collection focuses on evidence and a strengths-based approach. The collection is exciting in its challenge for service providers in that it illustrates the convergence and possible contradictions regarding some institutionalized health care practices; at times, these authors challenge mainstream approaches to care and open the door for new ways of offering and providing services to those living with chronic illnesses.

Mental wellness

Mental wellness evolved as a key concept in each of the chapters. Framing mental wellness as important to this collection, its presence in the chapters was most often set against the *gestalt* of a more traditional notion of biomedical dualities, meaning that study findings revealed experiences of living with chronic conditions in more diverse ways than measuring individual poor health as illness. Goals of strong and resilient mental wellness, our authors reflect, co-exist despite living with chronic illness, but these need to be re-constructed and re-imagined in an ongoing way, something we note reflects the work of Charmaz (1983, 1991). Charmaz set the stage for future researchers to reconsider how people can and do live well with chronic illness. In her ground-breaking work, Charmaz addressed early on how individuals engage in reflection and transformation as they learn to live with the trajectories of chronic illness, defining wellness for themselves, and thinking of recovery beyond a medical approach to what is otherwise considered at-risk, poor health.

Mental wellness emerged as a constant theme alongside various individual and collective practices associated with a range of faith groups and types of chronic illness. Wellness as an idea gave voice to a holistic and generative, positive view of otherwise challenging daily experiences. These diverse chapters, therefore, outline how mental wellness goes beyond what individuals alone can strive for. They also posit that we shift our thinking towards broader notions of the value of spiritual, religious, or faith-based practices and resources supporting mental wellness; that we address the challenges of interacting with service providers who may not share those perspectives; and, even further, that we engage with multiple cultural discourses, diverse geographic landscapes, and community-oriented collective experiences. Mental wellness is not a solitary pursuit.

In this way, mental wellness displaces a deficit model of health or mental health where subtractions are made for measurable gaps in one's health, and throughout the book the chapter authors refuse to focus primarily (or at all) on illness-oriented and medical diagnostic terms. As such, understanding chronicity as posited by Manderson and Smith-Morris (2010) means understanding the idea of mental wellness is also shaped by our surroundings, cultures, and histories (national and global) and – we mean this in the broadest sense – understanding the impacts of social determinants on our individual and global health through empirical research, of which this book represents a global diversity, and understanding that we do not always agree or share similar views on things. Certainly, mental wellness amidst chronicity is framed by our authors to include poverty/wealth or rural/urban dichotomies, designated spaces, and particular places of practice.

As suggested by Manderscheid et al. (2010), the terms "wellness" and "illness" have historically been placed on separate continuums, with the latter placed in tandem with terms such as "deficits," "disability," and "disorders." Ideally, "good health" indicates not having any of those disease-oriented diagnoses, but as Saracci posits (1997), this is far from practical or realistic. Manderscheid et al. (2010) further argued that previous foci on diagnosis have since shifted to more person-centered foci, and they state, "wellness refers to the degree to which one feels positive and enthusiastic about life" (1). The evolution of the terms themselves over time indicates a shift in the narrative and landscape of what it means to be well, and wellness includes spiritual health for these participants. Mental health has become a more contemporary concern in the Western world, but so too have the stigma experienced by those living with mental health issues and the invisibility of their daily realities (Centre for Addiction and Mental Health, 2020). People can gain from the respectful recognition that emerges when one has a specific diagnosis, but simultaneously, recasting poor mental health within a deficit model can potentially deepen its related stigma and associated discrimination. Broadening our understanding of institutional systems and discourses surrounding "mental health" is a valid and current concern, and perhaps discussions of Global Mental Wellness, as we explore in the concluding chapter, can help.

The National Wellness Institute (2020) suggests, "wellness is a conscious, self-directed, evolving process … encompassing spiritual well-being, [and it is] positive and affirming." It posits the following six dimensions of wellness: emotional, occupational, physical, social intellectual, and spiritual. These dimensions are evident in each of the chapters, and it is worthy to note that while the Institute does not include "mental" as one of their dimensions, the Institute does include spirituality. These six dimensions also refer to personal endeavors, contextual influences, strategies, and outcomes, as does our collection. The overall gaps in the literature point to the need to find better ways to understand mental wellness through spiritual, religious, or faith-based practices in contexts of chronicity. Given the evidence and thoughtful discussion presented by our chapter authors, spirituality and religion must be addressed in this context in that each occupies a central position for many communities around the globe.

We want to make a special note here of the role of community in mental wellness, as it emerged in our chapters. According to Absolon (2010) and Health Canada (2015), wellness must also incorporate being an individual in community with others. It became clear to us that all chapters reflected the invaluable role of community – relationships to friends, family, neighbors, social groups, and intentional collections of people that were able to share in the experience of trauma and suffering with the intention of healing. Being in community, and finally, hoping to be well in community, is empirically demonstrated in the diverse collection of chapters.

In departing from an explicit illness-good health dichotomy, this book offers further empirical discussion of the "fluid states" and more subtle ebb-and-flow narratives of striving for wellness amidst chronicity (Manderson and Smith-Morris 2010), not just physically but also mentally and spiritually, a life in which wellness is often self-defined and self-managed by those living with chronic illness. For example, our authors discuss the self as a way to house mental illness but not to identify with being ill. Illness can be seen as externalized, separate, and not core to one's being. They also reflect on the journey itself, the path of transformation, rather than a single state that achieves wellness. Being on a path is both metaphoric and physical – moving on a tangible, real landscape while reviewing one's movement in one's inner state. Thus, "fluid states" becomes a very poignant framework for our collection. As well, our authors discuss service providers as they struggle to find strategies and language to better work with their clients and as clients struggle to sustain strategies and language to help service providers work with them. As Manderscheid et al. (2010) state, "wellness" incorporates ideas beyond living with illness to include subjective experiences of happiness, hope, and personal definitions of well-being. We would argue that this balance, including hope and joy, is in fact more common to the human experience where traditional notions of poor health and mental illness are not always separated from experiencing and seeking wellness. Maintaining mental wellness is the territory in which most people are situated throughout their lives, at one time or another, in their own families and communities.

Typically good health and poor health are on a measurable continuum, a path directly linked to cures and treatments; however, this book explores mental wellness as it is defined by internal and external geographies of the spirit, through journeys and transformation, through aspects of self-management in relationship to others and in community, through the hope for individual wellness, and through the ongoing practice of seeking joy even while living with suffering and pain and the possibility of no cure but still with the goal of overall good health and mental wellness.

Chapter content

Chapter 2 frames well the tensions between service providers, the institutions they work in, and the people they serve. Freitas, Ruas, and Nwora describe and compare the findings of two studies carried out in a Brazilian context with psychologists working in mental health services, and with chaplains working in different contexts, including those involving chronic mental illness. Twenty-eight professionals (13 psychologists and 15 chaplains) were interviewed in-depth using a phenomenological approach to ascertain how they perceive the relationship between religiosity, spirituality, and mental health and illness, and how they address these issues when they arise in the context of mental health care. Freitas et al. analyze and discuss the convergences and divergences between their perceptions and experiences; they explore the implications arising from this for the training and formation of multidisciplinary teams for the care of chronic mental illness, with a special emphasis on the specific and complementary roles of psychologists and chaplains in both contexts. In the end, the chapter outlines considerations and implications for public mental health policies, considering that mental health services should be prepared to approach the various manners of expression of religiosity and spirituality and their roles in coping with mental illness and the recovery of health.

McGregor and McKinley, in Chapter 3, take us to Indigenous communities in eastern Canada. Among the most central teachings for the Anishinaabek is the understanding of having a *manidoowaadizi*, or spiritual-nature, experiencing a human or physical existence. The teachings continue to instruct that, in a holistic relationship of mind, body, emotion, and spirit, the spirit impacts the mind. This chapter explores this important ontological knowledge in order to articulate the importance of using local teachings to heal the spirit when the mind and brain are negatively impacted by colonization. During the ongoing era of colonization in Anishinaabek territory, various forms of violence, including the attempted destruction of local knowledge, were enacted on the Anishinaabek. The resulting increases in negative mental health outcomes continue to be treated using Western biomedical methods rather than valuing and applying Anishinaabek knowledge. In response, the authors move away from a biomedical construct that locates mental illness as a problem to be treated in the brain. Instead, drawing on teaching from Anishinaabek Knowledge Holders, they maintain a holistic, relational ontology to understand how the spirit is a key component in long-term mental health. Examples are drawn from the ongoing collaboration between the Health Centre at Whitefish River First Nation in Ontario, Canada and their non-Anishinaabek partners. The authors explore the importance of strength and relationship-based research and interventions to improve the quality of life for individuals and communities living with the impacts of colonization. The chapter also articulates an approach to community-based knowledge translation by detailing the process of an Anishinaabek knowledge holder (McGregor) working with a Western trained scholar (McKinley).

In Chapter 4, Moratz critically investigates discourses of modernization amidst experiences of chronic spirit possession, "mental illness," and Qur'anic healing practices in Burao, Somaliland, Northwestern Somalia. The research was based on ethnographic fieldwork between January 2013 and March 2020, conducted with the local help of the University of Burao. Data were collected through participant observation in the general society and of religious healers, as well as two rounds of semi-structured interviews in 2014–15 and 2018, respectively, involving a total of 26 participants and 42 interviews. Other relevant materials, such as a book manuscript by a local healer, a locally made movie, and several YouTube videos were also analyzed. This chapter argues that chronic possession experiences and healing practices are conceptualized as part of the modernization process in Somaliland society. In contrast to other research into spirit possession, the Somali experiences suggest that possession does not need to be designated as a traditional phenomenon but is often considered modern. Moratz outlines how Somali Islamic practice, as part of Somali culture, may be part of a larger modernization vision of the global Islamic movement. The chapter also proposes that embracing possession as a modern phenomenon offers new ways of treating underlying suffering, as the causes of suffering are externalized and personified.

In Chapter 5, Kurz situates research findings of healing from various forms of chronic illness based on a case study and builds on that while focusing on the Spiritist movement in urban environments of Brazil. Within the Brazilian Spiritist continuum, a veritable healing cooperation between health professionals, spirits, mediums, and clients constitutes a complementing space of medical and spiritual practices. Based on ethnographic field research in different regions of Brazil, this chapter explores practices and narratives regarding the spiritual aspects of illness, cure/healing, and well-being. It addresses the sphere of aesthetics both in the sense of sensory aspects of the healing experience as well as performative metacommunication in healthcare politics.

In Chapter 6, Goldingay, Dieppe, Warber, and Rahtz, explore healing, rather than curing of chronic health problems, at the Marian Catholic pilgrimage site of Lourdes in South West France. This is a multidisciplinary team (doctors and humanities scholars) that have been undertaking research in Lourdes for the past several years. Their interest is in well-being and healing, rather than the miraculous cures of disease, for which Lourdes is best known. Research methods are largely qualitative, including in-depth interviews and focus groups with a wide variety of pilgrims and visitors to Lourdes, as well as doctors, priests, and others who work there, novel visual research methods (asking people to draw pictures of their experiences), and ethnography. The authors obtained recorded interviews with 67 people, which have been transcribed, pictures from 19 participants, film recordings of two sick people describing their experiences, and a wealth of ethnographic material from the three visits made to collect data in Lourdes. They argue that whilst cures of diseases are rare, improvements in well-being and relief of symptoms from chronic illness are common. Many different factors contribute to the transformative changes that people experience in Lourdes, including spiritual or "noetic" moments, place, and nature, connecting with others, and the religious rituals that take place in Lourdes. This chapter concludes by stating that more research needs to be done on the ability of religious pilgrimage sites, such as Lourdes, to activate personal healing and facilitate relief of chronic symptoms, rather than on cures and that work of this sort can make an important contribution to the debate on how wellness might be improved.

Chapter 7 comes back to Canada with a discussion about sacred worldviews and spiritual practices of young Cree and Métis Indigenous Peoples. The chapter details 54 interviews with 36 youth that were partially drawn from two

Community-Based Participatory Research (CBPR) projects exploring Indigenous youth wellness within a mid-sized Canadian metropolitan city, Saskatoon, Saskatchewan. Globally, this context often involves intimate connections with land and nature that foster pathways for promoting mental health, resilience, and overall wellness. Drawing on chronicity theory to situate settler-colonialism as a persistent and relentless chronic condition of the body politic emerging through land dispossession, intergenerational trauma, racism, and structural violence, Morton, Bird-Naytowhow, and Hatala consider the role of anti-colonial and Indigenous perspectives that center positive transformations of Indigenous youth wellness identities within a contemporary urban context.

In Chapter 8, Remy-Fischler details an ethnography of Spiritual Peer-Support Networks' (SPSNs) community in the United Kingdom, encompassing organizations like Spiritual Crisis Network and Emerging Proud. SPSNs provide support for individuals who identify as having experienced a mental health and/or spiritual crisis. These crises range from what could be labelled psychotic episodes to mystical experiences and everything in between. SPSNs promote seeing these experiences on a spectrum, rather than as separate ontological categories. There is a growing body of literature on experiences of psychotic-like phenomena reported by clinical and non-clinical groups. These point towards a shift in diagnostic categories in favor of a psychotic continuum to better represent this diversity of experiences. Using a combination of narrative and affect theories, this chapter looks at how knowledge or *knowledges* are gained from lived experiences of crises but also from narratives interpreting these crises, re-shaping each other in looping effects. Furthermore, this study also explores the extent to which these knowledges are perceived to be beneficial or healing for individuals. The study includes participant observation in events, meetings, and peer-support groups as well as in-depth interviews with 20 members of the SPSN's community, mostly in the UK, from January to April 2019. Most participants had encountered psychiatric services, and all identified as having experienced at least one mental health and/or spiritual crisis. A thematic analysis was constructed primarily from narratives of SPSNs and individuals, whilst keeping in mind the emotions and affects imbued within these. Remy-Fischler discusses knowledges gained from narratives of experiences, and experiences themselves are beneficial insofar as they give meaning to individuals' crises – a teleological breakthrough after a breakdown. What seems most healing, however, is for the breakthrough to transcend individuals. It is not talking about knowledges gained from crises that is most healing but applying them to heal others. Individuals then become "wounded," or rather "scarred," healers.

In Chapter 9, Benyah discusses the conceptions surrounding the causal explanation of mental illness as a prevalent form of chronicity in Ghana. Mental illness is very prevalent in Ghana with an estimated population of about 3 million suffering from different forms of mental illness. However, the conceptions surrounding the causal explanation of mental illness make the approaches adopted in managing or remedying the illness nuanced and more complex. In Ghana and most parts of sub-Saharan Africa, mental illness is shrouded in witchcraft, curses, and supernatural, evil forces. This makes the sufferers of the illness, family relations, and sometimes health practitioners adopt not only biomedical care but also spiritual resources in remedying the illness. The journey to remedy the cause of a chronic mental health disease can sometimes be daunting and frustrating due to the complex narrative production of diagnostic trial and error in seeking both medical and spiritual resources in the management of the illness. Citing examples from two major prayer camps in Ghana and recounting the experience of individuals who have had a chronic mental health problem, this chapter examines how culture, spirituality, and faith influences the daily experience of people in the management of mental illness and well-being in Ghana.

In Chapter 10, Allen, Ellis, and Hatala explore the increasing prevalence in Belize, Central America, of Type 2 diabetes mellitus (T2DM) as a serious chronic illness and leading cause of preventable death. The purpose of this Grounded Theory study was to better understand how spiritual practices of people living with T2DM affects disease management and mental wellness in Belize. Semi-structured interviews with diabetes patients (n=11), discussions with key informants (n=20), participatory observation, and regular field notes occurred between February and March of 2020. In this chapter they observe that spiritual and religious practices, such as regular prayer, scripture reading, or communal worship, have been shown to improve patient emotional adjustments to T2DM diagnosis, psychological endurance with chronic illness, and improved mental health (including reduced depression and anxiety), glycemic control, and quality of life (QoL). This research suggests that health care providers (HCPs) in Belize can optimize diabetes care through collaboration with patients' spiritual frameworks and faith-based organizations. Similarly, T2DM prevention and education can likely be better facilitated by interdisciplinary efforts that take into consideration faith-based and spiritual perspectives.

Many mental disorders begin during adolescence and young adulthood, with symptoms and distress lasting many years. Chronic suffering and dysfunction are assumed for some diagnoses, such as psychosis, mood disorders and addictions. Chapter 11, prepared by Jarvis, Whitley, and Leblanc, identifies how religious practice and belief (1) challenge the notion of chronicity in mental illness, and (2) mitigate the suffering inherent to severe mental disorder. The literature on chronicity in mental illness is critiqued. Religious case material, derived from 41 patient histories in 2015, and from the Cultural Consultation Service (CCS) and First Episode Psychosis Program (FEPP) in Montreal, Canada is summarized and assessed thematically with respect to chronicity and the distress of mental illness. Findings highlight that religion 1) fosters cultures of recovery that reinterpret mental illness as episodic rather than chronic or degenerative in nature; 2) provides comforting coping strategies that reduce the distress associated with symptoms; and 3) offers meaning and purpose in the face of adversity. Religious variables have been neglected for decades in mental health research despite the consistent finding that religious beliefs and practices are associated with mental health on diverse measures. Religious cultures, beliefs and practices offer powerful tools to assist patients and their families in times of illness and suffering. The re-evaluation of notions of chronicity and wellness, as some belief systems encourage, permit reinterpretation of illness representations, reduce stigma, and foster recovery. Clinicians need to consider the religious resources that exist in the lives of their patients and plan interventions accordingly. Neglecting to do so may undermine the therapeutic relationship, or unwittingly may worsen suffering over the illness course.

In the concluding chapter, we (Hatala and Roger) highlight major themes that emerged across the diverse chapters in this collection, drawing attention to particular aspects of care and mental wellness, involving both individual and professionalized strategies as well as community approaches. We draw attention to future areas of research we find promising and use as a platform for our discussion concepts introduced by the authors in this collection. The concluding remarks are framed around the promotion of a compelling new concept, based on our discussion around global mental health, namely Global Mental Wellness. This framing of wellness and mental health in a global context is set within the contexts of chronicity and what we refer to as spiritual geographies of care, or the internal and external worlds that provide coping resources, cultural contexts of care, communities of normalcy, and frameworks for interpretation amidst experiences of persistent hardship, crisis, and struggle. This chapter argues that addressing concerning global rates of chronicity and mental illness can, in part, occur by advancing understandings of working relationships across epistemic divides, between biomedically informed health care practitioners and religious or spiritual-based faith practitioners. Overall, it is suggested that when such collaborations are formed through a Global Mental Wellness agenda, the global burden of chronicity and mental illness will be met in a more sustainable manner, appropriately aligned with, and accessing local cultural priorities, community resources, and endogenous solutions that may already be present and active in diverse communities around the globe.

References

Absolon, Kathy. 2010. "Indigenous Wholistic Theory: A Knowledge Set for Practice." *First Peoples Child and Family Review* 5 (2): 74–87. doi:10.7202/1068933ar

Ai, Amy, Bruce L. Rollman and Candyce Berger. 2010. "Comorbid Mental Health Symptoms and Heart Diseases: Can Health Care and Mental Health Care Professionals Collaboratively Improve the Assessment and Management?" *Health and Social Work* 35 (1): 27–38. doi:10.1093/hsw/35.1.27

Büssing, Arndt, and Harold G. Koenig. 2010. "Spiritual Needs of Patients with Chronic Diseases." *Religions (Basel, Switzerland)* 1 (1): 18–27. doi:10.3390/rel1010018

Centre for Addiction and Mental Health [CAMH]. 2020. "Mental Health Awareness Campaign leads to increase in the number of people seeking help, new CAMH study reveals." CAMH. Retrieved from www.camh.ca/en/camh-news-and-stories/awareness-campaign-leads-to-increase-in-people-seeking-help

Charmaz, Kathy. 1983. "Loss of Self: A Fundamental Form of Suffering in the Chronically Ill." *Sociology of Health and Illness* 5 (2): 168–195. doi:10.1111/1467-9566. ep10491512

Charmaz, Kathy. 1991. *Good Days, Bad Days: The Self in Chronic Illness and Time.* New Brunswick, NJ: Rutgers University Press.

Craig, Carol, Clarann Weinert, Joni Walton and Barbara Derwinski-Robinson. 2006. "Spirituality, Chronic Illness, and Rural Life." *Journal of Holistic Nursing* 24 (1): 27–35. doi:10.1177/0898010105282526

Estroff, Sue. 1993. "Identity, Disability, and Schizophrenia: The Problem of Chronicity." In *Knowledge, Power and Practice: The Anthropology of Medicine and Everyday Life*, edited by Shirley Lindenbaum, and Margaret Lock, 247–286. Berkeley, California: University of California Press.

Good, Byron, Carla Marchira, Nida Ul Hasanat, Utami Sofiati and Subandi Muhana. 2010. "Is 'Chronicity' Inevitable for Psychotic Illness? Studying Heterogeneity in the Course of Schizophrenia in Yogyakarta, Indonesia." In *Chronic Conditions, Fluid States: Chronicity and the Anthropology of Illness*, edited by Carolyn Smith-Morris and Lenore Manderson, 54–74. Ithaca, NY: Rutgers University Press. doi:36019/9780813549736-005

Hank, Karsten, and Barbara Schaan. 2008. "Cross-National Variations in the Correlation Between Frequency of Prayer and Health Among Older Europeans." *Research on Aging* 30 (1): 36–54. doi:10.1177/0164027507307923

Health Canada. 2015. *"First Nations Mental Wellness Continuum Framework."* Ottawa, Ontario: Health Canada. Retrieved from https://thunderbirdpf.org/wp-content/uploads/2015/01/24-4-1273-FN-Mental-Wellness-Framework-EN05_low.pdf

Koenig, Harold, Dana King and Verna Benner Carson. 2012. *Handbook of Religion and Health*. 2nd Edition. New York City, New York: Oxford University Press.

Kleinman, Arthur, and Rachel Hall-Clifford. 2010. "Afterword: Chronicity - Time, Space, and Culture." In *Chronic Conditions, Fluid States: Chronicity and the Anthropology of Illness*, edited by Carolyn Smith-Morris and Lenore Manderson, 247–252. Ithaca, New York: Rutgers University Press. doi:10.36019/9780813549736-015

Manderscheid, Ronald W., Carol D. Ryff, Elsie J. Freeman, Lela R. McKnight-Eily, Satvinder Dhingra and Tara W. Strine. 2010. "Evolving Definitions of Mental Illness and Wellness." *Preventing Chronic Disease* 7 (1): A19.

Manderson, Lenore, and Carolyn Smith-Morris. 2010. "Introduction: Chronicity and the Experience of Illness." In *Chronic Conditions, Fluid States: Chronicity and the Anthropology of Illness*, edited by Carolyn Smith-Morris and Lenore Manderson, 1–18. Ithaca, New York: Rutgers University Press. doi:10.36019/9780813549736-002

Mattingly, Cheryl, Lone Gron and Lotte Meinert. 2011. "Chronic Homework in Emerging Borderlands of Healthcare." *Culture, Medicine and Psychiatry* 35 (3): 347–375. doi:10.1007/s11013-011-9225-z

National Wellness Institute [NWI]. 2020. *"The Six Dimensions of Wellness."* National Wellness Institute. Retrieved from https://nationalwellness.org/resources/six-dimensions-of-wellness/

Pargament, Kenneth. 2002. "The Bitter and the Sweet: An Evaluation of the Costs and Benefits of Religiousness." *Psychological Inquiry* 13 (3): 168–181. doi:10.1207/S15327965PLI1303_02

Roger, Kerstin Stieber, and Andrew R. Hatala. 2017. "Religion, Spirituality and Chronic Illness: A Scoping Review and Implications for Health Care Practitioners." *Journal of Religion and Spirituality in Social Work* 37 (1): 24–44. doi:10.1080/15426432.2017.1386151

Saracci, Rodolfo. 1997. "The World Health Organization Needs to Reconsider its Definition of Health." *British Medical Journal* 314 (709): 1409.

Strauss, Anselm. 1990. "Preface." *Social Science and Medicine* 30 (11): v–vi. doi:10.1016/0277-9536(90)90254-P

Vigh, Henrik. 2006. *Navigating Terrains of War: Youth and Soldiering in Guinea-Bissau.* Oxford: Berghahn.

2 Religiosity and spirituality in mental health contexts

Perceptions of psychologists and chaplains

Marta Helena de Freitas, Evelyn Figueira Lima Ruas and Emmanuel Ifeka Nwora

Introduction

The concepts of health and mental illness in a Western context, and their relationship to religiosity and spirituality, have undergone significant cultural variation in the course of the history of civilization. These variations have been critically observed by different historians ranging from Foucauldian perspectives (Foucault 2005) to more recent historiographic approaches, such as that of Claude Quétel (2012). In the latter, for example, we find the development of Babylonian and Egyptian, mythological and Homeric, and Judeo-Christian reflections about the so-called "diseases of the soul", as well as the Hippocratic concept responsible for the inception of the medicalized definitions of mental health. This rational view of medicine is quite different from the magical/religious conception previously described, and it proposes that all diseases have a natural cause, rather than religious, in which its supposedly divine origin reflects human ignorance.

In the Middle Ages, in Europe, Saint Thomas Aquinas' influential theological approach was responsible for the definition of psychology as the "study of the soul" and important theological reflections about madness (Quétel 2012). In the Western context, during this period, chronic mental diseases tended to be associated with sin, demons, the Devil, or witchcraft. With the later development of scientific psychiatry and its diverse theoretical and therapeutic approaches aimed at the understanding and treatment of mental disorders, the relationship between mental health and spirituality suffered erosion and a specialized medical terminology was created to substitute the previous mystical or theological discourse (Quétel 2012). Thus, the lived spiritual and/or religious experiences of "patients" could be categorized in a medical manner – as deliriums, hallucinations, mental alienations, and so on, without attention being paid to other meanings or values. Furthermore, the treatment recommended was reduced to medication and other physiological or materialistic measures aimed at the elimination of symptoms.

The "anti-psychiatric movement" of the last decades of the twentieth century led to another change in the understanding of mental health. The ideas of mental disorder and various psychiatric classifications became the object of virulent attacks (Quétel 2012). Substituted in their place were new initiatives in mental health care, where people experiencing psychic suffering are considered as a unique and

DOI: 10.4324/9781003043508-2

indivisible whole – physical, mental, social, and cultural – and where treatment could be integrated with their social, cultural, religious and community reality.

One of the main challenges posed by the psychiatric reform stems from the fact that integral care demands a multi-, inter-, and transdisciplinary perspective (Alves and Freitas 2020). There is a need for the contributions of different competencies in an integrated manner, be it in the form of teamwork between different professionals or amplifying the scope of specific competencies to include other bordering competencies. Therefore, if we consider the relations between religiosity, spirituality, and mental health in terms of multi- and interdisciplinary actions, possible complementarities between the roles of the psychologist and the chaplain emerge. Nevertheless, according to literature in the area (Cunha and Scorsolini-Comin 2019; Gentil, Guia and Sanna 2011; Pereira and Holanda 2019) and recent research (Paulino 2019; Pereira 2018; Piasson and Freitas 2020; Nwora 2020; Ruas 2018), neither professional training nor the reality of mental health services, especially in Brazil, have been making contributions in this regard.

In light of this reality, this chapter focuses on a comparative study between the perceptions of Western-trained psychologists who work in mental health contexts and those of chaplains who work in various contexts where they similarly support and care for those with chronic mental disorders. The core of the comparison is the way both professionals perceive the relations between religiosity, spirituality, and mental health, and the way they approach care or address it. The convergences and divergences found between both, the implications for an integrated effort in the care of people with mental disorders, and the prevention and treatment of chronic mental disorders is later discussed in depth.

Mental disorders and chronicity

In a Western context, the notion of disorder, when applied to the psyche, stems from the medical concept of pathology introduced by Claude Bernard, as informed by Canguilhem (1966), creating significant ethical and epistemological problems. From the ethical point of view, one of the problems is the tendency of prejudice, marginalization, and stigma perpetrated by society toward people who present behavioural, social, and relational disorders. From the epistemological point of view, the possibility to distinguish, psychologically speaking, between "normal" and "pathological", as is often done with illness in the biological domain, is more complex and questionable. In other words, the distinction between a symptom of mental disorder and a natural reaction to specific life experience or a particularity of each person's manner of being, is always accompanied by the risk of pathologizing genuine human experiences, even though unusual, rare, eccentric, or sometimes inexplicable from the logical or functional point of view. These aspects are also in consonance with contributions from transcultural psychiatry (Ang 2016; Kirmayer et al. 2003; Kirmayer, Guzder and Rousseau 2014).

In accordance with contemporary psychopathology, people are considered to have mental disorders when they present serious alterations in thought, emotions, or behaviour, and when these alterations are unadaptable to their environments and/or accompanied by grave suffering to them and/or to people around them. According to the World Health Organization (WHO 2013), mental disorders encompass a wide spectre of problems, including different symptoms that impair people's performance, their interpersonal, family, social, and professional relations, studies, their capacity for self-evaluation, tolerance to normal life stresses, and joy in living.

The symptoms of so-called mental disorders may be temporary or long-lasting. The criteria employed to characterize their conditions of chronicity consider their more or less persistent character, and also the extent to which they may or may not be treated by recommended therapy, especially psychotherapy or psychiatric medication. The three criteria proposed by Bachrach (2006) – diagnosis, duration, and gravity of each case (disability) – have gained more ground and consensus among scholars and professionals in the definition of chronic mental disorder. Nevertheless, there is not yet a consensus with regard to its specific character, relative importance, and possible relations between these three elements, and the criterion of temporality tends to predominate, as Von Peter (2010) pointed out about ten years ago.

This lack of consensus about the chronicity criteria of mental disorders has been critically debated, either with regard to its turbulent historical evolution or to what is witnessed in contemporary environments of mental health care (Desciat 1999). In the first case, it is considered that the chronicity of mental disorders consists in a kind of socially constructed belief resulting from the psychiatric movement in the direction of the scientific model of mental health prevalent from the dawn of the twentieth century (Jimenez 1988). In the second case, it is understood that the classification of chronicity serves as "an instrument of description (of people or their conditions), regulation (of therapy, medical service, or management) and connection with infrastructures of customer service (technologies or standards practiced in different types)" involving "treatability production, organization of resources, demarcation of responsibilities, practice of rendering account and presence" in an environment "explicitly organized for 'chronic mental patients' as specific human type" (Bister 2017, 38).

In any case, irrespective of the lack of consensus, the chronicity of mental disorders elevates the level of stress in people with such a diagnosis, having an impact on and altering their existence as they incorporate it into their process of living that demands changes in their former lifestyle and identity. The different kinds of mental disorders classified today as chronic are complex and may appear in various forms. For example, if we consider the WHO's International Classification of Diseases (ICD-11) or the Diagnostic and Statistical Manual of Mental Disorders (DSM-5), we see that this wide definition ranges from neurological conditions, like epilepsy and Alzheimer's disease, through autism and mental retardation, including depression, anxiety, the so-called bipolar disorders, to drug addiction, eating disorders, and schizophrenia.

In terms of the prevalence of chronic mental disorders in the world population, in 2017, a total of 792 million people (10.7% of the world population) lived with some kind of persistent mental disorder (Ritchie and Roser 2018).

Globally, the rate of chronic mental disorders has been on the rise, and its prevention has constituted a tremendous challenge to mental health. In Brazil, approximately eleven thousand deaths are attributed to psychiatric causes per year, and 10% of the deaths occur in hospital infirmaries (Ribeiro, Melzer-Ribeiro and Cordeiro 2012). How many of these deaths could have been prevented if there had been measures of health improvement, including wider models of prevention and treatment of mental disorders in the country that are not restricted to the medical model? How much could a model that offers religious and spiritual care be helpful in saving lives and enhancing quality in mental health care?

Such considerations about the criteria for chronicity of mental disorders and their treatment are relevant to the study described in this chapter where we present a comparison between the perceptions of specific groups of professionals: a) psychologists that, in general, assimilate, in the course of their training, specific knowledge on psychopathology and afterwards can work in customer services specially directed to mental care; b) chaplains that undergo training based on the theological paradigm, and their work, as we shall see later, is carried out in wider contexts where they deal with people suffering from various mental disorders. This comparative study shows that, compared to chaplains, psychologists are much more involved with conceptual concerns, insofar as the concepts favour some measure of uniformity in the planning of services offered to people with mental disorders. Chaplains, in turn, are more committed to the experience of religiosity and spirituality, valuing pragmatic questions in their effort of offering spiritual assistance to people in various forms of psychological distress.

Spirituality, religiosity, and mental health

Going back to the etymological origins of the concept of spirituality, Koenig (2009) and Paiva (2015) remind us that the Latin term "spiritualis", derived from the Greek word "pneumáticos", is understood as it appears in the Letters of Paul to the Romans (Rom. 8, 9) and to the Corinthians (I Cor. 3,16); that is to say, a spiritual person is a person inhabited by the Spirit of God (e.g., Theresa of Avila and John of the Cross from a Christian framework). Even though the Greeks used it to distinguish what is human from what is irrational, the concept of spirituality has typically been related to religiosity in Western history and contexts.

More recently, the meaning of the term "spirituality" has expanded a lot in health contexts, with a strong tendency to give it a wider scope and not necessarily connect it to religion or religiosity. From the psychological point of view, this wider concept aims to validate personal dynamism based on the interior experience that impels the individual "beyond the limits of his or her earthly existence and the phenomic experience, with an attitude of hope, of search and/or attribution of meaning" (Aletti 2012, 166). Under this perspective, the concept of spirituality is reserved for the domain of the big questions of existential meaning, while religiosity and religion are situated in actual social contexts, with institutional practices, rights for inclusion, and historic rituals, where the domain of answers may be based on beliefs in the "sacred, transcendent, ultimate dimension" (Aletti 2012; Freitas 2017; Freitas and Vilela 2017; Roger and Hatala 2017).

Religiosity, as an answer to the quest for meaning, nurtured by spirituality, is based on the belief in a dimension that surpasses materiality and the human physical dimension but is not necessarily connected to a group, institution, or formal doctrine. It is also characterized by the subjective and inter-subjective experience but not necessarily in a shared manner. Religion is a kind of answer to the quest for meaning that is specifically institutionalized and shared. It is constituted, therefore, by a system or doctrine structured into principles, norms, codes, sacred texts, or other forms that enhance sharing and institutionalization. Such conceptions (Freitas 2017; Freitas and Vilela 2017) simultaneously permit adequate distinctions between each of the three concepts (spirituality, religiosity, and religion) as well as an understanding of their contiguities and inter-connections. They also make it possible to avoid incurring the three following difficulties: the tautology of the concept of spirituality as criticized by Koenig (2015); the excessive generality of the term, criticized by Paiva (2015); and the dichotomy between the terms religiosity and religion, criticized by Aletti (2012).

The role of religiosity and spirituality in supporting wellness amidst chronicity in general, and its relations to mental health in particular, can be considered from three complementary perspectives. The first stems from the plural-dimensional human condition, being that religiosity and spirituality are an integral part of the individual and are included in the global health scope as proposed by the WHO (1992) on considering the "non-material" or "spiritual" dimension of existence. The second has to do with religiosity and spirituality as fundamental elements of culture into which people are immersed and which exercise great influence on their habits and manners. They can positively or negatively affect, to a greater or lesser extent, people's mental health and wellness or that of those around them. The third, but no less important, is related to religiosity and spirituality as multi-dimensional constructs, associated with recommendations, practices, and strategies of intervention and protocol care in mental health, and resulting in concrete actions by professionals in their respective fields of operation. According to a recent integrative literature review on the subject (Cunha and Scorsolini-Comin 2019), these different perspectives are being approached in a more significant quantity of studies carried out in various countries, including Brazil.

As Koenig (2009) pointed out more than a decade ago, in spite of the fact that, during more than half of the twentieth century, spiritual and religious experiences, practices, and beliefs were associated with symptoms of hysteria, neurosis, and psychotic disorders, literature in contemporary Western psychology, psychiatry, and psychopathology has offered new insight on the subject and its positive influences. This insight is manifest in different contexts and countries and among different ethnic and age groups and suggests that spiritual and religious commitment is strongly related to coping positively with stress, and consequently, less associated with different chronic mental disorders like depression, suicide, anxiety, and drug addiction.

Brazil's policies of humanized care

In a country like Brazil, where more than 92% of the population declare themselves followers of some religion – being 64.6% Catholics, 22.2% Evangelicals, 2.7% Spiritists, 0.3% Afro-Brazilian religious, and 2% other (Brasil 2012), religiosity permeates almost all aspects of people's lives. It constantly appears in contexts of mental health services, especially in the *Centros de Atenção Psicossocial* (CAPS, Psychosocial Care Centres) (Henriques, Oliveira and Figueirêdo 2015; Freitas, Santo and Silva 2019). The CAPS multi-professional teams are composed of doctors, psychiatrists, psychologists, nurses, nursing technicians, social workers, and occupational therapists, who offer individual or group care to the beneficiaries of the service and to their families. As a team, these professionals need to work together in a spirit of "network care" involving other health institutions, and also other institutions and people connected with the patients and their families, including religious institutions and religious leaders (Brasil 2004).

The country's policies of humanized care (Brasil 2004; 2011) have granted as the right of the beneficiaries of the health system, a supportive service and competent network care. The professionals that operate in the system should, therefore, not only respect, but also, and above all, be guided by the ethical, cultural, and religious values of the beneficiaries. Such a responsibility evokes concerns related to the proper handling of religiosity and spirituality, especially by psychologists (Freitas, Santo and Silva 2019; Ruas et al. 2020). Research carried out with professionals and psychology students in the last decades show that the bias, silencing, and marginalization of religiosity and spirituality in the course of training tend to keep professionals insecure when addressing matters and experiences related to religiosity and spirituality brought up by patients and families in a clinical context (Pereira and Holanda 2019; Ancona-Lopez 2018).

The challenge becomes overwhelming in the face of the activities of religious groups and institutions committed to treatment – a growing trend in Brazil today – either in an independent or integrated manner with the *Sistema Único de Saúde* (SUS, Unified Health System), the Brazilian national health care system. There have been intense debates on this matter, charged with conflicts between secular ideological positions and other positions connected with specific religious denominations within and outside the community of mental health professionals (Freitas, Santo and Silva 2019). Even though the scientific-religious conflict may not be something new in mental health, the activities of religious therapeutic communities – including religious discourses regarding psychopathological phenomena – have triggered attitudes of mistrust from health professionals, especially from psychologists who tend to emphasize the negative aspects of the relations between religiosity and spirituality and mental health (Ribeiro and Minayo 2015). The tension is aggravated by the fact that, in spite of the wide range of psychological phenomena and their inseparability from other aspects of human life, the majority of psychology courses in the country continue to ignore phenomena related to religiosity and spirituality (Freitas and Piasson 2016).

Chaplaincy and mental health

About two decades ago, one of the most outstanding advocates of professional chaplaincy in the United States, Larry VandeCreek (1999), decried the lack of literature by chaplains on the relations between religiosity, spirituality, and mental health, as well as the lack of references made to chaplains in research about the subject. It appeared that chaplains' role was irrelevant in people's health care. Nevertheless, many authors have emphasized its importance in recent times. A study carried out in seven general hospitals in Brazil shows the importance of the services of the chaplain in health care (Francisco et al. 2015). In the last few years, studies in the country and around the world have drawn the attention of professionals and institutions to spiritual care as an essential component integrated in health care and mental health (Hefti and Esperandio 2016; Timmins et al. 2018). Such components are even envisaged in the process of accreditation of health institutions (Gentil, Guia and Sana 2011) where the chaplain's service is extended to patients, families, workers, and health professionals.

The policies of humanized health care in Brazil (Brasil 2004; 2011) seek to give adequate attention to different people involved in health care service – beneficiaries, workers, professionals, and managers – but do not currently envisage the chaplain as one of the professionals who should compose the multi-professional teams of the country's health care service. Nevertheless, the right to religious care is defended in Brazil by the 1988 Constitution. Article n° 5, section VII grants that "the service of religious care in civil and military institutions of collective internment is guaranteed by law". Federal Law n° 9.982, of 14th July, 2000 also grants the right of religious people to religious care in the country's health care services.

In spite of the fact that the chaplain is not legally envisaged as a component of the multi-professional teams in the mental health services provided by the CAPS, we argue that his/her services, in this context, parallel to the services of the psychologist and other health care professionals, are equally important and should be recognized as such. Some general hospitals in the country offer this service, but in a majority of Brazilian health care services, chaplaincy or religious-spiritual care is offered by religious organizations through voluntary activity. However, military organizations formally offer the services of a professional chaplain to patients and their families. Even though a majority of the services of chaplaincy in the country are carried out in hospitals, either in a voluntary or formal way, they include the spiritual and mental health care of patients and families in different contexts.

Considering the contemporary challenges posed to psychologists and chaplains in integral mental health care and their connections to religiosity and spirituality, this chapter aims to investigate and describe: a) how the relations between mental health and religiosity and spirituality are made manifest in the daily practice of both professionals; b) how they address this binomial in their professional practice and what they consider to be good or bad practice in the process; c) what are the main convergences and divergences between the conceptions and perceptions of these two groups of professionals.

Research method

Participants

The data explored in this chapter were obtained from three larger research projects[1] carried out in the work context of health professionals, with prior authorization of the hospitals, CAPS, and other institutions involved. The authorization was obtained after prior submission and approval of each research project by the *Conselho de Ética em Pesquisa* (CEP, Research Ethics Committee) of the Catholic University of Brasília, and by the Secretariat of Health of the Federal District. Each of the professionals previously signed a Free and Clarified Consent Term as the CEP demands.

Within the scope of the three projects mentioned above, about 200 health professionals of different areas (doctors, psychologists, nurses, social workers, occupational therapists, and chaplains), working in hospital contexts of mental health care were interviewed in depth. Within the scope of this chapter, we analyze only the interviews conducted with 13 psychologists working in the CAPS of the Federal District (five male and eight female, 12 Catholic and one Evangelical, their ages varying between 30 and 60 years) and 15 male chaplains working in military institutions (Navy, Army, Airforce, and Fire Brigade) of which nine are Catholic priests and six are Evangelical pastors also working in the Federal District. During the period of the interviews (2017 and 2018), there were no chaplains of other religious denominations in the military institutions.

Conducting the interviews

The methodology employed is the phenomenological perspective, philosophically grounded in the contributions of Husserl (2002), consisting of an essentially exploratory and qualitative study. A semi-structured interview was carried out with each participant, addressing the following thematic axes: demographical data; work context and client characteristics; how religiosity and spirituality manifest in the context of professional practice; perception of the relations between religiosity or spirituality and mental health and ways of approaching them; what participants consider to be good and bad practices in addressing this binomial; whether and how participants make connections and distinctions between spiritual experience and psychopathological symptoms; personal religiosity and spirituality and their influence in professional practice; whether and how religiosity and spirituality were addressed in professional training; and how young professionals are oriented towards the subject.

The interviews with psychologists were conducted by the first author and those with chaplains by the third. They were conducted in a spontaneous and natural manner, making it possible for the experiences lived by the professionals in their work contexts to be captured in act (Amatuzzi 2012). The duration varied between 30 and 120 minutes, respecting the pace of each interviewee. Some of them were more mobilized about the subject. This mobilization was respected, and care was taken to avoid interrupting the flow of their natural expressiveness. All the interviews were recorded, with due and prior consent of the participants, posteriorly transcribed and revised in view of a thorough and careful analysis. Pseudonyms were assigned to all participants in the presentation of the results to ensure confidentiality of all information provided.

Procedures of analysis

The analysis of the interviews was guided by the model described by Giorgi (2009). After successive reading of each interview and apprehending the sense of the totality of their experiences and perceptions, the thematic axes related to the specific objectives of this study and the respective discrimination of the meaning units (MU) were selected according to the psychological perspective. Then, the original expressions used by the interviewees were translated into psychological language in accordance with each thematic axis and the phenomenon under study. After that, as a synthesis of the meaning units, they were transformed into significant units (SU), which are expressions that agglutinate in a more consistent way, with more sensitive expressions. Finally, convergences and divergences between psychologists and chaplains were identified in comparing the results for both groups.

Results

For all the interviewees (chaplains and psychologists) religiosity and spirituality were perceived as being very present in their practice and in the lives of beneficiaries of their services. They considered that the respect of this dimension is of utmost importance in professional practice. They all reported that religiosity and spirituality are frequent issues emerging in the course of their service, and this has made them recognize the relevance of research about the subject. They demonstrated interest and enthusiasm in participating and were grateful for the opportunity of speaking about a subject that had been silenced during training and professional practice, especially for psychologists. They also demonstrated keen interest in the results of the research.

They were convergent in actively sharing lived experiences in the context of professional practice with beneficiaries and family members and strongly emphasized the importance of respecting their beliefs, values, religious, and spiritual experiences. Many of them continued talking about the subject even after the recorder was switched off at the end of the interview. This led us to the following three lines of thought: a) they were highly motivated about the subject and highly interested in continuing sharing their experiences; b) the subject had been much silenced, especially among psychologists, to the extent that, on having an opportunity to speak about it and being warmly received by the interviewers, they felt very much at ease to the extent that the duration of the interview appeared too short for much that needed to be shared; c) as the subject has been stigmatized and marginalized in mental health professional practice, especially among psychologists, the interviewees harboured some apprehension about speaking of the subject. They felt more at ease in sharing their experiences and reflections on the subject after the recorder was switched off.

Another significant aspect that emerged in the interviews, in the case of the chaplains, was the understanding that their practice crosses religious boundaries and that their service is not only spiritual, but it extends also to the mental health of their clients. In like manner, the work of the mental health psychologist often tends to cross the psychological boundaries of a service that revolves around, not only the cognitive, affective, or behavioural aspects of the individual, but also around the spiritual and religious issues that often emerge in the context of customer service.

After this general information about the various aspects that emerged during the interviews contextualizing the participants' lived experiences, the following sections will focus on two thematic axes: 1) the way psychologists and chaplains perceive the relations between religiosity, spirituality, and mental health; 2) the way they address it in daily professional practice.

Relations between religiosity and spirituality and mental health

The perception that religiosity and/or spirituality are related to mental health in a positive way, and in some situations in a negative way, was common among psychologists and chaplains. With regard to the positive aspects, many of them reported that religiosity offers a network of support, enhancing well-being and socialization between people, especially through the interactions and exchanges that occur through religious gatherings and celebrations (in churches, temples, and other places of worship). For example, a chaplain said: "Everybody needs a network of support...in the religious group, prayer and all that, you know, you have a network of support that encourages you to boldly face your problems" (Luís). Similarly, as a psychologist explained: "I think that a very healthy aspect is...the network that the individual finds in the church, among friends...They have some sense of belonging..." (Palma).

There are various references to positive impacts and healthy influences of religiosity and spirituality, including a source of hope, protection against suicide ideation and restraining people from taking their lives, redirecting existential struggles, and a coping strategy in stressful situations. As one chaplain shared: "A person that nurtures some religiosity...has a mental framework, a propensity to overcome that problem that is much bigger than the person that has no faith at all" (Eduardo). A psychologist said that: "We can consider it a positive influence. Positive because I think it offers a base, many a time, it gives a support, a direction to people's lives..." (Iris).

Some perceptions were convergent only among chaplains; religiosity and spirituality enhance solid values and principles, strengthen physical health, protect against depression, drugs, and violence, help with emotional disorder, and, in transformation of life, contribute to the success of surgeries and recuperation of health and offer confidence and existential guiding principles. One of the chaplains expressed this in the following terms: "Here we see the kind of recuperation, the recuperation is totally different… the time it takes to recover. It is impressive, in the person that has faith, the recuperation is much faster" (Cleisson).

For the psychologists, the influence of religiosity and spirituality on mental health is the solace it can offer through the practice of prayer. Based on the experience of some clients requesting prayers at the end of group activities, one of the psychologists said: "They frequently end the gathering with a prayer… and then we hug each other…I think this is seen as something rather strange… but I think it is good to them" (Palma).

Figure 2.1 illustrates convergences and divergences between psychologists and chaplains regarding their conceptions about positive aspects of the relations between religiosity and spirituality and mental health. It was observed that chaplains presented almost a double of positive aspects (13) than the psychologists did (7). Among the positive aspects mentioned by the psychologists, only one (Enhances comfort through praying) was not mentioned by the chaplains. However, this does not mean that the chaplains disagree on this. It only means it was not mentioned in the same terms by any one of them during the interviews. In contrast, the seven positive aspects mentioned by the chaplains were not mentioned by the psychologists. This shows that the chaplains' emphasis on the positive aspects of religiosity and spirituality tends to be greater than that of the psychologists.

As for negative aspects of the relations between religiosity and spirituality and mental health, both psychologists and chaplains reported they perceived, in specific cases that religiosity and spirituality disrupted the mental health of some clients and therefore was associated with the aggravation of psychic disorder. As one psychologist expressed: "I have a client…his psychotic deliriums

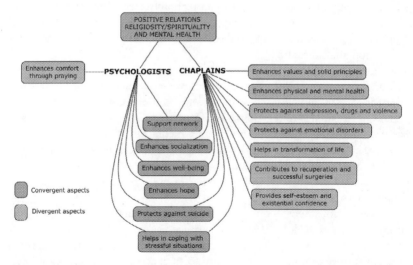

Figure 2.1 Positive relations between religiosity and spirituality and mental health.

started from religiosity, you see?" (Margarida), and as another chaplain explained: "There are pathologies that are triggered by religious experience, and this is a fact" (Airton). The chaplains reported that some ways of religious expression, based on excessively rigorous doctrines, may trigger a process of chronic psychical disorder. One of them affirmed that some kinds of doctrines and religious teachings assimilated by people may be disturbing in their lives. For him, "There are various forms of belief" and "Some forms of belief may trigger off disorders" (Cleisson). Another chaplain mentioned religious fanaticism, which can be harmful and detrimental to a healthy life: "A religiosity directed in a wrong manner from childhood may be pernicious to the individual instead of contributing to his personal growth" (Felipe).

Some psychologists perceived religion specifically as enhancing mental disorder, comparing it to religiosity: "I refer to religion and not religiosity…it contributes, in a certain way, to mental disorder" (Violeta); "It is always pernicious when the church maintains a very rigid position in relation to morality…When the church maintains rigid and severe positions, that really begin to cause mental disorder" (Lírio). Others said they perceive a negative relation between religiosity or spirituality and mental health when some clients did not adhere to or abandoned psychological and/or medical treatment as a result of their religious beliefs, which could enhance the chronic aspects of mental disorder: "Here at the CAPS, the question of religiosity, such as these more radical religions, think it is a spiritual problem, they end up not adhering to treatment" (Magarida). In other cases, for the patients who experience psychotic symptoms, a commanding voice typical of hallucinations and religious deliriums orders them to stop or not to start scientific treatment: "Commanding voice, for example, many people that suffer religious delusion…'Oh, no! God has ordered me to stop!' This happens. Deliriums, commanding voices, something like this happens" (Crisântemo).

The psychologists reported that religiosity may be harmful to mental health when it prevents people from considering other possibilities that might be helpful in dealing with their psychical disorder. One of them described the non-adherence to medication based on religiosity in the following way: "It often happens that, they close their eyes, the focus, the perspective of other possibilities, you know? And quite often, the possibilities of medication, it interferes in the possibility of medication" (Íris). References to religious proselytism were common among the psychologists as a negative aspect of the relation between religiosity and mental health. One of them reported that when he asked clients to speak about their spiritual experiences in groups, some of them engaged in religious debates and started giving "counsels" to other patients in the group. The "counsels" often involved recommendations to go to specific churches or religions to obtain a cure or improvement for their illnesses.

The perception of negative relations between religiosity and mental health in the form of religious violence, fanaticism, compulsive and obsessive praying, and mercantilist and triumphalist religiosity, all of which could contribute to psychic disorder, was common only among chaplains. As can be observed in Figure 2.2 concerning negative aspects of the relation between religiosity and spirituality and

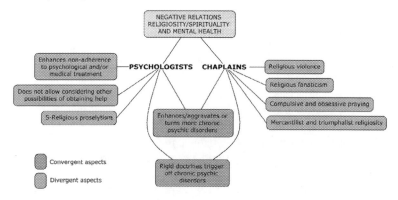

Figure 2.2 Negative relations between religiosity and spirituality and mental health.

mental health, the convergences between psychologists and chaplains are lesser (only two MU), and the specificities of each of them (divergences) increase, three for psychologists and four for chaplains. Even though the difference is little, chaplains report more negative aspects than psychologists.

Addressing religiosity and spirituality during mental health care

Psychologists and chaplains reported they are receptive and respectful to clients' religious and spiritual experiences through empathic listening, without disqualifying their beliefs. As one psychologist shared: "I think the first thing is respect... respect for what the other is saying, for his experience..." (Gérbera), and as another chaplain expressed: "I seek to maintain a relation with the person, to listen to him" (Evandro).

Psychologists often explained that they seek to understand the importance and the meaning of religiosity in the life of the client, to emphasize the importance of medical and psychological treatment, and to moderate religious debates in group sessions when they arise, thus avoiding religious proselytism: "I try to listen to and seek to understand the client's experience and what the experience means to him" (Gérbera); "I often tell clients: 'look, it is really important that you trust in God, say your prayers'. I reinforce the idea, but I also emphasize the importance of medical treatment" (Violeta). They also narrated that they avoid suggesting or imposing their own beliefs on clients: "I avoid bringing up my personal religious aspect" (Lírio). It was recounted they address the question of religiosity or spirituality only when the client brings it up: "From the moment that clients brings up the issue, it has to be considered…always respecting it as their instrument" (Crisântemo). To a lesser degree, psychologists also mentioned they avoid deconstructing clients' religious delirium; narrate using meditation in group sessions as a way of treating anxiety; try to change the focus of the debates about religion in group or individual sessions to something more concrete; say prayers before the sessions as a personal resource; address interpersonal relations and empathy based

Religiosity, spirituality, & mental health 29

on the religious questions that arise in the group sessions; and stimulate religious practice when it is observed that someone's religiosity is healthy. This last aspect is illustrated by one psychologist:

> When somebody, for example, has suicide ideation and says: "Oh, I go to church once in a while", then we encourage him, because, many a time, it is a way of establishing social networks whereby the individual gets some help.
>
> (Lírio)

Overall themes more frequently reported by the chaplains were: maintaining a relationship with the client, conducting biblical studies, talking to the client, offering counselling, orientations, and explanations, addressing existential issues, calling on the name of God, restoring self-esteem, offering hope, and organizing seminars and talks about drug and suicide prevention. As one a chaplain said: "The first thing is to be with them, by their side...I always seek to be with them, to know their problems, to listen to them, to rejoice, and to suffer with them" (Evandro). The chaplains tended to consider that this procedure brings comfort to clients as it assures them that they are not alone in their sufferings and dilemmas. They highlighted the importance of the support given by the spiritual dimension: "Besides giving spiritual support...we address its meaning in life, the connection with God, with the community, with the brothers and sisters of the church" (Eduardo).

Various chaplains reported they make referrals to other professionals and to other religious leaders; they highlighted the importance of working in multi-professional teams and spoke about their personal and independent search for

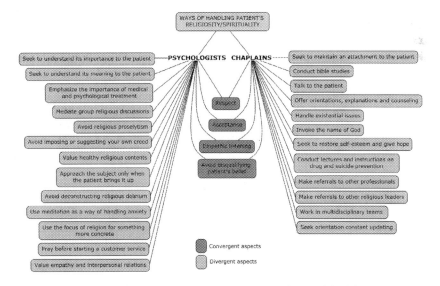

Figure 2.3 Ways of handling religiosity or spirituality and mental health.

updates and orientations through studies, research, participation in seminars, congresses, and consultation of peers.

Figure 2.3 shows convergent and divergent aspects between psychologists and chaplains regarding the ways of approaching religiosity or spirituality and mental health in their respective professional practices. A significant specificity in each professional category is observed here: 13 MU for psychologists, 12 for chaplains, and only four convergent between both, as outlined in the centre of the figure.

Discussion

The results presented here illustrate the role of psychologists and chaplains in addressing patients who are dealing with mental health concerns while practicing forms of religiosity and spirituality. The contents of their reports show that religiosity and spirituality are constantly present in their experiences of professional practice and corroborate results of other research carried out with other professionals or beneficiaries of mental health care services (Cunha and Scorsolini-Comin 2019; Henriques, Oliveira and Figueirêdo 2015; Freitas 2020).

The general finding, in consonance with findings of recent research carried out with more than four thousand Brazilian psychologists (Paulino 2019), counters the myth that psychologists are "anti-religious or anti-spiritual", which would create an expectation that the chaplains are more involved with the relations between religiosity or spirituality and mental health and would have much more to say about the subject. Even though a more technical discourse was found among the psychologists in their interviews, it was observed that all the psychologists recognized the positive role of spirituality and religiosity for the mental health of their clients and of their families. In spite of the fact that these professionals demonstrated concerns with situations where religiosity or spirituality could be harmful to mental health (see Figure 2.2), it was found that such concerns were not significantly more than those of the chaplains.

In general terms, we can say that the themes identified between psychologists and chaplains are directly related to the nature and specificity of their responsibilities, functions, and professional attributions in their respective domains of practice. A comparison between the data illustrated in Figures 2.1, 2.2, and 2.3 make it possible to identify a predominance of convergent aspects between religiosity or spirituality and mental health. With regard to the ways of engaging the subject, fewer convergences and more specificities are observed. In other words, psychologists and chaplains who engage in mental health practice experienced religiosity or spirituality in their professional practice and perceived its positive influence on the mental health of their clients in similar ways in a majority of cases. Nevertheless, they present distinct ways of approaching religiosity and spirituality in professional practice.

In view of the optimal care of the individual, the findings presented here show how the practices of chaplains and psychologists could, and we would argue should, be complementary in multi- and interdisciplinary mental health care. This demonstrates the relevance of the chaplain's presence in mental health institutions and not only in hospitals, reinforcing the idea of the creation of public policies that envisage the presence of professional chaplains, of different religions, in places where people seek assistance to treat their mental disorders, especially in the CAPS and as the mental disorders frequently go side by side with the spiritual and religious needs of these individuals. The service offered by chaplains, concomitant with that offered by psychologists and other mental health professionals in Brazilian institutions, will augment the multi- and interdisciplinary care of the individual that needs and seeks this care in these places. This would be in consonance with successful initiatives in other contexts that have been debated in consistent and well-grounded literature (Gentil, Guia and Sanna 2011; Gonçalves et al. 2015; Hefti and Esperandio 2016; Koenig 2013).

One way of thinking about the professional practice of psychologists in the context of mental health care is that stigma in relation to the religious or spiritual contents emerges in their practice. These ways of thinking, deriving from the misguided idea that religion and psychology are incompatible (Henriques, Oliveira and Figueirêdo 2015), suggest that psychologists should not venture into the domain of the religious or spiritual questions of their clients, which results in fear and difficulty in dealing with such contents in mental health practice and fear of speaking about the subject in interviews. On the other hand, the chaplains felt more at ease in speaking about these questions because they are directly related to their professional chaplaincy practice. Nevertheless, regarding addressing psychological questions, the service of the chaplain may be seen as unnecessary, which may explain the total absence of this professional in mental health care services.

There is a tendency to think psychologists should handle only questions of a psychological nature that emerge in their practice, leaving the spiritual questions of clients for religious leaders. This happens because, during psychologists' training, the subject of religiosity and spirituality is barely addressed, even though this situation has begun to change in recent years (Piasson and Freitas 2020). However, there is also a misguided idea that chaplains and religious leaders handle only spiritual and religious questions and should leave psychological questions to mental health professionals (psychologists and psychiatrists). However, in practice, our research shows that the landscape is quite different. The chaplains' work goes beyond spiritual care in the same way that clients' needs with which the psychologist must grapple, transcend the sphere of psychology. It follows then that it is required of these professionals to transcend the inherent approaches of their professional practices by way of adopting an attitude of integral or holistic care of the client, addressing psychological and religious or spiritual questions in such a way that one is connected with the other. This was manifest in the reports of the interviewees when they demanded interdisciplinary care or referral of clients with specific needs to one or the other domain.

It was also evident from the interviews that the chaplains, on perceiving that clients' specific necessities could be better handled by other mental health professionals, reported making due referrals in view of integral client care.

However, the psychologists, even in the face of clients' spiritual and religious struggles, and recognizing their limitations in handling such questions, did not report making referrals to chaplains or religious leaders of clients' traditions. Instead, the tendency to interpret religious or spiritual experiences and behaviours of clients as psychopathological symptoms (e.g., deliriums and hallucinations) was quite common. This shows the necessity of religiosity and spirituality being properly addressed in psychologists' training. It also shows the need to transcend the medical model present in the psychological discourse, even in the sphere of the CAPS, whose purpose is to create a "social support network, potentialize its actions concerned with the individual in his or her singularity, history, culture, and daily life" (Brasil 2004, 14).

A tendency of reproducing the dichotomy between religion and spirituality was also verified in the speech of some psychologists. Thus, even though they recognize the network of support offered by religion and all the positive aspects related to it, as a form of care for people with chronic mental disorders, they tend to associate spirituality with something healthy and meaning-enhancing and religion with something dangerous that can lead to mental illness and chronicity. On the other hand, the chaplains, even though they do not always make due conceptual distinctions between the three concepts (i.e., religion, religiosity, and spirituality), consider that what could be harmful is not religion in itself but the way it is lived by each individual. In other words, in consonance with what is recommended, based on the phenomenological perspective (Freitas and Vilela 2017), the formation of the chaplain appears to make him more prepared to qualify both the singularity of spirituality and the institutional sharing of religion based or not on a collective system of shared beliefs in their ways of evaluating the positive and negative relations of religiosity and spirituality with mental health.

The fact that the chaplains interviewed belong to the Christian religion even though Brazil is a country of outstanding cultural and religious diversity is worth considering. Naturally, chaplains' clients in various contexts of customer care profess different faiths, not only the Christian faith. This situation, therefore, needs to be reviewed in such a way that chaplaincy services be extended to other religious denominations in order to ensure a customer service that is consonant with the country's religious diversity and its respective historical-cultural roots. After all, as revealed by a multinational study (Zimmer et al. 2019), the relations between religiosity, spirituality, and mental health are subject to a wide spectrum of cultural diversity and cannot be generalized based on only one perspective.

Conclusion

The findings obtained and discussed in this study confirm and reinforce the relevance of the themes of religiosity and spirituality and their relations to mental health. We also highlight the necessity of both the professionals and the mental health services, especially psychologists and chaplains (though not only these), to be duly improved for more adequate and competent handling of this domain in professional care. Even though the study was carried out in the

Brazilian context and full of consequences for this particular reality and its respective national health policies, it also yields implications for mental health care in other countries, especially those that do not yet have this service sufficiently structured in an inter- and multidisciplinary perspective involving teamwork between psychologists and chaplains. The reports of the professionals interviewed can be interpreted here as excellent stimuli in this direction, encouraging and inspiring integrative models between both perspectives – scientific and spiritual/ religious – in the care of those that suffer severe mental disorders in body and soul.

Note

1 Identification of the three umbrella research projects:

   a) Religiosity and Spirituality in the Hospital Context – Perceptions of Multi-Professional Teams (RESCH) supported by the National Council of Development in Science and Technology (CNPq) and the Ministry of Science, Technology, Innovation, and Communications (MCTIC) through the Spontaneous Demand Announcement 2013.
   b) Religiosity of the Immigrant – Health or Symptom: Perceptions of Brazilian and Portuguese Mental Health Professionals (RISS) financed by Santander Universities (Phase I) and CNPq/MCTIC (Phase II) through the Universal Announcement 2014.
   c) Mental Health in Psychosocial Care Centres – Perceptions of Professionals about the Role of Religiosity (RESMCAPS) financed by the Foundation for Research Support of the Federal District (FAP-DF) through the Spontaneous Demand Announcement 2015.

References

Aletti, Mário. 2012. "A Psicologia Diante da Religião e da Espiritualidade: Questões de Conteúdo e de Método" [Psychology in the Face of Religion and Spirituality Questions of Content and Method]. In *Religiosidade e Cultura Contemporânea: Desafios para a Psicologia*, edited by Marta Helena de Freitas, Geraldo José de Paiva, 157–190. Brasília: Universa.

Alves, Cândida Helena Lopes, and Marta Helena de Freitas. 2020. "Reforma Psiquiátrica e suas Decorrências: Percepções de Profissionais da Saúde Mental Portugueses e Brasileiros" [Psychiatric Reform and its Outcomes: Perceptions of Brazilian and Portuguese Mental Health Professionals]. In press. In *Interfaces na Saúde Mental: Parâmetros e Desafios*, edited by Ana Patrícia Fonseca Coelho Galvão. Campo Grande: Inovar.

Amatuzzi, Mauro Martins. 2012. "Pesquisa Fenomenológica em Psicologia" [Phenomenological Research in Psychology]. In *Psicologia e Fenomenologia: Reflexões e Perspectivas*, edited by Maria Alves de Toleto Bruns and Adriano Furtado Holanda, 17–25. São Paulo: Alínea. doi:10.1590/S0103-166X2009000100010

Ancona-López, Marília. 2018. "Psicólogo Clínico e as Questões Religiosas" [Clinical Psychology and Religion Issues]. In *Tratado de Psicologia Clínica: Da Graduação à Pós-graduação*, edited by Andrés E. G. Antúnez and Gilberto Safra. São Paulo: Atheneu.

Ang, Winny. 2016. "Bridging Culture and Psychopathology in Mental Health Care." *European Child and Adolescent Psychiatry* 26: 263–266. doi:10.1007/s00787-016-0922-6

Bachrach, Leona L. 2006. "Defining Chronic Mental Illness: A Concept Paper." *Psychiatric Services* 39 (4): 383–388. doi:10.1176/ps.39.4.383

Bister, Milena D. 2017. "The Concept of Chronicity in Action: Everyday Classification Practices and the Shaping of Mental Health Care." *Sociology of Health and Illness* 40 (1): 38–52. doi:10.1111/1467-9566.12623

Brasil. 2004. *"Saúde Mental no SUS: Os Centros de Atenção Psicossocial"* [Mental Health in SUS: Psychosocial Care Centers]. Brasília: Ministério da Saúde. Accessed March 16, 2020 from www.nescon.medicina.ufmg.br/biblioteca/imagem/1212.pdf

Brasil. 2011. *"Carta dos Direitos dos Usuários da Saúde"* [Charter of the Rights of Health Beneficiaries]. Brasília: Ministério da Saúde, Conselho Nacional de Saúde. (Série E. Legislação de Saúde). Accessed March 16, 2020 from http://bvsms.saude.gov.br/bvs/publicacoes/cartas_direitos_usuarios_saude_3ed.pdf

Brasil. 2012. *"Censo Demográfico 2010: Características Gerais da População, Religião e Pessoas com Deficiência"* [2010 Demographic Census: General Characteristics of the Population, Religion and Handicapped People]. Rio de Janeiro: Instituto Brasileiro de Geografia e Estatística (IBGE). Accessed March 16, 2020 from https://biblioteca.ibge.gov.br/visualizacao/periodicos/94/cd_2010_religiao_deficiencia.pdf

Canguilhem, Georges. 1966. *Le Normal et le Pathologique*. Paris: Presses Universitaires de France. doi:10.3917/puf.cangu.2013.01

Cunha, Vivian Fukumasu, and Fabio Scorsolini-Comin. 2019. "A Dimensão Religiosidade/Espiritualidade na Prática Clínica: Revisão Integrativa de Literatura Científica" [The Dimension of Religiousity/Spirituality in Clinical Practice: Integrative Review of Scientific Literature]. *Psicologia: Teoria e Pesquisa* 35, e35419. doi:10.1590/0102.3772e35419

Desciat, Manuel. 1999. *A Reforma Psiquiátrica*. Rio de Janeiro: Fiocruz. doi:10.7476/9788575415436

Foucault, Michel. 2005. *Madness and Civilization: A History of Insanity in the Age of Reason*. London: Routledge.

Francisco, Daniel Pereira, et al. 2015. "Contributions of the Chaplaincy Service to the Care of Terminal Patients." *Texto e Contexto: Enfermagem* 24 (1): 212–219. doi:10.1590/0104-07072015003180013

Freitas, Marta Helena, and Douglas Leite Piasson. 2016. "Religion, Religiosity and Spirituality: Impact in the Media and Professional Training in Psychology." *Esferas* 5 (8). doi:10.19174/esf.v1i8.7909

Freitas, Marta Helena. 2017. "Religious Psychology, Psychology of Religion/ Spirituality, or Psychology and Religion/Spirituality?" *Revista Pistis and Praxis, Teologia Pastoral* 9 (1): 89–107. doi:10.7213/2175-1838.09.001.DS04

Freitas, Marta Helena, and Paula Rey Vilela. 2017. "Phenomenological Approach of Religiosity: Implications for Psychodiagnostic and Psychological Clinic Práxis." *Revista da Abordagem Gestáltica* 23 (1): 95–107.

Freitas, Marta Helena, Luciano Costa do Espírito Santo, and Rita de Cássia Silva. 2019. "Percepções de Psicólogos Sobre Religiosidade e Saúde Mental: Estudo Fenomenológico em um CAPS do Distrito Federal" [Perceptions of Psychologists about Religiosity and Mental Health: A Phenomenological Study in a CAPS of the Federal District]. In *Interfaces Entre Psicologia Clínica e Saúde*, edited by Jadir Machado Lessa, Simony de Sousa Faria, Auterives Maciel Júnior, and Eduardo Passos, 102–120. Curitiba: CRV. doi:10.24824/978854442378.3

Freitas, Marta Helena. 2020. "Religiosity, Spirituality and Wellbeing in the Perception of Brazilian Health and Mental Health Professionals." In *Spirituality and Wellbeing: Interdisciplinary Approaches to the Study of Religious Experience and Health*, edited by Bettina E. Schmidt, and Jeff Leonardi, 199–224. Oxford: Routledge.

Gentil, Rosana Chami, Beatriz Pinheiro Guia, and Maria Cristina Sanna. 2011. Organization of Hospital Chaplaincy Services: A Bibliometric Study." *Escola Anna Nery* 15 (1): 162–170.
Giorgi, Amedeo. 2009. *The Descriptive Phenomenological Method in Psychology: A Modified Husserlian Approach*. Pittsburgh: Duquesne University Press.
Gonçalves, Jilliane P. B., et al. 2015. "Religious and Spiritual Interventions in Mental Health Care: A Systematic Review and Meta-analysis of Randomized Controlled Clinical Trials." *Psychological Medicine* 45 (14): 2937–2949.
Hefti, René, and Mary Rute Gomes Esperandio. 2016. "The Interdisciplinary Spiritual Care Model: A Holistic Approach to Patient Care." *Horizonte* 14 (41): 13–47. doi:10.5752/P.2175-5841.2016v14n41p13
Henriques, Halline Iale Barros, Pedro Filho Oliveira, and Alessandra Aniceto Ferreira Figueirêdo. 2015. "Speeches of CAPS Users on Therapeutic and Religious Practices." *Psicologia e Sociedade* 27 (2).
Husserl, Edmund. 2002. "Philosophy as Rigorous Science." In *The New Yearbook for Phenomenology and Phenomenological Philosophy*, edited by Burt Hopkins and Steven Crowell, vol. 2: 249–295. Oxford: Routledge.
Jimenez, Mary Ann. 1988. "Chronicity in Mental Disorders: Evolution of a Concept." *Social Casework* 69 (10): 627–633.
Kirmayer, Laurence J., Jaswant Guzder, and Cécile Rousseau. 2014. *Cultural Consultation: Encountering the Other in Mental Health Care*. New York: Springer.
Kirmayer, Laurence J., Danielle Groleau, Jaswant Guzder, Caminee Blake, and Eric Jarvis. 2003. Cultural Consultation: A Model of Mental Health Service for Multicultural Societies". *Canadian Journal of Psychiatry* 48 (3): 145–153.
Koenig, Harold G. 2009. "Research on Religion, Spirituality, and Mental Health: A Review." *Canadian Journal of Psychiatry* 54 (5): 283–291. doi:10.1177/070674370905400502
Koenig, Harold G. 2013. *Spirituality in Patient Care: Why, How, When and What*. 3rd Edition. Philadelphia: Templeton Foundation Press. doi:10.1345/aph.1k479
Koenig, Harold G. 2015. "Religion, Spirituality, and Health: A Review and Update." *Advances in Mind-Body Medicine* 29 (3): 19–26.
Nwora, Emmanuel Ifeka. 2020. *Religiosidade, Espiritualidade e Saúde Mental na Percepção de Capelães Brasileiros* [Religiosity, Spirituality and Mental Health in the Perception of Brazilian Chaplains]. PhD diss. Universidade Católica de Brasília. doi:10.23925/1677-1222.2020vol20i2a14
Paiva, Geraldo José. 2015. "Classic Religiousness, Contemporary Spirituality and Quality of Life: A Psychological Discussion." *Relegens Thréskeia: Eestudos ePesquisa em Religião* 4 (1).
Paulino, Pedrita Reis Vargas. 2019. *Religiosidade/Espiritualidade em Psicólogos Brasileiros: Perfil e Implicações na Prática Profissional* [Religiosity/Spirituality in Brazilian Psychologists: Profile and Implications in Professional Practice]. PhD diss. Universidade Federal de Juiz de Fora, Minas Gerais. https://repositorio.ufjf.br/jspui/handle/ufjf/11257
Pereira, Sérgio Henrique Nunes. 2018. *Entre Cristandade e Psicanálise: Um Estudo Fenomenológico-hermenêutico sobre a Inveja e a Acídia* [Between Christianity and Psychoanalysis: A Hermeneutic-phenomenological Study about Envy and Acedia]. PhD diss. Universidade Católica de Brasília.
Pereira, Karine Costa Lima, and Adriano Furtado Holanda. 2019. "Religião e Espiritualidade no Curso de Psicologia: Revisão Sistemática de Estudos Empíricos" [Religion and Spirituality in Psychology Course: Systematic Revision of Empirical Studies]. *Interação em Psicologia* 23 (2): 221–235.

Piasson, Douglas Leite, and Marta Helena de Freitas. 2020. "O Senso Religioso na Formação do Psicólogo: Análise dos Currículos das Universidades Brasileiras" [The Religious Sense Formation of the Psychologist: Analysis of the Curricula of Brazilian Universities]. In press. In *Experiências Religiosas, Espirituais e Anômalas: Desafios Para a Saúde Mental*, edited by Thiago Avelar Aquino, Marta Helena de Freitas, and Letícia de Oliveira Alminhana. João Pessoa: Editora Universitária UFPB.

Quétel, Claude. 2012. *Histoire de la Folie: De l'Antiquité à nos Jours*. Paris: Texto.

Ribeiro, Rafael Bernardon, Débora Luciana Melzer-Ribeiro, and Quirino Cordeiro. 2012. Morbidity and Mortality due to Mental Disorders in Brazil. *Brazilian Journal of Psychiatry* 34 (2): 217–220.

Ribeiro, Fernanda Mendes Lages, and Maria Cecilia de Souza Minayo. 2015. "Religious therapeutic communities in recovering drug users: the case of Manguinhos, state of Rio de Janeiro, Brazil." *Interface* 19 (54): 515–526. https://doi.org/10.1590/1807-57622014.0571

Ritchie, Hannah, and Max Roser. 2018. "*Mental Health Disorders as Risk Factors for Substance Use*". Our World in Data. Accessed April 8, 2020 from https://ourworldindata.org/mental-health-disorders-as-risk-for-substance-use

Roger, Kerstin Stieber, and Andrew R. Hatala. 2017. "Religion, Spirituality and Chronic Illness: A Scoping Review and Implications for Health Care Practitioners." *Journal of Religion and Spirituality in Social Work* 37 (1): 24–44.

Ruas, Evelyn Figueira Lima. 2018. *Religiosidade de Pacientes Evangélicos nas Percepções de Psicólogos em Contextos Hospitalar e em CAPS* [Evangelical Patients' Religiosity in the Perceptions of Psychologists in Hospital and CAPS Contexts]. MSc diss. Universidade Católica de Brasília.

Ruas, Evelyn Figueira Lima, et al. 2020. "Manejo da Religiosidade/Espiritualidade em Contextos Clínicos: A Experiência de Psicólogos/as" [Handling Religiosity/Spirituality in Clinical Contexts: The Experience of Psychologists]. In *Clínica Política, Arte e Cultura: Subjetividades e a Produção dos Fascismos no Contemporâneo*, edited by Flávia Cristina S. Lemos, et al., vol. 8: 539–566. Transversalidade e criação – ética, estética e política. Curitiba: CRV.

Timmins, Fiona, et al. 2018. "The Role of the Healthcare Chaplain: A Literature Review." *Journal of Health Care Chaplaincy* 24 (3): 87–106.

VandeCreek, Larry. 1999. "Professional Chaplaincy: An Absent Profession?" *Journal of Pastoral Care* 53 (4): 417–432. doi:10.1177/002234099905300405

Von Peter, Sebastian. 2010. "The Temporality of 'Chronic' Mental Illness". *Culture, Medicine and Psychiatry* 34, 13–28. doi:10.1007/s11013-009-9159-x

World Health Organization [WHO]. 1992. "*The ICD-10 Classification of Mental and Behavioural Disorders: Clinical Descriptions and Diagnostic Guidelines*." World Health Organization. Accessed April 8, 2020 from https://apps.who.int/iris/handle/10665/37958

World Health Organization [WHO]. 2013. "*Mental Health Action Plan 2013–2020*". World Health Organization. Accessed March 15, 2020 from https://apps.who.int/iris/bitstream/handle/10665/89966/9789241506021_eng.pdf?sequence=1

Zimmer, Zachary, et al. 2019. "Religiosity and Health: A Global Comparative Study." *SSM: Population Health* 7.

3 Responding with Anishinaabek values

Understanding the importance of living as a spiritual being for mental wellness

Leslie McGregor and Gerald Patrick McKinley

Introduction

There is a lot that can be learned by sitting and listening to a good story. For example, stories about the Elder Brother, the atemporal Being Nanabijou, teach us about why the world is the way that it is. Telling these stories maintains a connection between Anishinaabek (Canadian Indigenous) people, the land, and the other Beings with whom they share the land. There are lessons that are seasonal and lessons that depend on where you are. There are lessons that arrive during the waking day and others while dreaming. The purpose of all of them is to provide guidance on how to follow a good path. This process, known in Nishnaabemwin, the Anishinaabek language, as *bimaadiziwin*, extends across a life-course and holistically feeds the physical, emotional, mental, and spiritual health of a person. *Bimaadiziwin* connects to an important truth, one of many truths, that to be Anishinaabek is to be a spiritual Being living in a physical world.

In this chapter, we discuss the nature of humans as *a priori* spiritual Beings given an Anishinaabek perspective and how this belief relates to chronic mental illness. We differentiate between being a spiritual Being and having a spiritual life by examining how we approach mental wellness. Like all good stories, this chapter has been through many iterations. We have worked with the general form of the chapter while keeping the main messages intact. This is not the only form that this story can take. We have decided on this version of an open, flowing narrative to reflect our ongoing conversations about spirituality and health in an Anishinaabek community. This is a version that flows out of the oral traditions of both our heritages. We come from places where people like to talk and laugh. LM is *Anishinaabekwe* (an Anishinaabek Indigenous woman) and GM is an Irish immigrant to Canada.

This chapter is about our understanding of mental wellness in the face of chronic mental illness. Assigning a definition to mental illness or wellness is challenging, particularly in a cross-cultural conversation. For us, mental wellness is about living a good life as often as you can. Mental wellness is strongly connected to *bimaadiziwin* as an ongoing process in life. In order to explore this, we approach two different cultural understandings of health and illness. The first is an Anishinaabek perspective on mental wellness and the second is a Western

DOI: 10.4324/9781003043508-3

biomedical perspective on chronic mental illness. For us, the distinction is simple; mental wellness is a focus on helping people live the best life possible for them (*bimaadiziwin*). We define mental illness or mental disorders as a language and science that focuses on, and works for the mitigation of, the symptoms of a disease believed to be based in the brain. Mental illness is deficit focused. Furthermore, chronic mental illness is defined when a person has symptoms that have had a duration of greater than six months or at least one episode of relapse (Nagel et al. 2009). Our central argument is that living *bimaadiziwin* helps to heal the individual spiritual Being in response to the ongoing stressors associated with colonization, and at the same time it helps to decrease the burden of chronic mental illness in a community.

A social aetiology of mental illness that originates with George W. Brown and Tirril Harris' (1978) work on depression, contends that chronic depression is the result of ongoing social stresses which accumulate over the life-course. The term chronic is based in a concept of time and derives from the Greek *khronos*. We both have seen the accumulation of stress on individuals and whole communities through our work together and separately, through LM's work in her community as the Director of Health and Social Services and GM's community engagement and research in the Office of the Chief Coroner for Ontario. The most common chronic mental illnesses impacting Indigenous communities in Canada include Post-Traumatic Stress Disorder, substance misuse, and major depression (Government of Canada, 2020). In response to the mounting chronic mental illnesses among Indigenous populations, Cynthia Wesley-Esquimaux and Andrew Snowball (2010) have called for the integration of traditional, cultural, and spiritual practices tied to the Seven Grandfather's teachings as a way of dealing with chronic mental illness and advancing *bimaadiziwin* in Indigenous communities. The Seven Grandfather's teachings are gifts of knowledge provided to the Anishinaabek to help them as they work towards living a good life (Kotalik and Martin 2016). We view, and have applied practices to support, *bimaadiziwin* as an appropriate response to chronic mental illness because it contains the key element of time and a process unfolding across the life-course. In the context of Indigenous communities, chronic mental health issues likely develop across the life-course and through intergenerational factors such as residential school trauma (Hatala, Desjardins and Bombay 2016). *Bimaadiziwin* is a life-course approach to wellness thereby making it a suitable response to chronic mental illness. Living and being well take time and practice. In addition, *bimaadiziwin* requires resilience to respond to the ongoing social determinants associated with historical and contemporary forms of Canadian settler colonization.

Linguistically, *bimaadiziwin* is constructed of the intransitive verb *bimaadizi* (he/she is alive) and the noun forming final *win*. More importantly, it is a unifying concept for what it means to be Anishinaabek (Gross 2002). It is a holistic concept that ties the spiritual, emotional, mental, and physical Self to the actions of a person. It expands out through a person's individual Self to their relations through the actions that they take in everyday life. It is, simply, following a good path, which, of course, is never simple. Following a good path depends on learning from others, taking part in ceremony, and feeding the spiritual Self through having a spiritual life. Local teachings hold that the Self is made up of four parts (the physical, mental, emotional, and spiritual), which are always connected. When we follow a good path through our good, embodied actions, we can have a good mind, which feeds good emotions that in turn nurture the spirit and enable a good life.

With *bimaadiziwin*, we focus on the importance of relationship. A holistic understanding of the Self means you cannot separate the components of that Self; we are spiritual, physical, mental, and emotional. It is a concept of Selfhood that extends out across generations and relationships, and inward to the core of who you are. A neuroscientist might find that a person experiencing depression has a specific part of their brain working (or not working) in a different way. They are connecting the physical and the mental through a reduction of the mind-to-brain function. Our lesson is that the spiritual (and other self-components) are also impacted in depression. Omushkego Elder Louis Bird (2007), for example, wrote that the spirit lives in the mind. It is a reminder that mental well-being and spiritual well-being are intimately connected. Together, these two aspects of the Self may also impact the physical (the brain) and the emotional (joy or sadness).

Like many before us who have engaged in a discussion about biomedicine, we view it as cultural (Good 1994; Kleinman 1981). However, we do not assume that everyone working in fields such as psychiatry are materialists or biological reductionists. We define the reductionist approach as a focus purely on the biological functioning of the brain apart from social and cultural determinants. Lawrence Kirmayer (2015, 622) clearly articulates three perspectives that have developed over the past 150 years of evolution in the field of psychiatry, namely the person as biological organism, the person as psychological self (i.e., psychoanalysis), and the person as shaped and contained within their social and cultural contexts. Furthermore, discussing the rise of the influence of the Diagnostic and Statistical Manual of Mental Disorders (DSM), Kirmayer laments a loss of context for patients and their social conditions as mental illness care is reduced to a checklist of symptoms that are added together for a diagnosis (Kirmayer 2015, 624). As we are strongly connected to Kirmayer's third perspective, which states that we develop as people based on our social environment and the cultural contexts that frame it, we argue for the importance of not just understanding culture, but also centring mental wellness programming around it. We view culture as the best way to understand the person, their context, and how they will interpret and act in the world. On the topic of culture and healing from chronic mental illness, one community member we work with noted,

> If the term culture encompasses our beliefs, our values, our way of seeing the world and our worldview, then…you talked about relationships…when you talked about traditional knowledge…that's what is important because it's not just you alone in the universe. You are not alone…you have all these different relationships…all those things tell you you are important.

We try to avoid simple dichotomies between Indigenous and Western knowledges. We both, in our personal and professional lives, draw on each knowledge system. However, we also do not consider an Anishinaabek Indigenous perspective as just another way of naming what Western science knows. We are purposeful when we make knowledges plural, as is common for a "Two-Eyed Seeing" epistemological approach (Martin 2012). In terms of chronic conditions, a Western approach to mental illness tends to focus on the individual patient's symptoms across time. *Bimaadiziwin*, in contrast, requires us to think about the individual and all their relations across a life-course. In other words, it is different to treat a person than it is to treat a symptom because the person is a web of relationships that contribute to wellness or illness. Chronic mental illness, like *bimaadiziwin*, is an accumulation of either negative or positive stressors.

In constructing this chapter, we draw on a number of perspectives and experiences. We believe in the importance of research being guided by lived experience. LM provides a strong degree of live experience, both as an *Anishinaabekwe* and as someone who has personal experiences within her relationship network of the impact of chronic mental illness and stresses. In her community, LM has worked as the Director of Health and Social Services and as the leader of the Crisis Response Team. GM, a Medical Anthropologist, trained as a researcher in the social aetiology of mental illness approach at the Centre for Addictions and Mental Health in Toronto, Canada. In this chapter, he draws on his experience working in school-based mental wellness programs, community-based suicide prevention programs, and his ongoing status as a learner of Anishinaabek culture. We met as part of a knowledge translation project funded by Canadian Biomarker Integration Network in Depression (CAN-BIND) and the Ontario Brain Institute (OBI), which were working to create a synthesis of Anishinaabek knowledge and biomedical research into depression and suicide prevention.

This chapter is an accumulation and continuation of our work together and our efforts to learn from each other. That work has included the development of knowledge translation programs with CAN BIND and the OBI for youth and their caregivers in LM's community. During the program we co-developed workshops that partnered local Indigenous knowledges with Western research into depression and suicide. In a typical workshop, youth and their caregivers spent time receiving teachings on seasonal aspects of Anishinaabek culture and strategies for responding to stressors that can lead to depression while learning how to respond to suicidal ideation in themselves and their peers. The goal of the workshops were to provide youth with tools they could use to respond to chronic stressors and the negative mental illness that resulted from them. The workshops consisted of four seasonal sessions. Traditional teachings and themes were integrated into the workshops depending on which season we were in. For example, certain older stories can only be told when there is snow on the ground and can therefore not be integrated during the spring and summer sessions.

In our current work together, we are adapting best practices from literature on "social prescription" to support community members who have responded to chronic stressors by becoming engaged in substance misuse. Social prescription is the practice of using social support networks and social inclusion to support individuals with chronic mental illness or who are engaged in substance misuse. With funding from the Canadian Research Initiative in Substance Misuse (CRISM), we are building programs around traditional knowledge and research into the positive impact of social inclusion and social support networks. Specifically, participants will learn how to make traditional Anishinaabek snowshoes and hear stories about living on their lands while learning to support each other in a positive way. We are measuring changes in the participants overall mental health and wellness throughout the process.

Methodology of working together

It is clear to us that what we are discussing in this chapter is not based in the context of academic research. Nor is it located solely in a community context. We are discussing relationships, which is a theme that runs through all the work that we do together. This is why we have focused our efforts on metaphors of relationships. The language of relationships ties us to *nishnaabemwin*. J. Randolph Valentine (2001, 335) wrote about metaphor in Anishinaabek language. He noted that meaning in *nishnaabemwin* is based on the component parts of a word each providing their meaning, stating that "relationships exist between the meaning of word components and the meanings of the words from which they are constituted." Furthermore, he adds that in some cases the components of the words are used metaphorically. He gives this example: *daapenim* or "taking a liking to someone" is constructed of the root *odaap* "take" and the final *enim* "in thought" (Valentine 2001, 336). Valentine is correct in his assessment that we do not actually take anything to someone when we like them. It is, like all language, a metaphorical language.

These concepts are present in how many Anishinaabek talk about positive relations and mental wellness. To be called or named as a sibling is a great honour. For "this person is my brother/sister" is not a connection of biological blood. Instead, it ties the spiritual Selves together in a journey of *bimaadiziwin*. Often the term is used to denote someone who plays a positive role in your life and someone upon which you know you can depend because they live their responsibilities to you. They live a good life, and you trust them. It is about connection and shared responsibility. Similarly, from a social determinants of health perspective, chronic mental illness is also a relationship of stressors that interact and accumulate over time before a person develops a condition, such as major depression. Relationships are always part of our mental well-being.

We wish to think and act more within the actions of relationships. Our work together is focused on learning; it is a process, and it is fluid. In *nishnaabemwin*, *inawem* or "to be related to," reflects not only how we work together but how knowledge about mental wellness can be considered. How do knowledge systems work in relationship? How do researchers work in relationship? It is from this position that our thinking shifts to the applied practice of community-based knowledge translation (CBKT) as a suitable response to chronic mental illness, a practice of implementation that holds relationships at its core and necessitates bidirectional knowledge sharing.

Most knowledge translation (KT) research and education are focused on the evidence-based science associated with clinical and hospital settings (Jenkins et al. 2016, 2). In short, medical science, including much mental health research, is geared towards the specific context of the hospital or clinical setting. The focus shifts the funding for research into this context and, as a result, favours evidence that is understandable within a narrow context. An emerging response to this constraint is community-based knowledge translation. CBKT acknowledges that under traditional bench to bedside KT, community or population-level knowledge and impact is often overlooked (Kitson et al. 2013).

The inequitable distribution of health outcomes and access to health care across all populations globally is very well documented (Ottersen et al. 2014). CBKT is an attempt to respond to inequity through increased participation of communities or populations that are often overlooked, such as global Indigenous populations. As a result, CBKT is often associated with public health approaches through the inclusion of health promotion techniques (Jenkins et al. 2016, 2). As defined by Kitson et al. (2013), CBKT, or CoKT in their terminology, moves through five stages: initial contact and refining the issue; knowledge refining and testing; knowledge interpreting, contextualising, and adapting; implementation and evaluation; and embedding in context, translating to other contexts. CBKT is similar in many ways to applied research approaches such as Participatory Action Research (PAR) where the community's needs are the driving force behind the research (Kitson et al. 2013). The work of CBKT moves between two main contexts. The local study context, where the population engaged in the research is based and the researcher context, where the research team is situated. In our case, the study context is Whitefish River First Nation and the research context is the University of Western Ontario.

The draw to CBKT is two-fold. First, the bidirectional knowledge sharing, which is the basis of CBKT, allows us to engage in learning together. CBKT has the potential to remove the top-down approach to research that has negatively impacted too many Indigenous communities in Canada. It prevents "helicopter research" or "break-and-enter research" where research teams visit a community to collect data and disseminate their results and the community is left with little or no direct benefit (Bird-Naytowhow et al. 2017). Through community participation and ownership of data, CBKT works to ensure that the community benefits directly from the research as the team responds directly to the health concerns in the community's context. Second, we consider the work that we do together to be relationship-based research. We define relationship-based research from Anishinaabek values focused on responsibilities to our relations. It encompasses a world larger than the data collection elements of a research project. It expands beyond the time and place of a single project to include the worlds that we live in and acknowledges that strong community-based research projects are built on a foundation of trust and mutual caring. Relationship-based research decentres the academy and places a focus on the Beings, largely defined, who are present in the context of the partnership. Relationship-based research allows us to respond to chronic conditions by ensuring that our partnerships are spread over a longer timeframe than the traditional length of a funded research project. The approach is beneficial because the causes of chronic mental illness are often cumulative or spread across a life-course.

In the context of our relationship-based work, we have tried to ensure that active listening is the core of our partnership. While partnered with CAN BIND and the OBI to develop the community-based mental wellness workshops for youth we needed to learn how to incorporate the values of relationships, identity, culture, and purpose/responsibility. It also provided a challenge in terms of "ethics" and what was understood within that context. The members of the research team were based in either hospital or university settings, which have a specific understanding of what ethics in research are. We experienced a degree of challenge from boards who are accustomed to clinical control trials rather than co-learning in a community. Our community partners also expected a degree of ethics derived from their perspective on relationships and responsibilities. One phrase GM has heard repeatedly is "we want you to do a good job for our kids." It means placing the community's priority to protect their youth first, ahead of paper writing and other academic priorities. The combination of these factors meant stepping away from a Western derived biological focus on chronic mental illness and adapting our approach to what we, as a team, were learning about working together. As will be discussed, an Anishinaabek understanding of mental wellness differs greatly from the biopsychosocial models that dominate much of the current research on chronic mental illness (Engel 1977), even including what has been referred to as a biopsychosocial-spiritual approach (Hatala 2013). In addition, the relationship-based approach means stepping away from the traditional research-participant power role. For the academic GM, it means assuming the role of learner and approaching the relationship with humility (Bird-Naytowhow et al. 2017). For Indigenous LM, it means being a patient teacher and allowing GM and the rest of the team time to process new important knowledge, an example of "Two-Eyed Seeing" in action (Martin 2012).

The scope of the project was to develop and evaluate a depression awareness and suicide prevention program for First Nations (Indigenous) youth in Ontario, Canada. It was a goal of LM's community to evaluate the effects of focusing on their values and culture with the goal of sharing the results with other Anishinaabek communities. It is worth noting that what might makes sense in an Anishinaabek community may be the wrong approach in another First Nation, even an Anishinaabek one. The process started with lots of meetings and relationship building in Toronto and in the community. We needed to trust each other before we would make progress. We included youth representatives in the development of the project. The relationship building process took about a year and included presentations to Chief and Council and the development of a memorandum of understanding to protect the rights of both sides of the relationship. The workshops were developed within a general framework, but content was decided on a workshop-by-workshop basis. In each workshop, community members and research team members presented on a variety of related topics. All content, both Anishinaabek and Western, was reviewed by a joint-team steering committee.

The evaluation of the project was qualitative in nature. At the second and fourth workshop, the research team recorded one-on-one and small group interviews with the community-based participants. The sessions at the second workshop focused on relationships, changes in behaviour, expectations for the project, and participants' understanding of why we were doing what we were doing. An example of the responses is drawn from a community staff member who said:

> They are turning to...connecting with their identity...they are turning to asking "who am I?"...and they are looking at...even ceremony. We just finished doing the fast and it is good to see our young people wanting...wanting to identify with that...whether they are asking for their spirit name, or their colours, or...even to participate in that ceremony of going through their stage in life which is youth now...and getting prepared and learning so that when they get to be an adult they'll have another stage, another ceremony. So, it is good to see that connection.

The fourth workshop evaluations focused on best practices we were seeing in providing a culture-based program, the role of different cultures, and the overall effectiveness of the team. On culture and healing, one staff participant noted: "[Its] important yeah...we lost that...but we are slowly getting that back...I feel that they don't know their identity and they're slowly getting that back too."

Step one of the CBKT process was given a great deal more time than most funding arrangements allow. It gave us time to figure out where each of our priorities came together and where there did not align. It helped establish an agreement on our values as partners and, most importantly, it helped with the development of trust. While most research funders may not understand the importance of spending time together for meals and getting to know each other, we were lucky that we had that opportunity. At times, we are working on projects together, such as the mental wellness workshops or our current focus on adapting social prescription practices to help community members engaged in substance misuse through the strengthening of positive social connections. Other times, most times, we are just staying in contact, sharing information, and considering when the relationship might work on a new project together. We agree that projects are short-term, but relationships are long-term. Like *bimaadiziwin*, CBKT is about partners following their paths which at times will come together and will at times flow apart. It is a process that allows us to consider mental wellness holistically.

Throughout the relationship we are attempting to ensure that Anishinaabek perspectives on mental wellness are our priority. But defining what that means continues to be challenging. We come from different cultural backgrounds but are trying to work together. We do not just know different things. We know differently. That is to say, we come from different epistemological traditions. However, we agree that learning together is an important component of relationship-based research, and we expand our definition beyond "Two-Eyed Seeing" to incorporate the importance of relationship building present in CBKT into our approach. We strongly believe that working to know from different perspectives, making mistakes, and adding to our knowledge from those mistakes is a key part of *bimaadiziwin*. This perspective also ties us to the important teaching of *dbaadendiziwin* (humility).

Relationships are not limited to other humans, nor are they limited to by a narrow understanding of what is living. The Anishinaabek world is composed of animate and inanimate Beings. Animate Beings include those that we can see and many that are not seen in the waking world. The former includes humans and animals. The latter is composed of Beings, including the Elder Brother and the Beings who are in and are the oldest stories or *aadizookaan*, where the story and the Being are the same. This includes Beings such as the four Winds and their brother Flint. Other Beings include the keepers of the animals such as Bear, and the *memengwesiwag*, or *pawagan*, the small but powerful Beings who reside in rock cliffs and visit in dreams. Humans most commonly interact while awake, but there are some who communicate through dreams. Some beings, like the *pawagan*, live on the land and communicate in dreams. While this is not an exhaustive list, it does demonstrate that the nature of Being takes on many forms. Some Beings are seen daily. Others live in and as stories. Others live in a spiritual realm, only accessible through fasting and dreaming. Each has their original instructions.

The spiritual Self

In Anishinaabek culture, an Elder or Knowledge Keeper (KK) is more than an older person. They are someone who holds knowledge and someone who has a responsibility for passing that knowledge on to others. An Elder can take a formal mentoring role or an informal teaching role. Sometimes, as GM has learned, the Elder will tell a story to correct and guide a learner. An Elder from Whitefish River First Nation provided us with a key teaching about the nature of what it means to be a spiritual Being. The teaching came while we were working away to prepare breakfast at one of our workshops. The Elder started to teach by telling stories about her life on the land, a common approach to teaching in Anishinaabek culture. During our conversation she said: "We are all spiritual Beings living a physical existence." She did not linger on the statement. Just a simple declaration of the facts, then on to a story about her life with her sisters. It was our responsibility to think about what she was sharing. It is not the Elder's responsibility to force us to act a certain way. She follows her path the best she can, and we must try to do the same. We understand that part of *bimaadiziwin* is making mistakes and owning them to learn from them. As such, what we write in this chapter is not a firm directive or fixed truth. It is a process we continue to learn.

How do we make connections between chronic mental illness, as mentioned above, and the spiritual Self? First, we start by defining the spiritual Self not as a set of actions, such as smudging or attending sweats. Those are the actions of having a spiritual life. They are important actions. Those actions are medicine for the person but are different from the spiritual Self. The spiritual Self is a priori to the physical Self but is dependent on the physical to experience life. Simply put, the spiritual is not something you tap into, it is who you are. Spiritual Beings experiencing a physical existence. Acting in a spiritual way does not make someone a spiritual Being because those actions take place after the spirit has taken a physical form. They are a reminder, a good way to follow your path, and should be thought of as a way of strengthening something that already exists.

The distinction between the spiritual Self and having a spiritual life is important. The Self can be divided into two related, but not always connected, forms. The body, or *miyó*, and the spirit, or *òtcatcákwin*, can be separated through ceremony or while dreaming (Hallowell 1955, 172–173). In Anishinaabek knowledge, many forms of illness take place with the spiritual Self, including forms of mental illness and chronic conditions such as depression and, in extreme cases, violent episodes associated with a person "going Windigo." The Windigo is an atemporal Being with a taste for human flesh whose story is told through the very old stories, the *aadizookaan*. To go Windigo is to lose your humanness. Illness of this form is often caused by others who are able to act against your spirit. For example, in discussion with A. Irving Hallowell, William Berens (2009) recalls a story about his development of a knee injury that was caused by his slighting a person who knew how to use his powers to harm the physical body through the spiritual.

Mental wellness, then, is a state where the spiritual Self is healthy and following a good path. The spiritual life is part of the process of keeping the spiritual Self well. If, for example, when forces, including direct attack from others or cumulative stressors, damage the spiritual Self, then only aspects of the spiritual life can help it heal. This understanding of sickness is present in many Indigenous communities globally. Healing practices can include sucking doctors, the use of traditional medicines, and ceremonies such as a sweat lodge, which are used to clean the spirit. It is a principle that we have worked into all our workshops. By focusing on aspects of the youths' lives that help them follow a good path and live their responsibilities to their relations, our experience clearly demonstrates that these workshops have positively enhanced their mental wellness and their spiritual Being.

We consider mental wellness through two key elements: your relationships and how you act towards those relationships. These relationships and actions are played out or develop as you follow your path across the life-course toward *bimaadiziwin*. Your path may also be guided by spirit helpers who provide knowledge and direction in dreams at different stages of life. The path to the "good life" starts at birth to seven years old. Here the child is cared for by their family. In the past, the family unit moved across the land together. Care for children was the responsibility of all adults, not just a child's parents. The child's role was to learn how to act from their families. The "fast life" includes ages eight to twelve years old. Here the child begins the rapid transformation into a young adult. For many, this is a time where Elders begin playing a more important role in their lives. It is a time to start learning more about the importance of their spiritual nature. For example, the traditional practice of fasting prior to the onset of puberty helps young people earn a spirit helper and receive guidance for the rest of their life. The "wandering life" is a time from 13 to 18 years old. It is a time of taking on greater responsibility for your own actions. During this time, a person may make many mistakes, might leave their good path, and might leave their community. However, it is understood that the wanderer can always return. Ages 19 to 55 years old are the "truth phase." It is a time of being an adult, learning who you really are, and showing children how to live. The final stage is the "planning stage." Here your responsibility may shift to the larger community. In this stage, you are now a person who others will look to as they journey along their own path. This was summarized by an Elder working with our program who said:

> These events...where I am today is sort of like, it parallels what this partnership means...to help out youth...[to] prepare their bundle...to get the skills...to recognize what is self-esteem...and to learn about problem solving... It enhances their stage of life...We all have a hand in helping our youth be who they are...It's our job and our responsibility to help them walk that good road.

Actions toward *bimaadiziwin* are often guided by several important teachings and stories. Perhaps the best known of these are the Seven Grandfather's teachings: *Dbaadendiziwin* (Humility), *Aakwa'ode'ewin* (Courage), *Gwekwaadziwin* (Honesty), *Nbwaakaawin* (Wisdom), *Debwewin* (Truth), *Mnaadendimowin* (Respect), and *Zaagidwin* (Love). In addition, depending on your clan or kinship connections, you may have additional responsibilities to your community. *Ajijaak* (Crane) and *Maang* (Loon) are responsible for leadership. *Bineshiinh* (Bird) are thoughtful or spiritual people. *Waabizkishi* (Martin) are brave and often act as hunters and warriors. *Wawashkes* (Deer) are peacemakers in the community. *Makwa* (Bear) are responsible for medicines and protecting the community. Finally, *Giigonk* (Fish) are wise.

Our perspective is that mental wellness ties the actions of a person to their relations. The stories about the Elder Brother, *Nanabijou*, are the *aadizookaan* which are old, sacred stories. But the word also means spirit because the stories and the Being are the same, an understanding of personhood that extends beyond a purely physical existence. In the *aadizookaan*, the Elder Brother is almost always walking or travelling, representing a culture that is largely place-based rather than time-based. The same is true of the spiritual Self. How we act as we move through time and across space impacts our whole Self. Over the years the accumulation of positive energy such as the emotions of love, humility, kindness, and hope, or negative energy such as hate, anger, despair, or misery contributes to the wellness of the spiritual Self. In other Indigenous contexts, this is sometimes referred to as a "soul wound" or the damage done to a person's spirit through the accumulation of unresolved grief connected to colonization and ongoing, day-to-day, stressors (Zimiles 2019). Our connection to our relations provides the resources that we can draw on to act our spiritual life in order to maintain wellness.

Relationships

Relational ontology carries into the world of wellness in an important way. In 1972, the anthropologist Adrian Tanner wrote a paper for the Sioux Lookout Indian Zone Hospital. The hospital is based northwest of LM's community but is the home to many Anishinaabek. As an internal report it was never published but is available via the University of Toronto Archives (Tanner 1971). In the paper, Tanner details what First Nations along the Albany River, an area where the population consists largely of Oji-Cree, or an Algonquin language and culture that blends Anishinaabek and Omushkego, knew about illness. The paper details four forms of "Indian" illnesses and of *pi:htaha:wtisu* (whiteman's illnesses) (Tanner 1972). *Inisna beh wa;biney, pa:hta:hsis, u:nchineh*, and *ki:wa:skweh* were understood to be different forms of "Indian" illnesses; however, all had within them a core spiritual illness (Tanner 1972). Tanner learned that white or Western medicines could relieve the symptoms of these illnesses but could never cure them because Western medicine only impacts the body. The reason being that traditional medicines are animate Beings. They work on specific ailments but only when the "prescriber," for lack of a better word, has a relationship with the medicine and knows the correct ceremony to accompany its use. Often the cure included working with the sick in their dreams (Tanner 1972). Much of the knowledge associated with healing in this manner is currently "sleeping," to use a term often heard in communities. The cultural knowledge and the relationships required for that knowledge to have meaning have been damaged by colonization. The conversion of many communities to Christianity has meant that practices such as the Shaking Tent or Bear Walking are no longer practiced in the open. A decrease in dreaming as a rite of passage means that Anishinaabek youth may not be making connections with their helpers' spirits and learning from them how to live a good life. See the work of A. Irving Hallowell for a complex discussion on the latter.

Cultural understandings and experiences with mental wellness and illness can be framed under the many approaches to phenomenology. However, it is important that when we consider this approach, we acknowledge that two people may use similar terms but mean completely different things. We have been using "holism" as a basis of our understanding of Anishinaabek wellness. Here we are concerned with the full integration of the body, mind, emotions, and spirit. Another take on holism is can be derived from George Engle's approach in 1977 to the biopsychosocial model of mental health (Borrell-Carrio, Suchman and Epstein 2004). This approach acknowledges that mental wellness and illness are the product of the interaction of biological, psychological, and social/cultural factors. There is not room enough in this chapter to consider or debate the extent to which social and cultural factors include the nature of Being versus the interpretation of experience based on belief. In this case, we suggest that the former incorporates the reality of being a spiritual Being for an Anishinaabek person, and the latter is an interpretation of experience based on a belief that you are such a being, regardless of actuality.

We believe that this is an important distinction. We adopt into our work together the understanding that to be an Anishinaabek person is to be a spiritual Being. This differs greatly from a perspective that assumes culture as purely a lens through which perception is formed. The former is about understanding the nature of wellness and illness at an ontological level while the latter is about interpreting context at an epistemological level. Two excellent examples of this are found in Arthur Kleinman's (1986) work on the social origin of disease in China and Bruce T. Bliatout's (2003) work with Hmong refugees on depression and nightmares. The implication is that there are certain forms of illness that can only be treated by incorporating a spiritual component, including mental illness, because the illness happens at the spirit level. As such, Western medicine may treat symptoms, but if the cause is spiritual then the cure must also be. In many ways, this is the challenge of aetiology research in health care. We must understand the cause before we can solve a problem.

Participants in our programs connected conditions like chronic depression to being alone. One adult from the community responded by saying: "They think they have no one…think that they can't handle life…isolation of themselves… they've got no one to talk to." Her response connected the youth in the program with local knowledge on the importance of relationships. Another adult described depression in terms of fire:

> I see it as the fire has gone out…like if you think passion, you're fiery… When that fire is low there's no passion…and there's no will…there's no drive. They're just going to exist…you're going to breath everyday…to do steps…do whatever you need to do and not enjoy life…and not enjoy what you are doing…It's all about their internal fire and keeping it going for them.

Both drew on a concept of relationships and responsibilities that extend beyond human interactions to include spiritual connections with the land, the animals, and the other-than-human Beings who share the territory. In this view, depression is caused by a history of colonial interference that reduced a youth's ability to see and act out their responsibilities to their relationships.

This approach is in keeping with a traditional Anishinaabek perspective on illness as something that originates outside of you and can be done to you. Michael Anthony Hart describes this holistic approach as "philosophies that concentrate on spirit, life in natural environments, fluxes, patterns and cycles, holism, diversity, relationships, interdependence, community, egalitarianism, and respectful individualism" (Hart 2019, 268). Spiritual Beings are in relationships with the land and the stories that are told in those places. We argue that one impact of colonization has been a change in those relationships which impacts the spiritual Being. Consider our earlier example of the pre-puberty fasting ceremony. With the introduction of Indian Residential Schools (IRS), youth were not with their families at this important time. As a result, the ceremony decreased in practice and youth lost an important part of their traditional knowledge. As the impact of change spreads across generations, the impact on the spiritual Beings involved will also grow. A loss of relationships contributes to a loss of resources for healing the spirit and lack of directions for following a good path.

The mental health and substance misuse challenges that are impacting Indigenous Peoples in Canada are a direct result of historical and ongoing settler colonization (Firestone et al. 2015). Suicide, self-harm, and substance misuse were never traditional aspects of Anishinaabek culture. Like diabetes and now certain cancers, suicide has a history of moving from non-existent or rare in First Nations populations to having very high rates in very short periods of time. Ward and Fox (1977) document the outbreak of suicide in the Manitoulin Island region starting in 1974. Documents from the Sioux Lookout Indian Zone Hospital demonstrated a concern over rapidly increasing suicide in the region starting in the mid 1980s (Fonseka, McKinley and Kennedy 2017). John Long (2010) mentions the earliest suicides in the James Bay region starting in the mid 1970s. Research into the Sioux Lookout Indian Zone Hospital shows a rise in substance misuse, first alcohol then gas sniffing, prior to the outbreak of suicide in that region (Fonseka, McKinley and Kennedy 2017).

Ours is an approach derived from Brown and Harris' (1978) research into the social aetiology of depression. The premise is straight forward. If you change people's social structure, you change how they can relate to others in their society. For example, consider traditional Anishinaabek social relationships. For a young boy, their uncle held the responsibility of teaching them how to be a member of society. Teaching was done through demonstrating *bimaadiziwin,* not in a classroom. It is the responsibility of the youth to watch the elder relation. It is the responsibility of the elder relation to follow a good path and demonstrate good relations with all classes of Beings. If, for a variety of reasons (including the Indian Residential Schools that occurred across Canada, loss of access to land, forced adoption or placement in Children's Aid care), the connection is broken, then the teaching cannot happen (Gracey et al. 2009; King et al. 2009; Wilks et al. 2017). The example of IRS, schools where First Nations youth were forcefully sent by the Canadian government from ages five to eighteen, inflicted a variety of traumas on First Nations individuals and their communities. The traumas have been passed through generations in numerous ways (Truth and Reconciliation Commission 2015, 115). These factors can increase stressors. Stress leads to several physiological and psychological responses associated with chronic mental illness and other diseases. Stress also damages the spiritual Self.

From a standard Western medical understanding, the physiological impact of stress is well documented. Environmental or chronic stress can place the body in a state of allostasis. The allostatic load is "biological adaptations to cumulative environmental demands" where the body releases stress hormones such as catecholamines and cortisol (McCaffery et al. 2012, e47246). Emotionally, stress, particularly the extreme stress associated with Post-Traumatic Stress

Disorder (PTSD), is linked to increased rates of anxiety and feeling loss of control over life situations (Sipple and Marshall 2013). LM adds that these emotions are carried with us, cumulatively adding to who we are. It is the accumulation of emotions that impacts our spirit. Adding too many negative emotions can lead to a damaged spirit. Because living *bimaadiziwin* is a practice in holistic health, it leads to an increase in positive emotions, which help in healing the Spirit. In our mind, our emotions are turned into memory. The mind solves problems for us and informs future actions. We use the expression "you heal with love, not with anger" to explain this approach. The combination of all aspects informs how a person follows their path.

A case of dreaming

We centre our argument of understanding chronic illness, spirituality, and health on the connected concepts of a spiritual Self and *bimaadiziwin*. Responsibilities and relationships are the mechanisms through which mental wellness is maintained. Guidance for living *bimaadiziwin* is held in stories, which exist on the land, or is provided in dreams by *memengwesiwag* or *pawagan*. We have been using the term "Western science" to denote research and evidence that originates from the narratives of a scientific method that dominates most health research in Canada. We do this to point out that if this is the lens through which you seek, it is the lens through which you will find. We extend this approach to the example of dreams to demonstrate the cultural difference in how dreams are understood in Western and Anishinaabek traditions.

Dreams continue to interest researchers and the general public around the world. Laura Palagini and Nicholas Rosenlicht (2011) provide a detailed review of how dreaming was thought to relate to mental health from a Western perspective across Western history. As expected, the way that health was understood greatly influenced how dreams were discussed. Most recently, from about the 1970s on, dreams have become a physiological activity studied using the techniques developed in neuroscience. Hobson and McCarley's (1977) activation-synthesis hypothesis (ASH) being a prime example of the transition from psychology to physiology in understanding dreams.

Another way to exist and to learn is through dreams. However, dreams are not a biproduct of the brain, in our view, they are a reality of the spiritual Self. Dreams can prefigure events that might happen to the dreamer (Brown and Gray 2009, 27), they are also a means of communication or healing, or they can be a way for other Beings to communicate. A common example is to consider dreams as a house. When you are in the different rooms, the other rooms are known to exist. Moving to another room does not make the experiences of the former unreal. The same applies for dreams and the waking world. Our actions in dreams are as real as the actions of the waking world. Others, living or dead, human or other, may visit and provide lessons to us on how to live *bimaadiziwin*. Dreams provide for us a way of understanding how the spiritual Self can exist and extend beyond the physical Self at times.

Other examples of this power include Bear Walking or Shaking Tents where, in both cases, the òtcatcákwin travels without the body or is visited by another spirit. Bear Walking allows an individual to travel as a bear between sites. Traditionally, Bear Walking was a healing practice that was later condemned by Christian churches as witchcraft. A Shaking or Conjuring Tent, *zhaaboondawaan* in Nishinaabemowin or *kwashapshigan* in Omushkego/Cree, is a small enclosure that permits communication with other tents across vast distances (Preston 2002, 80). William Berens, who taught A. Irving Hallowell (2009, 87) so much about Anishinaabek culture, recounts how he became sick through someone else's actions in a *zhaaboondawaan* in his story "The Rolling Head". While both practices are rarely discussed now, both authors have been in situations where their contemporary use was discussed, largely as part of cultural revival conversations. What follows is a detailed example of the relationship between dreams, reality, and the spiritual Self.

When LM first started as Health and Social Services Manager, she attended a workshop in Toronto on vicarious trauma. On the third day of the workshop, the instructor wanted to discuss the role of dreams in working with people who were traumatized. LM volunteered a dream she had about herself and a bear. For her it is an important dream because it helped her to feel powerful. At first, she was apprehensive about telling of the dream because it required her becoming vulnerable in front of others. The workshop facilitator brought her to the front of the circle and asked her to describe the dream.

The dream took place about six months after the death of her niece. In the dream, she was coming out of the back door at her parents' place and walking up from the water was a huge, black bear. At the same time, walking from her brother's place were her two nephews. Immediately, in the dream, she was afraid and worried about the boys. It has always been a fear of hers to encounter a bear, and she would often dream about them as a child. In the dreams, she would either be trying to get to the house, and a bear was between the her and the house, or she was in the house and the kids were outside playing, but the bear was in between house and the kids. In this dream, she says to the boys: "Walk slowly toward the basement door," and they do. She turns to the bear and says: "There is nothing for you here; you should go." She repeats this to the bear as it advances on the boys. Suddenly, the boys notice the bear and start to run for the basement door. As they do, the bear starts to charge at them, and one drops to the ground and plays dead. As she witnesses this, she intercepts the bear and says: "You will not get by me. There is nothing for you here. You should leave." Again and again, she says this to the bear, but the bear does not listen and continues to charge. Finally, the bear grabs her and puts her in a huge bear hug and starts to crush her while it bites the top of her head. She becomes enraged! She manages to get her arms out and forces her thumbs into the bears eyes. In pain, the bear lets go and runs away.

When she awoke from the dream, she felt powerful. The workshop facilitator asked her to repeat the dream time and time again. Finally, he asks: "Who died?" She looks at him quizzically. He asks again: "Who died?" and "By choice?" She is stunned and wonders how he is deriving that from this dream in which she is powerful. He continues to say that the young boy who drops to the ground dead is part of the message. Finally, she responds that her niece had died by suicide two years ago prior. He says: "Ahhhh...and you think it is your fault." She is taken aback when he says that. He continues and says, sarcastically: "You think you can read minds. You are one of the scarce few who can read minds." She is stunned (and crying), responding: "No." Then he says: "Oh, you can control people and what they do with your mind and words." Again, she responds with: "No." So, he says: "How could you have known? You cannot read people's minds. You cannot control what people do." Then he says: "Your family is lucky to have you. Your community is lucky to have you...You would fight a bear for them."

It is important to note that the bear in the dream is not symbolic in the way that psychoanalysis might view it. The bear was real. The consequences for not responding to the bear were real. LM would not have necessarily woken with scars on her body from the attack, although there are stories of people who have. Her spiritual Self was at risk in the dream. In asking who had died, the instructor was inquiring about who was sending LM the message. The dream was an important part of her healing from the loss of her niece two years before the workshop. It helped to heal her spirit and by doing so, allowed LM to make significant contributions to community's wellness.

Conclusion

Throughout this chapter we have put forward an argument that there is a key distinction between an ontological understanding of being a spiritual Being and the everyday practices of living a spiritual life. We do so in the context of ongoing settler colonization and the resulting traumas impacting too many Indigenous Peoples. We connect those traumas with a loss of broadly defined relationships. The process of *bimaadiziwin* requires living our responsibilities to our relations. The psychiatrist Bessel Van Der Kolk (2014) noted that social supports are a necessity rather than an option. We have worked to situate the spiritual Self within a larger understanding of social supports, one that includes classes of Being and relationships from Anishinaabek perspectives. Spiritual Selves are not limited to humans and extend to the many Beings who share the land, both in waking and in dreams, with the Anishinaabek. We believe that only by understanding the nature of being a spiritual Being can you start to understand a path forward to ending chronic mental illnesses in Anishinaabek communities. Not far from LM's home is a "dreamer's rock" where the Anishinaabek have come for generations to fast and receive instructions on how to follow their path from their relations. Other Beings, like the Elder Brother, live in and as stories that are told on the land. This knowledge of the spiritual Self provides multiple dimensions to how interactions contribute to wellness.

We, the authors, have agreed to a relationship based on mutual learning and positive actions so that we can continue to work towards positive change in LM's community. Our perspective is that a continued focus on deficits does not heal the spirit. Our work together has always been about finding a good way to work together. Sometimes we depend on Western knowledge, sometimes on Anishinaabek knowledge. Most often, we are negotiating and seeing with the two. We acknowledge the importance of relationship in living a healthy, holistic life and continue to develop and apply a CBKT model to support Indigenous young people finding mental wellness. Without understanding that, for the Anishinaabek, the Self is spiritual first, our attempts to combat the negative impacts of colonization are limited. We continue to learn that this holistic view provides a greater perspective on the aetiology of illness conditions and social problems and presents a richer context within which to restore and maintain mental wellness. *Chee Meegwetch* (Thank you).

References

Berens, William, as told to A. Irving Hallowell. 2009. *Memories, Myths and Dreams of an Ojibwe Leader*, edited by Jennifer S. H. Brown and Susan Elaine Gray. Montreal and Kingston: McGill-Queen's University Press.

Bird, Louis. 2007. *The Spirit Lives in the Mind: Omushkego Stories, Lives and Dreams*, edited by Susan Elaine Gray. Montreal and Kingston: McGill-Queen's University Press.

Bird-Naytowhow, Kelley, Andrew R. Hatala, Tamara Pearl, Andrew Judge and Erynne Sjoblom. 2017. "Ceremonies of Relationship: Engaging Urban Indigenous Youth in Community-Based Research." *International Journal of Qualitative Methods* 16 (1): 1–14. doi:10.1177/1609406917707899

Bliatout, Bruce T. 2003. "Social and Spiritual Explanations of Depression and Nightmares." In *Healing by Heart: Clinical and Ethical Case Studies of Hmong Families and Western Providers*, edited by Kathleen A. Culhane-Pera, Dorothy E. Vawter, Phua Xiong, Barbara Babbitt and Mary M. Solberg, 209–215. Nashville: Vanderbilt University Press.

Borrell-Carrio, Francesc, Anthony L. Suchman and Ronald M. Epstein. 2004. "The Biopsychosocial Model 25 Years Later: Principles, Practice, and Scientific Inquiry." *Annals of Family Medicine* 2: 576–582. doi:10.1370/afm.245

Brown, Jennifer S. H., and Susan Elaine Grey, eds. 2009. *Memories, Myths, and Dreams of an Ojibwe Leader, by William Berens as told to A. Irving Hallowell*. Rupert's Land Record Society series. Montreal: McGill-Queen's University Press.

Brown, George W., and Tirril Harris. 1978. *Social Origins of Depression: A Study of Psychiatric Disorders in Women*. New York: The Free Press.

Engel, George L. 1977. "The Need for a New Medical Model: A Challenge for Biomedicine Science." *Science (American Association for the Advancement of Science)* 196 (4286): 129–136.

Firestone, Michelle, Janet Smylie, Sylvia Maracle, Constance McKnight, Michael Spiller and Patricia O'Campo. 2015. "Mental Health and Substance Use in an Urban First Nation Population in Hamilton, Ontario." *Canadian Journal of Public Health* 106 (6): e375–381. doi:10.17269/CJPH.106.4923

Fonseka, Tehani M., Gerald P. McKinley and Sidney H. Kennedy. 2017. "Is Tetraethyl Lead Poison Affecting Contemporary Indigenous Suicides in Ontario, Canada?" *Psychiatry Research* 251: 253–254.

Good, Byron J. 1994. *Medicine, Rationality, and Experience: An Anthropological Perspective*. Cambridge, MA: Cambridge Press.

Government of Canada. 2020. "*Mental Health and Wellness in First Nations and Inuit Communities.*" https://www.sac-isc.gc.ca/eng/1576089278958/1576089333975

Gracey, Michael, and Malcolm King. 2009. "Indigenous Health Part 1: Determinants and Disease Patterns." *The Lancet* 374 (9683): 65–75. doi:10.1016/S0140-6736(09)60914-4

Gross, Lawrence. 2002. "*Bimaadiziwin* or the 'Good Life' as a Unifying Concept of Anishinaabe Religion." *American Indian Culture and Research* 26 (1): 15–32.

Hallowell, A. Irving. 1955. *Culture and Experience.* New York: Schocken Books.

Hart, Michael A. 2019. "Indigenist Social Work Practice." In *The Routledge Handbook of Social Work Theory*, edited by Malcolm Payne and Emma Keith-Hall, 268–281. London and New York: Routledge.

Hatala, Andrew. 2013. "Towards a Biopsychosocial-Spiritual Approach in Health Psychology: Exploring Theoretical Orientations and Future Directions." *Journal of Spirituality in Mental Health* 15 (4): 256–276.

Hatala, Andrew R., Michelle Desjardins and Amy Bombay. 2016. "Reframing Narratives of Aboriginal Health Disparity: Exploring Cree Elder Resilience and Well-Being in Contexts of "Historical Trauma."" *Qualitative Health Research* 26 (14): 1911–1927. doi:10.1177/1049732315609569

Hobson, John A., and Robert McCarley. 1977. "The Brain as a Dream State Generator: An Activation-Synthesis Hypothesis of the Dream Process." *American Journal of Psychiatry.* 134 (12): 1335–1348.

Jenkins, Emily K., Anita Kothari, Vicky Bungay, Joy L. Johnson and John L. Oliffe. 2016. "Strengthening Population Health Interventions: Developing the CollaboraK-Tion Framework for Community-Base Knowledge Translation." *Health Research Policy and Systems* 14 (65). doi:10-11864s12961-016-0138-8

King, Malcolm, Alexandra Smith and Michael Gracey. 2009. "Indigenous Health Part 2: The Underlying Causes of the Health Gap." *The Lancet* (British edition) 374 (9683): 76–85. doi:10.1016/S0140-6736(09)60827-8

Kirmayer, Laurence J. 2015. "Re-Visioning Psychiatry: Towards an Ecology of Mind in Health and Illness". In *Re-Visioning Psychiatry: Cultural Phenomenology, Critical Neuroscience, and Global Mental Health*, edited by Laurence J. Kirmayer, Robert Lemelson and Constance A. Cummings, 622–660. New York: Cambridge University Press. doi:10.1186/s13033-017-0134-6

Kitson, Alison, Kathryn Powell, Elizabeth Hoon, Jonathan Newbury, Anne Wilson and Justin Beilby. 2013. "Knowledge Translation within a Population Health Study: How Do You Do It?" *Implementation Science* 8 (54): 1–9. doi:10.1186/1748-5908-8-54

Kleinman, Arthur. 1986. *Social Origins of Distress and Disease: Depression, Neurasthenia, and Pain in Modern China.* New Haven: Yale University Press.

Kleinman, Arthur. 1981. *Patients and Healers in the Context of Culture: An Exploration of the Borderland Between Anthropology, Medicine, and Psychiatry.* Berkeley, CA: University of California Press.

Kotalik, Jaro, and Gerry Martin. 2016. "Aboriginal Health Care and Bioethics: A Reflection on the Teachings of the Seven Grandfathers." *American Journal of Bioethics* 16 (5): 38–43. doi:10.1080/15265161.2016.1159749

Long, John. 2010. *Treaty No. 9: Making the Agreement to Share the Land in Far Northern Ontario in 1905.* Montreal and Kingston: McGill-Queen's University Press.

Martin, Debbie H. 2012. "Two-Eyed Seeing: A Framework for Understanding Indigenous and Non-Indigenous Approaches to Indigenous Health Research." *Canadian Journal of Nursing Research* 44 (2): 20–42.

McCaffery, Jeanne M., Anna L. Marsland, Kelley Strohachen, Matthew F. Muldoon and Stephen B. Manuck. 2012. "Factor Structure Underlying Components of Allostatic Load." *PLoS One* 7 (10): e47246–e47246. doi:10.1371journal.pone.0047246

Nagel, Tricia, Gary Robinson, John Condon and Tom Trauer. 2009. "Approaches to Treatment of Mental Illness and Substance Dependence in Remote Indigenous Communities: Results from a Mixed Methods Study." *Australian Journal of Rural Health* 17 (4): 174–182. doi:10.1111/j.1440-1584.2009.01060.x

Ottersen, Ole Petter, Jashodhara Dasgupta, Chantal Blouin, Paulo Buss, Virasakdi Chongsuvivatwong, Julio Frenk, Sakiko Fukuda-Parr, Bience P. Gawanas, Rita Giacaman, John Gyapong, Jennifer Leaning, Michael Marmot, Desmond McNeill, Gertrude I. Mongella, Nkosana Moyo, Sigrun Møgedal, Ayanda Ntsaluba, Gorik Ooms, Espen Bjertness, Ann Louise Lie, Suerie Moon, Sidsel Roalkvam, Kristin I. Sandberg and Inger B. Scheel. 2014. "The Political Origins of Health Inequity: Prospects for Change." *The Lancet* 383 (9917): 630–667. doi:10.1016/S0140-6736(13)62407-1

Palagini, Laura, and Nicholas Rosenlicht. 2011. "Sleep, Dreaming, and Mental Health: A Review of Historical and Neurobiological Perspectives." *Sleep and Medicine Review* 15 (3): 179–186. doi:10.1016/j.smrv.2010.07.003

Preston, Richard. 2002. *Cree Narrative: Expressing the Personal Meaning of Events*. Montreal and Kingston: McGill-Queen's University Press.

Sipple, Lauren, and Amy D. Marshall. 2013. "Posttraumatic Stress Disorder and Fear of Emotions: The Role of Attentional Control." *The Journal of Traumatic Stress* 26 (3): 398–400. doi:10.1002/jts.21806

Tanner, Adrian. 1971. *Sickness and Ideology Among the Ojibway: Summer 1971*. (Unpublished). Sioux Lookout Zone Hospital Archives. University of Toronto.

Truth and Reconciliation Commission of Canada [TRC]. 2015. *What We Have Learned: Principles of Truth and Reconciliation*. Ottawa: Library and Archives Canada.

Valentine, J. Randolph. 2001. *Nishnaabemwin Reference Grammar*. Toronto: University of Toronto Press.

Van der Kolk, Bessel. 2014. *The Body Keeps the Score: Brain, Mind, and Body in the Healing of Trauma*. New York: Penguin Books.

Ward, J.A., and Joseph Fox. 1977. "A Suicide Epidemic on an Indian Reserve." *Canadian Psychiatry Association Journal* 22: 423–426.

Wesley-Esquimaux, Cynthia, and Andrew Snowball. 2010. "Viewing Violence, Mental Illness, and Addiction Through A Wise Practice Lens." *International Journal of Mental Health and Addictions* 8 (2): 390–407. doi:10.1007/s11469-009-9265-6

Wilks, Piotr, Alana Maltby and Martin Cooke. 2017. "Residential Schools and the Effects on Indigenous Health and Well-Being in Canada – A Scoping Review." *Public Health Review* 38 (1): 8. doi:10.1186/s40985-017-0055-6

Zimiles, Eleni. 2019. "Suicide and Soul Wound: Stress, Coping, and Culture in the American Indian and Alaska Native Youth Context." *Columbia Social Work Review* 11 (1): 57–68. doi:10.7916/d8nv9grm

4 Tradition and modernity in Somali experiences of spirit possession
An ethnographic exploration

Aaron Moratz

Introduction

> When I was a child, I didn't believe in spirits. I thought they were ghost stories. But now I have learned that they really exist, that the Qur'an teaches about them, and that they possess people.
>
> (male interviewee 1, unpublished data, 2015)

Experiences of spirit possession are common in Somaliland. In the past, possession was frequently studied as an exotic phenomenon within a cultural context that had little to do with the experience of the commonly Western-trained anthropologist (see Boddy 1994). While some recent studies (Pedersen 2011; Ram 2013) shifted the focus toward a more universal understanding of the underlying experience, allowing possession "to speak for itself," as Ram (2013) states, studies generally have not applied a diachronic perspective on the subject, in which ethnographic data consistently seem to suggest that possession is a traditional phenomenon to be seen in contrast with trends of modernization.

In this chapter, I analyze data that critically suggest an alternative interpretation. The population of Burao, a city in central Somaliland, understands its society as undergoing modernization, a process that is conceptualized as spirit-filled in that the existence of spirits is not questioned. As practicing Sunni Muslims, Somalis believe in the existence of *jinn* spirits who live parallel lives to humans (Ameen 2005, 38; see Qur'an 55:14–15). The major distinction between them is that humans are visible while *jinn* are invisible (Qur'an 7:27). Whereas there are believed to be good and evil *jinn*, in everyday life they usually appear as malevolent and deceptive. For part of the population, this belief in *jinn* spirits is currently being discovered for the first time, while for most people, the existence of spirits is reconceptualized according to the Somali understanding of an international Islamic modernity. It is also apparent that changes to this modernization process occur in the way that affliction by evil spirits is treated. While it used to be common in the Somali context to appease spirits with gifts and cooperate with them in various areas of life, the modern way is to consider them as enemies, to oppose them, and to drive them out with powerful Islamic religious methods considered to be "proper." This chapter offers a view of a "religious modernity" that considers itself

DOI: 10.4324/9781003043508-4

superior to a secular modernity and analyzes the advantages that a spiritual understanding offers in the area of mental health and chronic illness.

Possession frequently appears in the Somali cultural context as a chronic illness. Among my interviewees, several mentioned experiences in which they, or a close friend or family member, were possessed by a spirit (*jinn*), were "delivered" through methods of Qur'anic healing in so-called *cilaaj* clinics, but were then possessed again shortly after the deliverance had occurred, entering into a cycle of possession and healing that places the sufferer in a dependent relationship with the healer. An interviewee put it this way: "When a *jinn* is driven out, if ten years later he sees the door still open, he will enter again" (female interviewee 2, unpublished data, 2018). More common, however, are cases in which the person who is possessed attends an *cilaaj* clinic or has the Qur'an read over him/her in a private setting and is freed from possession by this treatment, but then the person experiences the same kind of possession again within days or weeks, prompting him/her to seek religious treatment again. An idiom used to describe this experience is that there remained an "open door," that is, the reason for the initial possession was not fully removed, reflecting a spiritual form of chronicity. According to common knowledge, this may be due to religious uncleanness or a general lack of religious practice, such as an irregular prayer routine, an unresolved conflict with another human being, a sin that is inherited from parents and grandparents, exposure to unclean places like rubbish dumps, or a number of other areas that leave the person vulnerable to or at "risk" from attacks by evil spirits.

Apart from this kind of recurring possession, there are also cases in which possession lasts for extended periods of time, sometimes years. In one case, the interviewee explained: "A spell was placed on her for eight years. After eight years the *jinn* would leave the body, but until then he would live inside her" (male interviewee 3, unpublished data, 2015). In this case, the possessed woman had frequent violent episodes. In another, a woman had several miscarriages until the influence of an evil spirit was removed, and she was then able to give birth to a number of healthy children. Frequently, I have observed those who suffer from spirit possession, especially when it is connected to violent behavior, being kept hidden in the back room of a house or even chained. Spirit possession, moreover, is always seen in a negative light in the contemporary Somali context. I agree with Lewis's (1998, 112) assessment that, for Somalis, possession is "essentially an illness ... spirits cause disease, they do not cure it." In the diverse contexts of my research population, therefore, spirit possession can be conceptualized as a somewhat unique chronic illness.

Literature overview and theoretical framework

The study of spirit possession in East Africa

To place the study of spirit possession among Somalis in its theoretical context, one must start with I. M. Lewis, whose work on possession has become known as deprivation theory, with the primary focus on the role of possession in the social structure of Northern Somali society (see Lewis 1998; 2003). By focusing on the circumstances in which people experience possession, he suggested that spirit possession was the functional equivalent of mental illness (2003, xiv).

Lewis (1998, 108) argued that the act of possession is "invoked to account for physical and mental distress in situations where those afflicted are in some sense deprived of secular efficacy … It is utilized by those who seek redress but find other means of effective action blocked or culturally inappropriate." Lewis (1966) also noted several contexts in which spirit possession occurred in Somali society at the time of his fieldwork in the 1950s to 1960s. The most common context is frustrated love and passion, which involves emotions that are not expressed openly in Somali culture, especially by men. This is described as the "entering" of a person on the part of their rejected lover. A woman, if showing "symptoms of extreme lassitude, withdrawal, or even more distinct physical symptoms of illness," is seen as "possessed by the object of her affections" (Lewis 1966, 311). Other contexts are the deprivation of food and company that young men often experience when they herd camels far away from home, the failure experienced by adult men to live up to their roles and responsibilities in the clan context, and the pressures experienced by wives who struggle with raising children in a harsh environment and who feel neglected by (often absent and polygamous) husbands (Lewis 1966, 313–16). Women, Lewis (1966, 314) argued, exhibit possession "as a limited deterrent against the abuses of neglect and deprivation in a conjugal relationship which is heavily based in favor of men." Lewis's interpretation of spirit possession is reflective of an "idiom of distress," a term developed by Mark Nichter (1981). Nichter (1981, 393) argued that in the South Indian context, "possession cults provide non-Brahmin women a variety of avenues for expressing affect, bringing to light sources of conflict and anxiety, mobilizing their families around socio-religious issues, manipulating social roles, and receiving security and moral support from other women." Like Lewis, Nichter (1981) contended that possession experiences are often a symbolic means for overtly expressing what is not socially acceptable to be expressed.

Lewis's deprivation approach, and by association Nichter's (1981) "idioms of distress," has been criticized by a number of scholars. Boddy (1989, 140) noted that Lewis assumed the intentionality of women who were described as using possession as a "strategy" to improve their life situation. Ram (2013, 82–83) similarly argued that the choice of using possession "may be regarded unsympathetically, as it is by local Somali men, … [or] it may be championed by men such as Lewis as a feminist stratagem in a sex war," but it remains a strategy that is "predicated on full consciousness" and requires us to see "a subject who is entirely whole" and unaffected by possession or gender inequality.

In my interpretation of spirit possession among my Somali research population, I have decided not to adopt an "idioms of distress" or deprivation framework. When I raised the possibility of an instrumentalist understanding, as Boddy (1994) labeled approaches based on Lewis's deprivation approach, with a number of interviewees, mainly those who were academically trained and who I assumed might be open to such an interpretation, I received only rejection. The issue is that interpreting possession as an "idioms of distress" would ontologically move a phenomenon that my research participants consider real and, to some degree, independent from circumstances, into the realm of metaphor, symbolism, and imagination. Ashforth (2005, as cited in Pedersen 2011, 32) summarized this interpretive problem well when he noted that "while this literature [of possession as a means to analyze social or cultural phenomena] has revealed much about African social life, it suffers from the singular defect ... of treating statements that Africans clearly intend as literal, or factual, as if they were meant to be metaphorical or figurative." In the East African case, Lewis (2003) considered spirit possession to be a strategy of the disadvantaged to alleviate their suffering by rising to a position of power, while Boddy (1989) saw in spirit possession a counter-hegemonic satirical allegory that allowed women to imagine an alternative reality. For these and other authors, possession is not considered as a phenomenon in and of itself but as a more instrumentalist means toward other ends. My research agrees with Ram (2013, 63) that giving possession a voice of its own instead of "mut[ing the] phenomenon" allows the experience of possession "to generate knowledge in its own right," which further enriches our understanding of the experience.

Foundations for a modernization framework for spirit possession

An assumption in the analytic framework that considers possession as a metaphor or symbol for other social or cultural phenomena is to firmly place it discursively in the realm of tradition as opposed to modernity, as well as ontologically in the realm of ideas as opposed to objective reality. A diachronic perspective of possession that investigates historical ruptures has generally not received much attention. This raises the question of whether spirit possession is in some way at odds with modernization.

Modernization theory, as originally conceived by Max Weber, involves the process of disenchantment or removing beliefs in spirits and demons that are active in this worldly realm. Weber (2009, 155) emphatically states: "The fate of our times is characterized ... by the 'disenchantment of the world.'" Two contemporary theories were based on Weber's (2009) thought, Fukuyama's (2002) end of history and Huntington's (1993) clash of civilizations. Fukuyama (2002, 3) argued that history had "culminated in modern liberal democracy and market-oriented capitalism" that "will continue to spread around the world." Huntington (1993, 48), in contrast, argued that the world is increasingly split along civilizational lines, that "differences between civilizations are real," and that "conflicts between civilizations" will become commonplace with a particular emphasis on conflict between "the West and the Rest" and an immediate focus on "the West and several Islamic-Confucian states." To sketch it broadly, Fukuyama (2002) envisioned a modernity that looks like the West at the turn of the millennium, while Huntington (1993) pictured the growth of a limited number of civilizations in conflict with each other.

The concept of multiple modernities, first developed by S. N. Eisenstadt (2000), shares elements of both these theories. It agrees with Fukuyama (2002) that modern societies have certain characteristics in common but disagrees that the world is on a trajectory toward a uniform world society and culture. It agrees with Huntington (1993) that societies will develop in different directions but disagrees that the expressions of civilization are based on some essential tradition. Most significantly, it suggests that "there is no single pattern of modernity" (Casanova 2011, 263–64). Instead, modernity is best understood as "a story of continual constitution and reconstitution of a multiplicity of cultural programs" and that "Western patterns of modernity are not the only 'authentic' modernities" (Eisenstadt 2000, 2–3). These different cultural programs, which align themselves with modernity by continually reinterpreting and reappropriating the discourse on their own terms, are based on "core transcendental visions" with the possibility that these visions may be contested (Eisenstadt 2000, 4). Specifically relevant to this chapter is Eisenstadt's (2000, 19) recognition that the transnational Islamic *ummah* community "transcends any specific place" and has "ideologically closed boundaries" but is at the same time continually changing so that its "cultural vision" can be proclaimed. Referring to Göle, Eisenstadt (2000, 20) notes that "Muslim fundamentalists ... share a preoccupation with modernity. It is their major frame of reference."

Brenner (1996, 679), as part of her research about veiling practices in Indonesia, described "Islamic discourses of modernity" that align with Eisenstadt's (2000) concept of a "core transcendental vision." While it needs to be recognized that Islam is expressed in a variety of forms around the world, certain similarities can be seen across contexts. When I use the term "global Islamic movement," I refer to the "core transcendental vision" of modernity that makes the transnational Sunni Muslim *ummah* community attractive to youth around the world. One key aspect of this vision "represents a conscious *disjuncture* with the local past in terms of its practices as well as in certain key ideological premises" (Brenner 1996, 679) so that certain Islamic practices are seen as proper, while other cultural practices are considered un-Islamic. This disjuncture is grounded in a common vision, or at least one that is believed to be common, of "a new society constructed on the principles of Islam," once again, whatever these principles might be once contextualized into a local context (Brenner 1996, 680). Brenner further suggests that the idea of reform or rupture with the past "may be fundamental to the ideologies and strength of the movement" (1996, 681) so that the foundation of the movement is "an essentially modernist vision ... [that] recasts modernity in a religious light" (1996, 682). I believe this description of the modern Islamic vision applies to Somaliland in a similar way.

Marja Tiilikainen conducted research into spirit beliefs and healing practices in Somaliland in the mid-2000s and suggested that "the emergence of Koranic healing clinics ... indicates a change in how the relationship between human beings and spirits is seen, and what is regarded as proper treatment" (2010, 164). The emphasis, especially for Qur'anic healers practicing in *cilaaj* clinics, is on using only "purely Islamic methods" (2010, 176), which stand in contrast to more traditional ways of healing practiced by *saar* possession cults common in East

Africa. The term *saar* can refer to "a type of spirit, the illness that spirits can cause by possessing humans, and the rituals necessary to their pacification" (Boddy 1989, 131). *Saar* ceremonies in which healers accommodate the spirits were the most common method of healing up to the turn of the century in Somaliland.

In order to illustrate the rupture between the traditional and the modern, Adam's (2010) detailed description of a *saar* ceremony she witnessed in Mogadishu, Somalia, in 1988 is helpful. She noted that appeasement and pacification were the goals of the event. Over the course of a week, social activities alternated with intense religious activities, such as the chanting of verses from the Qur'an, the anointing, mounting, and sacrificial slaughter of an ox, the tasting of the ox's meat by the healer to determine whether it was pleasant to *saar* spirits, and the "dancing of the *saar*," including "ecstatic rhythms," "monotonous chants," "fainting," "violent shaking," and the spirits being "called on by name and sung to" and fed with meat from the slaughtered animal (2010, 195, 198). The goal of the rhythmic dance was to invite the *saar* to possess the healer, while the dance was also "the means of release from [possession]" (2010, 195). The primary difference that Tiilikainen described was that Qur'anic healers consider spirits enemies to be rid of: "Force, violence and revenge have overtaken traditional ideals of negotiation, compensation, and collective responsibility" (2010, 178–79). Tiilikainen (2010, 180) saw in the organization of *cilaaj* clinics and their resemblance to medical clinics an aspect of "Somali modernity." My goal is to unpack this idea further and apply it, not only to the healing clinics but also to the conceptualization of recurring chronic possession and healing practices.

Based on these issues and previous literature, the main research questions I explore in this chapter are as follows: How do Somalis conceptualize modernity and modernization in the area of mental illness and as expressed in the affliction of chronic spirit possession? How does this conceptualization affect the approaches to Qur'anic healing as it is practiced in Somaliland? Finally, what may be gained from a perspective that allows spirits and spirit possession to be a modern Islamic phenomenon when offering care and support to people who suffer from chronic spirit possession and mental illness?

Context and methodology

The ethnographic context in which this project was conducted is the city of Burao, the regional capital of the Togdheer region in Somaliland, otherwise known as Northwestern Somalia, with a population of approximately 300,000 and an economic dependence on seminomadic livestock herding and trading (Bradbury 2008; Lewis 2008). Between January 2013 and March 2020, I spent approximately five years in Burao. I conducted ethnographic fieldwork with the goal of understanding the culture and worldview of central Somalilanders by taking their perspectives seriously to eventually focus on a specific research topic, which turned out to be the study of spirit possession. I was employed by the University of Burao, the largest university in the region, a public institution founded in 2004 as a cooperative project among the different clans in the city (http://uob-edu.net). Somaliland is a self-declared sovereign state that pronounced its independence from Somalia in 1991 after a civil war, basing its claim to independence on former colonial borders (Bradbury 2008). In contrast to its southern counterpart, Somaliland has achieved remarkable peace and development in the last twenty-nine years. It has been called "an island of stability in a sea of chaos" (Allison 2015) and "Africa's best kept secret, a challenge to the international community" (Jhazbhay 2003, 77). Religiously, Somalilanders almost exclusively follow Sunni Islam, although traditionally most Somalis also practice Sufism, a more mystical expression of the Muslim faith (Lewis 1955).

This chapter makes use of data collected for my thesis for a Master of Research in Religious Experience through the University of Wales Trinity Saint David whose ethics committee approved the research, while local approval and support was given by the University of Burao. The methodology aligns with ethnographic research, the most common approach in anthropological studies (Bernard 2006). Much of my knowledge on the topic was gained through participant observation in Burao society, particularly in my workplace at the University of Burao. I spent many work and leisure hours with my colleagues from the university, listened to stories in my classes of female students becoming possessed by spirits because of stress or love, complained with co-workers about spontaneously scheduled meetings for which no one was prepared, and laughed with them if no one turned up to the meeting except the one who called it "and his *jinn* [spirit]," as a Somali idiom goes. For two years, I took one-on-one language lessons with teachers who did not speak any English but who could explain to me the world of spirits, the places where they lived, the things we should avoid because they were unclean, and the preventative and curative measures for curses and dark magic. I drank sugary tea with friends in local cafes and heard the latest news from the world of politics and soccer, and I was also introduced to local movies that described how a *jinn* spirit can appear in the form of a snake or how the *jinn*'s invisible world can be found in the forests and on mountains. I sent my children to primary school in our neighborhood and was told by my wife that the school principal sent her and the children away one day because a commotion started around a teenage girl who was possessed by a *jinn* spirit and who had seizures. I tried to support my security guard when his wife ran off into the countryside because she had been possessed by a spirit, and I listened to explanations from men and women that, in everyday life, women experience possession more frequently than men due to their menstrual "uncleanness" and lesser access or commitment to so-called proper religious practice.

In an almost exclusively monocultural context, I remained an outsider to the culture. I attempted as much as possible to be an observer-as-participant (Knott 2005, 247) but never experienced possession myself, nor did I "become a curer" (Crapanzano 1980, 133). What united me with my Burao friends, and what I believe led to a deeper level of personal trust with my informants, was that I shared a religious worldview with them. As a Christian, I never questioned the power of healing prayer or the existence of God or invisible spirits, even though I had no experiential knowledge of the latter. I expect that all my research participants were aware of the fact that I was a Christian, as religion is not a private matter in Burao. My own background has meant that I have been open to supernatural understandings of reality and willing to take my informants' beliefs at face value, at least as a starting point for this investigation.

The material quoted in this chapter was collected through two rounds of semi-structured interviews with a total of 42 interviews by 26 interviewees. The interviewees covered age groups between early 20s and late 60s, as well as various educational levels from little to no formal education through to university graduates. The sample is not representative of the population, but the fact that I frequently reflected on my research with local friends as well as Somali academics from the University of Burao leaves me confident that the findings are reliable. The first round of interviews, conducted in 2014 and 2015, was a combination of language learning and a pilot study, and some of the material was used for a smaller project for one of my bachelor's degree units (ethics approval was granted by the Melbourne School of Theology). These interviews were mainly focused on beliefs about spirits and possession, and they provided helpful background material but little data in terms of experiential accounts.

In 2018, I conducted a second round of interviews with seven male participants, while my wife, Gloria Moratz-Kwan, interviewed five female participants, all focusing on personal experiences and direct observations of spirit possession: What have they experienced personally or observed first hand in terms of spirit possession? What was the bodily experience of possession and how was healing sought? My wife's involvement was made necessary when I discovered that cultural sensitivities would not allow female participants to share personal stories with a male researcher present.

Interviewees were identified through convenience and snowball sampling, with the purpose of finding people who were willing to share their experiences about spirit possession. Several of my colleagues at the University of Burao acted as informal gatekeepers, while connections with other interviewees were made through personal contact in the neighborhood where I lived. My wife and I met the interviewees in a variety of settings, such as tea shops, the university campus, and interviewees' living rooms, as well as our own living room. Except for two interviews that were conducted in English, the interviews were held in Somali. My grasp of the language is sufficient for conducting an interview, while my wife's Somali language ability exceeds my own, so her interviews were also conducted in Somali. In the transcription process, I enlisted the help of a language expert who transcribed the interviews in Somali and explained words and sentences to me that I was not able to understand. All interviews were conducted in confidentiality, and the names of interviewees are withheld for this reason.

The observations of two visits to a local *cilaaj* healing center for men and one visit to a female healer by my wife are included in this chapter. Both healers were also interviewees. Moreover, excerpts from another local Islamic healer's book manuscript on how to cure spirit possession (Xasan 2018) are included. Finally, I analyzed a number of local media productions and YouTube videos that were shared with me by participants in the research (see e.g., Horn Cable

TV 2012; Ojalan 2011; Sahamiye News 2018). The interview transcripts, observation notes, book manuscript, and notes from media productions were then analyzed through coding principles common to Grounded Theory methodology (Corbin and Strauss 2015).

Somali spirit possession in light of modernization theory

Moving on to the ethnographic data, I first outline two key areas, namely 1) the conceptualization of *jinn* as part of an Islamic modernization and a rupture between ignorance and knowledge, and 2) the practice of healing from spirit possession, contrasting traditional *saar* ceremonies and modern Islamic *cilaaj* methods. Following this, I offer some concluding thoughts about the potential health and wellness advantages of a spirit-filled vision of modernity that externalizes and personifies the source of suffering, especially when considering chronic conditions and mental health.

Reconceptualizing jinn *and their role in modern human life*

> We can't see them. They are hidden from us. But they are here. Not far from us. Wherever there are humans, there are also *jinn*. Some jinn and humans know each other. Some humans know the *jinn* language. Some religious men know. But we shouldn't learn. We should be afraid. They can see us; we can't see them. So, we're afraid. Don't learn it. Don't go close to them. Say, go in peace. It's dangerous. Don't look for it. Don't come close to it.
> (male interviewee 4, unpublished data, 2015)

In other ethnographic contexts in which anthropologists investigated discourses of modernity and their understanding of spirits, occurrences of possession were typically defined as pathology, stress, or mental illness (see e.g., Ram 2013, 63–65). In Burao and its surrounding region, however, becoming knowledgeable does not mean forfeiting a belief in spirits. Several interviewees related how they had lived without an awareness of the spirit world in their childhood and youth, but then they came to understand the place of spirits in God's creation. A man in his late twenties to early thirties put it this way:

> When I was young, I hadn't seen a *jinn* possess a person, but when I grew up, became part of society and learned the Qur'an, I realized that *jinn* exist and that they possess people. One time, I saw how a *jinn* possessed a person ... It was in 2008. A girl from my family came back from Hargeisa [the capital of Somaliland] and stayed in our house. She would fall [have a seizure]. She fell a lot of times, especially when she went to the bathroom. Then ... we brought her to the religious men who read the Qur'an over her and healed her. When we took her to the doctor, it was for nothing, but the reading [of the Qur'an] made her get better.
> (male interviewee 1, unpublished data, 2015)

This man's experience is typical for a significant number of young people in the community, as is his summary of his learning curve: "When I was a child, I didn't believe in spirits. I thought they were ghost stories. But now I have learned that they really exist" (male interviewee 1, unpublished data, 2015). The logic goes like this: Growing up, there was a lack of information and understanding on how the world works. As an adult who has seen more about life, has learned the Qur'an, and importantly, has been an eyewitness to experiences of spirit possession as well as the efficacy of religious healing, there is no more need to question the reality of *jinn* spirits, nor should it be a surprise that there are certain illnesses that cannot be healed with pharmaceuticals. More than that, it was evident to several of my interviewees that there are certain afflictions that cannot be attributed to a dysfunction of the patient's body but are instead caused by an external force that maliciously wreaks havoc on the person. The structure in which this coming-of-age narrative is presented is a direct equivalent to other personal modernization narratives: *jahli* (ignorance) leads to insight; the traditional and backward ways are replaced by modern and enlightened understandings founded on Qur'anic teachings.

If, however, becoming modern does not mean leaving behind a spiritual understanding of reality, then what does it mean to be modern in relation to spirit beliefs and chronic possession experiences in the Somali context? To start with, my research suggests that spirits are recategorized to create a uniform picture in line with what people consider proper orthodox Islam. The literature mentions a number of names for spirit beings in the Somali context, such as *roxaan, wadaado, mingis, boraane,* or *saar* (see e.g., Tiilikainen 2010, 171ff). When probing with my informants, there was a consensus that those spirits are in fact all *jinn* but were labeled wrongly in the past because of ignorance or lack of knowledge (see also Mölsä, Hjelde, and Tiilikainen 2010; Antoniotto 1984). It seemed to be significant to the interviewees that categories of *jinn* are aligned with what they understood to be correct Islamic theological teaching.

Aligning spirit beliefs with the supposed proper Islamic teaching is also a major theme on the internet. Somali websites and YouTube channels present numerous personal or eyewitness accounts of spirit possession as well as healing ceremonies with often passionate discussions in the comments section about how this experience should be interpreted and healed. While it can be assumed that the majority of commentators are located in larger cities, both in the Horn of Africa and globally where Somali diaspora populations have settled, several of my interview participants have mentioned these social media posts, and at numerous times, I have overheard informal conversations on the topic. Notably, the social media discourse is dominated by the perspective of Qur'anic healers and those who consider Islamic religious cures to be "proper." More traditional ways of healing spirit possession, as I describe below, are almost entirely absent. The voice of social media in Somaliland is predominantly the voice of the global Islamic movement and its vision of modernity. The knowledge of and belief in *jinn* and their potential to cause human harm and suffering, then, is embedded in the larger modernization discourse of the contemporary Islamic movement.

The bodily experience of possession by spirits, the perception of possession as an affliction, and the reasons for possession seem not to have changed since Lewis's research in the mid- to late-twentieth century. The primary idiom used to describe *jinn* spirit possession is "entering a person," frequently due to an "open door," as described previously. The physical symptoms of possession include falling or having seizures, screaming when exposed to verses from the Qur'an, and having violent outbreaks where the possessed person displays superhuman strength. Sufferers may also display weakness and extreme fatigue, social withdrawal, loss of appetite, sadness, and anxiety to the point of suicidal thoughts. In other contexts, possession may be considered positive and potentially give the possessed access to certain special abilities, superhuman knowledge, or extraordinary experiences. Lewis (2003) labeled possession in these contexts "central possession cults" (contemporary examples include Pedersen 2011; Schmidt 2016). For Somalis, however, possession is an affliction, which is not considered to be a symbol for an underlying disease but caused by the malevolent acts of *jinn* spirits. Possession may be a chronic experience that lasts for several years or recurs. It is commonly not a one-time event.

From saar *ceremonies to modern* cilaaj *healing*

Moving from the contextualization and discourse on spirits and possession to healing practices reveals another major historical rupture in Somali culture. In my time in Burao, I have not had the chance to attend an event such as the *saar* ceremony reported by Adam (2010). In fact, I found no indication that they are still being held in Burao, despite asking a significant number of people in the city. While the practice of *saar* ceremonies was most common up to the end of the twentieth century, it has since become increasingly marginalized in Somali society, particularly in Somaliland. It is interesting to note that already in the 1960s, at the beginning of her field work, Adam (2010, 187) observed that the small group of educated Somali women she related to "were disparaging of the practice and its efficacy, and indeed of its religious correctness." Contemporary sources, both from the literature and from my interview participants, confirm this sentiment and show that it has become socially normative. Johnsdotter et al. (2011, 743–744) found that among the Somali diaspora in Sweden, "many informants consider [traditional spirit ceremonies] to be 'un-Islamic.'" Mölsä et al. (2010, 293) conducted mental health research among the Somali diaspora in Finland and argued that "new Islamic interpretations originating both in and outside Somalia influence the ways traditional healing practices are seen," giving rise to "mental health conceptions and practices based on the Prophet's medicine." Traditional ways of healing, like *saar* ceremonies, "have been increasingly abandoned in favor of puritanical interpretations of Islam" so that one Qur'anic healer interviewed in their project called sorcery and witchcraft "grave sins" and *saar* possession "un-Islamic" (2010, 289). In contrast to these ceremonies, *cilaaj* clinics have sprung up all over Somaliland, which claim to heal people from *jinn* possession by using proper Islamic methods.

An academic from the University of Burao who I interviewed described the process of change in approaches to healing in the following way:

> The previous culture of Somalis didn't know the religious ways of healing. So, they used to give the *jinn* whatever they asked for, such as perfume, meat, blood to drink, the habits and desires of *jinn*, like giving presents to *jinn*. Sometimes the *jinn* request the humans to work with them. *Jinn* and human to work together to heal, to give medicine from overseas. For example, medicine from Germany or the United States [that was produced] only two days ago, the *jinn* can bring that to the person. You can know that it's not within the power of human beings to do this ... Before, the people with knowledge used to help people and spoke to *jinn*. What was inside the person used to say, "I want this, I want blood, I want meat." But afterwards the people learned the religion. They learned that reading the Qur'an helped the person ... With the previous traditional ways, they learned from experience that the *jinn* always came back when they gave things to the *jinn*. They tried and learned that the *jinn* kept coming again and again, never leaves. But this other one, when using Qur'an, he leaves and never comes back again. Maybe the rural people still do this [the appeasing ways of healing]. But now in the city, it's mostly stopped. [The transition] started in 1990; that's when *cilaaj* centers started, after the civil war. Before that, the people used the traditional ways. First, people conducted Qur'an readings without centers ... Then in the late 90s, they started centers.
>
> (male interviewee 5, unpublished data, 2018)

Discussions among the population of Burao about a change in treating spirit possession are couched in the discourse of modernization. There is an increasing moral dichotomy between traditional ways and modern practices. A further indication in support of an interpretation that the old ways are being left behind comes from a locally produced movie in which a *faaliye* (magician), a representative of the old ways, is being made to look familiar but ridiculous. There is a sense that the traditional methods of healing are backward, illogical, and absurd (Riwaayada Jinka 2012). Other research has suggested that this change in dealing with spirits may be due to a spread of more orthodox versions of Islam so that "in Islamic societies where traffic with spirits is formally discouraged, men's public religiosity may require them to handle possession via exorcism instead of mollification" (Boddy 1994, 415). The spread of an Islamic modernity, therefore, has a direct effect on local conceptualizations of Somali modernity and spirit possession. There is also a clear trend to label older animistic practices "traditional" in the sense of backward or immoral and recent Islamic methods of the *cilaaj* clinics as "modern," progressive, and right.

Cilaaj clinics are considered Islamic healing places and led by a religious expert, usually called a *sheikh* in the Somali context, who entered his profession from theological Islamic studies and not medicine. The training occurs in the format of an apprenticeship, sometimes abroad and at other times within Somaliland. The male religious healer in my research group summarized his journey in this way: "I started when I was little, the religious teachers taught me. Then I went to the college, run by an Egyptian man called Abul Fidaa. That's where I learned about the herbs and cupping and other techniques like that" (male *sheikh* interviewee, unpublished data, 2018). While his knowledge of the Islamic Scriptures originated from local religious men, his expertise in specific healing techniques was acquired at an Arab-run school. The female healer who was interviewed by my wife noted that she received her training "here in this city. Some people from outside, men and women, came to teach, and that's how I learned" (female healer interviewee, unpublished data, 2018). Both noted that no formal accreditation is required to practice *cilaaj* healing.

In a smaller *cilaaj* center in Burao, I observed a Qur'anic healer while he was treating patients who were suspected to suffer from possession. The entrance room served as a waiting room. A kiosk-style pharmacy sold herbal medicines, some pharmaceuticals, and a number of devices, such as cupping sets and massage devices. The main treatment room was furnished with a large sitting cushion for the patients and a plastic chair with legs half cut off for the *sheikh*. There was a bookshelf with Islamic literature in Arabic, a small spray pump, a massaging device, a small electric shock device, and some other seemingly random items. As the patients came in, the *sheikh* chanted the Qur'an. The *sheikh* used a pipe, held against the patient's ear, to intensify the words of the Qur'anic reading. He sprayed water on the patient's face, called *cashar* water, which had the Qur'an read over it so that it became holy water. Firm massages with an electric massaging device or electric shocks were also administered to "hurt the *jinn*," as the *sheikh* explained. Other reports indicate that some *sheikhs* use earphones to force the patient to listen to the words of the Qur'an. I observed patients who called out, "Stop! Stop!" Others tried to turn away from the pipe and cover their ears, and still others did not seem to mind the sound. The patient's reaction served as a diagnosis for what he/she was suffering from, based on the assumption that evil *jinn* hate the words of the Qur'an and experience "burning" when exposed to them. The *sheikh* then turned to presenting his diagnosis and prescribing a cure, which usually involved an exhortation to follow Islamic lifestyle practices (e.g., prayer, ritual washing, listening to the Qur'an at home) as well as an appropriate medicine. The latter may be pharmaceutical medicine, herbal medicine, or ointments of oil. An unpublished manuscript of another local Islamic healer's manual (Xasan 2018) includes detailed instructions on which Qur'anic verses need to be read out loud to cause maximum harm to certain *jinn* and force them to vacate the person. Significantly, throughout the consultation process, no animal sacrifice, dancing, or rhythmic drumming was used. These are considered improper and "against the religion," as a number of interviewees stated. Tiilikainen (2010) observed a similar healing process elsewhere in Somaliland.

The process of seeking healing at a *cilaaj* center follows a typical routine. Another interviewee described her experience when a relative was sick:

> When I went to her, she was a sick person who was lying down and really sick. She couldn't take or eat anything. She was finished. Then we took her in

a small car [to the *cilaaj*]. There were people in a hall, about a thousand people were there. People got tickets, and when we got our ticket, we entered, and when we got to the back gate, we stayed outside the gate ... Only the *sheikh*, who hit people and read the Qur'an over people, who ran the *cilaaj*, could be inside, other people were not allowed inside ... There were five men working in the place who held hoses, and those who went mad and ran away and had illnesses had the Qur'an read over them, water poured over them. The man [the healer] was called *Rusheeye* [literally, the sprayer] because of this ... So, he poured water and read the Qur'an and he said, "*Rusheeye.*" When the *jinn* hear, "It's *Rusheeye*," they become afraid and they run away... He had more power than the *jinn*, and they got scared, it's like that. When one says, "It's *Rusheeye*," they get scared and say to themselves, "Get up and run away! ..." Then he takes each one and puts earphones into their ears and he reads the Qur'an to them. The person goes crazy and yells, and the workers grab both legs and both arms and another worker stands above the man with a hose ... But yesterday, when he read over her [my cousin], she fell, then he put earphones into her ears, and he said, "Why?" She said, "The woman yesterday, we had an argument, it was [name of another woman]." He said, "Why did you enter?" and she said, "She yelled at me and hit me." Then we took her home. She was walking [now], but when we brought her to *Rusheeye* [before the treatment], she was finished.

(female interviewee 6, unpublished data, 2018)

The affliction in this case originated in an interpersonal conflict, yelling and hitting, which caused the *jinn* person who belongs to a lady to possess the interviewee's cousin. This is one of two types of *jinn* common in Somali experience. While some jinn are called "independent *jinn*," the type causing the suffering in this case is a person's *qareen jinn*, a spiritual companion or double of the human who normally stays at their human's side but can leave the human in an act of retribution. Because the cause of the conflict is externalized onto the *jinn*, healing can be prompt, as can be seen in the lady's situation dramatically improving in the course of a short session with the healer. The healing power comes from two sources. On the one hand, the constant reading of the Qur'an and the pouring of holy water that had been imbued with the power of the Qur'an inflicts pain on the *jinn*, which expresses itself in the crying of those who are possessed. On the other hand, the healer, nicknamed "the sprayer," appears to have special powers so that *jinn* who hear his name run away in fear.

As was outlined by my interviewees and in the observation notes above, the religious healer's approach to healing is a pragmatic use of "whatever works" medicine, a healer may prescribe religious treatment, herbal medicine, or pharmaceuticals. This pragmatic attitude is also expressed in the action of a sick person and those who care for him or her. It seems reasonable to conclude that Somalis in Burao and other places in Somaliland do not see religious ways of treating illness and secular-scientific means in conflict with each other. Rather, a pragmatic approach is employed as a feature of the *cilaaj* healing process. It may be the case that no dichotomy between religious healing and physical healing is conceptualized in this ethnographic context, but this conclusion would require further research.

Discussion and conclusion

Potentials of a modern belief in spirit possession

A number of Somalis interviewed in this study and ethnographic data from other studies suggests there may be a benefit to conceptualizing symptoms commonly understood as mental illness as spirit possession. When I asked two medical professionals from Burao what people in the population thought about mental illness and spirit possession, their answer was clear that people would always prefer to be diagnosed as being possessed by a *jinn* over being mentally ill. One of them explained: "If someone is possessed by a *jinn*, he may be healed in one minute. A person with a mental illness can't be healed in one minute. *Jinn* possession is much easier to cure" (male interviewee 7, unpublished data, 2015). A participant in Johnsdotter et al.'s (2011, 749) study in Sweden also exclaimed: "In our country, people may be mentally ill, but they get well again with the Koran and medication, and when they have recovered, nobody will notice that they've been ill. But here they make you take medicine till the day you die."

The rationale behind this is firmly rooted in worldview. In Somali culture, as in many other cultures (see Crapanzano 1980; Hatala and Waldram 2016), malevolent spirits are a way of speaking about states of being by externalizing them. The potential of a modern belief in spirit possession is, however, not limited to an increased sensitivity to local explanatory frameworks. Rather, there are potential benefits to "externalizing" medical discourses (Young 1976), namely that attributing causation to spirits allows the sufferer to externalize the suffering, while personifying the cause of suffering locates the blame outside the person and in an entity that can be influenced, taken control of, and overcome (Hatala and Waldram, 2016). As a result, the person is not permanently damaged and doomed to live in perpetual chronicity. In an informal conversation, a Somali university colleague who was educated abroad shared his opinion on *jinn* possession with me: "When people, after the war, explained their mental issues with *jinn* possession, as a result, the responsibility of their madness is not inside them but placed outside themselves" (personal communication, 2015).

A range of experiences are conceptualized in an externalized and personified manner in Somaliland, such as instances of perceived personal guilt or shortcoming, of fragile and hurt emotions, and of simple ill health. Conceptualizing these experiences as possession allows for interpersonal tensions or violations in human-to-human relationships to be blamed on the activities of *jinn* spirits. In the Indian context, Ram (2013, 130) suggests that "once a malady is diagnosed as the work of troublesome spirits, new kinds of engagement with curative practices are opened up … The problem is external, and so is the cure." The sufferer remains intrinsically whole. The practical benefit of a spiritual conceptualization of these aspects of suffering does not automatically go hand in hand with an "idioms of distress" framework (Nichter 1981). Ontologically, it could be argued that there is an underlying spirit-filled dimension to the experiences.

Spirit possession as a modern experience

The suggestion I put forth in this chapter is an application of Eisenstadt's (2000) theory of multiple modernities to the context of the spiritual realm in Somaliland. In the area of possession experiences and healing practices, Somalilanders in Burao conceptualize the present as fundamentally different from the past, modernity from tradition, or in local Somali terms, the "age of ignorance" from the "age of knowledge." Using these possession and healing practices in a heuristic sense as a Weberian ideal type, that is, focusing on certain characteristics of the phenomenon that are useful for comparative analysis, gives the phenomenon a voice that reveals a new aspect of an alternative modern vision. As in Weber's (2009) original modernization theory, this vision of modernity needs to be implemented through "intentional acts" in Weber's words, through "rationalization" (Kim 2007), by aligning certain everyday experiences and practices to a larger vision.

The literature in this area has largely assumed that possession is a traditional phenomenon essentially at odds with modernity. Reflecting on "Islam and the Languages of Modernity," Eickelman (2000, 120) notes: "Common to all variants of modernization theory is the assumption of a declining role for religion, except as a private matter." While the thesis of a decline of religion has been challenged, the notion that modern worldviews necessarily are disenchanted, in the sense of being freed from a belief in a densely populated this-worldly realm of invisible spirits, has proven more persistent. The Somali context of my ethnographic research challenges this notion and likely aligns with other contexts in which Islam is the dominant religious worldview. More research in other Muslim societies undergoing a similar development of actively aligning themselves to a vision of a global Islamic modernity would add to the picture.

In studies conducted in other Muslim-majority contexts, observations have been made about women who exercise agency by meeting in groups to study the Qur'an, choosing to wear the hijab (Brenner 1996) and submitting themselves to male leadership as well as "feminine virtues, such as shyness, modesty, and humility" (Mahmood 2012, 6), all to intentionally refashion their identities in a Foucauldian sense. This has led to questions about an Islamic modernity that is deeply religious. In both Brenner's (1996) and Mahmood's (2012) case, the language of becoming aware of correct practices and rejecting those that are so-called backward is prevalent. The Somali material adds to the understanding of the modernist vision of the global Islamic movement. Modernization, as it is understood in the Somali case, means intentionally regulating practices, beliefs, and discourse in the way of Weber's (2009) rationalization of society. In the striking ways that this vision of modernity differs from a Western, mostly secularist, utopia, Eisenstadt's (2000) thesis of Somali modernity as one of multiple modernities provides a good framework.

As shown above, imagining a modernity that is spirit-filled or enchanted opens up new ways of approaching the treatment of chronic spirit possession and other areas of chronic mental illness. In a study from 1974, Waxler compared studies of healing efficacy of schizophrenic patients in Mauritius and the United Kingdom and found that, despite limited treatment facilities, Mauritian patients recovered significantly better than their fellow British sufferers. Rejecting theories that societies cause different rates of disorder or have varying tolerance for deviance, she suggested that the societal response had a significant effect on the outcome of the treatment. She summarizes:

> Of greatest importance ... are the belief systems of the society and the extent to which the patient has power over his own role as a sick person. In societies ... where beliefs about mental illness center on supernatural causation, where the person is not held responsible for his illness, where his "self" remains unchanged, he can shed the sick role quickly and easily.
>
> (Waxler 1974, 379)

While in Waxler's time, this seemed to be a question of a native healing system, we now face the possibility that a global modern vision embraces a similar worldview. Unmuting the discourse of spirit possession may offer an alternative for chronic illness and mental health that is worth further exploration in Islamic contexts and beyond.

References

Abdel Haleem, Muhammad A.S., ed. 2005. *The Qur'an*. New York: Oxford University Press.

Adam, Anita. 2010. "A Saar Gaamuri in Somalia: Spirit Possession as Expression of Women's Authority?" In *Peace and Milk, Drought and War: Somali Culture, Society and Politics; Essays in Honour of I. M. Lewis*, edited by Markus Virgil Höhne and Virginia Luling, 185–203. London: Hurst.

Allison, Simon. 2015. "Somaliland: Losing Patience in the World's Most Unlikely Democracy." *Daily Maverick*, April 7, 2015. Retrieved from www.dailymaverick.co.za/article/2015-04-07-somaliland-losing-patience-in-the-worlds-most-unlikely-democracy/

Ameen, Abu'l-Mundhir Khaleel ibn Ibraaheem. 2005. *The Jinn and Human Sickness: Remedies in the Light of the Qur'an and Sunnah*, edited by Abdul Ahad. Translated by Nasiruddin Khattab. Riyadh: Darussalam.

Antoniotto, Alberto. 1984. "Traditional Medicine in Somalia: An Anthropological Approach to the Concepts Concerning Disease." In *Proceedings of the Second International Congress of Somali Studies: Studies in Humanities and Natural Sciences*, edited by Thomas Labahn. Hamburg: Helmut Buske Verlag.

Bernard, H. Russell. 2006. *Research Methods in Anthropology: Qualitative and Quantitative Approaches*. 4th edition. Lanham, MD: AltaMira Press.

Boddy, Janice. 1989. *Wombs and Alien Spirits: Women, Men, and the Zār Cult in Northern Sudan*. New Directions in Anthropological Writing. Madison, WI: University of Wisconsin Press.

Boddy, Janice. 1994. "Spirit Possession Revisited: Beyond Instrumentality." *Annual Review of Anthropology* 2: 407–434.

Bradbury, Mark. 2008. *Becoming Somaliland*. London: Progressio.

Brenner, Suzanne. 1996. "Reconstructing Self and Society: Javanese Muslim Women and 'The Veil.'" *American Ethnologist* 23 (4): 673–697.

Casanova, José. 2011. "Cosmopolitanism, the Clash of Civilizations and Multiple Modernities." Edited by Reimon Bachika and Markus S Schulz. *Current Sociology* 59 (2): 252–267. doi:10.1177/0011392110391162

Corbin, Juliet M., and Anselm L. Strauss. 2015. *Basics of Qualitative Research: Techniques and Procedures for Developing Grounded Theory*. Los Angeles: Sage Publications.

Crapanzano, Vincent. 1980. *Tuhami: Portrait of a Moroccan*. Chicago: University of Chicago Press.

Eickelman, Dale F. 2000. "Islam and the Languages of Modernity." *Daedalus* 129 (1): 119–135.

Eisenstadt, Shmuel N. 2000. "Multiple Modernities." *Daedalus* 129 (1): 1–29.

Fukuyama, Francis. 2002. "Has History Started Again?" *Policy* 18 (2): 5.

Hatala, Andrew R., and James B. Waldram. 2016. "The Role of Sensorial Processes in Q'eqchi' Maya Healing: A Case Study of Depression and Bereavement." *Transcultural Psychiatry* 53 (1): 60–80. doi:10.1177/1363461515599328

Horn Cable TV. "Riwaayada Jinka Sooraan iyo Jawaan by HCTV." August 28, 2012. Video, 49:57. https://youtu.be/ynXaMIGFGQM

Huntington, Samuel P. 1993. "The Clash of Civilizations?" *Foreign Affairs* 72 (3): 22. doi:10.2307/20045621.

Jhazbhay, Iqbal. 2003. "Somaliland: Africa's Best Kept Secret, A Challenge to the International Community?" *African Security Review* 12 (4): 77–82. doi:10.1080/10246029.2003.9627253

Johnsdotter, Sara, Karin Ingvarsdotter, Margareta Östman and Aje Carlbom. 2011. "Koran Reading and Negotiation with Jinn: Strategies to Deal with Mental Ill Health among Swedish Somalis." *Mental Health, Religion and Culture* 14 (8): 741–755. doi:10.1080/13674676.2010.521144

Kim, Sung Ho. 2007. "Max Weber." In *The Stanford Encyclopedia of Philosophy (Winter 2019 Edition)*, edited by Edward N. Zalta. Retrieved from https://plato.stanford.edu/archives/win2019/entries/weber/

Knott, Kim. 2005. "Insider/Outsider Perspectives." In *The Routledge Companion to the Study of Religion*, edited by John R. Hinnells, 569. New York: Routledge. doi:10.1177/0952695115594099

Lewis, I. M. 1955. "Sufism in Somaliland: A Study in Tribal Islam - I." *Bulletin of the School of Oriental and African Studies* 17 (3): 581–602.

Lewis, I. M. 1966. "Spirit Possession and Deprivation Cults." *Man* 1 (3): 307–329.

Lewis, I. M. 1998. *Saints and Somalis: Popular Islam in a Clan-Based Society*. Lawrenceville, NJ: Red Sea Press.

Lewis, I. M. 2003. *Ecstatic Religion: A Study of Shamanism and Spirit Possession*. London: Routledge.

Lewis, I. M. 2008. *Understanding Somalia and Somaliland: Culture, History, Society*. London: Hurst and Company.

Mahmood, Saba. 2012. *Politics of Piety: The Islamic Revival and the Feminist Subject*. Princeton, NJ: Princeton University Press.

Mölsä, Mulki Elmi, Karin Harsløf Hjelde and Marja Tiilikainen. 2010. "Changing Conceptions of Mental Distress Among Somalis in Finland." *Transcultural Psychiatry* 47 (2): 276–300. doi:10.1177/1363461510368914

Nichter, Mark. 1981. "Idioms of Distress: Alternatives in the Expression of Psychosocial Distress: A Case Study from South India." *Culture, Medicine and Psychiatry* 5 (4): 379–408. doi:10.1007/BF00054782

Ojalan Jr. "*Nin Naag Jin Ah Guursaday.*" April 20, 2011. Video, 1:07:28. Retrieved from https://youtu.be/rH8o1hpxpWg

Pedersen, Morten Axel. 2011. *Not Quite Shamans: Spirit Worlds and Political Lives in Northern Mongolia*. Culture and Society after Socialism. Ithaca: Cornell University Press.

Ram, Kalpana. 2013. *Fertile Disorder: Spirit Possession and Its Provocation of the Modern*. Honolulu: University of Hawaiʻi Press.

Riwaayada Jinka. 2012. Comedy. Horn Cable TV. Retrieved from https://youtu.be/ynXa MIGFGQM

Sahamiye News. "*Sheikh Rusheeye Muqaalka Burco ee Maanta oo dhamaystiran.*" May 28, 2018. Video, 13:36. https://youtu.be/hmXwRI0SDVs

Schmidt, Bettina E. 2016. *Spirits and Trance in Brazil: An Anthropology of Religious Experience*. London: Bloomsbury Publishing.

Tiilikainen, Marja. 2010. "Spirits and the Human World in Northern Somalia." In *Peace and Milk, Drought and War: Somali Culture, Society and Politics; Essays in Honour of I. M. Lewis*, edited by Markus Virgil Höhne and Virginia Luling, 163–184. London: Hurst.

Waxler, Nancy E. 1974. "Culture and Mental Illness: A Social Labeling Perspective." *The Journal of Nervous and Mental Disease* 159 (6): 379–395. doi:10.1097/00005053-197412000-00001

Weber, Max. 2009. *From Max Weber: Essays in Sociology*. Translated by Hans Heinrich Gerth and C. Wright Mills. New York: Routledge.

Xasan, Sh. Abdiwahaab Xaashi. 2018. *Untitled*. Book. Burao, Somaliland.

Young, Allan. 1976. "Internalizing and Externalizing Medical Belief Systems: An Ethiopian Example." *Social Science and Medicine* 10: 147–156.

5 Politics and aesthetics of care
Chronic affliction and spiritual healing in Brazilian Kardecism

Helmar Kurz

Introduction

An illness narrative of chronic illness and spiritual healing

Simone is thirty-five years old and additional to her profession as an administrator in public finance services, she works part-time in the library and bookstore of a Spiritist center in Marília, São Paulo/Brazil.[1] Even though in religious terms, she is of Catholic background and denomination, she has engaged with Spiritism for the last twenty years for "the sake of learning", as she puts it. She is unmarried due to the fact that her former long-time boyfriend would not cope with her increasing involvement with Spiritism. She admits that ever since a healing experience regarding a chronic condition, she indeed has taken her spiritual obligations more seriously than "earthly" promises and seductions. For years, Simone had suffered from a bladder infection, which "conventional therapy" was not be able to cure. She complains about biomedical practitioners whose various forms of treatment from nutritional adaptation to long-term pharmaceutical therapy helped to control her symptoms but did not provide any chance of sustained relief. It also implied economic challenges, as the biomedical treatment was very expensive, and her prognosis suggested that she would have to take it for the rest of her life, having to succumb to surgical interventions twice a year. One day, she attended the famous daily television show *Mas Voce* ("More You") hosted by Brazilian celebrity Ana Maria Braga who reported about *Grupo Soccorista*, a Spiritist group in the city of São Paulo providing "far-distance spiritual healing". Braga revealed that she had experienced successful spiritual cancer treatment and suggested everybody at least try to seek support there.[2]

Simone decided to give it a try and, through their website, communicated her illness experience and marked a Friday night for treatment. She learned about some rules to be followed, such as four days before and three days after she should not consume any meat, alcohol, or other "chemical" substance besides her regular medication. She avoided physical and sexual activity and other "materialistic" behaviors, like going out with friends or to the cinema. Instead, she engaged with her spirituality; for one month and at least once a week, she visited a Spiritist center to listen to lectures and to receive a *passe* (a treatment of her "energetic body"). On the marked day, she still had lunch but afterward just drank water. She read Spiritist

DOI: 10.4324/9781003043508-5

literature for the rest of the day, took a shower, put a white sheet on her bed, and put on comfortable, white clothes. She made sure that nobody would disturb her and placed three bottles of water close by to "fluidize", having to drink it after the treatment three times a day until it was finished. When the marked hour approached, she laid down in her bed and prayed. After some time, she felt a comfortable sensation as if somebody were touching and pressing her bladder. Then she fell asleep until her mother woke her up after a few hours. Since the treatment, she suffered from severe pain in the respective body parts, but it would continuously reduce in the following days. Her permanent urge to urinate reduced, too, and she decided to go two weeks without her medication to verify the effect of the surgery. Simone experienced it as "eighty percent better" and, therefore, decided to repeat the treatment, following the same instructions and procedures. Ever since the second treatment, she has not suffered from her chronic affliction, nor has she continued with her medication. She has been even able to consume food and drinks she never could before. Simone concludes:

> My doctor could not believe it, and it is crazy because you do not see anybody as everything is online. I believe that over there, they connect with the spirits and provide a certain vibration. Our belief and prayers are so powerful, our trust that there are spiritual doctors and that you deserve to be cured ... I do not know if it was something emotional or spiritual; it came out of the blue and stayed chronic. However, who usually has these problems are older women who already gave birth. Neither am I old, nor do I have kids, so maybe there was a spirit involved.

Politics and aesthetics of care

Anthropologist and psychiatrist Arthur Kleinman (1988) reminded us to take the "illness narratives" of patients with chronic afflictions seriously. Doing so would support therapists in understanding their patients' experiences of suffering and related explanatory models. It would also help them to develop coping strategies in psychosocial and/or religious-spiritual terms. From an anthropological perspective, illness narratives also allow us to explore cultural aspects of healing practices, their socio-political contexts, and their effectiveness. Simone's account provides rich information on the political-economic implications of the Brazilian health care system and also on the performativity (both in terms of media production and ritual action) and sensory aspects of Spiritist healing in the context of chronic affliction and spirituality. I take her narrative as a starting point for exploring the politics and aesthetics of care in Brazilian Spiritism, which are two intersecting aspects of relevance when investigating chronicity in spiritual terms. I will return to Simone's case and the involved politics and aesthetics of care in the conclusion of this chapter, but first I intend to further investigate patient-therapist interactions and care in Spiritism as forms of social practice.

Regarding the politics of care, Drotbohm and Alber (2015) argue that "care" is a relevant and timely tool for examining multiple dimensions of social relations, for example, between classes, genders, and generations. The anthropological gaze reveals cultured perceptions of certain types of care work, but also aspects of actively chosen and maintained social belonging (Drotbohm and Alber 2015, 2). Thelen (2015) takes a slightly different perspective as she understands care as a practice of social organization encompassing these alleged dichotomies between private and public, traditional and modern, or even micro and macro levels. Inferentially, "care" reveals links and overlaps between relations that are usually analyzed within different spheres of social life, such as economics and politics, and, therefore, mirrors correlations, dynamics, and experiences of, for example, age, migration, neoliberal restructuring, changing notions of uncertainty and responsibility, or social instability and change beyond public-private binaries (Thelen 2015, 497f). Care as a practice for the (re)production of significant relations would serve the social organization (as opposed to social structure) and the establishment of social order as it *should* be, and maybe as opposed to what it *is* (Thelen 2015, 498). Accordingly, she states that public debates in the context of economic rationalization of care reveal the utmost importance for self-understanding and moral sensibilities regarding visions of a "good life" and a "good society" (Thelen 2015, 499).

From this point of view, the concept of "politics" extends from the level of institutional regulations to any aspect of social negotiation regarding gender, age, ethnicity, social status, and the hegemony of certain sociocultural ideals as sometimes opposed to people's needs and their problems accessing care resources. It implies that specific practices within certain care relationships are to be negotiated on the individual and societal level:

> Conflicting values become especially clear in situations of accelerated change when many care practices lose their former meaningful embedding. In such situations, they are reworked according to changing notions of uncertainty and responsibility, thereby acquiring new meanings, and shaping emerging social formations.
>
> (Thelen 2015, 505)

Thelen also stresses the political impact of care regarding the inclusion or exclusion of (vulnerable) social groups and the aspect of solidarity as a practice of affection (Thelen 2015, 508f). Thiesbonenkamp-Maag (2014), in this regard, impressively illustrates, with the example of a diasporic Philippine religious community in Frankfurt/Main (Germany), how charitable care is also a form of self-care, as I similarly argue in the case of Brazilian Spiritism (Kurz 2017; 2018a,b). These religious-spiritual aspects are widely ignored in the aforementioned debates on "care" but are of special interest in the Brazilian Spiritist context.

Political and aesthetic aspects of care in Brazil

As I have already indicated elsewhere (Kurz 2018a), the Brazilian health care system lacks sufficient infrastructure to organize sustained treatment, especially for psychiatric and chronic patients. It is a bifurcated system of state-financed basic care and additional private health plans for those who can afford them. The basic official *Sistema Única de Saúde* (SUS, "Single Health System") provides free treatment for anyone but lacks significant infrastructure and resources. Some patients have to wait for weeks or months before receiving care or being attended, and far too often, the treatment is insufficient. After having attended these patients for just a few minutes and without paying attention to their illness narratives in any significant manner, many of the medical staff within SUS prescribe heavy medications that are not included in the free care approach. As the example of Simone illustrates, this is even a burden for patients with regular income, but it is especially problematic for the vast economically disadvantaged classes of Brazilian society. Further, most health resources are located far away from the *favelas* (shantytowns), where most of these vulnerable groups live. This lack of health resources, especially for the poor, reveals another connotation of chronicity, namely that of chronic social crisis (Vigh 2008) and structural violence (Farmer 2002, 2003). Farmer argues that the embodied experience of discrimination and poverty as a "normal" larger social matrix further translates into, or exacerbates, chronic personal distress and disease (Farmer 2002, 424; Caldwell 2017; Biehl 2018; Das 2008; Huschke 2013; Scheper-Hughes 1994).

In Brazil, religious institutions often step in to fill this care gap, some of them engaging in practices of mediumship and discourses on possession (or in Spiritist terms, obsession) as spiritual causes or aspects of affliction. Especially in cases of chronic affliction and alleged incurable diseases, such institutions provide "coping" more in terms of transformational healing (Kurz 2015, 2017, 2018a, 2018b; Schmidt 2015, 2016a, 2016b, 2017; Seligman 2005, 2010, 2014; Pierini 2016, 2020; Waldram 2013).

Practices of mediumship and possession (obsession) have attracted the attention of many medical and religious anthropologists in different places. They trigger theoretical interpretations related to discourses on social functionalism and/or psychological adaption. Either way, most of these approaches share a symbolical, if not performative, perspective that addresses the socio-political environment of the afflicted self and its interaction within respective frames. These approaches imply the notion that symbolic acts would, in a way, "heal" people by establishing/maintaining/restoring a sense of social community, metaphorically representing relevant problems and alleged solutions by reframing the social context and symbolically reintegrating the patient (back) into it (Dow 1986, Moerman 1979). Related dynamics have been interchangeably referred to as aesthetic role plays, social dramas, context- and earmarked interactions, multimedia communications, and meta-communicative displays of problems that relate current circumstances and problems to accounts of history, memory, or tradition. From this perspective, healing rituals are both culture-specific treatments of distress *and* its communication in terms of criticism of related and alleged circumstances. Symbolical ritual practices would generate multivocal meanings that relate to a certain social context with a certain political connotation and the aim of transforming individual experience (Arpin 2003; Bell 1992, 1997, 2006; Boddy 1988, 1994; Desjarlais 1992;

Douglas 1975; Hatala and Waldram 2016; Kapferer 1979, 1983, 1984, 2004; Köpping, Leistle and Rudolph 2006; Köpping and Rao 2000; Kurz 2013; Laderman and Roseman 1996; Levi-Strauss 1963; McClean 2013; Nichter 1981; Reuter 2004; Sax 2004, 2009; Tambiah 2002; Turner 1968a, 1968b, 1982, 1992; Walker 1972; Wulf and Zirfas 2001, 2004).

Huizer (1987) extends this perspective from the local to a translocal level. He argues that the global expansion of Western cultural and economic forms of care trigger asking for Indigenous, traditional, cultural, and/or religious healing practices as a form of resistance against hegemonic cosmopolitan medical discourse and practice. As a consequence of colonial and postcolonial relationships and interactions between alleged, distinct "modern" and "traditional"[3] populations, classes, nations, and opposed global political-economic powers, "Indigenous healing" would serve as an emancipatory practice to deny patronage. It would support local problem-solving capacities in terms of passive resistance to and a substitute for Western medical hegemony and its insufficiency in the context of capitalist modernization and its socio-political maladaptation. In Brazil, this aspect of sociocultural resistance has been widely discussed regarding Afro-Brazilian religions like Umbanda (Brown 1986, 1999; Maggie 1992; Montero 1985; Negrão 1996) and Candomblé (Hofbauer 2002a, 2002b; Kurz 2013; Schmidt 2016a, 2016b; Seligman 2005, 2014; van de Port 2005; Wiencke 2006, 2009), and sometimes also in terms of medical implications (Araújo 1991; Budden 2010; Leibing 1995; Loyola 1984, 1997; Luz 1979; Rabelo 1993, 2005; Rabelo and Souza 2003; Wintrob 2009). Kardecist Spiritism, on the other hand, is more often mentioned regarding its importance for therapeutic ends (Aureliano and Cardoso 2015; Greenfield 2008, 2016; Hess 1991, 1995; Krippner 1987; Rocha 2009, 2017; Stoll 2002; Prandi 2012) but hardly regarding its socio-critical potential (Kurz 2015, 2017, 2018a, 2018b), and Theissen (2006, 2009) even interprets it as a form of social discipline.

Current discussions regarding an "anthropology of the senses" provide new perspectives in healing and also further support performative approaches to care by investigating how sensory modulations and or "somatic modes of attention" affect experiences of (spiritual) well-being and healing (Csordas 1993; Hatala and Waldram 2016; Howes 2009; Nichter 2008; Pink 2015). I theoretically frame this nexus of performativity and sensory perception in the context of health, illness, and therapy as "aesthetics of healing/care" to analyze spiritual healing practices related to chronic affliction in Brazil in terms of both the negotiation of social organization and political frameworks, as well as the effectiveness of these practices. Accordingly, I will explore how Spiritist practices refer to both the politics and aesthetics of care in an attempt to negotiate chronic illness in spiritual terms.

Methodological approaches

I base my argument on fieldwork I conducted and data I collected in a Spiritist hospital and affiliated Spiritist centers in Marília, São Paulo (Brazil) during 2015 and 2016, and in other Spiritist institutions located in Itabuna, Bahia (Brazil), and Munich (Germany) during 2016 and 2017.[4] Marília, with its approximately

200,000 inhabitants, is an administrative, economic, educative, political, and religious center within an agricultural environment in the periphery of the relatively and economically well-developed Brazilian state of São Paulo. It has also been a historic center of Spiritism in Brazil, resulting in a high density of related institutions and a certain influence in local politics, economics, and health care. In this environment, I performed participant observation, or rather observing participation, to explore the impact of Spiritist knowledge and practice on (mental) health care in Brazil and abroad. In Marília, I conducted about thirty qualitative, unstructured, and narrative interviews with psychiatric and Spiritist therapists, patients, and adepts of Spiritism. This distinction, however, is a difficult one as most of my interlocutors fit at least two of the categories in Spiritism; care and self-care blend.

My data analysis and interpretation surpass the formerly intended approaches of thick description (Geertz 1973), the identification of actor-networks (Latour 2005), and the coding, clustering, and categorization of related information (Glaser and Strauss 1967). Especially after my participation and emotional response to mediumship practices (Kurz 2017, 2019), I decided to integrate aspects of sensory ethnographic methods (Pink 2015), that is, evaluating my personal perception as "data" to reflect upon in comparison with my interlocutors' accounts. The advantage of this approach is that I am able to generate knowledge beyond observation and "hearsay", comparable to other participants' narratives. The epistemological problem, or maybe also the strength, is, of course, that as an ethnographer and alleged medium, I am "betwixt and between" emic and etic perspectives. However, after initially having been in doubt of the validity of my accounts, I have concluded that a credible account of the "aesthetics of healing/care" *has* to integrate experience with observations, data interpretation, and related theoretical models and concepts. As a result, I do not intend to discuss my data as universally valid for the intersection of chronicity and spirituality in Spiritism, but instead will analyze snapshots in time and space that allow us to explore certain dynamics in the haze of chronic affliction and aspired spiritual solutions. Apart from Simone's illness and healing narrative cited in the introduction, I will focus here on narrative expert interviews with a therapist and my observations and experiences regarding his interaction with patients.

Accordingly, in this chapter, I will address practices of "spirit doctors" engaging with chronic patients in Brazil. It has been *the* branch of Brazilian Spiritism that attracted the most attention of both public media and social anthropologists. The focus has been on cases of surgeries on the material body of patients without providing any anesthetic or hygienic precautions, as for example, by "Dr. Fritz" (Greenfield 2008), and "John of God" (Rocha 2017). Here, I intend to address the question of how healers perform and adapt to the experiences of patients in their environment. How do "spirit doctors" engage with chronicity at the intersection of spiritual healing and official health care in Brazil? How do the experiences of chronicity and structural violence intersect with sensory-performative approaches of spiritual healing? Finally, how can we apply considerations regarding the "aesthetics and politics of care" to the context of "chronicity and spirituality"?

In addressing these questions, I will first introduce the development of Spiritist health care throughout the 20th century in Brazil. Then I will share some fieldwork experiences and data regarding health-seeking behavior and healing practices in the context of Brazilian Spiritism. In my conclusion, I will come back to the question of how the experience of chronic illness and spiritual healing is not just a question of personal transformation but also one of attention and care in an environment that lacks official health care resources and provides antagonistic/alternative approaches to substitute and/or to complement social practices resulting in a "care gap".

Spiritism and health care in Brazil

The Brazilian Spiritist continuum (Camargo 1961) constitutes a large veritable healing cooperation between health professionals, spirits, mediums, and clients and a complementing space of medical and spiritual practices. Especially patients medically diagnosed with chronic conditions of somatic illness or mental health issues seek support in Spiritist institutions that exist all over the country and start to flourish abroad, like, for example, in the United States and Germany. They partly substitute and complement the official (mental) health care distribution in Brazil, and, lately, abroad too (Kurz 2018a). The philosophy of Spiritism marks a "religious-spiritual modernization" in the context of rationalization and political reorientation in 19th-century Europe (Sharp 2015, Sawicki 2016). Different from its neighboring countries, France, with its divergent sociocultural and political reformations, provided a context where scholar Hippolyte Léon Denizard Rivail (1804–1869), with the pseudonym of "Allan Kardec", was able to create a Spiritist doctrine, referred to as "Kardecism", gaining increasing global importance throughout the 20th century and at the beginning of the 21st. The impact of enlightenment, revolution, and reactionism produced culturally specific perspectives on society, humanity, human and social progress, and especially human suffering.

Kardec stressed individual responsibility for moral development by personal effort and progress; he preached solidarity, charity, and fraternity. His doctrine fell on fertile ground in Latin America, and especially in Brazil. Different theories exist about the fact that Kardecist Spiritism (in opposition to Anglo-Saxon Spiritualism) became so attractive to Latin American populations. Sharp (2015, 221f) argues that in addition to the possibility of communicating with beloved ancestors, the prospect of progressive development towards perfection throughout many lifetimes would appear promising to humans living in the colonies with all their injustice, violence, and social stratification. Moreover, Spiritist concepts of reincarnation and spiritual progress also aligned with Indigenous and Afro-Brazilian concepts and were easily adapted (Engler and Brito 2016; Kurz 2013; Stubbe 1987).

According to the "Book of Spirits" (Kardec 1996), a human spirit leaves its perishing biological body and remains in the spiritual realm until reincarnating for the sake of continuous moral development and correcting past life errors. In a fusion of Buddhist, Christian, and contemporary philosophical approaches to human existence, Kardec deemed reincarnation crucial for the immortal spirit within mortal material bodies; within several subsequent incarnations one might learn how to deal with issues of hostility, guilt, and other interpersonal problems, which are transported from one lifetime to another until they are resolved. He dismissed contemporary practices like "table-turning" as useless entertainment but instead proclaimed the importance of communication with spirits for the sake of education, knowledge, and moral instruction. He preached the ideal of spiritual progress throughout many lifetimes but also acknowledged that some spirits are so attached to "materiality" that they would not accept the fact of their biological death and, therefore, keep interfering with the world of the living. This way, they would not only counteract their spiritual progress but also afflict the living they attach to (Sawodny 2003, 15). For the sake of their and their human target's benefit, these "obsessing" spirits would have to be supported in a caring and moralizing way, a practice called "dis-obsession" (Sawodny 2003, 16f), while at the same time, the afflicted persons have to change their habits so as not to attract them anymore, supported by practices of "evangelization" and charity (Sawodny 2003, 19ff). In Brazil, mediumship practices have been elaborated throughout the 20th century to facilitate and control spirit-human communication or interaction, and they became essential for practices of Spiritist health care.

The emergence of Spiritism in Brazil by the second half of the 19th century coincided with the demarcation and professionalization of medical institutions, which, ever since, would compete with Spiritist healers and seek persecution of them as "quacks" (Aureliano and Cardoso 2015, 284). It was the psychographic medium Francisco Cândidio "Chico" Xavier (1910–2002) and his psychographic "ghostwriters" *Emmanuel* and *André Luiz* who, from the 1930s onward, had a significant impact on the rapprochement of medical and spirit doctors and elaborated a theoretical and practical frame for Spiritist healing practices (Kurz 2017, 2018a, 2018b; Xavier 1944). Contemporary medium and figurehead of the internationally active *Federação Espírita do Brasil* (FEB, "Brazilian Spiritist Federation") Divaldo Ferreira Franco argues that independent from social, biological, psychological, or spiritual factors of health affliction, there are three interrelated aspects to be considered in any case of affliction and healing, namely 1) there are organic causes that respond to medical treatment, 2) spiritual aspects are always involved, and their solution supports medical treatment, and 3) the concept of reincarnation is crucial to understanding these aspects (Franco 2009, 12f). He develops a tripartite model of the human person, which consists of a material body, an immaterial spiritual body, and a subtle energetic body (or "perispirit") to connect these two spheres. Even though he does not define it as such, as a logical consequence, "mind" is not an independent sphere as depicted in Cartesian models but a conglomerate of (materially, spiritually, and energetically) embodied experiences and memories of all three bodies.[5] As a resource for prophylactic and therapeutic (self-) care, Franco suggests mental hygiene by the lecture of the "Gospel According to Spiritism" (Kardec 2008) and the practice of "Christian discipline" (Franco 2009, 20f), including moral reformation, education, and training towards the practice of love and charity "in the name of Jesus" (Franco 2009, 25ff, 48, 101).

Spiritual development, self-examination, and self-empowerment (Franco 2009, 37) by Spiritist doctrine, prayer, and fraternal care would help to recognize one's own mistakes and to alter the self's behavior and mental attitudes (Franco 2009, 102f, 115), supported by the bio-energetic fluid therapy (or *passe*) and the consumption of "fluidized" water (Franco 2009, 33, 66, 115).[6]

An increasing number of Brazilian medical professionals organize in the *Associaçao Medico-Espírita* (AME, "Spiritist Medical Association") to integrate these concepts into their daily practice and scientific research. The medical doctor and adept of Kardecism, Moreira (2013) currently investigates how aspects of spiritual-energetic healing can be linked to Asian practices such as "chakra treatment", which I will refer to in more detail in the subsequent paragraphs. He summarizes his underlying preoccupations and hoped-for effects of the integration of biomedical, psychological, and spiritual approaches to health, illness, and health care as follows:

> The contemporary practice of health, despite all scientific progress, presents itself as a fragmented overspecialization. It often lacks the individual support regarding resources of self-knowledge, wisdom, and (self-) love, which should be the base of any health-seeking behavior seeking permanent, effective treatment. The majority of patients wish anesthesia instead of conscience. It is all right that the effects of their symptoms are reduced for the sake of avoiding unnecessary and unproductive suffering, but an educational process that frees individuals from their ignorance and dependencies is fundamental to the reconstructional process of health and as a prophylaxis against the diseases of body and soul.
> (Moreira 2013, 23f; translated by HK)

One of his colleagues in Marília shares this perspective and attempts to integrate spirituality into the treatment of patients with chronic affliction. I will refer to him as "Dr. Alexandre". My conversations with him and my observations of his practices appear to be crucial for the understanding of chronic affliction and healing at the intersection of medical and spiritual treatment.

Healing cooperation of "earthly" and "spirit doctors"

The health care infrastructure of Marília consists of numerous pharmacies and private clinics, several public health centers, a center for psychosocial assistance (CAPS), a public hospital with a psychiatric emergency unit, a university clinic, and the *Hospital Espírita de Marília* (HEM, "Spiritist Hospital of Marília"), a primarily psychiatric hospital administrated by a council of the Kardecist Spiritist community of Marília. With its high density of related institutions, Marília is one of the historic centers of Kardecism in Brazil and currently consists of about twenty-five Spiritist centers spread all over the town. They all engage in similar activities, such as lectures and study groups, fraternal and family care, mediumship training and practice, and charity. They provide a friendly atmosphere, and upon arrival, members welcome the newcomers and introduce them to the environment and related customs. The *Centro Espírita Barsanulfo* (CEB, "Spiritist Center Barsanulfo") has existed since 1980 and was founded by young adepts of the more well-established Spiritist centers of town with the aim to apply more profound practice to the theoretic study of Spiritism. It is located between the economic center of Marília and its poorer suburbs, and it offers free day care for the children of this special environment so that they do not hang around in the streets, and instead receive healthy nutrition and learn about charity and solidarity through group activities and playful learning. The project is funded by the administration of Marília, private donations, and a network of restaurant owners who organize the "catering" using leftovers. A garden of self-grown vegetables and fruits provides further healthy nutrition and income, as does a small bookstore with essential Spiritist literature. The vast territory also consists of buildings for lectures, courses, mediumistic sessions, and spiritual healing. Here, many younger people of Marília's Spiritist community like to engage with Dr. Alexandre, a medical doctor who academically engages with Spiritism and organizes courses on the interrelation of energetic healing (or "psycho-physio-fluido-therapy") with somatic and psychological aspects of illness, health, and healing. In his discourse on Spiritist practices of healing, he especially stresses the importance of concepts such as "chakras" and "energy fields", as derived from Asian knowledge systems such as "Reiki", "Yoga", or "Kundalini".

Every Monday night, Dr. Alexandre provides the free treatment of "spiritual surgery" in CEB, and after I attended some of his classes, he invited me to participate in these sessions. He is a 44-year-old clinician and homeopath who turned to Spiritism at the age of sixteen, looking for rational explanations for spiritual experiences. He is part of the AME and is planning a research project on the correlation of "psycho-physio-fluid-therapy" and cellular renewal but so far lacks funding. Some of his assistants in the spiritual treatment are medical professionals and psychologists, and many participate in his courses on Tuesdays, where they reflect on their experiences from the previous day and learn about the spiritual-energetic aspects of illness and treatment. Patients provide a variety of chronic afflictions, but he only treats them if he detects spiritual-energetic issues. Then they receive at least a two-month treatment structured through different consultations, mediumistic sessions, lectures on the Spiritist doctrine, an "extended *passe*", and if indicated, spiritual surgery on their "perispirit". An important detail is that in the therapeutic context, Dr. Alexandre does not act himself but instead as a medium who allows the spirit of the deceased "Dr. Wilhelm" to use his body to perform therapy and communicate related information to the patients.

Psycho-physio-fluid-therapy

From seven o'clock in the evening onward, people start to gather in the entrance area of the Spiritist center, chatting and having tea or water before entering a hall with eighty chairs, some of them marked with numbers. Some patients sit down there, others receive a paper with a number at the entrance and find their space in the rows of chairs, staying quiet and trying to contemplate. In the background, meditative music is playing. An elderly man greets everybody personally and offers explanations and support for first-time participants. He advises them to relax, offers them something to read, and clarifies any doubts about the procedure. He tells me that he has been a patient himself and that he experienced support here, which is why he now engages in supporting others. By eight in the evening, the room is packed, and Dr. Alexandre enters a little stage in the front, turns off the music, and greets everybody. He says a prayer to ask for the guidance of God, Jesus, and "all the good spirits", before announcing that today's lecture will be on suffering and different perspectives on it.

He explains different forms of suffering, namely 1) limitation (to be surmounted by technology), 2) fear (due to ignorance and overcome by knowledge), and 3) frustration (manageable through work and progress). Even though everybody would be free in their decision to progress, there would be some "divine laws" framing it, including that fraternity and charity would serve personal evolution and therefore, satisfaction and happiness. Egoism and vanity, as provided in capitalism, would not support any progress but instead escalate in materialism and competition, leading to moral decline, violence, segregation, indifference, and consequently more suffering and expiration. In conclusion, humans would create suffering by their proper acts and habits, but there would always be a way out and a chance for repentance and change: the study of Spiritist doctrine would help to progress and interrupt the vicious cycles of suffering. He stresses the fact that "sharing is caring" and that charitable practice provides more advantages than accumulation, that hope brings progress, and that sustained healing is an act of self-transformation.

Apart from the rational argument, however, it is also his performance as a speaker that affects me. His speech is rather monotonous but with rhythmic waves of speeding up and slowing down, taking the listener to another level of perception, and thus somehow subtly influencing me. At times, I lose the thread and feel taken by his voice and a certain atmosphere in the room, instead of really paying attention to a message that I have listened to already many times before in similar environments. At some point, Dr. Alexandre turns on the meditative music again and finishes with another prayer, thanking Jesus and the enlightened spirits for their support and the possibility of development and knowledge. Throughout this lecture of exactly one hour, participants have been called into another room to receive energetic treatment according to their *fichas* (the numbers they received upon arrival), and some still wait to do so while chatting with each other. Others wait for the scheduled spiritual surgery, which will take place from ten in the evening onward.

Only separated by a tiny hallway and two doors, in a smaller, darkened room, which is only illuminated by a blue light on top of a desk, about fifteen participants of different ages and genders sit in a semi-circle of chairs around four stretchers. Patients come in four by four after a woman on the desk reads out of their "patients files" including their name, age, affliction, diagnosis, therapy aims, and development. She outlines today's treatment, which usually consists of special energetic manipulation of afflicted body parts by "mentalizing colors" and "giving *passe*". Accordingly, she selects two people to stay at each stretcher. Those are alleged mediums, affiliated with Dr. Alexandre's project to integrate spiritual and therapeutic skills, being trained under his supervision. Another person at the door calls in the patients who lay down on the stretchers, or, when to do so would be too difficult for them, sit down in a chair. Still, meditative music is playing in the background, and a person says a prayer, asking for spiritual support and "all the fluids and energies, belief, and hope" they would need. Then, the two persons at each stretcher perform an intensive *passe* for "their patient". They focus on the before-mentioned body parts and finish with a "wiping off" towards the feet. Other participants not actively involved in this practice concentrate and "donate" energy until, after a few minutes, another thanksgiving prayer is performed, and the four patients are released by having a cup of "fluidized" water; they also take home bottles of it. After the patients' departure, the chairperson at the desk asks if anyone has made any special observations and asks everyone to freely comment so that their perceptions can be integrated into the patients' files. Altogether, there are four cycles of ten minutes each. Common issues include experiences of depression, anxiety, sadness, and emotional distress, but I also witness cases of vision loss, kidney stones, psychosis, auto-aggression, cancer, and auto-immune issues. Regarding these conditions, Dr. Alexandre explains that treatment never only addresses certain body parts, but rather aims at related "chakras" as mediators between the material, energetic, and spiritual bodies. Referring to Mesmerism and Buddhism as further sources of Spiritist practice (Kurz 2017), the energetic treatment would aim at the dispersion of negative and the donation of positive energy waves called "fluids" being generated through the imagination of colors.

It is only with time and participation in various sessions that I learn that as soon Dr. Alexandre engages as a lecturer and/or participant of energetic healing, he transforms and acts as a medium for "spiritual healers" who he "incorporates" and who allegedly "talk and act" through him. He explains to me that it is a "team" of a hospital in the spiritual sphere called *Esperança* (Hope), and that would consist of "strong spirits", most of them having been medical doctors or healers in one of their previous lifetimes. In the spiritual world, many spirits would suffer from chronic issues yet to be resolved, thus many would decide to cooperate for mutual support; the "spirit doctors" help to treat the incarnated and the mediums help to guide afflicted spirits. Dr. Alexandre declares that he usually incorporates Dr. Wilhelm, a German medical doctor from Bavaria who practiced during World War I. He perceives it as very compelling and a strong connection, as Dr. Wilhelm "allows" Dr. Alexandre to stay conscious throughout incorporation. Together, they would try to not just "work on people" on the energetic level but also in psychotherapeutic ways, for example, in the discussion of "spiritual messages" handed in throughout treatment and the provision of hints on spiritual issues needing to be resolved.

Spiritual surgeries

The aspect of spiritual support becomes even more prominent through the "spiritual surgeries" provided twice a month in the same room but after the regular *passe* and with a slightly different team. The procedure starts in a similar manner to the previous one, with the difference that there is only one stretcher at the center of the room. Around the stretcher, a circle of chairs provides space for twelve participants (including me), while another chair between the desk and the stretcher is reserved for Dr. Alexandre/Wilhelm. He sits there rather isolated, highly concentrated, and allegedly in a trance. The others gather in groups of two to four people, everybody in silence. I learn that today only two patients will be treated. The man at the desk invocates a prayer for the support of benevolent spirits and then discusses the case of the first patient who suffers from osteonecrosis in his femur. Three mediums are instructed which colors to direct to which body parts. The patient comes in, takes off all metal devices so as to "not disturb energies", and lays down on the stretcher. One medium at his head invokes another prayer. Then, one after another, the three mediums perform their treatment from the left side of the patient, while Dr. Alexandre/Wilhelm stays at the right side, observes, and only occasionally stretches out his hands as if to direct beams of energy. What they mainly do is move their hands over the patient's body in repeated movements. It looks as if they remove certain energies and implement others.

Dr. Wilhelm speaks in a voice that is significantly different from Dr. Alexandre in tone, speed, and accent, and he also appears in a different posture, performing significant and strange body habits like repeated shrugs and clasping of hands. He "waves" from his belly towards the patient as if "donating energy" and then forms his hands into a tube and seems to blow and suck at the afflicted body part of the patient. He asks two assistants to help him and orders the light to be extinguished. The room stays completely dark for a few minutes, and I can only listen to murmurs. When the blue light is on again, all three have their hands placed on the right upper leg and hip of the patient. Dr. Wilhelm explains that they implanted a prosthesis in his perispirit. He asks the patient to cancel physiotherapy for the following two weeks so that it can heal. He also prescribes some homeopathic remedies and minerals, stressing the fact that these suggestions come from the spiritual work. After half an hour, the treatment is finished.

The second patient suffers from multiple sclerosis. Her treatment starts with a similar procedure with the slight difference that, throughout the prayer, she already receives energetic treatment in the form of the brushing away of energies by Dr. Alexandre/Wilhelm and his assistants. In between, they repeatedly rub their hands as if dis/charging energies. She then is asked to turn around and, facing down, receives a massage by Dr. Alexandre/Wilhelm before turning back with visible effort. Now, everybody in the room is asked to mentalize "green" and direct it to her whole body but especially to her lungs. Interestingly, I have no problems visualizing a pair of lungs in front of my inner eye, which slowly transform in their diffuse appearance from a dirty, see-through, colorless quality to green and then to something I can best explain as a multisensory soothing experience of peace, harmony, and satisfaction.

Dr. Wilhelm starts a conversation with the patient as a spirit who allegedly was her mother in an earlier incarnation and who, ever since, obsesses her for the sake of resolving spiritual problems with her. I am hardly able to understand what is going on, but Dr. Alexandre/Wilhelm seems to persuade her in terms of spiritual issues, and she cries and poses questions. The conversation focuses on moral behavior and karmic issues. Even though his voice is comforting, the message is not as he refers to the earlier lecture and stresses that this case is about obsession and spiritual development. What shocks me most are his final words; she will not be cured in this life, but she has the chance to work on her spiritual progress to suffer less in her future lifetimes. Her affliction would be auto-immune, her body not accepting the spirit. She would have to change her spiritual vibration. Having her obligatory cup of water, she leaves the rooms under excuses and sobs. She was the last patient of the day, and participants start to analyze her case as they have experienced it as disturbing. Whereas Dr. Alexandre/Wilhelm defends his approach of spiritual diagnosis and clarification, some of his "earthly" team members request a more soothing approach. There is a long discussion about it until finally, Dr. Alexandre/Wilhelm addresses me, pointing out how important my research would be and asking my opinion. However, I am hardly able to pay any attention or to speak, and I leave the scene with hammering headaches (Session CEB 2016-02-22).

Aesthetic and political implications of chronicity and spiritual healing

My reaction that day was partly due to my shock concerning how the last patient allegedly has had all of her hope taken away and, moreover, is held responsible for her experience. The latter aspect of "guilt" in Spiritist health care has already been sharply criticized by Theissen (2009), but it relativizes when reflecting on it. The patients who Dr. Alexandre/Wilhelm treats all have chronic conditions and are deemed incurable by cosmopolitan medicine; they are often refused further therapy by the official health care system (SUS) and/or are unable to pay expensive treatment costs. Many find their way to CEB as a point of last hope, and Dr. Alexandre/Wilhelm negates any illusion of miracle healing. He provides spiritual support that actually does not address the topic of "guilt" but of "self-responsibility". He facilitates the agency of the patients to learn how to cope with their affliction and offers guidelines on how to alleviate their situation, even if it is only the prospect of an alleviate reincarnation. Moreover, CEB provides a space where people with similar experiences interact and care for each other. Those who have experienced some form of healing start to engage as mediums or assistants to support others who are in despair. Overall, sense is made of the affliction, which helps the person to cope with it, and it triggers experiences of transformational healing (Waldram 2013).

Apart from these psychological aspects often attributed to Spiritist healing (Brody 1973; Figge 1973; Spinu and Thorau 1994; Stubbe 1987; Wiencke 2006), there are also the sensory ones, and they offer another explanation for my reaction. When I share my experiences (feelings of dizziness, altered states of consciousness, headaches) with Dr. Alexandre, he is sympathetic and stresses the energetic aspects of therapy. He interprets my perceptions as mediumistic and declares that for me not to suffer from it, I would have to share it to help others. I will not negate nor support this opinion in this discussion, but I argue that it is the sensory manipulation in this context that triggers these experiences that are interpreted as mediumship, and also those of alleviation and, in the best case, healing. The long periods of lectures and waiting, the dim light and meditative music, the prayers and *passes* create an environment where participants relax, focus on themselves, reflect on their life situation and relations, and maybe release and/or sense feelings and issues they are not able to otherwise give space to in a busy, hectic cultural environment like Brazil that provides little room for self-reflection and verbal communication of personal distress (Laplantine 2015; Kurz 2017 for the example of Brazil; Farb et al. 2015; Howes 2015; Kirmayer 2015 for the aspects of inner senses and self-perception). The aesthetics of care in Brazilian Spiritism provide a space to become at ease with oneself and one's (chronic, incurable) affliction and, therefore, at least reduce psychological/mental/emotional/spiritual side effects, if not even reduce or adapt certain symptoms. However, the open question remains of how exactly this process is initiated and maintained. Accordingly, I have asked Dr. Alexandre about the aspect of "colors" in therapy. I quote his rather extensive answer uncommented here, as I believe that it speaks for itself, clarifying how, in his opinion, the imagination of colors helps to alleviate or heal chronic affliction; it is not something "symbolic" but related to scientific discourse, and is thought of as a complement to cosmopolitan medicine. He said:

> Colors make a central part of our studies; it is called the fluidic-spectral analysis. Colors are a way to differentiate fluids; the color is nothing more than identifying the patterns of vibrations, the pattern of waves, their frequency, their speed. So, it is about certain local energies; it relates to the energetic patterns of our organs. If, for example, the liver is afflicted, it sends out an antagonistic vibration, and this we try to deal with. It has nothing to do with the color you see, but it is a reference for our consciousness to focus on certain vibrations. When we say: "let us give green to the liver of the patient", what we really are doing is to mentalize and to send fluids to influence the vibrational state of that organ. It is not that a certain color can be identified with certain organs; it is more like a certain energetic lack in the metabolism that has to be adjusted to support biochemical processes in the body. Let us just take the example of yellow in the treatment of dementia; it is not because yellow is related to the brain but to the recovery of cells. If we send yellow to the brain, we support the cellular renewal in the brain via the perispirit ... Whereas chromotherapy is related to certain cultural meanings applied to colors and thus has more symbolical and psychological effects, we work with radiation and their manipulation. Of course, certain lights have physiological effects, but their meaning differs; here green is hope, yellow is wealth, red is love, white is health and purity. If you go to Tibet, yellow is poverty, red is insight, and white is death. We do not work with that. The same way we use the blue light for merely practical reasons; the less you see,

the better it is for our concentration, but you need some light to see what is necessary to see ... It might also have the sight effect of relaxing the patients, just like the music we are playing.

(Session Dr. Alexandre 2016-02-15)

Besides adding up aspects to a biopsychosocial-spiritual understanding of human beings, their afflictions, and ways to heal them, Dr. Alexandre indirectly supports my interpretation of the importance of the sensory environment and also contributes another aspect to the aesthetics of care that I perceive through the theoretical lens of "performance" in the sense of a symbolical transformation of the participants' experiences (Bell 1992, 1997; Turner 1968a,1968b, 1982, 1992; Kapferer 1979, 1983, 1984, 2004; Köpping and Rao 2000; Kurz 2013; Laderman and Roseman 1996; Wulf and Zirfas 2001, 2004). Apart from the issue that many patients are not aware of these implications mentioned by Dr. Alexandre, he complains that one of the biggest problems is the belief of people who expect that some kind of spirit doctor would "magically" heal them "right here, right now". It would be this popular delusion that feeds performative distraction and suggestion by implementing hospital mimicry (Kurz 2015). Only by symbolically copying medical procedures in terms of waiting and treatment rooms, long waiting hours and the provision of (Spiritist) literature and journals, and certain applications and prescriptions in an environment that resembles a hospital or clinic, would patients perceive that they are attended to at all. Even though the support is spiritual, it needs certain triggers to have them convinced that they are treated, such as using treatment rooms, "surgeries", and prescriptions of remedies (e.g., homeopathic and/or fluidized water).

Accordingly, besides substituting for official health care institutions, spiritual support is also a critical performative meta-commentary on official health care politics with its failed infrastructure, unequal resources related to economic status, and long waiting but short treatment times; here, everybody *is equally treated for free*, not only once but as often as needed, and especially when in a chronic condition. This fact already promotes a transformation of experience for many chronic patients in Brazil. My data does not allow me to develop any interpretation that would generalize their illness experiences as socially caused (in terms of "idioms of distress", Nichter 1981, 2010; or "sociosomatics" Jenkins and Cofresi 1998; Kirmayer and Young 1998), or only if we define "spiritual" as social relationships. I leave this question for future investigations. What my discussion *does* illustrate is how Spiritist care is a form of social organization and (re)structuring (Drotbohm and Alber 2015; Thelen 2015) in an environment of (permanent) social- and health-political crisis and related forms of structural violence (Farmer 2002, 2003; Kurz 2013, 2015, 2017, 2018a, 2018b; Vigh 2008).

Conclusion

The introductory illness narratives of Simone and others detailed throughout this chapter uncover the interaction of chronic patients and spiritual healers in

Brazil, with a focus on the politics and aesthetics of care. This analysis reveals problems or limitations within the Brazilian health care system regarding expensive and/or insufficient therapies, especially of chronic illnesses and among the less advantaged members of society. It also reveals a certain dynamic of socially and politically negotiating this "care gap" by providing a free alternative (or complement) in the shape of Spiritist therapy, which is even "advertised" in public mainstream media. The Simone case and other healing encounters introduce the cosmos of Spiritist therapy where explanatory models and concepts of a healthy self, divergent from cosmopolitan medicine, are provided, such as mediumship, obsession, and an energetic body. Experiences of healing are partly located within the transformation of self in terms of learning coping strategies and developing agency, where self-care also implies care for others. It is not so much about resistance to the hegemony of cosmopolitan medicine or a contest between "tradition" and "modernity" but, to a certain degree, healing cooperation where spiritual approaches complement and sometimes substitute unsuccessful or insufficient medical treatment, especially of chronic conditions. A certain affinity for fashionable, Buddhist-derived, complementary, and alternative medical practices (CAM) (Baer et al. 2013; Kirmayer 2015) intensifies the impression that different medical systems create a "third space" (Bhabha 1994) of negotiation and integration of diversified treatment approaches.

The perception of interaction of cosmopolitan medicine and Spiritism is also produced on a performative level by acts of "hospital mimicry". Different Spiritist procedures and equipment resemble practices in hospitals and clinics, and, therefore, facilitate the experience of being cared for and, in the best case, healed. However, the performance of healing also integrates critical symbolical meta-commentary on a health care and political system experienced as insufficient, for example, by turning to "spirit doctors as more effective" and implementing CAM (like homeopathy, chakra-therapy), which are hardly supported within SUS. The malfunctions of modernity in an economic and political capitalist system are contested by practices of charity and care that cushion the equally long (and often unbearable) waiting hours for patients with a chronic condition and low income in Brazil.

Complementing this performative aspect, the aesthetics of care in Brazilian spiritual surgeries and "psycho-physio-fluid therapies" also provide somatic modes of attention, which, by the modulation of sensory experience, produce experiences of spiritual well-being and healing. Again, I cannot develop any trustable suggestion as to how far afflictions have been socially produced, but it is evident that the reduction to a few sensory stimuli facilitates the perception and reflection of self within a soothing and relaxing social environment often so different from the daily life-world experienced as sickening. The aesthetics of care in Spiritist healing practices, therefore, reflect on and contest official politics of care, providing experiences of belonging, care, and healing within a larger environment that, if not facilitating chronicity of suffering, at least does not provide sufficient measurements of healing.

Notes

1 In December 2015, in the course of my anthropological investigation regarding the intersection of mental health and spirituality in Brazil, Simone shared her experience of a "spiritual surgery" with me. She was one of my first interview partners, but as her narrative did not appear "psychiatric enough" for my research project, I have dismissed it for too long. With the opportunity to now discuss chronicity and spirituality, her report appears to me as a perfect starting point to investigate and discuss practices and experiences of healing in Brazilian Spiritism, especially when it comes to chronic affliction.
2 It is worth mentioning here that, while Braga usually advertises entrepreneurs and their products on an economic basis, in this case, the treatments, as most Spiritist healing practices in Brazil, are free of charge.
3 Gaonkar (2001) for the discussion on "alternative modernities" instead of obsolete dichotomies of "modernity" and "tradition".
4 This qualitative research was part of the DFG-funded project "Diversification of Mental Health – Therapeutic Spaces of Brazilian Spiritism" and applied to the ethical guidelines of the German Research Association (DFG, www.dfg.de/download/pdf/foerderung/rechtliche_rahmenbedingungen/gute_wissenschaftliche_praxis/kodex_gwp_en.pdf [last accessed 21 September 2020]) and the German Association of Social and Cultural Anthropologists (DGSKA, www.dgska.de/dgska/ethik/ [last accessed 21 September 2020]). Accordingly, all mentioned interlocutors and representatives of institutions consented in the publication of my observations and their narratives and statements.
5 Not to be confused with, but maybe comparable to, the concept of the "mindful body" by Scheper-Hughes and Lock (1987).
6 Franco does not take these practices as a substitute to neuro-pharmaceutical drugs, but due to their side effects, suggests a strategy of gradual substitution by spiritual engagement and smoother treatments such as phytotherapy, acupuncture, Bach flowers, and bio-energetic practices (Franco 2009, 131).

References

Araújo, Annette. 1991. "Herr Doktor, es sind die Nerven: Zur Relevanz 'Traditioneller' Erklärungsmodelle in der Schulmedizin am Beispiel Brasiliens." In *Traditionelle Heilsysteme und Religionen: Ihre Bedeutung für die Gesundheitsversorgung in Asien, Afrika und Lateinamerika*, edited by Robert Wiedersheim *et al.*, 157–167. Saarbrücken: Dadder.

Arpin, Jacques. 2003. "Masters of their Conditions: At the Crossroads of Health, Culture and Performance." *Transcultural Psychiatry* 40: 299–328. doi:10.1177/13634615030403001

Aureliano, Waleska, and Vânia Z. Cardoso. 2015. "Spiritism in Brazil: From Religious to Therapeutic Practice." In *Handbook of Spiritualism and Channeling*, edited by Cathy Gutierrez, 275–293. Leiden: Brill. doi:10.1163/9789004264083_014

Baer, Hans A., Merrill Singer, and Ida Susser. 2013. *Medical Anthropology and the World System: Critical Perspectives*. 3rd Edition. Santa Barbara: Praeger.

Bell, Catherine. 1992. *Ritual Theory, Ritual Practice*. New York: Oxford University Press.

Bell, Catherine. 1997. *Ritual: Perspectives and Dimensions*. Oxford: Oxford University Press.

Bell, Catherine. 2006. "Embodiment." In *Theorizing Rituals: Issues, Topics, Approaches, Concepts*, edited by Jens Kreinath *et al.*, 533–543. Leiden: Brill. doi:10.1163/9789047410775_027

Bhabha, Homi K. 1994. *The Location of Culture*. New York: Routledge.

Biehl, João. 2018. "*Care and Disregard.*" In *Legitimidades da Loucura: Sofrimento, Luta, Criatividade e Pertença*, edited by Mônica Nunes and Tiago Pires Marques, 249–284. Salvador: EDUFBA. doi:10.7476/9788523220242.0010

Boddy, Janice. 1988. "Spirits and Selves in Northern Sudan: The Cultural Therapeutics of Possession and Trance." *American Ethnologist* 15 (1): 4–27. doi:10.7476/9788523220242.0010

Boddy, Janice. 1994. "Spirit Possession Revisited: Beyond Instrumentality." *Annual Review of Anthropology* 23: 407–434. doi:10.7476/9788523220242.0010

Brown, Diana. 1986. *Umbanda: Religion and Politics in Urban Brazil*. Michigan: UMI.

Brown, Diana. 1999. "Power, Invention, and the Politics of Race: Umbanda Past and Future." In *Black Brazil: Culture, Identity and Social Mobilization*, edited by Larry Crook and Randal Johnson. Berkley: University of California Press.

Brody, Eugene B. 1973. *The Lost Ones: Social Forces and Mental Illness in Rio de Janeiro*. New York: International University Press.

Budden, Ashwin. 2010. *Moral Worlds and Therapeutic Quests: A Study of Medical Pluralism and Treatment-Seeking in the Lower Amazon*. PhD diss. San Diego: University of California, Department of Anthropology and Cognitive Science.

Caldwell, Kia L. 2017. *Healthy Equity in Brazil: Intersections of Gender, Race and Policy*. Urbana: University of Illinois Press. doi:10.5406/illinois/9780252040986.001.0001

Camargo, Cândido P.F. 1961. *Kardecismo e Umbanda*. São Paulo: Pioneira.

Csordas, Thomas J. 1993. "Somatic Modes of Attention." *Cultural Anthropology* 8 (2): 135–156.

Das, Veena. 2008. "Violence, Gender, and Subjectivity." *Annual Reviews of Anthropology* 37: 283–299. doi:10.1146/annurev.anthro.36.081406.094430

Desjarlais, Robert R. 1992. *Body and Emotion: The Aesthetics of Illness and Healing in the Nepal Himalayas*. Philadelphia: University of Pennsylvania Press.

Douglas, Mary. 1975. "The Healing Rite." In *Implicit Meanings: Essays in Anthropology*, 142–152. London: Routledge and Paul.

Drotbohm, Heike, and Erdmute Alber. 2015. "Introduction." In *Anthropological Perspectives of Care: Work, Kinship, and the Life-Course*, 1–19. New York: Palgrave MacMillan. doi:10.2307/j.ctt18mvnwk.4

Dow, James. 1986. "Universal Aspects of Symbolic Healing: A Theoretical Synthesis." *American Anthropologist* 88 (1): 56–69.

Engler, Steven, and Ênito Brito. 2016. "Afro-Brazilian and Indigenous-Influenced Religions." In *Handbook of Contemporary Religions in Brazil*, edited by Bettina E. Schmidt and Steven Engler, 142–169. Leiden: Brill. doi:10.1163/9789004322134_010

Farb, Norman, et al.2015. "Interoception, Contemplative Practice, and Health." *Frontiers in Psychology* 6 (763): 1–26. doi:10.3389/fpsyg.2016.01898

Farmer, Paul. 2002. "On Suffering and Structural Violence: A View from Below." In *The Anthropology of Politics. A Reader in Ethnography, Theory, and Critique*, edited by Joan Vincent, 424–437. Malden: Blackwell.

Farmer, Paul. 2003.*Pathologies of Power: Health, Human Rights, and the New War on the Poor*. Berkeley: University of California Press. doi:10.1525/9780520931473-toc

Figge, Horst H. 1973. *Geisterkult, Besessenheit und Magie in der Umbanda-Religion Brasiliens*. Freiburg: Alber.

Franco, Divaldo P. 2009 [2003]. *Aspectos Psiquiátricos e Espirituais nos Transtornos Emocionais*. Salvador: LEAL.

Gaonkar, Dilip P. 2001. *Alternative Modernities*. Durham: Duke University Press. doi:10.1215/08992363-11-1-1

Geertz, Clifford. 1973 [1966]. *The Interpretation of Cultures*. New York: Basic Books. doi:10.4324/9781912128310

Glaser, Barney G., and Anselm L. Strauss. 1967. *The Discovery of Grounded Theory: Strategies for Qualitative Research*. Chicago: Aldine. doi:10.4324/9780203793206-1

Greenfield, Sidney M. 2008. *Spirits with Scalpels: The Culturalbiology of Religious Healing in Brazil*. Walnut Creek: Left Coast. doi:10.4324/9781315419855

Greenfield, Sidney M. 2016. "The Alternative Economics of Alternative Healing: Faith-Based Therapies in Brazil's Religious Marketplace." *Research in Economic Anthropology* 36: 315–336. doi:10.1108/s0190-128120160000036012

Hatala, Andrew R., and James B. Waldram. 2016. "The Role of Sensorial Processes in Q'eqchi' Maya Healing: A Case Study of Depression and Bereavement." *Transcultural Psychiatry* 53 (1): 60–80. doi:10.1177/1363461515599328

Hess, David J. 1991. *Spirits and Scientists: Ideology, Spiritism, and Brazilian Culture*. University Park: PSU.

Hess, David J. 1995. "Hierarchy, Heterodoxy, and the Construction of Brazilian Religious Therapies." In *The Brazilian Puzzle: Culture on the Borderlands of Western Culture*, edited by David J. Hess and Roberto A. DaMatta, 180–206. New York: Columbia University Press.

Hofbauer, Andreas. 2002a. "Candomblé: Der Weg einer ethnischen Religion ins globale Zeitalter. "*Anthropos* 97 (1): 127–145.

Hofbauer, Andreas. 2002b. "Von Farben und Rassen: Macht und Identität in Brasilien." *Zeitschrift für Ethnologie* 127 (1): 17–39.

Howes, David. 2009. "Introduction: The Revolving Sensorium." In *The Sixth Sense Reader*. 1–52. Oxford: Berg. doi:10.1215/9780822372455-001

Howes, David. 2015. "Sensation and Transmission." In *Ritual, Performance, and the Senses*, edited by Michael Bull and Jon P. Mitchell, 153–166. London: Bloomsbury. doi:10.5040/9781474217712.ch-008

Huizer, Gerrit. 1987. "Indigenous Healers and Western Dominance: Challenge for Social Scientists?" *Social Compass* 34: 415–436. doi:10.1177/003776868703400407

Huschke, Susann. 2013. *Kranksein in der Illegalität: Undokumentierte Lateinamerikaner/-inneni in Berlin: Eine medizinethnologische Studie*. Bielefeld: Transcript. doi:10.14361/transcript.9783839423936

Jenkins, Janis H., and Norma Cofresi. 1998. "The Sociosomatic Course of Depression and Trauma: A Cultural Analysis of Suffering and Resilience in the Life of a Puerto Rican Woman." *Psychosomatic Medicine* 60 (4): 439–447. doi:10.1097/00006842-199807000-0 00009

Kapferer, Bruce. 1979. "Introduction: Ritual Process and the Transformation of Context." *Social Analysis* 1: 3–19.

Kapferer, Bruce. 1983. *A Celebration of Demons: Exorcism and the Aesthetics of Healing in Sri Lanka*. Bloomington: Indiana University Press. doi:10.2307/2802353

Kapferer, Bruce. 1984. "Introduction: Ritual Process and the Transformation of Context". In *The Power of Ritual: Transition, Transformation and Transcendence in Ritual Practice*, 3–19. (Reprint of *Journal of Cultural and Social Practice* 1979/01). Adelaide: Department of Anthropology.

Kapferer, Bruce. 2004. "Ritual Dynamics and Virtual Practice: Beyond Representation and Meaning." In *Ritual in its Own Right: Exploring the Dynamics of Transformation*, edited by Don Handelmann and Galina Lindquist, 35–54. New York: Berghahn. doi:10.3167/015597704782352591

Kardec, Allan. 1996 [1857]. *The Spirits' Book*. Rio de Janeiro: FEB.

Kardec, Allan. 2008 [1864]. *The Gospel According to Spiritism*. Brasilia: ISC.
Kirmayer, Laurence J. 2015. "Mindfulness in Cultural Context." *Transcultural Psychiatry* 52 (4): 447–469. doi:10.1177/1363461515598949
Kirmayer, Laurence J., and Allan Young. 1998. "Culture and Somatization: Clinical, Epidemiological, and Ethnographic Perspectives." *Psychosomatic Medicine* 60 (4): 420–430.
Kleinman, Arthur. 1988. *The Illness Narratives: Suffering, Healing, and the Human Condition*. New York: Basic Books.
Köpping, Klaus P., and Ursula Rao. 2000. "Einleitung: Die 'performative Wende'. Leben - Ritual - Theater. " In *Im Rausch des Rituals: Gestaltung und Transformation der Wirklichkeit in Körperlicher Performanz*. 1–31. Münster: Lit.
Köpping, Klaus P., Bernhard Leistle, and Michael Rudolph. 2006. "Introduction." In *Ritual and Identity: Performative Practices as Effective Transformations of Social Reality*. 9–30. Berlin: Lit.
Krippner, Stanley. 1987. "Cross-Cultural Approaches to Multiple Personality Disorder: Practices in Brazilian Spiritism." *Ethos* 15 (3): 273–295.
Kurz, Helmar. 2013. *Performanz und Modernität im brasilianischen Candomblé: Eine Interpretation*. Hamburg: Dr. Kovač.
Kurz, Helmar. 2015. "'Depression is not a Disease. It is a Spiritual Problem': Performance and Hybridization of Religion and Science within Brazilian Spiritist Healing Practices." *Curare* 38 (3): 173–191.
Kurz, Helmar. 2017. "Diversification of Mental Health: Brazilian Kardecist Psychiatry and the Aesthetics of Healing." *Curare* 40 (3): 195–206. doi:10.7476/9788523220242.0006
Kurz, Helmar. 2018a. "Transcultural and Transnational Transfer of Therapeutic Practice: Healing Cooperation of Spiritism, Biomedicine, and Psychiatry in Brazil and Germany." *Curare* 41 (1,2): 39–53. doi:10.7476/9788523220242.0006
Kurz, Helmar. 2018b. "Affliction and Consolation: Mediumship and Obsession as Explanatory Models within Brazilian Kardecist Mental Health Care." In *Legitimidades da Loucura: Sofrimento, Luta, Criatividade e Pertença*, edited by Mônica Nunes and Tiago P. Marques, 129–154. Salvador: EDUFBA.
Kurz, Helmar. 2019. "Aesthetics of Healing: Working with the Senses in Therapeutic Contexts." *Curare* 42 (3,4).
Laderman, Carol, and Marina Roseman. 1996. *The Performance of Healing*. New York: Routledge.
Laplantine, Francois. 2015. *The Life of the Senses: Introduction to a Modal Anthropology*. London: Bloomsbury. doi:10.5040/9781474219204
Latour, Bruno. 2005. *Reassembling the Social: An Introduction to Actor-Network-Theory*. Oxford: Oxford University Press. doi:10.17323/1726-3247-2013-2-73-87
Leibing, Annette. 1995. *Blick auf eine Verrückte Welt: Kultur und Psychiatrie in Brasilien*. Münster: Lit.
Levi-Strauss, Claude. 1963. *Structural Anthropology*. New York: Basic Books.
Loyola, Maria A. 1984. *Médicos e Curandeiros. Conflito Social e Saúde*. Sao Paulo: Difel.
Loyola, Maria A. 1997. "Social and Cultural Hierarchies and Different Ways of Healing in Brazil." *Curare* 12 (97): 59–65.
Luz, Madel T. 1979. *As Instituições Médicas no Brasil: Instituição e Estratégia de Hegemonia*. Rio de Janeiro: Graal.
Maggie, Yvonne. 1992. *Medo de Feitiço: Relações entre Magia e Poder no Brasil*. Rio de Janeiro: Arqivo Nacional.

McClean, Stuart. 2013. "The Role of Performance in Enhancing the Effectiveness of Crystal and Spiritual Healing." *Medical Anthropology* 32 (1): 61–74. doi:10.1080/01459740.2012.692741

Moerman, Daniel E. 1979. "Anthropology of Symbolic Healing." *Current Anthropology* 20 (1): 59–66. doi:10.1086/202409

Montero, Paula. 1985. *Da Doença à Desordem: A Magia na Umbanda.* Rio de Janeiro: Editora Graal.

Moreira, Andrei. 2013. *Cura e Autocura: Uma Visão Médico-Espírita.* Belo Horizonte: AME. doi:10.22568/jee.v3.artn.010205

Negrão, Lísias N. 1996. *Entre a Cruz e a Encruzilhada: Formação de Campo Umbandista em São Paulo.* São Paulo: UDESP.

Nichter, Mark. 1981. "Idioms of Distress: Alternatives in the Expression of Psycho-social Distress: A Case Study from South India." *Culture, Medicine and Psychiatry* 5: 379–408.

Nichter, Mark. 2008. "Coming to our Senses: Appreciating the Sensorial in Medical Anthropology." *Transcultural Psychiatry* 45 (2): 163–197. doi:10.1177/1363461508089764

Nichter, Mark. 2010. "Idioms of Distress Revisited." *Culture, Medicine and Psychiatry* 34: 401–416. doi:10.1007/s11013-010-9179-6

Pierini, Emily. 2016. "Becoming a Spirit Medium: Initiatory Learning and the Self in the Vale do Amanhacer." *Ethnos* 81 (2): 290–314. doi:10.1080/00141844.2014.929598

Pierini, Emily. 2020. *Jaguars of the Dawn: Spirit Mediumship in the Brazilian Vale do Amanhacer.* New York: Berghahn.

Pink, Sarah. 2015. *Doing Sensory Ethnography.* London: Sage Publications. doi:10.4135/9781446249383.n1

Prandi, Reginaldo. 2012. *Os Mortos e os Vivos: Uma Introdução ao Espiritismo.* São Paulo: Três Estrelas.

Rabelo, Miriam C.M. 1993. "Religião e Cura: Algumas Reflexões sobre a Experiência Religiosa das Classes Populares Urbanas." *Cadernos da Saúde Pública* 9 (3): 316–325. doi:10.1590/s0102-311x1993000300019

Rabelo, Miriam C.M. 2005. "Religião e a Transformação da Experiência: Notas sobre o Estudo das Práticas Terapêuticas nos Espaços Religiosos." *Ilha* 7 (1,2): 126–145.

Rabelo, Miriam C.M., and Iara Souza. 2003. "Temporality and Experience: On the Meaning of Nervoso in the Trajectory of Urban Working-Class Women in Northeast Brazil." *Ethnography* 4 (3): 333–361. doi:10.1177/146613810343003

Reuter, Julia. 2004. "Körperinszenierungen: Zur Materialität des Performativen bei Erving Goffman und Judith Butler." *Argument* 254: 102–115.

Rocha, Cristina. 2009. "Seeking Healing Transnationally: Australians, John of God and Brazilian Spiritism." *Australian Journal of Anthropology* 20: 229–246. doi:10.1111/j.1757-6547.2009.00028.x

Rocha, Cristina. 2017. *John of God: The Globalization of Brazilian Faith Healing.* Oxford: Oxford University Press. doi:10.1093/acprof:oso/9780190466701.003.0001

Sawicki, Diethard. 2016. *Leben mit den Toten: Geisterglauben und die Entstehung des Spiritismus in Deutschland 1770–1900.* Paderborn: Schöningh. doi:10.30965/9783657782796_001

Sawodny, Heike. 2003. *Die Kardecistische Bewegung in Deutschland: Spiritistische Praxis, Weltbild und Lebenseinstellung.* Universität Hamburg: M diss.

Sax, William S. 2004. "Healing Rituals: A Critical Performative Approach." *Anthropology and Medicine* 11 (3): 293–306. doi:10.1080/1364847042000296572

Sax, William S. 2009. *God of Justice: Ritual Healing and Social Justice in the Central Himalayas.* Oxford: Oxford University Press. doi:10.5860/choice.46-6288

Scheper-Hughes, Nancy. 1994. "Embodied Knowledge: Thinking with the Body in Critical Medical Anthropology." In *Assessing Cultural Anthropology*, edited by Robert Borofsky, 229–242. New York: McGraw-Hill.

Scheper-Hughes, Nancy, and Margaret M. Lock. 1987. "The Mindful Body: A Prolegomenon to Future Work in Medical Anthropology." *Medical Anthropology Quarterly* 1 (1): 7–41.

Schmidt, Bettina E. 2015. "Spirit Mediumship in Brazil: The Controversy about Semi-Conscious Mediums." *Diskus* 17 (2): 38–53.

Schmidt, Bettina E. 2016a. *Spirits and Trance in Brazil: An Anthropology of Religious Experience*. London: Bloomsbury. doi:10.5040/9781474255707

Schmidt, Bettina E. 2016b. "Spirit Possession." In *Handbook of Contemporary Religions in Brazil*, edited by Bettina E. Schmidt and Steven Engler, 431–447. Leiden: Brill. doi:10.1163/9789004322134_027

Schmidt, Bettina E. 2017. "Varieties of Non-ordinary Experiences in Brazil: A Critical Review of the Contribution of Studies of 'Religious Experience' to the Study of Religion." *International Journal of Latin American Religions* 1: 104–115. doi:10.1007/s41603-017- 0006–0005

Seligman, Rebecca. 2005. "Distress, Dissociation, and Embodied Experience: Reconsidering the Pathways to Mediumship and Mental Health." *Ethos* 33 (1): 71–99. doi:10.1525/eth.2005.33.1.071

Seligman, Rebecca. 2010. "The Unmaking and Making of Self: Embodied Suffering and Mind- Body-Healing in Brazilian Candomblé." *Ethos* 38 (3): 297–320. doi:10.1111/j.1548- 1352.2010.01146.x

Seligman, Rebecca. 2014. *Possessing Spirits and Healing Selves: Embodiment and Transformation in an Afro-Brazilian Religion*. New York: Palgrave MacMillan. doi:10.1057/9781137409607_4

Sharp, Lynn L. 2015. "Reincarnation: The Path to Progress." In *Handbook of Spiritualism and Channeling*, edited by Cathy Gutierrez, 221–247. Leiden: Brill. doi:10.1163/9789004264083_012

Spinu, Marina, and Henry Thorau. 1994. *Captação – Trancetherapie in Brasilien: Eine ethnopsychologische Studie über Heilung durch telepathische Übertragung*. Berlin: Reimer.

Stoll, Sandra J. 2002. Religião, Ciência ou Auto-Ajuda? Trajetos do Espiritismo no Brasil. *Revista de Antropologia* 45 (2): 361–402. doi:10.1590/s0034-77012002000200003

Stubbe, Hannes. 1987. *Geschichte der Psychologie in Brasilien: Von den Indianischen und Afrobrasilianischen Kulturen bis in die Gegenwart*. Berlin: Reimer.

Tambiah, Stanley J. 2002. "Eine performative Theorie des Rituals." In *Performanz: Zwischen Sprachphilosophie und Kulturwissenschaften*, edited by Uwe Wirth, 210–242. Frankfurt/Main: Suhrkamp. doi:10.1007/978-3-322-95615-6_12

Theissen, Anna J. 2006. "Spiritismus und Psychiatrie in Brasilien: Eine Anthropologische Perspektive." In *Transkulturelle Psychiatrie, Interkulturelle Psychotherapie: Interdisziplinäre Theorie und Praxis*, edited by Ernestine Wohlfart and Manfred Zaumseil, 325–330. Heidelberg: Springer. doi:10.1007/978-3-540-32776-9_21

Theissen, Anna J. 2009. *The Location of Madness: Spiritist Psychiatry and the Meaning of Mental Illness in Contemporary Brazil*. Ann Arbor: Proquest.

Thelen, Tatjana. 2015. "Care as Social Organization: Creating, Maintaining and Dissolving Significant Relations." *Anthropological Theory* 15 (4): 497–515. doi:10.1177/1463499615600893

Thiesbonenkamp-Maag, Julia. 2014. *'Wie eine Quelle in der Wüste': Fürsorge und Selbstsorge bei der philippinisch-charismatischen Gruppe El Shaddai in Frankfurt*. Berlin: Reimer. doi:10.5771/0257-9774-2017-2-713

Turner, Victor W. 1968a. *The Forest of Symbols: Aspects of Ndembu Ritual.* Ithaca: Cornell University Press. doi:10.2307/1498807
Turner, Victor W. 1968b. *The Drums of Affliction: A Study of Religious Processes Among the Ndembu in Zambia.* Oxford: Oxford University Press. doi:10.4324/9780429486012
Turner, Victor W. 1982. *From Ritual to Theater: The Human Seriousness of Play.* New York: PAJ. doi:10.2307/1385776
Turner, Victor W. 1992 [1987]. *The Anthropology of Performance.* New York: PAJ.
van de Port, Mattijs. 2005. "Candomblé in Pink, Green and Black: Re-scripting the Afro-Brazilian Religious Heritage in the Public Sphere of Salvador, Bahia." *Social Anthropology* 13 (1): 3–26. doi:10.1017/s0964028204001077
Vigh, Henrik. 2008. "Crisis and Chronicity: Anthropological Perspectives on Continuous Conflict and Decline." *Ethnos* 73 (1): 5–24. doi:10.1080/00141840801927509
Waldram, James B. 2013. "Transformative and Restorative Processes: Revisiting the Question of Efficacy of Indigenous Healing." *Medical Anthropology* 32: 191–207. doi:10.1080/01459740.2012.714822
Walker, Sheila S. 1972. *Ceremonial Spirit Possession in Africa and Afro-America: Forms, Meanings, and Functional Significance for Individuals and Social Groups.* Leiden: Brill.
Wiencke, Markus. 2006. *Wahnsinn als Besessenheit: Der Umgang mit psychisch Kranken in spiritistischen Zentren in Brasilien.* Frankfurt/Main: IKO.
Wiencke, Markus. 2009. "Performative Therapie in einem Candomblé- und Umbanda-Tempel. " In *Differenz und Herrschaft in den Amerikas: Repräsentationen des Anderen in Geschicht und Gegenwart*, edited by Anne Ebert et al., 199–204. Bielfeld: Transcript. doi:10.14361/9783839410639-015
Wintrob, Ronald. 2009. "Overview: Looking toward the Future of Shared Knowledge and Healing Practices". In *Psychiatrists and Traditional Healers: Unwitting Partners in Global Mental Health*, edited by Mario Incayawar et al., 1–11. Chichester: Wiley-Blackwell. doi:10.1002/9780470741054.ch1
Wulf, Christoph, and Jörg Zirfas. 2001. "Die performative Bildung von Gemeinschaften: Zur Hervorbringung des Sozialen in Ritualen und Ritualisierungen. " *Paragrana* 10 (1): 93–116.
Wulf, Christoph, and Jörg Zirfas. 2004. "Performative Welten: Einführung in die historischen, systematischen und methodischen Dimensionen des Rituals." In *Die Kultur des Rituals: Inszenierungen - Praktiken - Symbole*, 7–45. München: Fink.
Xavier, Francisco C. 1944. *Nosso Lar.* Brasilia: Federacao Espirita Brasileira.

6 Nourishing exchanges
Care, love, and chronicity in Lourdes

Sarah Goldingay, Paul Dieppe, Sara Warber and Emmylou Rahtz

Introduction

The Marian Catholic pilgrimage site of Lourdes in South West France is renowned for its miraculous cures, whether one believes in their truth or not. The shrine's Medical Bureau is responsible for the identification and validation of these unexplained cures, which are then examined for their miraculous qualities by the local Bishop of Tarbes et Lourdes. Only when an inexplicable cure has been approved for its spiritual component can it be declared a miracle. The Bureau, with its roots in the *fin de siècle* height of Scientism, is focused on medical science. There is a logic in this pairing; modern medicine assumes conditions can be cured never to return. This allopathic belief is that pathological changes in body and mind result in health problems, the causes of which can be explained (diagnosed), and for which there will be some medicine, device, or operation that can alleviate or rid the person of the offending pathology (Dieppe, Roe and Warber 2015). This strategy has been spectacularly successful for many conditions, particularly acute diseases (e.g., appendicitis, heart attack, many types of infectious disease) but has not enjoyed the same success with many chronic diseases, the majority of mental health problems, or the highly prevalent general "dis-ease" and suffering amongst us. Moreover, even for acute disorders, the intervention of modern medicine will often leave people with chronic problems and suffering (Roberts et al. 2015). Despite a focus in the stories told about Lourdes on the acute cure, many of the pilgrims who go there have chronic conditions that cannot be "cured" per se. Seldom do the pilgrims expect a miracle; however, they are seeking care and relief. These qualities, we argue, are central to healing. For us, the potential in Lourdes in the twenty-first century is not about acute conditions needing a cure; it is instead an opportunity to understand how people with chronic conditions seek and often find healing through somatic, social, and sacred experiences. This chapter opens with two complex and contested binary oppositions for examination, namely healing versus curing and chronic medicine versus acute medicine. However, these binaries can only be temporary placeholders, a way of setting out the chapter's territory. Having argued that Lourdes can be distilled in such a way, we then complicate that oversimplification.

DOI: 10.4324/9781003043508-6

Acute and chronic: Healing versus curing

For cultural convenience, acute and chronic, healing and curing are binaries, typically placed far apart. The language, taxonomy, and bureaucracy of Western medicine drive much of this. They are, in fact, lived experiences in a fluid continuum and, at times, are encountered simultaneously. It is helpful then to think of acute and chronic states of health not as fixed, but sometimes separate, sometimes overlapping, always moving. For example, there are many relapsing and remitting conditions (such as multiple sclerosis) in which much of life is lived coping with chronic, perhaps minor problems, interspersed with "flares" demanding acute medical interventions. Acute conditions can often be cured while chronic conditions, in the vast majority of cases, cannot. Therefore, while being cured of an acute condition, a person can also be seeking relief from a chronic condition. Simple binaries are unhelpful here.

Chronic and non-communicable diseases and multi-morbidity are now the major health problems of the Western world (Bernell and Howard 2016; Chan 2011). We are living longer, which results in the development of a variety of chronic, age-related health problems that are incurable. In addition, many people describe mental health issues that are not easily delimited and boxed into convenient diagnostic categories. Chronicity is rising. But chronic physical and mental health problems cannot be thought of in the same simple terms of diagnosis and treatment that we use for acute health issues, the terms of reference that underpin modern Western medicine. There are often no obvious causes for chronic disorders, and no available interventions.

It is also important to acknowledge that the majority of older people have more than one chronic health problem; so-called "multi-morbidity" or "co-morbidity" contributes to the difficulty we have with the simple categorization of chronic health or mental health issues. Having several conditions is commonplace, particularly in an aging population. Yet, co-morbidity is seldom addressed in popular culture and is seen as an unwanted complication in the execution of medicine's principal measure of validity, the randomized controlled trial. These trials only consider treatment for a single condition. Chronic health problems affect body/mind/soul together. They are hard to explain and hard for other people to understand (Goldingay 2018). People look to different ways of dealing with chronicity, such as in the case of Lourdes, religion, spirituality, and practices of pilgrimage.

Many of those who come to Lourdes, referred to as pilgrims, have a chronic illness or disease (Lourdes Sanctuary, n.d.). Those trying to help such people often assist them in finding ways of coping with their problems, allowing them to live fulfilling, flourishing lives despite physical, mental, and social difficulties. Pilgrims may hope for, but not expect, a miraculous cure of their condition. However, contrary to everyday cultural assumptions, you do not have to find a cure to gain help and relief; you can heal without being cured of your chronic disease (Waldram 2013). Healing is a complex construct; it means different things in different languages and cultures. In English, the word can be used variably, as a verb, a noun, or an adjective. As authors, we think of healing as a positive change towards a state of greater integration of mind/body/soul, as a journey, and as a process that leads to more harmony and wellness, as well as to our being able to function more fully, and to flourish (Dieppe et al. 2015; Rahtz, Warber and Dieppe 2019; Scott et al. 2017). We were interested to see if healing, thought of in this way, was something that might be promoted by visits to Lourdes. And importantly, rather than seeing pilgrimage as an activity entirely "set apart" in a sacred realm, with no relevance to the pilgrims' quotidian lives, we asked how what is taking place in Lourdes could benefit the care of those with chronic conditions of various kinds.

From here, we focus on the relationship between healing and chronicity to highlight the necessary centrality to this discussion of the "whole-person" who changes over time within shifting communities and contexts. For us, these contexts are the totality of the immersive interpretative material and ephemeral experiences and beliefs from which people make meaning of their lives. They are, broadly, but not exclusively, a web of things, material and immaterial, such as people, places, practices, beliefs, memories, and expectations (Dieppe 2016; Greville-Harris and Dieppe 2015; Goldingay 2018).

From this conceptual framework, we examined the experiences of people visiting, volunteering, or working in Lourdes. Our interest was not in miraculous cures, the rare phenomena for which Lourdes is popularly known (Duffin 2014; François et al. 2014). Instead, we took a holistic approach to explore the more generalized day-to-day benefits people experience in Lourdes by considering the relationships between individual and collective, social and devotional practices in a complex "therapeutic" landscape. Lived religious or spiritual experiences are intensely contested, and we are not suggesting that pilgrimage to Lourdes is universally or uniformly beneficial to those who experience it. Without denying this complexity, the work within this chapter has a primarily positive focus. This decision to emphasize a strengths-based or beneficial perspective was further underpinned by our work on the relationship of context interpretation and healing to placebo and nocebo responses (Dieppe et al. 2014a, 2014b, 2016; Greville-Harris and Dieppe 2015).

Healing, both somatic and social, is a common term in pilgrimage studies[1] but is seldom defined (Eade 2018; Gesler 1996; Harris 2013), and, increasingly, reference is being made to wellness and well-being (Courtney 2013). Here, we set out to offer a working definition of healing as a journey with a positive trajectory enabled by a whole-person interpretive response to and within a context. Below, we provide a background to Lourdes, our ontological and epistemological positions, and describe what we found on our field research at Lourdes. Underpinned by a phenomenological frame, we also identify a nexus of beneficial factors that enable the healing process, synthesized into a novel framework of analysis, "nourishing exchanges," used to examine our findings.

Lourdes and the Bureau (colloquially known as the Office of Miracles)

Lourdes is a Roman Catholic, Marian pilgrimage site, a shrine developed as a sanctuary for healing following a series of apparitions of the Virgin Mary seen by

Bernadette Soubirous in 1858. These visions subsequently gave rise to the creation of a distinctly modernist shrine that was directly influenced by late-nineteenth-century innovations, including railways, advertising, mass production and, importantly, the contested relationship of medicine and science (Kaufman 2005; Harris 1999). This modern foundation underpins much of Lourdes' religious life during the current April to September pilgrimage season. Daily, weekly, and festival-centered practices shape it. Its activities are open to tourists, individual pilgrims, and those travelling in large groups; cohorts of two thousand or more are common. These large groups come annually to spend about a week together as a diocese (Lourdes Sanctuary, n.d.). They bring their medical support staff, volunteers, and priests to supplement the emergency assistance provided by the resident doctors, nurses, and clergy in Lourdes. While in our work we spoke to tourists and small groups of pilgrims (typically families), the focus of this chapter is three large groups described below. To understand how miracles are the framework of possibility upon which the healing infrastructure of Lourdes is built, it is helpful to consider not the miracles themselves but their codification by the Office of Medical Observations, or "the Bureau."

Established in 1883 to examine reported cures, the Bureau applies to the question of miracles a series of clinical criteria with a methodology increasingly refined over its history. It has investigated more than seven thousand cases of an inexplicable cure, seventy of which have been deemed miraculous by the local Bishop. It is worth noting that this measurement and ratification of unexplained cures only addresses those reported to and authorized by the Medical Bureau: many more pilgrims and tourists report experiencing a "benefit" from being in Lourdes that is not recorded. These are termed, by some, "mini-miracles" (Higgins and Hamilton 2016) or "minor miracles" (Harris 2013). Within the formal system, if a pilgrim believes they have benefited from an exceptional cure and wish to bear witness to this, they approach the Bureau des Constatations Médicales (Office of Medical Observations) to make a declaration. The Bureau is separate from, but works for, the Church and is overseen by the Bishop of Tarbes et Lourdes (Lourdes Sanctuary, n.d).[2] In 1862, the Bishop declared the first seven miracles. By then, in addition to the cures of the body, his criteria were the reliability of the seer and the spiritual fruits of the miracle. Here, regardless of the extraordinary nature of the scientific evidence, medicine yields to religion. Throughout our work, like many others, we have found the interrelationship of medical science and religion in Lourdes to be complex but fruitful (Spirituality and Health, n.d.). A point of continued reflection during our research was the pilgrims' ease in combining these realms through their daily lived experience. In contrast, for academics, medicine and religion typically exist in separate discourses, worlds, buildings, and often campuses.

The Bureau's formalized system of registering and testing exceptional cures limits those who declare their healing experience and therefore which cases become part of the "authorized discourse." In its measurement methods, not its understanding of and engagement with people, the Bureau is only concerned with the body, not the mind. And, with its allopathic underpinning, its focus is more acute than chronic. Yet, much of the "benefit" we encountered was a generalized sense of increased, and often incremental, mental, emotional, and spiritual wellness. Symptomatic relief, such as reductions in chronic pain or anxiety, in the absence of any major change in any underlying pathology, appear to be common results of visits to Lourdes. These generalized benefits were acknowledged by the Bureau's staff who often described these phenomena as "the real miracle of Lourdes." The Bureau's doors are open to all; however, it is not universally known or accessible. Therefore, of Lourdes' reported six million annual visitors, those who present their healing experience at the Bureau are limited in several ways: people who know of its existence and that it is possible to register a cure; those who know how to access the Bureau; those who could, or would, want to describe their experience to a stranger; those who want their experience recorded; and importantly, those who believe in the idea of the exceptional cure as a sign of faith. Although miraculous cures seem like metaphysical anomalies beyond measure, the structures put in place at Lourdes to capture and, perhaps, limit them are in many ways constraining to our more productive understanding of how people benefit from their time there. To only speak of official miracles is to deny the site's potential to facilitate non-miraculous healing.

To some extent, therefore, the power of the Lourdes' miracle is controlled by medicine. This process of attributing scientific credence to the benefits experienced by pilgrims is central to Lourdes' broader narrative, namely the power of science to prove the miraculous in the modern world. While we recognize that the polemics of science and religion continue, we saw in the activities of the town and the temporary communities who go there a holism. While some of the infrastructures might separate physical and mental health from spiritual and community well-being, we experienced a rich integration of these worlds amongst the pilgrims we met and interviewed. This holistic integration of worldview is central to our concept of nourishing exchanges.

Research objectives and methods

The research team

The authors of this chapter comprise an international, transdisciplinary team with expertise in biomedicine, complementary medicine, human health, social science, and the humanities. All four authors work in academia, each pursuing somewhat different goals but with shared interests in lived human experience, humanity, healing, and wellness. While working mainly within a medical framework, two of the team members have a broader knowledge of other literatures and practices, and we all remain open to different ways of thinking about the world; we are pluralistic and combine systemic approaches with reductionist materialism.

Our team's strengths involve the proactive consideration of researcher positioning and careful examination of our cultural beliefs along with a sensitive exploration of best practice in the studying and representing the religious "near" and "other" (Albera and Eade, 2019; Asad 1986, 2009; Geertz 1974,

1988; Eade and Albera, 2015; Hufford 1993, 1995; McCarthy Brown 1999). SG and PD had visited Lourdes previously to study pain relief there (Goldingay 2010; Goldingay et al. 2014a) and had become fascinated by stories they heard of people having life-changing experiences rather than the miraculous cures of disease (Agnew 2019; Harris 2013; Higgins and Hamilton 2019). They then teamed up with SW and ER to submit a successful research grant application to the Institution of Public Utility (Fundacao BIAL)[3] to explore these observations further. Ethical approval was granted by the ethics committee of the College of Humanities, University of Exeter (19-04-2017). Funded by the BIAL Foundation in the summer of 2017, all four authors went to Lourdes for eight days to better understand people's experiences at Lourdes and how they support individual journeys of wellness and healing.

Methodology

Our overarching methodological framework was phenomenology (Maso 2001; Moustakas 1994; Van Manen 2016). We used qualitative methods that we have used previously in our work on healing (Rahtz et al. 2019). These include recorded, in-depth interviews (n=33 people), focus groups (n=10 pairs or groups), and pictorial representations of what people thought was happening to them in Lourdes (n=19 pictures). Seventy-two percent of the participants were women. Participants were aged between 15 and 87. Forty-one percent were under 25 years old, and 19% were over 75 years old, with an even spread of ages between these two groups.

In addition to the interviews, which included both verbal and drawn responses using a range of ethnographic modes including sensory, visual, organizational, and auto-ethnographic, each of us did a large amount of ethnographic work (Atkinson et al. 2001; Atkinson and Delamont 2010; Curtis and Curtis 2011; Given 2008; Lewis-Beck et al. 2004; Madden 2017; O'Reilly 2009; Pink 2015; Salkind 2010; van Donge 2006). This fieldwork included immersion in the Lourdes rituals, observation of others attending them, and taking photographs of activities and notable sights. Before, during, and after our time in Lourdes, individually and collectively, we reflexively considered our positioning as researchers along with our and findings. Staying together in the same hotel enabled extensive discussions about our methods and findings each day. As much of the fieldwork was undertaken by each of us alone, rather than as a group, we found this approach challenging and informative, illuminating and enriching. Subsequently, we undertook a thematic analysis of our findings, to be reported elsewhere (Rahtz et al., in submission). As we write, we have had further group discussions about these findings, along with photographs and pictures drawn by participants. What follows is a phenomenological analysis informed by our thematic analysis and ethnographic work.

Spiritual and noetic experiences

Previous research trips led us to believe that many pilgrims to Lourdes come for reasons other than a miraculous cure, and people we spoke to had described profound spiritual experiences resulting in relief from chronic pain (Goldingay et al. 2014a). We found the concept of the noetic to be central to this. We acknowledge the important work in psychological research and studies concerning "meaning in life," perhaps best defined by the SONG test, "Seeking of Noetic Goals" (Garcia-Alandete et al. 2020). Our approach is more closely aligned to Husserl's phenomenological understanding of the noetic (2018; 2019) and James' definition of "noetic quality" (1925), along with the emerging field of Noetic Science (Institute of Noetic Sciences, n.d.).

Derived from "gnosis" or knowledge, a "noetic experience" describes something special, profound, and associated with a sense of knowing about the Universe. It also includes being connected with the Universe and feeling part of something bigger than ourselves. While such experiences occur for many of us at some time in our lives, they are usually fleeting but can leave a profound mark on us. Their attribution depends on our world view, our ontology. Scholarship in pilgrimage studies has moved towards holistic spirituality with its associated emphasis on well-being (Harris 2013). This holistic well-being was central to our understanding of our participants' world view and associated contextual interpretation because it is a critical component in healing. Our prior belief was that many visitors to Lourdes would have a noetic experience. We also thought that they might interpret their experience in an ontological way, and that finding a clearer sense of meaning would help them on their journeys to improved physical, mental, and spiritual health and well-being, in other words, to help them heal (Rahtz et al. 2017). Nourishing exchanges, as we will explain, are valuable in this healing process.

Participants

Everyone we spoke to self-identified as a "pilgrim" rather than a "tourist." These self-identified roles are not a fixed, clean-cut matter of being either a pilgrim or a tourist but rather markers of behavior; most tourists visit for a day or two to experience the spectacle of Lourdes as secular observers, but while there, they typically engage in a "spiritual activity" such as the candle-lit procession, which is part of the regular sacred activities in the Domain. Pilgrims travel to the site as a practice of sacred journeying, but they too enjoy shopping, tasting the local food, and travelling outside the shrine to places of interest. In the large pilgrimage groups, taking part in "secular" activities with their fellow group members like fancy dress competitions and talent shows are part of the weekly schedule each year and are relished as part of the pleasure and tradition of the diocese. Beyond this, it was not always possible, or indeed useful, to distinguish between "*malades*/assisted pilgrims" and other pilgrims. To do so would have reaffirmed the inaccurate assumption that "the well" aid "the sick." Many people who travel to assist others have long-term conditions themselves, and many people who require daily medical care as part of their pilgrimage provide significant care and support for others. Below, we problematize this issue further. Within the groups' categorization of pilgrims were people described collectively as "assisted pilgrims/*maladies*," medical volunteers, other volunteers, clergy, and family members. While the large pilgrimage groups we worked with were led and facilitated by Catholic Diocese and the vast majority of pilgrims are Catholic, it is essential to note that all faith is a lived and personal experience that should not be generalized.

Using pseudonyms, we offer extracts from those interviewed here for analysis. When in Lourdes, we chose to not try to label our informants according to what health problems they might want to disclose to us. We saw people who told us they were living with cancers, chronic neurological issues (e.g., the consequences of strokes), renal failure, cardiac failure, arthritis, and compromised sight and hearing. Some told us about living with more than one chronic condition. Some of our respondents would probably be labelled as having mental health disorders by conventional Western medicine, but in our experience such terminology was not used in Lourdes. People spoke of crises of faith, loss of spirituality, and emotional distress rather than mental health problems. But both their and our emphasis was on living a good life despite physical, mental, or spiritual issues, and the value of Lourdes to them on their healing journeys (Scott et al. 2017).

Locations of our research and pilgrimage groups

Our work took place in several locations within the town: three within The Domain (e.g., the Grotto, the procession way, and the Medical Bureau), and multiple locations outside (e.g., hotels, chapels, the riverside, and the Accueil Saint-Frai). Colloquially known as "the Domain" the Sanctuary of Our Lady of Lourdes is fifty-one hectares of carefully managed land that encloses the Grotto site of Saint Bernadette's apparitions. This fenced enclosure includes much of the explicitly medical infrastructure of the town, the Bureau described above and the Accueil Notre Dame, which opened in 1997. There are two Accueils in Lourdes, Notre Dame inside the Domain and Marie Saint-Frai, just outside. It was here, at the Saint-Frai, that we conducted some of our fieldwork and interviews. The Accueils are specialist buildings for pilgrims who have demanding medical needs. Their architecture, structures, and staffing are redolent of a small cluster of hospital wards. They are spread across six floors over two wings, with a refectory and social spaces, and each week one of these wings, or even a whole level, is taken over by a large pilgrimage group. Much of our work was with the Westminster Pilgrimage from London, England who took over a floor of the Accueil Marie Saint-Frai for their annual pilgrimage, from the 21st to the 27th of July 2017. We also worked with a group of pilgrims who had come from Malta, and with the two doctors who travelled with them, as well as the English-based Order of Malta Volunteers (OMV), each of whom used the Accueil for their sickest pilgrims. The majority of the other pilgrims who do not have demanding medical needs but who need help with their basic care and to facilitate travel stay together in large hotels with their supporting volunteers, again taking over entire floors or buildings. These large pilgrimage communities come together for Mass, prayer, processions, outings, and entertainment, and we joined them in many of these activities. Elsewhere we have spoken about the importance of community and connectivity to the process of healing (Goldingay et al. 2014a; Goldingay et al. 2014b). And within these well-functioning communities, a number of elements come together to create the nexus of a nourishing exchange.

Research findings: Nourishing exchanges

In our findings we foreground particular attributes that we think facilitate healing along with a sense of community and belonging, namely, 1) equality as nourishment, which includes a recognition of the importance of feeling safe, 2) compassion, loving hospitality, and the rejection of cultural norms (medical, spiritual, and societal), and 3) valuing of self-care and appreciation. These attributes add nuance to Gesler's observation that "[h]ealing takes place at Lourdes because the site is a focus for meaning" created by cultural expectation (1996, 104). Place holds open a space where meaning can be made, but as we have described elsewhere, meaning-making in response to cultural expectation can both enable and retard healing (Dieppe et al. 2016; Moerman 2012). As our participant Kevin (male, volunteer, 24) explained, Lourdes is more than a site:

> It's a community whereby people feel they can come here, and they can express their worries. So, it's a place where they feel at peace whether that's if they're sick, or if they just simply want some time to reflect with their faith. And, they allow you to be with them as well so you actually get the experience from that as well.

Place, however, is not the whole story. Narrative also matters. Community matters. Sharing time with others matters. We thus illustrate that the activation of these qualities by people in nourishing exchanges brings about positive benefits, especially to those with chronic conditions that cannot be cured who find healing relief and improved daily wellness through the currency and exchange of care and love. We also observe that these qualities are transferable to the quotidian world and offer a means to better harness and value the excellent care work that is already taking place in a time of chronicity.

Equality as nourishment

In Lourdes, since its inception, collectively sick pilgrims have been termed *malades*. While the term *des malades* is difficult for politically reconstructed ears, within the vernacular of The Domain it is unproblematic and as acceptable as *Brancadier*, the name for male volunteers, or the similarly complex term for female volunteers, "Hand Maiden." And, as we will see below, this is not because it is ignored as a non-issue, but rather, because in a place of necessary equality, collective nouns are more often than not a means of shared identification; they are a matter of pride, rather than a tool for objectification.

All the large pilgrimages, for example, strongly identify with their group, and this is something that is supported by the common clothing they wear, which is often national dress or traditional to their region. It is worth noting that groups such as the OMV have taken the explicit decision to call their pilgrims with special needs, "Guests," and the Westminster Diocese "Assisted Pilgrims." This decision is, in formal, policy-driven language, a clear indication of the informal ways that disability and infirmity are valorized and celebrated at the shrine. In our previous work, we noted that in Lourdes social power structures are inverted and the *malades*, who are often hidden away when the pilgrims return home, are celebrated (Goldingay et al. 2014a). This power inversion is indicative of how the *malades* are perceived more widely in Lourdes; others have noted that "for the week they were VIPs. They were special, they were the whole reason the place existed" (Lille 2005, 238).

In our latest research, we have also noted there were two ideas worthy of further nuance. First, like many visiting Lourdes for the first time, we may have thought the daily, public processing of people in wheelchairs to be exploitative and mawkish. From the outside looking superficially in, it would be reasonable to see the processions as a matter of objectification. But as observers, participants, and interviewers, we found that this shared celebration of humanity, a public performance of community, is central to establishing the conditions by which healing might take place. The complexity of how ill and disabled people are limited by dominant narratives of difference, tragedy, and loss is ably discussed in the work of Petra Kuppers (2003) and Kuppers and Marcus (2008).

Susan (female, *malade*, 81), who has visited Lourdes many times for what she called "spiritual refreshment" commented as follows:

> I feel I belong to a huge community and together we venerate Mary. That is what I feel. The pleasure of being a part of such a big community, and of hearing the "Ave, Ave" of the candlelight procession.

The experience of being understood of equal value to another is central to nourishing exchanges as vehicles for healing (Greville-Harris and Dieppe 2015). This ethos was also reflected through the views shared with us by the *malades* we spoke with, and with the rhetoric shared by group leaders in the briefings and worship we observed. There is something vital here, the potential of Lourdes as a model of equality. And, this equality was not only evident in the valorization of the *malades*. It was also apparent in the importance placed on community. There was a prevailing ethos that to be in community is to care for one another reciprocally. To be in a well-functioning community, therefore, is to be in a perpetual nourishing exchange of care and love that enables healing.

This reciprocal exchange enabled by equality moves beyond a trite neoliberal rejection of altruism, where someone "does good" as an instrumental expression of power and gives to a person whom they perceive to be weaker or with a greater need (Agrawal 2001). It also moves beyond a presumption that universally The Church or The Faithful are exploitative or exploited. This beneficial environment is about a series of mutually nourishing exchanges repeated throughout the long course of the pilgrimage from the early moments of planning and fundraising to the friendships that continue after the pilgrims return home. There is a sense of equality and reciprocal understanding from which, through mutual care given by both the *malades* and volunteers, everyone benefits. Beyond this complexity, there is, as John shared, a simplicity to the pilgrimage that shifts pilgrims into a state where they can step aside from their everyday lives and surrender space and time to giving and receiving nourishment:

> It's a very simple way of block booking a week or two where I can just come and give back without agenda, without an ulterior motive. It's very, very, very simple (laughs).

What John alludes to here is a freedom, afforded by Lourdes structures, to be released from the social expectations of a complex home life and to find space for different kinds of relationships where nourishment is central. As Lewis Hyde (2019, 52) notes, the gift economy can only function if there is an equality between giver and recipient. He explains, "a gift that has the power to change us awakens a part of the soul […] but we cannot receive the gift until we meet it as an equal." Equality in a nourishing exchange is not a linear process but a matter of giving and receiving. Nourishing exchanges are part of an extended, circular process built on equality and certainly, in part, a sense of being part of something larger than yourself, social, temporal, or spiritual.

Prosocial behavior: Reciprocity, altruism, and beneficence

Prosocial behavior was important to our respondents, who often came on several occasions in groups to share the Lourdes experience. As Marta (female, *malade*, 53) explained:

> I have come with my children as a family outing in the past, rather than with a group like this, and it is a completely different experience. It is much more valuable if you come with a group, because people get to know each other, and they share, and work together and help each other, it is much better.

Furthermore, we heard of many examples of pilgrims helping each other. Joan (female, *malade*, 72) who has had a stroke said:

> Yesterday I was talking to this man in our group, and told him about my troubles, and he said something that I really understood, and it made me look upon myself differently, he told me not to fight the problem, but to accept it and work with it, and that way I would get better. And that has changed everything, I see now that I have been approaching this in the wrong way, that I need to accept and be grateful for what I still have, rather than railing against what I have lost.

Significant research exists on the topic of prosocial behavior, it is important in evolutionary biology, anthropology, and economics. In the Social Sciences, it is underpinned by the work of Durkheim, Mauss, and Bordieu (Blogowska et al. 2013; Norenzayan et al. 2016; Penner et al. 2005; Simpson and Willer 2007). Much of the literature explores the motivation for reciprocity and assumes that, while you might give away your resources for no benefit now, you expect compensation later. This "tit-for-tat" is termed "reciprocal altruism" (Marsh 2016). It assumes both parties share an objective equality in their perception of materials or time exchanged. In Lourdes, it is not reasonable to assume that people see the same value in things and experiences. For example, the Domain operates in six languages, and what is being shared is often ephemeral and immediately rewarding, for example, eye contact, a smile, assistance from strangers. This process is not then about reciprocal altruism. What we saw taking place in the daily exchanges between the volunteers and the *malades* was not done with an expectation of repayment.[4] We also considered the common Christian trope of self-sacrifice, where you give now so that you might be rewarded later in heaven. While important in Christian dogma and personal belief, the causal relationship of being in service to another to receive heavenly reward was not expressed by any of our participants. Many volunteers who were travelling in service spoke explicitly of the benefits they experienced in caring for another without expectation of a specified reward.

Nor is this straightforward altruism. Altruism places one person in a position of power to "do good" for another – even if that other person has not been consulted or can communicate their needs. Medicine offers a helpful way to unpack this prosocial complexity which can be a problematic issue. For example, in the U.K. in 2005, following the discovery that a doctor (Harold Shipman) had murdered some of his patients, the Royal College of Physicians rejected medical altruism as problematic because "it is the claim of altruism that allows the medical profession to claim moral superiority" (Royal College of Physicians 2005). Medical ethics has been dominated, instead, by the concept of beneficence (acting in the patient's best interest/duty of care), alongside the other principles of patient autonomy, justice, and non-maleficence (not doing harm) (Gillon 1994).

While we recognized this ethos of beneficence in many of the Lourdes' interactions, a problem remains, namely the underpinning sociocultural dynamic remains where the powerful (e.g., the medical expert, the priest, the young, fit volunteer) aid the weak, the *malades*. And while this dynamic does of course exist, we found that this phenomenon was perceived by the external observer rather than the people involved in the prosocial interaction. Therefore, our understanding is that in Lourdes, this prosocial behavior is not an exchange (doing a single action in order to be rewarded later) but more a matter of "gift-giving" within the social and cultural context of a "gift economy."

Care, love, and the possibility of a deep-gift economy

The most interesting work in the field of the gift economy has come out of scholarship exploring gender and economic inequality (Cheal 2017; Mauss 1990; Simpson and Willer 2007). In pilgrimage studies, too, the importance of anglophone, political-economic processes are coming to the fore (Coleman and Eade 2018; Eade 2020). As with many things in Lourdes, this ethos of gift-giving bypasses the dominant assumptions of a capitalist economy: categorization and qualification, competition and measurement, scarcity and self-interest. The exchanges we observed were not "tit-for-tat;" there was deeper nurturance at work.

After an early discussion about our planned research with one of the medical staff working with the *malades*, author PD noted:

> She also said that she thought that many of their group would benefit from sharing things about their visits with us, and that taking part in our research could be an additional beneficial part of their pilgrimage.

The currency of exchange we observed was one of care. Mutual care is central to all activities for these large pilgrimage groups. We would argue that the primary animating force underlying this exchange of care is love. In a refinement of the field of the gift economy, critic and writer Ronald Grimes speaks of the possibility of a deep-gift economy that undermines or suffuses "THE economy" (Grimes 2002). We see this as central to Lourdes' potential as a model of care in a time of chronicity. Grimes argues that to live in the twenty-first century is "a dialectical dance" with the planet and all its inhabitants. We term the manifestation of Grimes' global dialectical dance that we observed in Lourdes a nourishing exchange. From a deep-gifting perspective, these exchanges are not about an objective reward but rather about the mutual benefit received in nourishing one another. Perhaps the Lourdes' "mini-miracle" then is a dialectical dance of nourishing exchange that suffuses behaviors foregrounded by the economy and its associated cultural norms. As poet Gary Snyder (2007) explains, "the real heart of a gift economy [is] an economy that would save, not devour, the world" (34). While Lourdes is, of course, imperfect, and not universally beneficial, the activities there bring significant benefit to many pilgrims. In a time of chronicity, where cures are not available, the possibility of the nourishing care we saw in Lourdes offers a rich locus of potential.

Loving hospitality and care

After attending one of the regular social events for priests, doctors, and nurses, held in the Medical Bureau, SG made the following note:

> The tiny room was packed with people passing cups over each other's heads, laughing, and waving as new people squeezed in from the overflow that took the party into the corridor. I was chatting with a Phillipino nurse from an Islamic family who was travelling with the London pilgrimage. "I love it," she said. "We work hard. But we play harder. It sets me up for the rest of the year."

While its focus is the *malades*, the Bureau facilitates and nurtures the registration and collaboration of health care professionals who visit Lourdes as volunteers. Anyone can register, whether they are travelling as part of a group or as individuals. During this research trip, we were based in the Bureau where we observed two important factors enabling nourishing exchanges, namely collegiate collaboration along with hospitality and care.

The intimate interactions of staff with visitors, the worship in the Bureau's chapel, and end of day socials, all of which we observed and participated in, created important collaborative spaces for health care practitioners. They were from a dynamic variety of fields, trainings, nations, and spoken languages. People valued the opportunity to meet in a supportive environment to share experiences and facilitate support in a compassionate and safe setting that promotes openness. Compassion enabling professional transparency and vulnerability is a quality we have noted elsewhere in the work of health care professionals volunteering in the Baths in Lourdes (Goldingay 2010; Goldingay et al. 2014a). The Bureau's Director, Dr. Alessandro de Franciscis, a Harvard-trained physician and Naples-born former politician, sets this nourishing tone. While each large pilgrimage group has their approach and tradition, the Bureau echoes, or perhaps enables, an ethos of loving support that we found in all of the pilgrimages we encountered. We note it because it is indicative of the importance of care, deep-listening, and gifting, which we found to be common practice within these large pilgrimage groups. Kevin explained the importance of "togetherness" and "bonding" with strangers:

> I find that even people that are struggling with their faith, or you know not even the Catholic belief, there's almost like a togetherness, a bonding between people from all over the world. You see different pilgrimages and different religions and different languages come together, and it's a real sense of community, which I really love.

This context is indicative of the importance of care, deep-listening, and gifting which we found to be common practice within these large pilgrimage groups.

Both the idea and experience of community are felt intensely during the pilgrimage. It then takes on a different form as pilgrims return home. The Bureau's care of this transient community extends beyond the actual pilgrimage time in Lourdes, with remote support available during preparations to travel for the Directors of Medicine for each pilgrimage, and a quarterly in-house journal, *Fons Vitae*, circulated to its forty thousand international professional members. There is a commonality in two critical areas of life for those who interact with the Bureau, medicine, and religion: the vast majority of those registered are Roman Catholic. Both medicine and religion therefore provide a framework of commonality and community that transcends the limits of spoken language, culture, or geography, thereby fostering a sense of collective purpose. We observed that, because the interactions were taking place across nationality and areas of health care specialization, the focus and professional dialogue was not siloed into the minutiae of developments in specific fields. Instead, it fell into the commonly shared area of interest, patient care, conviviality, and compassion. These, coupled with equality, enable nourishing exchanges.

Assumptions about care and medicine

While spending time in the Accueil Saint-Frai, SG made the following note:

> Kneeling by the wheelchair, the volunteer asked for help, looking worried about the distress of the person they were with. And there it was again from the Medical Team Lead. No words. Eye contact. Smile. Walk over. A guiding hand. A nod. Another smile. The calm care of a low-tech, high-touch environment. No need to shout instructions across the ward. No machine going ping. Kind laughter echoing from the corridor. Distress eased, not amplified.

Lourdes is a shrine for the sick.[5] This purpose is supported by the town's infrastructure of hotels and restaurants, besides its religious center, that facilitates the movement of thousands of wheelchairs to the daily activities in "an economy of caring exchange" (Goldingay et al. 2014b), akin to Higgins and Hamilton's (2019) conception of a "therapeutic servicescape." This sympathetic collaboration between the care needs of the pilgrims, the operational needs of the Domain's infrastructure, and the socio-economic needs of the town might appear tangential to healing. It is, however, this complex network of long-established relationships and collaboration that provides the rich locus of potential for nourishing exchanges. These ephemeral structures are easy to dismiss. Yet, they enable and nourish care. For people with chronic health needs, a cure is not always available, but care is.

As we have explored elsewhere, Lourdes ethos is underpinned by the beneficial practices of deep-listening, attentive and well-intentioned care, along with a low-tech, high-touch environment (Goldingay 2010, Goldingay et al. 2014a). These qualities both construct and are an expression of the operational norms of Lourdes. Progress in medical technology is not a driving force. And while some may see this as detrimental, the people we spoke with valued this person-centered, calm kindness of care. Moreover, the potential of Lourdes' low-tech, high-touch environment as a training ground for developing high-quality patient care is well-established.[6] In our experience, healthcare in our modern hospitals and communities is often routine and somewhat "soulless," being dominated at times by protocols and bureaucracy. Palliative care stands out as something of an exception. The very fact that the patients are dying, and the recognition that medical science cannot cure the problem, frees up the carer to work within a spiritual, caring ethos, rather than a goal-driven one that is searching for a materialistic solution. As Lille (2005, 239), in a case study exploring the practice of pilgrimage, concluded, her participants identified the reasons for accompanying pilgrims to Lourdes because they:

> closely reflect the aims of palliative care [...] enabling patient choice and respecting patient autonomy [...] provision of spiritual care [coupled with] benefits that are not readily available within a hospice setting [...] the experience of communitas, of belonging and friendship, which formed during the pilgrimage and chance of a holiday.

Lourdes provides a model of healing that is freed from medical buildings and infrastructure; it is instead built on nourishing exchanges that exist in the experience of people facilitated by a convivial, caring environment of equality and safety. This sense of safety, equity, and care was central to another aspect of nourishing exchange, namely nourishing the self.

Assumptions about self-care

> What I found at the grotto was pure – err – silence in the sense [...] that someone, and that probably is Mary – is there with us, based on the fact that it's so still, and it's so peaceful, and you almost feel like if you have anything that you need to get off your chest and explain that's the place where, you know, someone is watching and someone is saying it's going to be all right.
>
> (Kevin, male 24)

It would be reasonable to expect that in a community orientated towards care for another that self-care would be rare, especially one that is Christian, where narratives of self-sacrifice are common. However, we found that self-care remains an important factor in the nourishing exchanges. While mental health is not part of the popular medico-miraculous narrative of Lourdes, many of our participants noted an increase in mental wellness and feelings of appreciation. As Sharon (female, 35) explained,

> I am an amputee, I have lost my right leg to cancer, so travelling is a bit limited, so my very first trip after my treatment in the U.K. was Lourdes. So, it is something that helps. It fills me, so during the year if my battery is running low and I have to refill it (laughs). It makes me live, it is a place that really and truly adds life, a lot. And I feel I can really relate with the heavens above. I know that God is everywhere, but being here gives me some very good me time [...] quality time with God.

She describes how her self-care, her "me time," is entwined with quality time with God and that a nourishing relationship both with Lourdes and the divine "adds life, a lot." As another participant succinctly expressed, "The craziness of the rest of the world keeps going, but whilst I'm here it's yes, you're content with what you're doing." Participants' narratives about self-care focused on two primary sources: times of quiet reflection afforded by the religious infrastructure in the town and the wider landscape, and, as with Sharon above, a stronger connection to a sense of the divine.

There are two points worth noting here. First, the volunteers' schedules, published in the large pilgrimage groups' handbooks, are relentless – in particular, if the assisted pilgrim the volunteer is working with needs assistance with personal care, like dressing. 5:30 am team briefings and prayers are common. Second, although the days start early, Lourdes has a vibrant nightlife, and the bars are full of pilgrims until the early hours. Each large pilgrimage group "adopts" a bar for the duration of their trip. "Feeling knackered" is common (Kevin, male, 24). We were surprised then that individuals choosing to set time aside for personal reflection, quietude, and self-care was frequently referred to as part of pilgrims' beneficial experience.

The Grotto is the site of Saint Bernadette's apparitions and is the sacred center of Lourdes. While it is in the busy heart of the Domain during the day, Mass is conducted here in the open air throughout the day and pilgrims sit in silence to pray and contemplate. Many volunteers we spoke with described going to the Grotto after leaving bars and restaurants late into the night. In our interviews, the qualities attributed to therapeutic landscapes are in evidence, but beyond this, there is a nourishing exchange that facilitates a sense of personal centeredness, safety, and fortitude. As Kevin explained, this self-focused, nourishing exchange is built on deep-listening to the landscape and in it finding the divine's presence and response:

> The Grotto is shaped in the sense that the water runs down and you know, you can hear the river at the back behind you. It just feels like someone is there and someone is listening to you and then that's always reassuring [...] Although, you've got all of the masses and you've got your life outside of Lourdes there's a time when you can just say you know, I need somewhere to think and someone to just make sure that I'm okay. And, that's what I think the Grotto gives you. It gives you a place of stillness and prayer where you can really try and look for a Mary and try and look for God and to allow them to just – [...] to feel that someone is listening to you. And, I've got enriched by that every year. I feel that the Grotto is the most special part, especially at night time [...] that's when I feel that I'm most calm so I'm actually in touch with my faith then. And, also, I feel that with the stillness then that's when I can feel much closer to God.

Kevin conveyed the ways that these nourishing exchanges with focal places in Lourdes can be single high-point noetic moments. Still, for him, it is a slow development over years with the river and the rocks and the stillness of the landscape.

Remaining with self-care while returning us to questions of equality, John explained that not all of the self-realizations in Lourdes are comfortable. However, through the process of spacious reflexivity and self-care afforded by the pilgrimage, he shared that there is a chance not only to recognize but also to try out "the best version of yourself" (Goldingay 2010). And, in so doing, recognize the ways you can reflect that positive change in quotidian life:

> If you walk along any of the streets and look at the cafes and the hotels, you're as likely to see someone who's in an electric wheelchair than you are an able-bodied person having a cappuccino, having a beer, having a – whatever! And, [...] no one would bat an eyelid you know. No one would look twice at someone, anyone – whether they were in a stretcher, you

know – whatever [...]. They would think good for them [...] the situation we're in in the U.K. now where I feel that we push and we aim for an equal society, but even myself, I catch myself doing it. Someone is out in a bar in an evening in a wheelchair and having a good few [...].

We found this complex and thoughtful reflexivity seeking self-development expressed in many ways by several participants included realizations around being more patient, less self-centered, more compassionate.

Another aspect of self-care that participants noted was a quality of self-development emerging from their nourishing exchanges. As Kevin expressed:

In the U.K., I'm a police officer. So, obviously, I deal with different religions and different communities, and no matter what community I would deal with, being at Lourdes gives me an understanding of different people. So, like we've got people who are elderly and people who are sick. We've also got young people this year in terms of a new community and some with learning difficulties. And, I feel that it gives you patience. I feel that I'm a lot more patient coming back from Lourdes and it gives me a time where before I think I wouldn't necessarily have – be the best person to approach and I feel that it gives me time to reflect and to, you know, to understand people who are different. People come from different communities. People you know share different values. Lourdes, I think it makes you reflect on how you are as a person, I think. And, you know no one's perfect and I feel that people in Lourdes, they get a sense that they've done a good duty for the week and they want to instill that in their lives.

Individuals are nourished within these communities; this is in part enabled by collectivity and in part by the immersion in the actuality and imaginative landscape of Lourdes, its history, its symbology. The well-functioning community is made up of cared for individuals – and that care is in turn shared between self and others. Nourishing exchanges in Lourdes take many forms but share a common thread of a well-functioning community with an ethos of equality, simplicity, and commitment to each other and one's self. This may help explain why so many pilgrims come so often.

Conclusion

Seen from the outside, Lourdes is a place of complex dualities. At first glance, it belongs to a residual culture, one formed in the past yet still active in the present. In many ways, the outsider's understanding of the present now appears to be at odds with this past. Certain things seem out of place, an expression of something we have, as a society, now moved beyond. Superficially, Lourdes is explicitly Christian, Catholic, predominantly white, patriarchal, and hierarchical. Its landscape has been tamed, and the river formalized. It is built on old symbols and practices of medicine; such as white coats and nurses' caps. It is, to all intents and purposes, anachronistic to our postmodern or late modern view. However, this is not its totality. There are paradoxes and complexity here too, hardly surprising in light of much scholarship discussing the incommensurability between the sceptic and the believer (MacIntyre 1964). While these complexities from a residual culture appear to be in opposition to the equality, safety, and ease necessary for nourishing exchanges to support healing, they become important in the intimate care taking place in these loving communities. We found much that is anachronous to being positive. This systemic understanding moves our work from the realms of empirical evidence to consider positive experiences, described by François et al. (2014) as, "anticipation and hope, belief and confidence, fervor and awe, meditation and exaltation, [...] compounded by the spiritual atmosphere of the place, ritual gestures, hymns, and prayers." And while we agree with their conclusions, we do not simply place these experiences together under "mental" effects (2014, 162). Instead, we argue that it is the unique, intersecting, and systemic combination of social, somatic, atmospheric, experiential, geographical, historical, intellectual, temporal, and spiritual elements that create an integrated system of nourishing exchange. And that system, experienced by each individual, enabled by a willing community, has the rich potential to bring about healing.

Healing here has the potential to be enabled by nourishing exchanges in four principal ways, namely, 1) a whole-person interpretative response is invited in relationship to a context, in this case, Lourdes, 2) the possibility of positive change and growth towards a state of greater integration of mind, body, and soul is supported, 3) a journey and a process that can lead to more harmony and wellness is being facilitated, 4) carers intend to help people to function more fully in their lives. Nourishing exchanges are beneficial for meaning-making in the context of chronic illness; they are enabled by prosocial behavior; they disrupt rather than reject social norms. Within nourishing exchanges, equality and feeling safe are possible; hospitality and care are central; love and appreciation are primary; intelligent self-awareness and reflexivity are fundamental.

Our conclusions about the key components in the nexus of beneficial factors that facilitate nourishing exchanges and thus healing in Lourdes is summarized in Table 6.1. Nourishing exchanges are a gift. Lourdes' "mini-miracles" occur in the dialectical dance between people and ideas, each other, sacred places, symbolism, themselves, and the Divine. By thinking about the process of gifting rather than the action of altruism or reciprocity, we might turn towards an ethical community where expectation is not a condition for treating someone as an end in itself, but rather a localized exchange that is nourishing and a catalyst for transformation, growth, and healing. It is then a matter of hope. And perhaps that is where the principle benefit of Lourdes lies, that in this immersive environment participants live a different version of their better selves; they are living in a state of reflection, appreciation, and hope, and in so doing enabling healing for themselves and others.

Table 6.1 The nexus of beneficial factors

Nourishing exchanges enable healing by:

- Facilitating a whole-person interpretative response to and within a context
- Enabling positive change and growth towards a state of greater integration of mind, body, and soul
- Supporting a journey and a process that leads to more harmony and well-being
- Helping people function more fully

Nourishing exchanges are beneficial nexuses of meaning-making:

- They are enabled by prosocial behavior
- They are expressions of a deep-gift economy
- They disrupt social norms

Essential attributes:

- Equality and feeling safe
- Hospitality and care
- Love and appreciation
- Intelligent self-awareness and reflexivity

Notes

1 Pilgrimage Studies is a well-established international, transdisciplinary discourse examining the motivations for and experiences of sacred and secular pilgrimage. The *Ashgate Studies in Pilgrimage* series (www.routledge.com/Ashgate-Studies-in-Pilgrimage/book-series/APILGRIM) and Centre for Pilgrimage Studies offer core resources (https://pilgrimagestudies.ac.uk).
2 The complexity of this process, as much social as scientific, is ably described in Ruth Harris's excellent book *Lourdes: Body and Spirit in a Secular Age* (1999).
3 The Fundacao BIAL supports research into what enables a healthy human being, both from the physical and spiritual point of view. It works particularly in fields largely still unexplored but which warrant further scientific analysis.
4 *Malades* is the Lourdes' collective term for pilgrims with health care needs. We will return to this complex idea in later sections.
5 Many religious traditions have shrines. They are places set apart as sacred, often marking an important location. They can be small, a simple altar for votive offerings, or large landscapes such as Lourdes. In many traditions they are dedicated to certain groups of people; in Lourdes the shrine is dedicated to the healing of the sick.
6 This is exemplified by Dr Anne Solari-Twadell's clinical placement programme at Loyola University's Marcella Niehoff School of Nursing.

References

Agnew, Michael. 2019. "'This is a Glimpse of Paradise': Encountering Lourdes through Serial and Multisited Pilgrimage" *Journal of Global Catholicism* 3 (1): article 3. doi:10.32436/2475-6423.1048

Agrawal, A. 2001. "Kin recognition and the evolution of altruism." *Proceedings of the Royal Society London B* 268: 1099–1104.

Albera, Dionigi, and John Eade. 2019. *New Pathways in Pilgrimage Studies: Global Perspectives*. London: Routledge.

Asad, Talal. 1986. "The Concept of Cultural Translation in British Social Anthropology." In *Writing Culture: The Poetics and Politics of Ethnography*, edited by James Clifford and George E. Marcus, 141–164. Oakland: University of California Press.

Asad, Talal. 2009. *Genealogies of Religion: Discipline and Reasons of Power in Christianity and Islam*. Baltimore: Johns Hopkins University Press.

Ashgate Studies in Pilgrimage website. n.d. Accessed February 14, 2020 from www.routledge.com/Ashgate-Studies-in-Pilgrimage/book-series/APILGRIM

Atkinson, Paul, and Sarah Delamont. 2010. *Sage Qualitative Research Methods*. Thousand Oaks, California: Sage Publications.

Atkinson, Paul, Amanda Coffey, Sara Delamont, John Lofland and Lyn Lofland. 2001. *Handbook of Ethnography*. New York: Sage Publications. doi:10.4135/9781848608337

Bernell, Stephanie, and Steven W. Howard. 2016. "Use Your Words Carefully: What is a Chronic Disease?" *Frontiers in Public Health* 4 (159). doi:10.3389/fpubh.2016.00159

Blogowska, Joanna, Catherine Lambert and Vassilis Saroglou. 2013. "Religious Prosociality and Aggression: It's Real." *Journal for the Scientific Study of Religion* 52: 524–536. doi:10.1111/jssr.12048

Chan, Margaret. 2011. "The Worldwide Rise of Chronic Noncommunicable Diseases: A Slow-Motion Catastrophe". World Health Organization. Accessed February 2, 2020 from www.who.int/dg/speeches/2011/ministerial_conf_ncd_20110428/en/

Cheal, David. 2017. *The Gift Economy*. London: Routledge.

Coleman, Simon, and John Eade. 2018. *Pilgrimage and Political Economy: Translating the Sacred*. Oxford: Berghahn Books.

Courtney, Michelle. 2013. "New Opportunities for Occupational Therapy Through the Occupation of Contemporary Pilgrimage." *British Journal of Occupational Therapy* 76 (6), 292–294. doi:10.4276/030802213X13706169932987

Curtis, Bruce, and Cate Curtis. 2011. "Ethnographic Research: Studying Groups in Natural Settings". In *Social Research*, edited by Bruce Curtis and Cate Curtis, 78–98. London: Sage Publications.

Dieppe, Paul, and Maddy Greville-Harris. 2014a. "Are We Dispensing Nocebos to Patients in Pain?" *International Musculoskeletal Medicine* 36 (4): 128–129. doi:10.1179/1753614614Z.00000000083

Dieppe, Paul, Debbie Marsden, and Sarah Goldingay. 2014b. "Placebos, Caring and Healing in Rheumatology." In *Rheumatology* (6th ed.), edited by Marc Hochberg, Alan J. Silman, Joseph Smolen, Michael Weinblatt and Michael A. Weisman, 390–394. Toronto: Elsevier. doi:10.1016/B978-0-7020-6865-2.00057-9

Dieppe, Paul, Chris Roe and Sara L.Warber. 2015. "Caring and Healing in Health Care: The Evidence Base." *International Journal of Nursing Studies* 52 (10): 1539–1541. doi:10.1016/j.ijnurstu.2015.05.015

Dieppe, Paul, Sarah Goldingay and Maddy Greville-Harris. 2016. "The Power and Value of Placebo and Nocebo in Painful Osteoarthritis." *Osteoarthritis and Cartilage* 24 (11): 1850–1857. doi:10.1016/j.joca.2016.06.007

Duffin, Jacalyn. 2014. "Religion and Medicine, Again: JHMAS Commentary on 'The Lourdes Medical Cures' Revisited." *Journal of the History of Medicine and Allied Sciences* 69 (1): 162–165. doi:10.1093/jhmas/jrt045

Eade, John. 2018. "Healing Social and Physical Bodies: Lourdes and Military Pilgrimage." In *Military Pilgrimage and Battlefield Tourism: Commemorating the Dead*, edited by Dionigi Albera and John Eade, 15–34. London: Routledge.

Eade, John. 2020. "Moving, Crossing, and Dwelling: Christianity and Place Pilgrimage." In *The Wiley-Blackwell Companion to Religion and Materiality*, edited by Vasudha Narayanan, 209–225. New Jersey: Wiley-Blackwell.

Eade, John, and Dionigi Albera. 2015. *International Perspectives on Pilgrimage Studies: Itineraries, Gaps and Obstacles*. London: Routledge.

François, Bernard, Esther M. Sternberg and Elizabeth Fee. 2014. "The Lourdes Medical Cures Revisited." *Journal of the History of Medicine and Allied Sciences* 69 (1): 135–162.

Garcia-Alandete, Joaquin, César Rubio-Belmonte and Beatriz Soucase Lozano. 2020. "The Seeking of Noetic Goals Revisited Among Spanish Young People." *Journal of Humanistic Psychology* 60 (1): 77–98.

Geertz, Clifford. 1974. "From the Native's Point of View: On the Nature of Anthropological Understanding". *Bulletin of the American Academy of Arts and Sciences* 28 (1): 26–45.

Geertz, Clifford. 1988. *Works and Lives: The Anthropologist as Author*. Cambridge: Polity Press.

Gesler, Wil. 1996. "Lourdes: Healing in a Place of Pilgrimage." *Health and Place* 2 (2): 95–105.

Gillon, Raanan. 1994. "Medical Ethics: Four Principles plus attention to Scope." *British Medical Journal* 309: 184–188.

Given, Lisa M. 2008. *The Sage Encyclopedia of Qualitative Research Methods (Vols. 1–0)*. Thousand Oaks, CA: Sage Publications.

Goldingay, Sarah. 2010. "How is Contemporary English Spiritual and Religious Identity Constructed and Reconstructed by Performance?" PhD diss. University of Exeter. Retrieved from https://ore.exeter.ac.uk/repository/handle/10036/106819

Goldingay, Sarah, Miguel Farias and Paul Dieppe. 2014a. "'And the Pain Just Disappeared into Insignificance': The Healing Response in Lourdes. Performance, Psychology and Caring." *International Review of Psychiatry* 26 (3): 315–323. doi:10.3109/09540261.2014.914472

Goldingay, Sarah, Paul Dieppe, Michael Mangan and Debbie Marsden. 2014b. "(Re)acting Medicine: Applying Theatre in Order to Develop a Whole-Systems Approach to Understanding the Healing Response." *Research in Drama Education: The Journal of Applied Theatre and Performance* 19 (3): 272–279. doi:10.1080/13569783.2014.928007

Goldingay, Sarah. 2018. "Act Like It Hurts: Questions of Role and Authenticity in the Communication of Chronic Pain." In *Painscapes*, edited by Elena Gonzalez-Polledo and Jen Tarr. London: Palgrave Macmillan. doi:10.1057/978-1-349-95272-4_4

Greville-Harris, Maddy, and Paul Dieppe. 2015. "Bad is More Powerful than Good: The Nocebo Response in Medical Consultations." *The American Journal of Medicine* 128 (2): 126–129. doi:10.1016/j.amjmed.2014.08.031

Grimes, Ronald L. 2002. "Performance is Currency in the Deep World's Gift Economy: An Incantatory Riff for a Global Medicine Show." *Interdisciplinary Studies in Literature and Environment* 9 (1): 149–164. doi:10.1093/isle/9.1.149

Harris, Alana. 2013. "Lourdes and Holistic Spirituality: Contemporary Catholicism, the Therapeutic and Religious Thermalism." *Culture and Religion* 14 (1): 23–43. doi:10.1080/14755610.2012.756411

Harris, Ruth. 1999. *Lourdes: Body and Spirit in the Secular Age*. London: Viking.

Higgins, Leighanne, and Kathy Hamilton. 2016. "Mini-Miracles: Transformations of Self from Consumption of the Lourdes Pilgrimage." *Journal of Business Research* 69 (1): 25–32. doi:10.1080/14755610.2012.756411

Higgins, Leighanne, and Kathy Hamilton. 2019. "Theraputic Servicescapes and Market-Mediated Performance of Emotional Suffering." *Journal of Consumer Research* 45 (6): 1230–1253. doi:10.1093/jcr/ucy046

Hufford, David. 1993. "Epistemologies in Religious Healing." *The Journal of Medicine and Philosophy* 18 (2): 175–194.
Hufford, David. 1995. "The Scholarly Voice and the Personal Voice: Reflexivity in Belief Studies." *Western Folklore* 54 (1): 57–76.
Husserl, Edmund. 2008. *Introduction to Logic and Theory of Knowledge: Lectures 1906/7*. Translated by Claire Ortiz Hill. New York: Springer.
Husserl, Edmund. 2019. *Logic and General Theory of Science*. Translated by Claire Ortiz Hill. New York: Springer.
Hyde, Lewis. 2019. *The Gift: How the Creative Spirit Transforms the World*. New York: Vintage.
Institute of Noetic Sciences. n.d. Accessed February 14, 2020 from https://noetic.org
James, William. 1925. *The varieties of religious experience: a study in human nature / being the Gifford Lectures on Natural Religion delivered in Edinburgh in 1901–1902*. London: Longmans Green.
Kaufman, Suzanne. 2005. *Consuming Visions: Mass Culture and the Lourdes Shrine*. Ithaca: Cornell University Press.
Kuppers. Petra. 2003. *Disability and Contemporary Performance: Bodies on Edge*. London: Routledge.
Kuppers, Petra, and Neil Marcus. 2008. *Cripple Poetics*. Ypsilanti, MI: Homofactus Press.
Lewis-Beck, Michael S., Alan Bryman and Tim Futing Liao. 2004. *The Sage Encyclopedia of Social Science Research Methods (Vols. 1–0)*. Thousand Oaks, CA: Sage Publications.
Lille, A.K. 2005. "The Practice of Pilgrimage in Palliative Care: A Case Study of Lourdes." *International Journal of Palliative Nursing* 11 (5): 234–239. doi:10.12968/ijpn.2005.11.5.234
Lourdes Sanctuary website. n.d. Lourdes Sanctuary Official Website. Accessed February 14, 2020 from www.lourdes-france.org/en/
Macintyre, Alasdair. 1964. "Is Understanding Religion Compatible with Believing?" In *Faith and the Philosophers*, edited by John Hick, 115–133. London: Palgrave Macmillan.
Madden, Raymond. 2017. *Being Ethnographic*. London: Sage Publications.
Marsh, Abigail A. 2016. "Neural, Cognitive, and Evolutionary Foundations of Human Altruism." *WIREs Cognitive Science* 7 (1): 59–71. doi:10.1002/wcs.1377
Maso, Ilja. 2001. "Phenomenology and Ethnography". In *Handbook of Ethnography*, edited by Paul Atkinson, Amanda Coffey, Sarah Delamont, John Lofland and Lyn Lofland, 136–144. London: Sage Publications.
Mauss, Marcel. 1990/1950. *The Gift: The Form and Reason for Exchange in Archaic Societies*. Translated by W.D. Halls. London: Routledge. First published in 1950 by Presses Universitaires de France in Sociologie et Anthropologie.
McCarthy Brown, Karen. 1999. "Writing about 'The Other'." In *The Insider/Outsider Problem in the Study of Religion*, edited by Russell T. McCutcheon. London: A&C Black.
Moerman, Daniel. 2012. *Meaning, Medicine and the "Placebo Effect"*. Cambridge: Cambridge University Press.
Moustakas, Clark. 1994. *Phenomenological Research Methods*. London: Sage Publications.
Norenzayan, Ara, Azim Shariff, Will Gervais, Aiyana Willard, Rita McNamara, Edward Slingerland and Joseph Henrich. 2016. "The Cultural Evolution of Prosocial Religions." *Behavioural and Brain Sciences* 39 (1): 1–65. doi:10.1017/s0140525x14001356
O'Reilly, Karen. 2009. *Key Concepts in Ethnography*. London: Sage Publications.
Penner, Louis A., John F. Dovidio, Jane A. Piliavin and David A. Schroeder. 2005. "Prosocial Behavior: Multilevel Perspectives." *Annual Review of Psychology* 56 (1): 365–392. doi:10.1146/annurev.psych.56.091103.070141

Pilgrimage Studies website. n.d. Accessed February 14, 2020 from https://pilgrimagestudies.ac.uk

Pink, Sarah. 2015. *Doing Sensory Ethnography*. London: Sage Publications.

Rahtz, Emmylou, Sian Bonnell, Sarah Goldingay, Sara Warber and Paul Dieppe. 2017. Paul "Transformational Changes in Health Status: A Qualitative Exploration of Healing Moments." *Explore* 13 (5): 298–305.

Rahtz, Emmylou, Sara L. Warber and Paul Dieppe. 2019. "Understanding Public Perceptions of Healing: An Arts Based Qualitative Study." *Complementary Therapy in Medicine* 45: 25–32. doi:10.1016/j.ctim.2019.05.013

Rahtz, Emmylou, Sara L. Warber and Paul Dieppe. 2020. "Transcendent Experiences Among Pilgrims to Lourdes: A Qualitative Investigation." In submission.

Roberts, Karen, Deepa Rao, T.L. Bennett, Lidia Loukine and G.C. Jayaraman. 2015. "Prevalence and Patterns of Chronic Disease Multimorbidity and Associated Determinants in Canada." *Health Promotion and Chronic Disease Prevention in Canada* 35 (6): 87–94. doi:10.24095/hpcdp.35.6.01

Royal College of Physicians, working party. 2005. "Doctors in society: medical professionalism in a changing world." *Clinical Medicine London* 5 (6–1):S5–40.

Salkind, Neil J. 2010. *Encyclopedia of Research Design*. Thousand Oaks, CA: Sage Publications.

Scott, John G., Sara Warber, Paul Dieppe, David Jones and Kurt Stange. 2017. "Healing Journey: A Qualitative Analysis of the Healing Experiences of Americans Suffering from Trauma and Illness." *BMJ Open* 7 (8): e016771. doi:10.1136/bmjopen-2017-016771

Snyder, Gary. 2007. *Back on the Fire*. Berkley: Shoemaker and Hoard.

Simpson, Brent, and Robb Willer. 2007. "Altruism and Indirect Reciprocity: The Interaction of Person and Situation in Prosocial Behavior." Berkley Greater Good. Accessed February 2, 2020 from https://greatergood.berkeley.edu/images/uploads/Simpson-AltruismReciprocity.pdf

Spirituality and Health database. n.d. Accessed 18 July 2020 from https://spiritualityandhealth.duke.edu

van Donge, Jan Kees. (2006). "Ethnography and Participant Observation". In *Doing Development Research*, edited by Vandana Desai and Rob Potter, 180–188. London: Sage Publications.

Van Manen, Max. 2016. *Researching Lived Experience: Human Science for an Action Sensitive Pedagogy*. New York: Routledge.

Waldram, James B. 2013. "Transformative and Restorative Processes: Revisiting the Question of Efficacy of Indigenous Healing." *Medical Anthropology: Cross-Cultural Studies in Health and Illness*, 32 (3), 191–207. doi:10.1080/01459740.2012.714822

7 Miyo-wîcêhetowin in the city

Indigenous youth spirituality, good ancestors, and mental wellness through healing journeys on the land

Darrien Morton, Kelley Bird-Naytowhow and Andrew R. Hatala

Introduction

> There is a medicine that grows on the sidewalk called plantain. It grows anywhere—in dusty lots, the cracks of sidewalks—and if you pick it up and clean it and put it on a wound, it will take infection out and promote healing. In a lot of ways, the plantain is very similar to the history of Indian people in the city. They may be obscure and they may be sort of growing in the cracks in the sidewalk, but when they are brought back to who they are, then there is an immense amount of power, and there's an immense amount of healing.
>
> (Alan Bobiwash, Anishinaabe teacher and community leader as quoted in Johnson 2013)

Relationships with the natural world, including stars, mountains, waterways, landscapes, airways, animals, and plants, continue to shape the spiritual worldviews, beliefs, values, institutions, laws, and practices of many Indigenous[1] communities across the globe (see discussions in North America by Deloria 2003; Ermine 1995; Grande 2015; Simpson 2011). From these views, "spirit" is not a static, anthropocentric, or monotheistic category linked to discrete inner workings of souls independent of culture, politics, and geography. Instead, it is *all our relations* that we hold and become a part of. Notwithstanding devastating legacies of colonization across "urban" and "remote" landscapes for many Indigenous nations in Canada and globally, these sacred relationships with the natural world have persevered to provide meaning, resilience, and wellness amidst challenging aspects of contemporary existence (Simpson 2011).

Despite *land* being a fundamental Indigenous determinant of health (Greenwood and Lindsay 2019; Redvers 2018), as well as literature demonstrating how spiritual practices and worldviews can foster pathways to wellness (Clark 2018; Dylan and Smallboy 2016; Kirmayer, et al. 2009; Marquina-Marquez, Alfonso and Ruiz-Callado 2016; Mikraszewicz and Richmond 2019; Wilson 2005), there is limited research illustrating how the sacredness of land is understood and

DOI: 10.4324/9781003043508-7

experienced within urban geographies. This oversight is significant considering that 52% of Indigenous Peoples in Canada reside in cities, with those under 24-years-old comprising approximately half the population (Statistics Canada 2016). Young people are accessing job markets, reclaiming Indigenous lifeways, and identifying cities as "home," even where strong attachments to "remote" communities and ancestral homelands still exist (Environics Institute 2010).

The research presented here explored Indigenous youth spirituality, human-nature relations, and pathways to mental wellness in a central Canadian city through the framework of chronicity while considering the role of *place*, or land, from anti-colonial and critical Indigenous perspectives (Tuck and McKenzie 2015). Following healing journeys of 36 youth growing up and enduring what we refer to as "settler-colonial chronicities," Indigenous young people often negotiate a contemporary sense of themselves as healing across urban landscapes that involves creative exchanges of ancestral, contemporary, and adopted spiritual practices (Hatala et al. 2019). We illustrate that, by embodying practices within their daily lives and securing Indigenous futures in cities, youth understand themselves as "good ancestors" and value their bodies and environments positively in aesthetic and spiritual terms of beauty and acceptance. Mobilizing our findings through the Cree Indigenous concept of *miyo-wîcêhetowin*, meaning "to have or possess good relations" (Cardinal and Hildebrandt 2000), we argue that the uptake of land-based wellness interventions, as important as they are in Canada and elsewhere, should not only engage the sacredness of land in "remote" or "traditional" places and spaces outside of cityscapes, but equally strengthen sacred and good relationships with creation in and through urban geographies.

Chronicity theory, settler-colonization, and thriving as context

Chronicity theory problematizes social or structural inequities unevenly distributing chronic illness, mental disorder, and impairment in society (Manderson and Smith-Morris 2010). Places mired with persistent poverty, war, and environmental devastation, as well as precarity, structural violence, or oppression, manifest not as singular events but relentless and stress-inducing conditions of the body politic, or "crisis *as* context" (Vigh 2008). Limiting agency and wellness, people enduring these contexts struggle against injustices heightened by intersecting health risks and medical conditions (Weaver and Mendenhall 2014). Over time, chronic social conditions fluctuate to shape the functioning and capabilities of people grappling with mortality, morality, meaning, and action as part of daily routines of survival (Vigh 2008). Chronicity theory here moves beyond clinical matters of disease management and health care toward diverse sociocultural manifestations and places of distress and injustice (Heinemann 2015; Read and Geest 2019; Yates-Doerr and Carney 2016).

To date, however, researchers utilizing chronicity theory have not explicitly engaged anti-colonial and Indigenous perspectives of *place* that reframe oppressive histories and geographies of settler-colonization as chronic social conditions and articulating home*land* as central to its transformation. While focused on resource extraction and land settlement, settler-colonization institutes a slave or migrant workforce to guarantee settler futures and instigate Indigenous erasure that slowly manifests as persisting illness and mortality across remote and urban lands (Rifkin 2017; Wilson and Peters 2005). Settler-colonization has devastated land-based economies and lifeways for many Indigenous Peoples in Canada, and propagated systemic racism, intergenerational trauma, and poorer mental health, educational, and socio-economic outcomes (Greenwood et al. 2018; Waldram et al. 2006). Canadian settler-colonization has attempted to sever connections to land while at the same time being transformed through land, spiritual knowing, human-nature kinship, and ancestral ties (Hatala et al. 2019).

As the Truth and Reconciliation Commission (TRC) of Canada observed, Indigenous youth in Canada bear the brunt of intergenerational effects of collective trauma experienced by previous generations (TRC 2012). Indeed, health research indicates direct links between historical and contemporary impacts of settler-colonization, and higher rates of alcohol and substance use, suicide, and mental illness and disorder among Indigenous youth today (Nelson and Wilson 2017; Waldram 2004; Wilson and Cardwell 2012). When compared to non-Indigenous youth, contemporary Indigenous realities are also characterized by higher rates of child welfare involvement, gang violence and violent victimization, and inadequate living conditions due to poverty (De Leeuw, Greenwood and Cameron 2010). Increasingly relocating to urban centers both voluntarily and unwillingly, youth encounter the "front-lines" of social, economic, and political inequities of a settler-colonial urban welfare state; thus, further exacerbating their precarious health and wellness status (DeVerteuil and Wilson 2010).

With trends moving Indigenous health research and practice toward health promotion, social determinants of health, and Indigenous ways-of-healing, health and wellness are understood as holistic, and encompass an important balance among diverse dimensions, including the spiritual (Allen et al. 2020; Kirmayer and Valaskakis 2009). Recently, mental health interventions and cultural revitalization movements addressing inequities understand land as a site and practice that can improve pathways to holistic wellness for youth enduring settler-colonial chronicities of the body politic and significant health risks (Greenwood and Lindsay 2019). Among Indigenous determinants of health and resilience, *access to* and *stewardship over land* are often understood as central, if not the most important, determinant shaping wellness directly (e.g., Lines et al. 2019) and indirectly (e.g., Ladner 2009; Nesdole et al. 2014). Furthermore, as biomedical reductionism and deficit-based thinking are critiqued for deflecting settler-colonization (see Clark 2016; Hatala et al. 2016), *environmental repossession* frameworks become relevant when referring to processes whereby Indigenous Peoples improve wellness pathways by reclaiming ancestral homelands and revitalizing Indigenous lifeways (Big-Canoe and Richmond 2014; Morton et al. 2020). As such, these frameworks shift land and mental health away from a "crisis *as* context" toward a "thriving *as* context."

Histories and geographies of Indigenous youth spirituality

Indigenous communities in Canada have had to contend with religious influences and doctrines of Christianity since the 1600s (Friesen and Heinrichs 2017).

Prior to European contact, many communities maintained cultural practices, rituals, and customs through spiritual ways-of-knowing occurring from the inside out, instead of the outside in (Ermine 1995). Through moral and sentient connections to Mother Earth and spiritual beings, spirituality did not exist as a corpus of knowledge akin to dogmatic biblical scripture, but was situated within corporeal and experiential acts of sacred knowing transmitted across generations through oral traditions, connections with nature, and subsistent ways-of-life (Deloria 2003). Continuing into present-day Canada, distinctions between the "sacred and profane," although diverse among various Indigenous spiritualities, are often less apparent and contribute to all aspects of society unlike the institutional arrangements of Western religion (Collard and Palmer 2015). Counter to dualistic utopian religions of Europe conceiving spirituality as universal, innate, and independent of locality, Indigenous spiritualities generally associate spirit with the particularities of one's homeland and kinship ties to humans, land, and nature (Collard and Palmer 2015).

Although Indigenous Peoples generally upheld values of non-interference considering it inappropriate to impose one's views on another people, an openness and inquisitiveness existed to other ways-of-being and ways-of-seeing, therefore allowing Christianity to travel widely (Miller 2017). This openness expedited the syncretization of belief systems while maintaining sovereignty over communities' spiritual lives and geographic territories (Bradford and Horton 2016). Without successfully replacing Indigenous spiritual values, it was only later that the necessary conditions and attitudes to propel evangelizing missions toward indoctrination became possible. This involved the Confederation of Canada (1867) and Indian Act (1876), which established race-based policies governing those classified as "Indians." These events consolidated Canadian national unity, bolstered constitutional sovereignty, and secured control over First Nations lives and territories to make space for settler resource extraction and settlement (King 2017). Foremost among strategies of expanding control of an emerging settler-colonial state was an assimilationist agenda supporting Indian Residential Schools (IRS). IRS acted as a state-sponsored and church-administered educational, cultural, and spiritual intervention into the everyday lives of Indigenous communities, where attendance was legally and detrimentally enforced for some hundreds of thousands of children (TRC 2012).

Although state laws at the time restricted mobility, fragmented identity, and demonized spiritual expression, an unrelenting perseverance and resistance to intrusive settler-colonial religious domination occurred in various ways; for instance, communities practicing spiritual ceremonies in secrecy (Haig-Brown 1988; Hatala et al. 2016). Despite the revitalization of Indigenous spiritualities across Canada post-1950s based on legislative changes and cultural movements, Indigenous people continue today to confront and challenge settler-colonial rationalities that act on, bound, and legitimize Indigenous spirituality (Friesen and Heinrichs 2017). While coping with effects of settler-colonization and Christianization in present-day Canada, considering what is traditional, sacred, and "good" within specific local contexts such as cityscapes, biographical histories also complicate discourses on who counts as being authentically "Indigenous" *and* "spiritual" and *where* such authenticity manifests and flourishes (Bakht and Collins 2017; Buch 2017; Deerchild 2003).

Although important for addressing contemporary health inequities for Indigenous young people in Canada, research has narrowly conceived Indigenous Peoples' connections to land as being centered on "remote" home communities and ancestral homelands while negating urban landscapes from discussions of land and human-nature connections as being a potential source of healing (Davie 2019). Focusing on geographies of Indigenous youth spirituality, we maintain that despite shifts in research articulating urban landscapes as sources of wellness (e.g., Wilson and Peters 2005), the "where" of contemporary land-based mental wellness interventions must also acknowledge how youth resist and challenge chronicities of settler-colonization and thereby maintain connections with the land, nature, and traditional spirituality within contemporary urban realities, spaces, and places.

Towards spiritual encounters and Miyo-wîcêhetowin in the city

When considering Indigenous youth spirituality, chronicity, land, and mental wellness within cityscapes, Adelson's (2000) reflections on reimagining Indigeneity for the James Bay Cree in Northern Canada becomes particularly relevant. Although juxtaposing descriptions of cultural "Gatherings" on remote land to restore Indigenous lifeways against a colonized urban space or "village" located nearby, Adelson's (2000, 28) insights highlight negotiations of contemporary Indigenous identity based on "melding of concepts and practices" and "conscious fusion of old and new." These hybridized cultural identity transformations offer departures to reimagine, understand, and observe spiritual pathways to mental health and wellness for urban Indigenous youth.

Furthermore, referring to enactments of youth spirituality through sacrilege and encounter, Olson and colleagues (2018) also suggest shifting our analytical repertoire away from spiritual beliefs to more explicit groundings in a *spiritual encounter*. Within settler-colonies, spiritual encounters might express hybrid transformations of spirituality at the intersection of traditional Indigenous cosmology, European religious philosophy, and contemporary spiritual imaginaries (Collard and Palmer 2015). Through a chronicity framework attuned to anti-colonial and Indigenous conceptualizations or practices of place, we therefore interpret Indigenous youth spirituality as a *healing journey* whereby youth become actively entangled in a fusion of "old and new" relations to spirit, time, culture, nature, and land that enhance pathways to mental health, resilience, and wellness within urban contexts.

Following healing journeys in urban lands through youth narratives from two Community-Based Participatory Research (CBPR) projects in Saskatoon, Saskatchewan Canada, two interrelated questions are explored in this chapter, 1) how do urban Indigenous youth encounter spirituality through land and nature within urban contexts? and 2) how are connections to spirit, nature, time, and land contributing to their perceived mental wellness? In addressing these questions, we illustrate how healing journeys are not merely functional processes of reoccupying physical and objectively constructed spaces (e.g., Woodgate and Skarlato 2015), but invite youth to become "good ancestors," that is, to positively view themselves in urban landscapes with moral responsibilities flowing from aesthetic and spiritual values. We also interpret youth narratives through *miyo-wîcêhetowin* to demonstrate how settler-colonial chronicity of the urban politic endures and youth reimagine good relationships not only to thrive-in-place but ensure places themselves thrive over generations. When regarding *miyo-wîcêhetowin* through instruction by the "Old Ones" (or "Elders") we situate it within the overarching principles of *wâkôhtowin*, or Natural Laws, that govern the world and human nature. Relationships and their core values emerge as morally responsible acts of experience that generate power, knowledge, and action. As Settee (2011, 9) notes: "Indigenous Knowledge Systems do not encompass a singular body of knowledge but reflect many layers of being, knowing, and expressing." Although, socio-ecological systems models of wellness and resilience theoretically reflect holistic unity between humans and nature, they often fail to acknowledge and explore the dynamic interactions and agential capacities of non-human spiritual beings (Morton et al. 2020). Therefore, they resort to spatialized explanations that demand human control and ownership over nature through intervention in contrast with spiritual and moral values of non-interference and reciprocity (Tobias 2015). As such, this chapter does not seek to encapsulate a definition of *miyo-wîcêhetowin*, but employs it as an analytical heuristic to surface processes of repatriating good relationships with spirit and nature in urban lands, by seeking out Elders, listening to community, engaging with tradition, teachings, learning about *wâkôhtowin*, and thereby promoting mental wellness, resilience, and prosperity.

Methods and analysis

The research presented here involved 54 interviews with 36 youth that were drawn from two CBPR projects exploring Indigenous youth wellness within a mid-sized Canadian metropolitan city, Saskatoon, Saskatchewan (see Bird-Naytowhow et al. 2017; Hatala and Bird-Naytowhow 2020; Morton et al. 2020). The research projects emerged from several years of conversations, relationship building, and engagement with youth, community organizations, parents, and Elders identifying the need to build on existing community strengths. They were carried out in 2014–15 and 2018–19, involving youth-serving organizations, high schools, and the University of Saskatchewan Community Engagement Centre.

Directed by Elders, the research followed a "Two-Eyed Seeing" approach whereby Indigenous and Western paradigms worked alongside one another (Wright et al. 2019). Applied to our research teams consisting of Indigenous and non-Indigenous researchers, academics, community partners, and youth collaborators, this approach created spaces for open discussions regarding roles and responsibilities of both ways-of-seeing and ways-of-doing, enhancing our overall methods and sensibilities when interpreting spiritual encounters and pathways to mental wellness (Bird-Naytowhow et al. 2017). The projects were approved by the University of Saskatchewan's and University of Manitoba's Behavioural Research Ethics Boards, and local ethical approval and guidance was upheld by youth serving community-based organizations.

Positioning ourselves

Darrien Morton is of Anglo-African descent and originally from Zambia. Living in Winnipeg, Central Canada (Treaty 1 Territory), he works as a health researcher, community helper, and ally alongside Anishinaabe and Cree grassroots youth activists and advocates. His research focuses on topics related to youth participation, social movements, and health services and policy. He not only works in service to the urban Indigenous communities in which he has come to belong, but works from a position that recognizes, confronts, and leverages the "terrible gifts" he must exchange to live on these lands as a soon-to-be Canadian citizen whose citizenship will ultimately be gifted through the scholarly and economic labor of doing research with Indigenous youth as an international student and permanent resident. Darrien primarily draws on critical-interpretive and relational methodological frameworks that center youth voice and posthumanist philosophies from a cross-cultural and localized standpoint with various communities in the prairies.

Kelley Bird-Naytowhow is known in a spiritual or ceremonial context as Black Buffalo Man. He uses Bird-Naytowhow to honor his biological parents who he still yearns to get to know. He was born in Montreal Lake/Sturgeon Lake, Saskatchewan. Kelley is of Cree descent and has learned to keep his mind and heart open to all things while also paying mind to protect what knowledge comes to him. His positionality comes from places and stories that have helped shape his paradigm, the way he perceives the world. Positioning himself in this way speaks to the powerful acts of how principles can be put into practice. Kelley feels that it is only right for him to display his position, for this position comes from the very principles that his community(ies) have taught him. This is also his way to give back in hopes that he has paid attention to and acknowledged his teachers in a good way. Kelley completed his Bachelor of Social Work degree at First Nations University of Canada and has more recently completed his Master's of Social Work. Kelley is passionately committed to working with Indigenous youth and local organizations serving youth in Saskatoon. Kelley also has extensive community-based research experience on diverse projects with Indigenous youth in Canada.

Andrew R. Hatala was born in central Canada with Polish, English, and Finish ancestry. After growing up primarily in Treaty 7 area on Blackfoot lands (outside Calgary Alberta), Andrew is now settled on Treaty 1 Territory (Winnipeg), the lands where First Nation Peoples have been living since time immemorial, and where the Métis have established their Homeland. As part of his work as an Associate Professor at the University of Manitoba, he endeavors to be a good visitor on these lands by doing his part in decolonizing his worldviews and dismantling systemic white supremacy, while building good and respectful relations with Indigenous Peoples. Andrew is forever grateful for the land, the water, and the skies that have taught him so much and shown him the beauty of this place and its people. His community-based participatory research explores Indigenous youth wellness, health, and resilience within urban Canadian contexts and diverse healing practices for mental illness and chronic conditions in both Canadian and Belizean Indigenous contexts.

Methodological considerations

Situated within a social constructionist epistemological perspective, this qualitative research adapted Indigenous Methodologies (IM) (Kovach 2009) alongside a modified Grounded Theory (GT) approach (Charmaz 2006) for data collection (see Table 7.1), interpretation, and analysis. An IM framework infuses decisions concerning choices of methods, how methods are employed, and how data are analyzed through Indigenous ontological and epistemological perspectives prioritizing relationality (Kovach, 2009). They not only consider knowledge in itself, but together with relationships we share during its creation (Wilson 2008).

Table 7.1 Data collection procedures for CBPR Project 2014–15 and CBPR Project 2017–18

Data Collection Procedures	CBPR Project (2014–15)	CBPR Project (2017–18)
Sampling Methods	Combination of purposeful/snowball sampling was used to recruit youth self-identifying as Indigenous through partnering organizations.	Convenience sampling was used to recruit youth self-identifying as Indigenous through partnering organizations.
Sample Population Demographics	28 participants; ages 15–25 years (16 females, 12 males), and self-identifying as Nêhiyaw Plains Cree (n=21) and Métis (n=7)	8 participants; ages 18–24 (6 females, 2 males), and self-identifying as Nêhiyaw Plains Cree ($n = 6$) and Métis ($n = 2$)
Conversational Interviews	Interviews were audio recorded with youth permission and later transcribed. As recommended by our Elders, interviews began by creating safe spaces where Nêhiyaw and Métis cultural lifeways or protocols were followed, including smudging with sacred medicines if desired and offering non-commercial tobacco to youth to respect the sacredness of their stories, experiences, and knowledge. Interviews were conducted with at least two university researchers and/or Indigenous youth research assistants to ensure meaningful conversations, intergenerational mentorship, and diverse perspectives. We allowed time and space for participants to build relationships with researchers outside interview settings.	
Total Interview Transcripts	n=38, including 10 follow-up interviews	n=16, including 8 follow-up interviews

Synthesizing methodological frameworks was achieved by strengthening and honoring relationships among people and landscapes we were working with and on (see discussion on relational validity, Tuck and McKenzie 2015). They included, but were not limited to, collective decision-making processes reflective of urban Indigenous sovereignty; intergenerational mentorship; building cultural, personal, and professional capacities of youth as co-collaborators; ensuring appropriate introductions and preparations were performed with all collaborators to create safety, share sacred stories, and work on one's healing journey; and extending relationships beyond the two projects to involve ongoing research partnerships, ceremonial and community engagement, and sustaining friendships (see Bird-Naytowhow et al. 2017; Hatala and Bird-Naytowhow 2020; Morton et al. 2020).

Data analysis

Utilizing constructivist GT techniques during analysis (Charmaz 2006), the interpretation of interview data allowed for an inductive approach integrating the research team's knowledge as well as inspiration from youth (as co-creators of knowledge). Data summaries, coding, theme generation, and writing memos occurred iteratively as data were collected. Initial themes were coded using Dedoose software Version 8.1 (2018) by the third author and checked for consistency by others. As categories and themes emerged from stories, they were checked with participants and team members (i.e., member checking). The approach generated key concepts and processes discussed by youth participants related to perspectives of land, time, spiritual encounter, and natural environments, and how they engaged wellness pathways.

Results: Mental wellness through healing journeys on the land

Results illustrate *healing journeys* of urban-dwelling Nêhiyaw Plains Cree and Métis youth experiencing settler-colonial chronicities in various ways. Beginning in childhood and described by youth as cyclical and intergenerational (e.g., Indian Residential Schools, Child Welfare Systems), these social chronicities were outlined by youth as "a continuous cycle of this horrible, horrible genocide towards a person's soul, to a person's being." We convey these social challenges and hardships elsewhere as the "normalcy of negativity" propelling youth to renegotiate identity, futures, and health under distressing conditions (Hatala et al. 2017). However, as youth described, such negative "life-cycles" perpetuating settler-colonial chronicities were not permanent and inevitable, but could be "broken" and positively transformed. During their encounters with spirituality, chronicity, and land, three main themes emerged from this analysis involving how youth *perceive, enact,* and *value* their cultural and spiritual identities, futures, and pathways to mental wellness, and how breaking negative life-cycles transform youth wellness through *miyo-wîcêhetowin* in cityscapes, namely 1) locating geographies of spiritual encounter, 2) growing up on the land as a "good ancestor," and 3) valuing the aesthetics and spirituality of body and land.

Locating geographies of spiritual encounter

The geographies of spiritual encounters among urban-dwelling Indigenous youth occurred in everyday places, such as homes, schools, community centers, organizations, workplaces, streets, churches, and other topographic features of landscapes that were an extension of people and cities. Both naturally occurring or human-made, places of spiritual encounter were not a backdrop for social human activity or an abstracted site possessing supernatural beings and valued for their grandiosity, such as a tourist attraction or shrine. Rather, they became intimately tied to corporeal acts and bodily senses (e.g., smell, touch, hearing, taste, dreams, intuition), and emerged through "sacred" places that were returned to, ritualized, held personal and ancestral significance, and constituted being-in-place that made particular understandings about self and the world possible. As one youth explained:

> Even when I realize I'm in an urban setting I try my hardest to find a secret spot where no one will walk [s]o that I can twist up some tobacco [as a sacred medicine] and stuff it there... I'm in Saskatoon. The people who have their reserves, they have their sacred places to go to... But Saskatoon is sacred to me. It's my home. I dream of this place and protecting it. [I]n a powerful sense Saskatoon is in the middle of everything, it is a real strong place.

Spiritual encounters were not necessarily bound to religious institutional arrangements or cultural community membership. Discussing her spirit name signifying a horse that guides her healing journey, a Nêhiyaw Cree youth explained her name as grafted across tribal, community, family, and personal geographies:

> I definitely accepted it [spirit name] and hold it so closely to who I am... It all depends on the Elders and who's giving the name and your teachings and your understandings. My name is in Dakota. But I'm Nêhiyaw, I'm a Cree person. But I didn't grow up learning Cree ways, and there are definitely differences, but similarities too. I feel comfortable with learning Lakota and Dakota. Because that's part of my family, my adopted family that I kind of adopted myself into.

Accordingly, understanding *who I am* and *where I come from* at the intersection of different Indigenous teachings, Christian religious doctrines, and Indigenous spiritual values was also expressed as "confusing" at times. Especially difficult during childhood, processes of "learning from both worlds" occurred in different ways for all youth as they grew up. Over time, a strategy of syncretizing both worlds emerged from shifting relations between family, community, and belief systems ranging from growing up with parents, grandparents, and caregivers raised in a Christian or "traditional" way; carrying an Indigenous language, attending ceremonies, and being connected to (remote) reserves; feelings of not belonging in the church or culture; and meaningfully connecting to other non-fundamentalist sacred ways-of-knowing. As another youth similarly shared:

> My dad never went to church but my mom did, very Catholic... Then my dad's side and my mom's dad's side grew up very spiritual, on the reserve. Of the beliefs I definitely got good sides of both, experiencing them and then having the choice to choose a course. Going to church helped in listening to pastors and then listening to Elders.

In various ways, this kind of syncretization limited yet also assisted youth to reimagine *miyo-wîcêhetowin*. However, spiritual encounters with land and nature were unequivocally evoked when describing "culture" and not "religion" to make *miyo-wîcêhetowin* possible in urban environments. Religion was perceived as imposing doctrines separate from the natural world, whereas culture animated relationships with the Creator and all of creation, including the land. As a source of morality, action, and wellness, *miyo-wîcêhetowin* emerged in the city not from scripted rules but ancestral values transmitted over generations.

Another aspect of spiritual encounters in the city came from connections with ceremony. Although in many Canadian Indigenous contexts ceremony can often involve larger events and gatherings outside of the city occurring over multiple days (e.g., Powwows or Sun Dance Ceremonies), many youth also expressed a "personal" ceremony done (or made) with prayer, smudging, or fasting that can subtly punctuate the day-to-day movements and challenges of life within urban spaces. As one youth explained:

> I think ceremony is more of a personal thing. You can make anything into a ceremony... And there are times that like, "Oh, I can't get to a Powwow" or "Oh, I can't dance today" or "Oh, I don't have smudge [act of burning sacred medicines like sage or sweetgrass]." Just because I don't have access to do certain things, you're automatically like, "Life's so unfair. I'm just going to go back to my old ways now [harmful coping strategies]. How am I going to cope with this?" So, what I've really learned is that you've got to kind of make your own ceremony with whatever you're given in that time. Because you're not always going to have a Powwow to run to [when difficulties emerge]. You're not always going to have what you need available to you... So, for me, it's even just going to sit down somewhere outside to clear my mind that can help me out, like meditate or smudge, and just even that ceremony, just making the best of any situation with a positive mind and a positive heart and you're asking for help [from Creator, spirit world] and you're humbling yourself.

Since larger ceremonies or sacred gatherings may not always be the most appropriate or possible for many Indigenous youth in the city, these subtle forms of *ceremony-making* and creative reimaginations of "where" ceremony and spirituality can occur can be supportive of mental wellness, identity, and relationality. Since young people acknowledge that they're "not always going to have what you need available to you," this agential use of "making the best of any situation" with "whatever you're given in that time" becomes an important spiritual practice and innovative part of one's healing journey involving a fusion of "old and new" within the urban context. In the end, it is a relocating of the spiritual encounter to occur within local urban geographies that becomes a core theme from our interviews with young people.

Growing up on the land as a good ancestor

Without essentializing and romanticizing Indigenous Peoples connections to land as genetic, mythical, or purely performative, we observed them as sources of mental wellness with long-standing ways of being-in-place that denote an "ecocentric self" (Kirmayer et al. 2008). Connecting with land in the city emphasized connections with natural environments including "backyards," "urban parks," "wilderness," "bush," and "Turtle Island" more broadly (North American continent). Land, or "Mother Earth," was conceived as having a female, sentient, and spiritual presence signifying care and interconnectedness. The land emerged through daily routines such as walking, travelling, breathing, eating, menstruating, praying, crying, tree-hugging, storytelling, playing, gift-giving, fasting, and sweating (see Hatala et al. 2019; Hatala et al. 2020).

Accompanying negotiations of place, time, identity, and health, these everyday practices on and connections with the land were often characterized by reciprocity, generosity, spiritual connection, and non-interference to reimagine *miyo-wîcêhe-towin*, which we interpret through the notion of being and becoming a "good ancestor," and not simply being a good person. Rejecting and disrupting the settler-colonial chronicles pervading unhealthy and negative relationships, becoming a "good ancestor" for youth during their healing journeys often meant nurturing good relationships with themselves, their families, and their communities, thus promoting mental wellness. As Justice (2018, 140) poignantly explains on becoming a "good ancestor":

> [I]t's about those who imagined actual futures for us, those who didn't accept the settler colonial "vanishing Indian" as a given... for it's only in the looking backward and forward—and in the imaginings of different possibilities than the one's we've inherited—that a viable future is made possible.

In many instances, the land and nature became a teacher for youth that transmitted personal and cultural teachings. These teachings informed youth how to conduct good relationships with others, as well as inspired them to achieve their aspirations in life. While observing zig-zagging ducks on the city river, a young woman described how ducks teach her about love, gentleness, and slowing down time to reflect, and remind her to be a patient daughter and friend for her mother as she slowly improves her life circumstances, which created much hardship when growing up in the city. As she outlines:

> Ducks remind me of my mom when we were younger and would travel. I remember being in the car and we'd see a duck. She believed that when ducks

fall in love, they stay with that love forever... When I was observing two lovebird ducks I noticed they were swimming zig-zaggy. It reminded me of a teaching because I eventually want to dance jingle [a form of powwow dance and prayer]. When you're dancing jingle you're supposed to dance like zig-zag. Every person, there is ups and downs in life and you're never given a straight road. I was looking at these ducks [while walking by the rivers] and thinking of my mom and her passion... She's had so many obstacles in her life. She's always been in an unhealthy relationship, too. I mean my step-dad's an amazing man but their relationship is not that healthy... I think of ducks and of my relationships and how I never had a healthy relationship either and that is kind of the main reason for my ups and down.

Land and nature, however, were not only teachers but also became caregivers for many youth who experienced loneliness, abandonment, and trauma that had been inherited over generations through deep persistent loss and adversity. Through a recurring dream throughout her life about the river running along her grandmother's reserve and the city, another youth explained how the river has shown her love in ways that her family has not. The river, in many ways, further emboldened her to become a good parent for her children who are currently in foster care, which was exemplary of other youth who had children and wanted to raise them better than their parents did. As she expressed:

I would find my children [near the river]... There is petrified wood along where there is trees and condominiums and there's no bridge. It's like showing all these symbols of whatever my life is facing... It brought me comfort and understanding especially in my spirit or in walking in my dreams and it's always constant... It's distorted, like nature showing me unconditional love that wasn't shown to me through my family or my parents... I have been given recommendations that I must heal, uncover my past feelings, that I must comply to these things [loving people] and understand them for the hope of my children returning home. I put too much displacement on them, anxiety on them, like, I love them. I know that I have to heal for them in order to be a good parent. I must heal from all these traumas.

While land and nature served to teach and care for youth, they also acted as direct sources of wellness as healers. Through spiritual practices of smudging with sacred medicines (such as sage, cedar, sweetgrass) and drumming with hand drums (made of animal hide and wood), many youth engaged in these practices as they were seen as portable and self-sufficient when ceremonies or ceremonial spaces were unavailable to them, especially in urban or secular spaces. Smudging accompanied by prayer sought to cleanse negative spiritual energy originating from a person or place. As one youth shared:

So, for me, it's just like when I can't go anywhere, I have nowhere to turn, or I feel kind of hopeless, for me I just—I have my own drum and I just sit there with my drum and I smudge and just pray and hold my drum and if I need to cry, I cry. I just kind of let myself feel whatever I need to feel in that moment to let it go, and just take deep breaths, and try not to overthink anything, because I know once I'm done the answer will come to me and guide me in what the next step is… So yeah usually when I'm upset or anything, I just smudge. I smudge, and that just makes everything feel better.

Drumming, which is often said to signify the sacred heartbeat of Mother Earth, allowed one to listen to their spirit, use their voice, connect with others through joy or comfort, and pass on oral traditions. For one young man in this research, these practices of smudging and drumming did not simply serve to heal himself given hardships he had faced in life, but allowed him to help "heal the community" and "give back." Recognizing higher rates of crime near a community park that once was considered part of an "Old Indian Village" in Saskatoon, he hosted a recurring event to share drum songs, food, and smudge the city park area to bring about healing:

We started singing at the [park]. And we didn't realize what the group was bringing to [the park]. We didn't realize it at first. We're just jamming, whatever, and where else to jam. We started noticing that the crowds were getting bigger. More and more people started to come. I always remember this one lady she told us boys… she came to the top of that hill [at the park]. She gave us a cigarette [a form of sacred tobacco offering] while her granddaughter said, "You know, my grandmother wants to tell you something." They gave us a tobacco and she said, "Do you guys know what they call this hill?" We're like, "No." She's like, "They call this Gangster Hill… because there's so much fighting, there's so much drinking, there's so much bullying, and just negative stuff happen on this hill at night-time and during the daytime. I'm scared to come out here with my grandkids." She said, "I'm scared someone is going to come hurt us or rob us or something like that." She said, "But what you boys are doing—you guys are balancing out that feeling. It's not just bad people who are making poor choices… So, you guys are going to change this neighborhood," she said.

The varied ways youth grew up on urban lands whereby land became a source of wellness (a teacher, a caregiver, and a healer) broke, in several ways, the chronic, negative life-cycles interfering with their ability to live a good life and have good relationships. Merely being a good person and having hopes, wishes, and aspirations (something to look forward to in the near future, which many youth discussed and considered important) was not always enough to compensate for deep and persistent biographical and historical losses and trauma in their lives. Common across the young people's healing journeys, therefore, were wellness identity transformations whereby youth assumed personal, cultural, and spiritual responsibilities on becoming "good ancestors" while ceremony-making. Yet, overcoming this loss and trauma while remaining resilient was no easy feat. Becoming "good ancestors" to oneself and others followed with deeper commitments to and negotiations of *miyo-wîcêhetowin* with past, present, and future generations within their families, communities, and nations. They served to creatively imagine alternative possibilities than the ones they and their families experienced while growing up. These identity transformations on being and becoming a "good ancestor" that emerged from connections with land and nature not only allowed youth to thrive-in-place, but came along with moral responsibilities for youth to act on "urban" places in positive and transformative ways.

Valuing the aesthetics and spirituality of body and land

For many youth, connecting with the land in urban contexts also provided joy, inspiration, companionship, belonging, purpose, healing, and self-preserving; it was life-giving. Providing more than psychological or economic *benefits* that were instrumental and utilitarian (e.g., leisure, pleasure, sustenance, sightseeing), becoming a "good ancestor" meant deriving personal, cultural, and moral value upholding *responsibilities* that acknowledge and positively sustain identity transformations in relation to the Creator and all of creation. From subjectively and positively valuing one's body and environment in aesthetic (i.e., beauty) and spiritual (i.e., acceptance) terms, responsibilities to be a "good ancestor" and pathways to wellness, or *miyo-wîcêhetowin*, also emerged.

The aesthetic qualities of bodies and nature within urban landscapes were subjectively described as "powerful," "incredible," "elegant," "strong," "resilient," "still," and "beautiful." They did not only suggest youth learn from the land and nature, but that bodies "look like" and "act like" the land and nature. For one youth who stopped attending ceremonies and dancing Powwow for "a long time because [she] wasn't comfortable in [her] own skin," she found beauty and cultural pride in looking and dancing like a goose when describing her Powwow regalia. As she expressed:

> I wanted black fringe to go on my headband so that my eyes are covered... and only my nose and my mouth are showing. Then I wanted to paint all this black, but you're not supposed to because that means you're hiding from God, from something bad, so you shouldn't. Some guys do it. That's their own choice and they have a different spiritual meaning. Everyone's given [regalia] for different reasons. And yeah. I'm going to look like a goose. I'm going to dance like a goose. And people will be like, "Look at that girl, she's a goose (laughter)."

Although beautiful things often provide function (Cooper et al. 2016), invocations of beauty alone did not necessarily incite embodied moral responsibility, which limits value to matters of aesthetic appreciation and environmental awareness. Rather, an "ugliness" or "nastiness" moved youth to act positively on what appeared "bad" and "wrong" while assuming responsibility over their bodies, communities, and homelands, which encompassed cities. When marked on the body, ugliness related to those negative life-cycles, including the "pain," "suffering," "addiction," "depression," "boredom," "abandonment," "wasted time," "shame," "trauma," and morally irresponsible actions of the past: "I'd still be this ugly guy." Alternatively, when marked on the land or nature, ugliness related to things such as polluted waterways, unsafe parks, traffic-generated noise, and grief during winter months due to family loss and loneliness. Many of the youth understood these negative social and natural environments as sites of transformation and reasons to give back to their communities and homelands.

While Indigenous cultures and Christian doctrines both disrupted negative life-cycles and promoted mental wellness, ugliness characterized Christianity for many youth (and to an extent Indigenous cultural practices when commodified, as one youth explained when referring to the competitive and monetary aspects of some cultural activities and ceremonies). It was not that European religious philosophies were inherently "evil" or "incompatible" with Indigenous cultures, but, instead, harsh judgements accompanying everyday fundamentalist expressions of Christianity and failures of adherents to accept difference and live in harmony: "I trusted the Aboriginal perspective of healing because we shouldn't judge anyone when we go into ceremony." As another youth explained about Christianity:

> It was too judgey. This is the way, or else no way, or else you burn in hell. I think what really affected me was how my grandma told me that. Not all the time, but she told me three times in my life that really stuck with me and hurt. I don't ever want to hear people say that to anybody because religion is not about that. It's about connecting spiritually with God and all of creation.

Accordingly, *acceptance* was deemed beautiful, positive to one's existence, and morally righteous. Acceptance was not sacrilegious, a defiant act against religion or culture. It is historically and culturally rooted in aesthetic, moral, spiritual, affective, and personal commitments on what it means to become a "good ancestor." Traversing urban landscapes through good relationships with and responsibilities to the natural world and natural law, or *miyo-wîcêhetowin*, younger generations reimagined alternative possibilities to settler-colonial chronicles of the urban politic and negative life-cycles experienced in the city. In Saskatoon, a growing resurgence of land-based and culture-based initiatives have sought to sustain such pathways (e.g., Powwows, drumming, Round Dances, Sweat Lodges, gardening, etc.). Nevertheless, land-based interventions Indigenizing urban landscapes should progress with caution. They may not bring significant transformations in the absence of strong and trusting Indigenous-settler relationships, respecting Indigenous Peoples rights to self-determination, and ensuring shared responsibilities to care for the natural world and laws governing it (Hatala et al. 2019; Peach et al. 2020).

Discussion

Scholarship locating the "where" of contemporary Indigenous mental wellness interventions has largely failed to examine youth spiritual encounters with land across urban geographies mired by the chronicities of settler-colonialism. This conceptual oversight is predicated on assumptions that the sacredness of land exists "out there" and "on the land," and does not occur "here" in the city (Hatala et al. 2019). Such assumptions do not reflect contemporary healing journeys that interrupt cycles of negativity and repatriate land-based spiritual practices within urban geographies and places where Indigenous youth live. This research highlights a few aspects of transformative processes that promote pathways to youth wellness and Indigenous futures in the city. Our considerations for Indigenous mental health and wellness interventions in Canada not only challenge geographies that bound Indigenous young people's spirituality and wellness to "remote" and "traditional" places, but also consider the anthropocentric divisions that separate culture from nature in settler societies and urban places.

Tuck and McKenzie (2015) have engaged conceptualizations or practices of "place" enduring settler-colonization through "critical place inquiry" (CPI). While taking "place" to be synonymous with "land" and "first teacher," CPI envisions an intellectual project transgressing place as an objective backdrop for human activity that is bounded or trivialized, notwithstanding globalizing and secularizing identities (Tuck and McKenzie 2015). Rather, it is a "land-we" ontology that is incommensurable with (Western) notions of place (Tuck and McKenzie 2015, 38). Departing from allied theories of place long used in service of Indigenous struggles by researchers and activists, Western notions of place remove Indigenous identities and bodies from the land (Tuck and McKenzie 2015). The removal of "mind from body, body from land" locates nature as separate from the study and social activity of humans, or questions epistemology to the exclusion of ontology, thus accentuating discursive constructions of place in the spiritual and corporeal absence of materials, species, and bodies native to place and holding it together (Tuck and McKenzie 2015). When foregrounding land as cosmologically complex sets of relations among and between humans and nature, these relations interrupt settler presence and domination, and repatriate Indigenous imaginaries and possibilities in "remote" and "urban" lands (Bang et al. 2014; Hunt 2014; Nxumalo and Cedillo 2017; Watts 2013). Theses insights center urban land and places as sites from which people, nature, other kinds of life, and ancestral ties together produce and transform wellness identities amidst colonial chronicities.

With mental health literature having admirably documented the effects of temporality through cultural psychology and a developmental lens (e.g., Chandler and Lalonde 2008), which infer self-continuity and cultural continuity as forms of future-seeking and self-persistence (Hatala et al. 2017), the ways youth embodied wellness through their healing journeys conceive of land, wellness, and spirituality in subjective, non-linear, and locally situated ways. Based on urban Indigenous youth narratives, "thriving-in-place" and ensuring places themselves thrived, as in the protection of local parks via cultural practices and expressions, occurred through spiritual encounters with nature, becoming a "good ancestor," and submitting to moral responsibilities to the natural and spiritual world through beauty and acceptance. Connection here was not about re-inhabitation of land or prescribing to dogmatic scripture, but repatriating *miyo-wîcêhetowin* by learning from and relating with the land and nature to reimagine it and alternative pathways to wellness, even in contested "urban" land that is at once debilitating and life-giving (Bang et al. 2014).

Nevertheless, when operationalizing land through health and mental health interventions, and by extension cultural revitalization movements, questions remain about the colonization of spaces offering access to land and nature by neoliberal and settler-colonial logics (Longhurst 2006). The depoliticization and instrumentalization of civilizing discourses have typically constructed greenspace as ordered, domesticated, and separate from or replaceable of natural ecosystems, in turn, producing exclusive kinds of citizenship and inclusion, especially in urban settler-colonial contexts (Bang et al. 2014; Longhurst 2006). Such questions are apparent when considering public and community health transformations that have linked nature to urban health (Sandifer, Sutton-Grier and Ward 2015), and witnessed the proliferation of greenspace and outdoor excursions through the simulated and limited experience of "programs" (Panelli and Tipa 2009; Riley 2020).

These important conceptual moves to critically uncover Indigenous-settler power relations, however, can oversimplify place-making and future-seeking that redirects healing in important ways (Mattingly et al. 2011). Based on healing journeys of urban Indigenous youth we engaged, spirituality became tied to personal, communal, ancestral, and human-nature relations within urban lands that are considered as both homeland and "hostile-land." As a place-based turn in studying religion and spirituality pursues spiritual encounters, mental wellness, and identity through spatialized mobilities ranging from pilgrimages to virtual reality (e.g., Scriven 2014; Wigley 2018), bounding the sacredness of land to an abstracted greenspace, such as a park or garden, would be irresponsible to and inappropriate for fully exploring such reimaginations and re-directions. For researchers, framing settler-colonial chronicity through histories and geographies of Indigenous youth spirituality, however, must ensure the event of place not only centers and focuses metaphorical abstractions of land, but engages with ontology and human-nature differences from a culturally grounded positioning that reveals localized and subjective ways of knowing-as-being (Morton et al. 2020).

Conclusion

The countless examples of refusal or denunciation of settler-colonial chronicity rendering geographies of Indigenous youth spirituality vulnerable to control and commodification are profound among Indigenous youth as they have reimagined Indigenous futures and sovereignties in Canadian cities by reclaiming traditional cultural lifeways from the past and re-fashioning adopted and new possibilities for the future (Simpson 2017). When describing a series of street Pipe Ceremonies led by two Anishinabek youth and other helpers over the summer of 2015 in Winnipeg, Canada, an Ininew (Cree) community organizer explained:

> Doing ceremony doesn't always entail leaving an urban center and going to an isolated community to visit ceremonial grounds. Sometimes it means

making the land that is before us sacred… The streets are land too. For us who are displaced from our home communities, the inner-city is our land, that's our First Nation, that's our home community… This is a timely and needed conversation, not only for non-Indigenous people to understand, but also for First Nations, Métis, and Inuit people that are now urban dwellers. They are now the roses growing through the concrete.

(Wirch et al. 2017)

Based on the healing journeys explored here of Indigenous youth living in a mid-sized Canadian city, these acts of refusal are made visible through the liveliness of human-nature relations, spiritual encounter, and wellness identity transformations that see youth enact *miyo-wîcêhetowin* as they grow up and thrive on urban land as "good ancestors." Reimagining the histories and geographies of previous generations and re-envisioning better possibilities for future generations of their children, families, communities, and nations. In so doing, being and becoming a "good ancestor" not only allows for youth to thrive-in-place but ensure contexts and places themselves confront and outgrow settler-colonialism to thrive. These acts of refusal and reimaginings of better futures did not emerge as pious or humanitarian duties of good, youthful democratic or religious citizens living in urban spaces, but were passed on over generations to fulfil moral and ancestral responsibilities to the natural and spiritual world. As such, when approaching youth mental wellness through programmatic land-based interventions that can be constrained by institutional logics, researchers and health practitioners should consider how such interventions may unintentionally reproduce settler-colonial relations while acknowledging how youth can resist, redirect, and transform their commodification and capacities to act as technologies of social control.

Note

1 The term "Indigenous" refers collectively to the heterogeneous groups of status/non-status First Nations, Inuit, and Métis Peoples in Canada, unless specific nation-based identities are referred to (e.g., Nêhiyaw Plains Cree). The term "Indian" is enrolled when referring to historical or legal definitions to describe status First Nations (more recently the term includes non-status First Nations and Métis).

References

Adelson, Naomi. 2000. "Re-Imagining Aboriginality: An Indigenous Peoples' Response to Social Suffering." *Transcultural Psychiatry* 37 (1): 11–34. doi:10.1177/136346150003700101

Allen, Lindsay, Andrew R. Hatala, Sabina Ijaz, Dave Courchene, Burma Bushie. 2020. "Indigenous-led Health Care Partnerships in Canada." *Canadian Medical Association Journal* 192 (9): E208-E216. doi:10.1503/cmaj.190728

Bakht, Natasha, and Lynda Collins. 2017. "'The Earth is Our Mother': Freedom of Religion and the Preservation of Indigenous Sacred Sites in Canada." *McGill Law Journal/Revue de droit de McGill* 62 (3): 777–812. doi:10.7202/1042774ar

Bang, Megan *et al*. 2014. "Muskrat Theories, Tobacco in the Streets, and Living Chicago as Indigenous Land." *Environmental Education Research* 20 (1): 37–55. doi:10.1080/13504622.2013.865113

Big-Canoe, Katie, and Chantelle A.M. Richmond. 2014. "Anishinabe Youth Perceptions about Community Health: Toward Environmental Repossession." *Health and Place* 26127–135. doi:10.1016/j.healthplace.2013.12.013

Bird-Naytowhow, Kelley, Andrew R. Hatala, Tamara Pearl, Andrew Judge, and Erynne Sjoblom. 2017. "Ceremonies of Relationship: Engaging Urban Indigenous Youth in Community-Based Research." *International Journal of Qualitative Methods* 16 (1): 1–14. doi:10.1177/1609406917707899

Bradford, Tolly, and Chelsea Horton. 2016. *Mixed Blessings: Indigenous Encounters with Christianity in Canada*. Vancouver: University of British Columbia Press. doi:10.1353/gpq.2018.0020

Buch, Barbara. 2017. "Canada/North America: Shame Between Indigenous Nature-Connectedness, Colonialism and Cultural Disconnection." In *The Value of Shame: Exploring a Health Resource in Cultural Contexts*, edited by E. Vanderheiden and C.H. Mayer, 157–184. Cham: Springer International Publishing. doi:10.1007/978-3-319-53100-7_7

Cardinal, Harold, and Walter Hildebrandt. 2000. *Treaty Elders of Saskatchewan: Our Dream is That Our Peoples Will One Day be Clearly Recognized as Nations*. Calgary: University of Calgary Press. doi:10.2307/j.ctv6gqwq3

Chandler, Michael J., and Chris E. Lalonde. 2008. "Cultural Continuity as a Moderator of Suicide Risk Among Canada's First Nations." In *Healing Traditions: The Mental Health of Aboriginal Peoples in Canada*, edited by L.J. Kirmayer and G.G. Valaskakis, 221–248. Vancouver: University of British Columbia Press.

Charmaz, Kathy. 2006. *Constructing Grounded Theory: A Practical Guide Through Qualitative Analysis*. London: Sage Publications. doi:10.7748/nr.13.4.84.s4

Clark, Natalie. 2016. "Shock and Awe: Trauma as the New Colonial Frontier." *Humanities* 5 (14):1–16. doi:10.3390/h5010014

Clark, Natalie. 2018. "Cu7 me7 q'wele'wu-kt. Come on, let's go berry-picking." *Revival of Secwepemc Wellness Approaches for Healing Child and Youth Experiences of Violence*. PhD dissertation. Vancouver: Simon Fraser University. https://summit.sfu.ca/item/18083

Collard, Len, and Dave Palmer. 2015. "Koorlankga Wer Wiern: Indigenous Young People and Spirituality." In *Handbook of Children and Youth Studies*, 875–888. Singapore: Springer. doi:10.1007/978-981-4451-15-4_41

Cooper, Nigel *et al*. 2016. "Aesthetic and Spiritual Values of Ecosystems: Recognising the Ontological and Axiological Plurality of Cultural Ecosystem 'Services'." *Ecosystem Services* 21: 218–229. doi:10.1016/j.ecoser.2016.07.014

Davie, Jenna. 2019. *An Exploration of Connections with the Land in an Urban Sport Context among Indigenous Youth, Faculty of Kinesiology, Sport, and Recreation*. PhD dissertation. Edmonton: University of Alberta. doi:10.7939/r3-1y64-5j64

De Leeuw, Sarah, Margo Greenwood, and Emilie Cameron. 2010. "Deviant Constructions: How Governments Preserve Colonial Narratives of Addictions and Poor Mental Health to Intervene into the Lives of Indigenous Children and Families in Canada." *International Journal of Mental Health and Addiction* 8 (2): 282–295. doi:10.1007/s11469-009-9225-1

Deerchild, Rosanna. 2003. "Tribal Feminism is a Drum Song." In *Strong Women Stories: Native Vision and Community Survival*, edited by Kim Anderson and Bonita. Lawrence, 97–105. Toronto: Sumach Press.

Deloria, Vine. 2003. *God is Red: A Native View of Religion*. Golden: Fulcrum Publishing. doi:10.2307/1185399

DeVerteuil, Geoffrey, and Kathi Wilson. 2010. "Reconciling Indigenous Need with the Urban Welfare State? Evidence of Culturally-Appropriate Services and Spaces for Aboriginals in Winnipeg, Canada." *Geoforum* 41 (3): 498–507. doi:10.1016/j.geoforum.2010.01.004

Dylan, Arielle, and Bartholemew Smallboy. 2016. "Land-Based Spirituality among the Cree of the Mushkegowuk Territory." *Journal of Religion and Spirituality in Social Work: Social Thought* 35 (1–2):108–119. doi:10.1080/15426432.2015.1067589

Environics Institute. 2010. *Urban Aboriginal Peoples Study – Main Report*. Environics Institute.

Ermine, Willie. 1995. "Aboriginal Epistemology." In *First Nations Education in Canada: The Circle Unfolds*, edited by M. Battiste and J. Barman, 101–112. Nanaimo: University of British Colombia Press. doi:10.20361/g22g7r

Friesen, Jeff, and Steve Heinrichs. 2017. *Quest for Respect: The Church and Indigenous Spirituality*. Altona: Mennonite Church of Canada.

Grande, Sandy. 2015. *Red Pedagogy: Native American Social and Political Thought*. Maryland: Rowman and Littlefield.

Greenwood, Margo, Sarah De Leeuw and Nicole Marie Lindsay. 2018. *Determinants of Indigenous Peoples' Health*. Toronto: Canadian Scholars' Press. doi:10.5663/aps.v6i1.27374

Greenwood, Margo, and Nicole Marie Lindsay. 2019. "A Commentary on Land, Health, and Indigenous Knowledge(s)." *Global Health Promotion* 26 (3): 82–86. doi:10.1177/1757975919831262

Haig-Brown, Celia. 1988. *Resistance and Renewal: Surviving the Indian Residential School*. Vancouver: Arsenal Pulp Press.

Hatala, Andrew R., and Kelley Bird-Naytowhow. 2020. "Performing Pimâtisiwin: The Expression of Indigenous Wellness Identities through Community-Based Theater." *Medical Anthropology Quarterly* 34 (2): 243–267. doi:10.1111/maq.12575

Hatala, Andrew R., Michel Desjardins, and Amy Bombay. 2016. "Reframing Narratives of Aboriginal Health Inequity: Exploring Cree Elder Resilience and Well-Being in Contexts of Historical Trauma." *Qualitative Health Research* 26 (14): 1911–1927. doi:10.1177/1049732315609569

Hatala, Andrew R.*et al*.2017. "'I Have Strong Hopes for the Future': Time Orientations and Resilience Among Canadian Indigenous Youth." *Qualitative Health Research* 27 (9): 1330–1344. doi:10.1177/1049732317712489

Hatala, Andrew R.*et al*.2019. "Re-Imagining Miyo-Wicehtowin: Human-Nature Relations, Land-making, and Wellness among Indigenous Youth in a Canadian Urban Context." *Social Science and Medicine* 230: 122–130. doi:10.1016/j.socscimed.2019.04.012

Hatala, Andrew R., Chinyere Njeze, Darrien Morton, Tamara Pearl, and Kelley Bird-Naytowhow. 2020. "Land and Nature as Sources of Health and Resilience among Indigenous Youth in an Urban Canadian Context: A Photovoice Exploration." *BMC Public Health* 20 (538): 1–14. doi:10.1186/s12889-020-08647-z

Heinemann, Laura L. 2015. "Accommodating Care: Transplant Caregiving and the Melding of Health Care with Home Life in the United States." *Medicine Anthropology Theory* 2 (1): 32–56. doi:10.17157/mat.2.1.211

Hunt, Sarah. 2014. "Ontologies of Indigeneity: The Politics of Embodying a Concept." *Cultural Geographies* 21 (1): 27–32. doi:10.1177/1474474013500226

Johnson, Jon. 2013. "The Great Indian Bus Tour: Mapping Toronto's Urban First Nations Oral Tradition." In *The Nature of Empires and the Empires of Nature:*

Indigenous Peoples and the Great Lakes Environment, edited by K.S. Hele, 279–298. Waterloo: Wilfred Laurier University Press.

Justice, Daniel Heath. 2018. *Why Indigenous Literatures Matter*. Waterloo: Wilfred Laurier University Press. doi:10.1111/cag.12598

King, Thomas. 2017. *The Inconvenient Indian Illustrated: A Curious Account of Native People in North America*. New York: Penguin Random House.

Kirmayer, Laurence J., Christopher Fletcher, and Robert Watt. 2008. "Locating the Ecocentric Self: Inuit Concepts of Mental Health and Illness." In *Healing Traditions: The Mental Health of Aboriginal Peoples in Canada*, edited by L.J. Kirmayer and G. G. Valaskakis, 289–314. Vancouver: University of British Columbia Press.

Kirmayer, Laurence J.*et al*.2009. "Community Resilience: Models, Metaphors and Measures." *Journal of Aboriginal Health* 5 (1): 62–117. doi:10.3138/ijih.v5i1.28978

Kirmayer, Laurence J., and Gail Guthrie Valaskakis. 2009. *Healing Traditions: The Mental Health of Aboriginal Peoples in Canada*. Vancouver: University of British Colombia Press. doi:10.1177/070674370004500702

Kovach, Margaret. 2009. *Indigenous methodologies: Characteristics, conversations, and Contexts*. Toronto: University of Toronto Press. doi:10.1111/j.1541-0064.2012.00420.x

Ladner, Keira. 2009. "Understanding the Impact of Self-Determination on Communities in Crisis." *International Journal of Indigenous Health* 5 (2): 88–101. doi:10.3138/ijih.v5i2.28984

Lines, Laurie-Ann, Yellowknives Dene First Nation Wellness Division, and Cynthia G. Jardine. 2019. "Connection to the Land as a Youth-Identified Social Determinant of Indigenous Peoples' Health." *BMC Public Health* 19 (176): 1–13. doi:10.1186/s12889-018-6383-8

Longhurst, Robyn. 2006. "Plots, Plants and Paradoxes: Contemporary Domestic Gardens in Aotearoa/New Zealand." *Social and Cultural Geography* 7 (4): 581–593. doi:10.1080/14649360600825729..

Manderson, Lenore, and Carolyn Smith-Morris. 2010. *Chronic Conditions, Fluid States: Chronicity and the Anthropology of Illness*. New Jersey: Rutgers University Press. doi:10.36019/9780813549736

Marquina-Marquez, Jorge VirchezAlfonso, and Raul Ruiz-Callado. 2016. "Postcolonial Healing Landscapes and Mental Health in a Remote Indigenous Community in Subarctic Ontario, Canada." *Polar Geography* 39 (1): 20–39. doi:10.1080/1088937x.2016.1155673

Mattingly, Cheryl, Lone Grøn, and Lotte Meinert. 2011. "Chronic Homework in Emerging Borderlands of Healthcare." *Culture, Medicine, and Psychiatry* 35 (3): 347–375. doi:10.1007/s11013-011-9225-z

Mikraszewicz, Kathleen, and Chantelle Richmond. 2019. "Paddling the Biigtig: Mino Biimadisiwin Practiced Through Canoeing." *Social Science and Medicine*240: 112548. doi:10.1016/j.socscimed.2019.112548

Miller, J.R. 2017. "A Mixed Record: Indigenous-Christian Encounters in Canada." In *Quest for Respect: The Church and Indigenous Spirituality*, edited by Jeff Friesen and Steve Heinrichs. Altona: Mennonite Church of Canada.

Morton, Darrien*et al*.2020. "'Just Because They Aren't Human Doesn't Mean They Aren't Alive': The Methodological Potential of Photovoice to Examine Human-Nature Relations as a Source of Resilience and Health Among Urban Indigenous Youth." *Health and Place* 61: 102268. doi:10.1016/j.healthplace.2019.102268

Nelson, Sarah E., and Kathi Wilson. 2017. "The Mental Health of Indigenous Peoples in Canada: A Critical Review of Research." *Social Science and Medicine* 176: 93–112. doi:10.1016/j.socscimed.2017.01.021

Nesdole, Robert *et al.*2014. "Reconceptualizing Determinants of Health: Barriers to Improving the Health Status of First Nations Peoples." *Canadian Journal of Public Health* 105 (3): 209–213. doi:10.17269/cjph.105.4308

Nxumalo, Fikile, and Stacia Cedillo. 2017. "Decolonizing Place in Early Childhood Studies: Thinking with Indigenous Onto-Epistemologies and Black Feminist Geographies." *Global Studies of Childhood* 7 (2): 99–112. doi:10.1177/2043610617703831

Olson, Elizabeth, Peter Hopkins, and Giselle Vincett. 2018. "Rethinking Youth Spirituality Through Sacrilege and Encounter." In *Spaces of Spirituality*, edited by N. Bartolini, S. MacKian and S. Pile, 1–20. New York: Routledge. doi:10.4324/9781315398426-12

Panelli, Ruth, and Gail Tipa. 2009. "Beyond Foodscapes: Considering Geographies of Indigenous Well-being." *Health and Place* 15 (2): 455–465. doi:10.1016/j.healthplace.2008.08.005

Peach, Laura, Chantelle A.M. Richmond, and Candace Brunette-Debassige. 2020. "'You Can't Just Take a Piece of Land from the University and Build a Garden on it': Exploring Indigenizing Space and Place in a Settler Canadian University Context." *Geoforum* 114 (3): 117–127. doi:10.1016/j.geoforum.2020.06.001

Read, Ursula M., and Sjaak van der Geest. 2019. "Introduction to Special Issue on Intimacy, Morality, and Precarity: Globalization and Family Care in Africa - Insights from Ghana." *Africa Today* 65 (3): vii–xxi. doi:10.2979/africatoday.65.3.01

Redvers, Nicole. 2018. "The Value of Global Indigenous Knowledge in Planetary Health." *Challenges* 9 (2): 30. doi:10.3390/challe9020030

Rifkin, Mark. 2017. *Beyond Settler Time: Temporal Sovereignty and Indigenous Self-Determination*. Durham: Duke University Press. doi:10.1515/9780822373421

Riley, Kathryn. 2020. "Posthumanist and Postcolonial Possibilities for Outdoor Experiential Education." *Journal of Experiential Education* 43 (1): 88–101. doi:10.1177/1053825919881784

Sandifer, Paul A., Ariana E. Sutton-Grier, and Bethney P. Ward. 2015. "Exploring Connections Among Nature, Biodiversity, Ecosystem Services, and Human Health and Well-being: Opportunities to Enhance Health and Biodiversity Conservation." *Ecosystem Services* 12: 1–15. doi:10.1016/j.ecoser.2014.12.007

Scriven, Richard. 2014. "Geographies of Pilgrimage: Meaningful Movements and Embodied Mobilities." *Geography Compass* 8 (4): 249–261. doi:10.1111/gec3.12124

Settee, Priscilla. 2011. "Indigenous Knowledge: Multiple Approaches." In *Indigenous Philosophies and Critical Education: A Reader*, edited by G.J.S. Dei, 434–450. Bern: Peter Lang Publishing. doi:10.3726/978-1-4539-0131-1/37

Simpson, Leanne. 2011. *Dancing on Oour Turtle's Back: Stories of Nishnaabeg Recreation, Resurgence and a New Emergence*. Winnipeg: Arbeiter Ring Publishing.

Simpson, Leanne Betasamosake. 2017. *As We Have Always Done: Indigenous Freedom Through Radical Resistance*. Minneapolis: Universty of Minnesota Press. doi:10.5749/j.ctt1pwt77c

Statistics Canada. 2016. *Aboriginal Peoples in Canada: Key Results from the 2016 Census*. Ottawa: Statistics Canada.

Tobias, Joshua K. 2015. "'We are the Land': Researching Environmental Repossession with Anishinaabe Elders." PhD dissertation. Electronic Thesis and Dissertation Repository. 2784. London, ON: University of Western Ontario. https://ir.lib.uwo.ca/etd/2784

Truth and Reconciliation Commission of Canada. 2012. *They Came for the Children: Canada, Aboriginal Peoples, and Residential Schools*. Winnipeg: Truth and Reconciliation Commission of Canada.

Tuck, Eve, and Marcia McKenzie. 2015. *Place in Research: Theory, Methodology, and Methods*. New York: Routledge.

Vigh, Henrik. 2008. "Crisis and Chronicity: Anthropological Perspectives on Continuous Conflict and Decline." *Ethnos* 73 (1): 5–24. doi:10.1080/00141840801927509

Waldram, James B. 2004. *Revenge of the Windigo: The Construction of the Mind and Mental Health of North American Aboriginal Peoples*. Toronto: University of Toronto Press. doi:10.3138/9781442683815

Waldram, James Burgess, Ann Herring, and T. Kue Young. 2006. *Aboriginal Health in Canada:Historical, Cultural, and Epidemiological Perspectives*. Toronto: University of Toronto Press.

Watts, Vanessa. 2013. "Indigenous Place-Thought and Agency Amongst Humans and Non Humans (First Woman and Sky Woman go on a European world tour!)." *Decolonization: Indigeneity, Education and Society* 2 (1): 20–34.

Weaver, Lesley Jo, and Emily Mendenhall. 2014. "Applying Syndemics and Chronicity: Interpretations from Studies of Poverty, Depression, and Diabetes." *Medical Anthropology Quarterly* 33 (2): 92–108. doi:10.1080/01459740.2013.808637

Wigley, Edward. 2018. "Everyday Mobilities and the Construction of Subjective Spiritual Geographies in 'Non-places'." *Mobilities* 13 (3): 411–425. doi:10.1080/17450101.2017.1342972

Wilson, Kathi. 2005. "Ecofeminism and First Nations Peoples in Canada: Linking Culture, Gender and Nature." *Gender, Place and Culture* 12 (3): 333–355. doi:10.1080/09663690500202574

Wilson, Kathi, and Nicolette Cardwell. 2012. "Urban Aboriginal Health: Examining Inequalities Between Aboriginal and Non-Aboriginal Populations in Canada." *The Canadian Geographer* 56 (1): 98–116. doi:10.1111/j.1541-0064.2011.00397.x

Wilson, Kathi, and Evelyn J.Peters. 2005. "'You Can Make a Place for It': Remapping Urban First Nations Spaces of Identity." *Environment and Planning D: Society and Space* 23 (3): 395–413. doi:10.1068/d390

Wilson, Shawn. 2008. *Research is Ceremony: Indigenous Research Methods*. Black Point: Fernwood.

Wirch, Jenna, Michael Redhead Champagne, and Steve Heinrichs. 2017. "Street Ceremony and Activism: A North End Conversation." In *Quest for Respect: The Church and Indigenous Spirituality*, edited by J. Friesen and S. Heinrichs, 95–97. Altona: Mennonite Church of Canada.

Woodgate, Roberta L., and Olga Skarlato. 2015. "'It is About Being Outside': Canadian Youth's Perspectives of Good Health and the Environment." *Health and Place* 31: 100–110. doi:10.1016/j.healthplace.2014.11.008

Wright, A.L., C. Gabel, M. Ballantyne, S.M. Jack, and O. Wahoush. 2019. "Using Two-Eyed Seeing in Research with Indigenous People: An Integrative Review." *International Journal of Qualitative Methods* 18: 1–19. doi:10.1177/1609406919869695

Yates-Doerr, Emily, and Megan A. Carney. 2016. "Demedicalizing Health: The Kitchen as a Site of Care." *Medical Anthropology Quarterly* 35 (4): 305–321. doi:10.1080/01459740.2015.1030402

8 Psychosis, spiritual crisis, and narrative transformation

An ethnography of spiritual peer-support networks in the United Kingdom

Raphaëlle Remy-Fischler

Introduction

Psychiatry, or biomedicine more generally, and religion have a strongly intertwined relationship in European history. Biomedical authority can be seen to have replaced religious authority in the 19th century, reframing certain phenomena as diseases and medicalizing many behaviors and practices. Foucault's work has been particularly influential in this domain, demonstrating in *The Birth of the Clinic* (1973) and *Madness and Civilisation* (1965) how "madness" became an object of science in the 19th century through the birth of the clinic as a state apparatus to control and discipline deviant bodies.

In the context of what has been called the "medicalization of society", mental disorders, their diagnostic categories, and their treatment have been particularly problematized as being constructed (Conrad 1992; Illich 1975; Szasz 1972). Many mental health problems were construed as fluctuating and thus chronic, but schizophrenia and other psychotic disorders have a particularly long-standing history with terms like "chronic" and even "degenerative" (Good et al. 2010, 54). Treatment usually consists of prescribing antipsychotics on a long-term basis and often involves being hospitalized, sometimes by force, or "sectioned" as per the UK's Mental Health Act's (1983) terminology (Rethink Mental Health 2017). An increasing amount of research is showing that prolonged usage of some of these drugs causes concern for physical health and brain structure (Murray et al. 2016; Tobert 2018). Furthermore, the UK's Mental Health Act has been under scrutiny in the last few years, with reports by Rethink Mental Illness (2017) and the Royal College of Psychiatrists (Government of United Kingdom 2018) exposing that service users have felt "imprisoned [and] not cared for" (Campbell, 2018). Luhrmann (2007, 146) has suggested the way patients are treated in current Euro-American systems and institutions might worsen their condition and turn a brief or singular psychotic episode into "chronic clienthood".

Psychotic episodes can be triggered by multiple factors but, for individuals concerned, they often carry meaningful or even spiritual aspects. What if individuals were to recover from the crises by looking at what they mean and how they can learn from them, instead of seeking medical treatment to suppress symptoms? This idea was already popularized by the emergence of service-user movements in the

DOI: 10.4324/9781003043508-8

1960s, notably the anti-psychiatry one led by Ronald Laing (1960) in the UK. It has seen a resurgence with trauma-informed care and the Recovery Movement, a direct stance against the claim that psychotic disorders are chronic conditions (Luhrmann 2016b, 19). User-led organizations like the National Hearing Voices Network (2020) also emerged in the 1980s, promoting alternative positive narratives to find meaning in these experiences. Within medical anthropology, there has been some criticism of peer-support groups as "confessional technologies" (Nguyen 2013), as they can be seen to replace one discourse or label with another (e.g., "psychotic" with "voice-hearer").

There is a growing body of literature on these types of experiences, sometimes called "psychotic-like phenomena" (Heriot-Maintland et al. 2011), "psychotic-like anomalous experiences" (Brett et al. 2013), "hallucination-like events" (Luhrmann 2011), which considers both clinical and non-clinical groups reporting these experiences. These studies point towards a need to better understand the diversity and heterogeneity of these experiences, without pathologizing them systematically.

Luhrmann (2016b, 9) points out again that "romantic" readings of anthropology have argued that people diagnosed with schizophrenia might in fact be considered shamans in "less modern settings", implying that "'our' schizophrenia is 'their' shamanism". A documentary called *Crazywise* (Borges and Tomlinson 2017), popular amongst the community of user-led movements, explores this idea of how so-called Western cultures identify hallucinations as pathological whereas shamans in "other" cultures see it as a "gift" or sign of becoming a healer. The homogenization of "our" culture and "theirs" is problematic, as is the romanticizing of shamanic societies as void of mental illnesses and their stigmatization. However, reference to shamanism can be relevant to a discussion of psychosis and spirituality, as types of "states" (Luhrmann 2016b, 10). It can also allow diagnosed individuals to consider an empowering alternative narrative, which can, if not make them shamans, help with their healing process and promote overall mental wellness.

Chronicity and "psychosis"

The *Diagnostic and Statistical Manual of Mental Disorders V* (DSM, 2013) includes a chapter entitled "Schizophrenia Spectrum and Other Psychotic Disorders" and describes the key symptoms as: "delusions, hallucinations, disorganized thinking (speech), grossly disorganized or abnormal motor behavior (including catatonia), and negative symptoms" (Bhati 2013, 409). Psychotic disorders can encompass, and medicalize, a wide variety of behaviors and practices. Experiencing hallucinations in Euro-American contexts is often framed in a negative light because of its association with psychosis, notably schizophrenia, as one of the main symptoms. However, anthropological works (Cassaniti and Luhrmann 2011, 2014; Kirmayer and Sartorius 2007) have shown that hallucinations and other types of unusual sensory experiences can be understood and lived in a multitude of ways, and are often influenced by cultural perceptions of the mind and ontology.

Since the 1980s, schizophrenia has mostly been seen through the "lightning bolt" prism as cases of "random bad genetic luck" (Luhrmann 2007, 140). This has added to its "hopelessness" (Good et al. 2010, 55) and stripped individuals and families of their agency to potentially stop its course or recover (Luhrmann 2007, 140). Nonetheless, the last two decades have seen changes in the understanding of psychotic disorders, due to psychiatric and epidemiological longitudinal studies initiated by the WHO (1973) (Bleuler 1978; Good et al. 2010). These demonstrated socio-environmental and cultural factors might have more impact than biological ones on the development and, most importantly, the prognosis of many psychiatric disorders (Good et al. 2010; Luhrmann 2007, 2012, 2016a). These studies combined with the "Recovery movement" have sought to replace a discourse on "chronicity and deficits" with one of recovery as a reasonable goal (Anthony 2000).

Spirituality and mental health

Spirituality and religiosity's impacts on chronic physical and mental problems appear to be both positive and negative (Roger and Hatala 2017, Moreira-Almeida et al. 2016). Negative impacts can materialize through religious doubts or guilt linked to difficulties maintaining or adhering to beliefs or practices (Roger and Hatala 2017). However, positive impacts can often outweigh negative ones, with reports of increased quality of life, self-esteem, sense of meaning, purpose, hope, and emotional comfort (Roger and Hatala 2017). Positive impacts of spiritual and religious practices have also been observed amongst psychotic patients as "coping mechanisms", including for patients whose beliefs and symptoms overlapped (Huguelet et al. 2006, 366). An increasing amount of research being done on psychotic-like experiences in non-clinical populations also show not only that these states are not inherently distressing (and are made to be by certain factors), but also that a spiritual appraisal of the experiences can be protective against distress (Brett et al. 2013).

Spirituality and religion have relatively recently gained prominence on the psychiatric agenda. The World Psychiatry Association defines spirituality as relating to the transcendent, the sacred, the quest for an ultimate reality, and to finding meaning and purpose in life (Moreira-Almeida et al. 2016, 87). The idea of spirituality as a quest for meaning and purpose is also advocated by Isabel Clarke, co-founder of the Spiritual Crisis Network. She argues that the concept of God or the sacred has survived partly because it provides a framework for people to create meaning and order out of messy lived experience, a basic human need (Clarke 2008).

On the one hand, spirituality can be seen as a human need and desire for meaningfulness (Clarke 2008) and on the other it can be seen as taking shape through sharing experiences (Haidt 2012). These perspectives hold spirituality not as extraordinary or magical belief systems, but rather as a basic feature of human experience and socializing (Clarke 2008). In this chapter, I will focus on how participants use the peer-support groups, their specific narratives, and their sharing practices to find purpose and meaning in their psychotic experiences.

Context and emergence of SPSNs

As part of user-led movements, there has been an emergence of networks I refer to as Spiritual Peer-Support Networks (SPSNs) for people going through what is called a spiritual "crisis" or "emergence", who might have been diagnosed as suffering from psychotic disorders by biomedical practitioners or who simply feel this crisis is related to mental health as well as spirituality.

Although the SPSNs are about a decade old in the UK, their discourse is rooted in older ideas like Laing's (1960) anti-psychiatry movement, a Recovery approach[1] (Clarke 2008), the psychiatric survivor movement (International Mental Health Collaborating Network 2020), or the National Hearing Voices Network (2020). It is also inspired by Jung's work on the collective unconscious and archetypes (Lucas 2011, 54–55), but also Grof and Grof's (1989, 59) work, which popularized transpersonal psychology (Psychology Today 2020) and the term "spiritual emergency". In these ways, the SPSNs frame and reframe psychotic and spiritual experiences through different narratives or perspectives. These were disseminated via their websites, resources, and email support and reflected in language used by participants, including during groups. This chapter will focus on their narrative of transformation.

Transformation narrative

The narrative of transformation that was present in SPSNs' discourse considers the emerging mental health "crisis" as a part of a process or journey towards an end goal: transformation. The transformation narrative is present on both Spiritual Crisis Network and Emerging Proud websites with phrases such as a "spiritual crisis is a turbulent period of psychological opening and transformation" and "reframing mental distress as a potential catalyst for positive change" (Spiritual Crisis Network UK 2020). The first metaphor in this narrative is of the process as journey, and the second of transformation as breaking down to breakthrough.

The "journey" metaphor sometimes referred to identifies specifically with Campbell's Hero's Journey. Campbell (1949) conceptualized the Hero's Journey narrative as an overarching, collective myth drawing from research of heroic stories from various eras and cultures. It was a commonly used narrative within SPSNs and was specifically mentioned by many participants themselves. Catherine Lucas (2011, 151–152), cofounder of the SCN, also uses it as a model to "mak[e] sense of it all". The journey is not necessarily considered linear, but seeing a crisis as part of this journey contributes to highlight learning gained from it (i.e., if I had not gone through this journey, I would not be where I am today).

The metaphor of "breakdown to breakthrough" presented by SPSNs and participants was already present in Laing's and Grof's writings. Laing wrote that "madness need not be all breakdown. It may also be break-through" (Laing 1967, 86). Grof went further by calling a crisis "an opportunity to "emerge", to rise to a higher level of psychological functioning and spiritual awareness" (Grof 2000, 137). It allows individuals to see the benefits in the breakdown as leading to a breakthrough. From this perspective, the breakthrough is seen as the teleological, meaningful purpose of the breakdown, although it is only formulated in hindsight of the (first or only) experience.

Research questions and theoretical concepts

This research ethnographically explored how individuals who have gone through what they identify as mental illness or spiritual crises replace the biomedical narrative of chronicity associated to these crises with a narrative of transformation as shared myth or archetype within SPSNs' community, and how, through practices of meaning-making and sharing within the groups, they can challenge and shape future crises and ultimately heal. To illuminate important aspects of these experiences, I will draw on narrative theories, approached also as rooted in affect, since I explore how participants' narrative and experiential realms both affect and are affected by each other. The narrative and experiential realms can be seen as inextricable because they are "entangled in embodied action being bound up with talk at some point in a flow of activity" (Wetherell 2013, 360).

Narrative theory

The turn to narrative theory to frame illness experience in anthropology was first initiated by Kleinman (1988) and has been used increasingly since (Ezzy 2000). It is particularly potent for illness experiences thanks to its teleological aspect, which allows individuals to re-appropriate or reframe their experiences of illness in positive ways (Ezzy 2000, 605). Similar to the way illness narratives are constructed, through the encounter with SPSNs rather than the clinic, the metaphors of "breaking down to breakthrough" and of "the journey" help construct a plot (Kirmayer 2000). Kirmayer (2000, 29) stresses the importance of interlocutors as one does not tell stories "in a vacuum", and stories are actively shaped by different agents in an "ongoing exchange or contest". Narratives in this study were co-created by different agents interacting with individuals in this setting, including peers, literature that resonated with them, and even myself as interlocutor, through a palette of discursive meaning-making practices, including talking, listening, reading, and writing.

Participants' crises represent an important biographical disruption or "critical situation", which impacts their lives chronically or in a lasting manner, and involves challenges to prior explanatory systems and a "rethinking of the person's biography" (Bury 1982, 169). This rethinking calls for a search for meaning and more profound explanation of events, which is done by the individual and their "circle" (Kirmayer 1993, 162). The fact that psychotic disorders are characterized and rhythmed by episodes or crises engages with the notion of chronicity in a particular way. Anthropological focus on psychosis has often looked at how the label or diagnosis triggers a fundamental shift in selfhood and identity for individuals (Estroff 1989; Lurhmann 2016b). In this research, I am particularly interested in how the crises or experiences themselves might create a shift as a "biographical disruption" (Bury 1982) in their life narratives.

If spirituality is understood as a quest for meaning and purpose, a narrative can be understood as a spiritual framework as it is the "primary scheme by means of which human existence is rendered meaningful" (Polkinghorne 1988, 11). SPSNs' narrative(s) of transformation will be explored as archetypal, in the sense that it is a shared "myth" or story. It is both a singular "narrative" and plural "narratives" as it is both archetypal and multiplied by individuals' interpretations.

The transformation narrative is prototypical as it represents a smoother ideal rather than the messiness of complex lives, but it resonates enough with individuals that they can identify with it and create their own interpretation of it. Individuals' lived experiences will always escape, to a certain degree, linguistic and narrative frameworks used to describe them (Borch-Jakobsen 1992, 109). Yet, these frameworks can still help to create order out of the messiness of life, and since they are shared, they serve to receive recognition and validation from the group (Kirmayer 1993, 170). In this chapter, I will explore how participants' narratives and meaning-making practices modulate their psychophysiological experiences allowing "to organize and transform meanings and memories in a way that modulate emotional experience" (Kirmayer 2006, 595).

Methodology

Overview of fieldwork activities

To address the main research questions, I participated in local peer-support groups in London (n=2) and Oxford (n=3) and conducted interviews with attending individuals (n=20), most of them across the UK in London, Oxford, Bristol, Norwich, Birmingham, and Yorkshire, with a couple in the Netherlands. All participants in this study have been diagnosed with a psychotic disorder at some point of their lives, although they did not necessarily identify with it. Participants in this study used different terms to refer to their experiences: episode, psychosis, experience, transpersonal state, mystical experience. Throughout this chapter, I will use "crisis" or "experience", unless quoting from participants themselves.

Participants had all taken part in peer-support groups with the Spiritual Crisis Network or Emerging Proud and/or attended some of their events. I also conducted informal interviews (n=4) with professionals in the field (e.g., founders of SPSNs, conference organizers, psychiatrists) and attended related events in London (n=2). I took part and observed Skype meetings with the Spiritual Crisis Network core team (n=4) and joined their Annual General Meeting in London.

Recruitment and sample

I recruited participants through the organizations' (Spiritual Crisis Network and Emerging Proud) group facilitators, groups themselves, and events attended. Criteria for interviews were for participants to identify as having experienced a mental health/spiritual crisis and to attend SPSNs groups and/or events regularly.

Eleven participants had been "sectioned" (i.e., hospitalized by force) at least once, and 13 had been diagnosed as suffering from a psychotic disorder by psychiatrists, making the majority of the sample "clinical" (i.e., having gone through the psychiatric system). A few others were diagnosed with bipolar, depression, or anxiety disorder, whilst a couple felt they had gone through a mental health crisis but were not forced to get psychiatric help. Nine were still in contact with the psychiatric system, either through regular follow-ups with a psychiatrist and/or having been sectioned in the last few months. About 16 of them had jobs, studied, or had social activities at the time of the interview and could be considered "stable", although it may have changed for some since.

I spoke to ten men and ten women, which fell out naturally and broadly reflected the population I observed during groups and events. There was a majority of middle-aged participants (between 35 to 55 years old), five in their twenties and three in their late fifties. Almost all came from white, British backgrounds and were not necessarily raised in religious homes but were familiar with Christianity (mainly Anglican). A couple came from Catholic Irish families, a couple were Latin American British, and one was Black African British. About four were part of a religious institution, but a rather homogeneous pattern emerged around participants' current (at the time of the interview) relationship to spirituality, as almost everyone defined themselves as agnostic or hermetic. They often believed in "a higher force" or the existence of "something more than me".

About 15 participants would be considered as highly educated, with a majority having gone to college or university, a few completing masters and a couple with PhDs. Although not many seemed to come from high socio-economic backgrounds, most did have high cultural capital, were intellectually driven and well-read. About 15 worked or had worked in mental health services, both within the UK National Health Service (NHS) and alternative services. A couple worked in community services and a few had sporadic jobs in the creative or retail industries. Many were active, in addition to participating in the groups, in lay expert movements and/or mental health activism.

Ethical considerations

My research was approved by the ethics board of the University of Amsterdam, Department of Medical Anthropology. Ethical considerations follow the American Anthropological Association (AAA) Statement on Ethics as well as Green and Thorogood's (2004, 51) recommendations for ethics and responsibilities in qualitative health research.

Group facilitators were approached with an abstract describing my research, as well as a letter explaining to group members what my research entailed, and asking for consent, in principle, to let me participate in the group. Participants were given consent forms both in the groups attended and before starting interviews. All my participants have been anonymized in this research with pseudonyms, which most chose themselves.[2] It felt important to give them the opportunity to do so, given the focus on narratives in this study.

I remained aware of participants' degrees of vulnerability and potential fluctuations, depending on individuals and moments. Since talking about experiences can be triggering, perhaps re-traumatizing, interviews were kept as flexible as possible. I directed participants to safeguarding documentation on the SPSN's websites when needed and relied on SPSNs' teams for assistance in the case of one participant, who reached out a few weeks after the interview to say she had been sectioned (again). The SPSN's teams gave me advice about how to respond to her email and let her local group know so they could support her if necessary. Her interview was used as she gave consent and was supportive of the research in our last exchanges.

Apart from demographic features (e.g., age, gender, nationality) having an impact on my relationship to the field and participants, my prior experience as a peer-support group facilitator and my interest in both spirituality and wellbeing allowed me to gain participants' trust and build rapport, but they may have acted as a potential bias in favor of the groups' usefulness. Having my own experiences as a facilitator and member of a peer-support group, albeit different, I had experiential knowledge of the groups' potential benefits, and it may have been more difficult to assess usefulness objectively.

I made my position as researcher clear and reminded participants that I was not conducting research for them but about their community. This said, I do believe that anthropological research, as Butler (2009) has brought to the fore, should not only commit to not harming the community studied, but further, is only justifiable if the results benefit the community. I hope to demonstrate my research remains nuanced whilst benefitting the community as a contribution to literature on the use of positive and spiritual narratives as helpful tools for mental health challenges.

Analysis

The ethnographic data collected were based on field notes taken during meetings or events or after peer-support groups, and interview transcripts, as well as any extra material participants shared with me (e.g., films, poetry, plays, paintings). Narrative, for Kleres (2010, 188), can give access to "human experience as it is inextricably meaningful and emotional at the same time" and thus argues for an extension of narrative analysis to emotion analysis. There is a limitation in this narrative and emotion analysis; participants told me that there is an important part of the experience, an emotional or affective aspect, that they struggle to put into words. However, being able to analyze the expression of this struggle might already be a step in the right direction.

I coded my transcripts, field notes, and extra material "by hand" (rather than using specific data coding software). I conducted a framework analysis, which was thematic and mostly inductive (Green and Thorogood 2004, 184). I ran informal member checks by sending participants chapters and the full thesis for review during and after my writing process, via email and phone, as well as face to face. Specific feedback was rare but was included as it helped to refine my analysis.

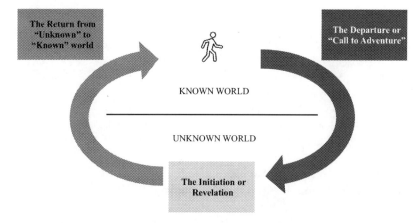

Figure 8.1 Campbell's Hero's Journey Narrative.

Results

The presentation of the stories and experiences of SPSNs can be organized based on Campbell's Hero's Journey narrative (1949) (see Figure 8.1). I will focus on the three major phases, which are the Departure, the Initiation, and the Return. I will start with an outline of the SPSNs community and meeting structure and participants' relationships to spirituality to illustrate the setting in which the Hero's Journey unfolds. The first section on the Departure will focus on the context in which participants' first experiences took place as well as specific events and triggers that may have been tipping points. The Initiation section will delve into the experience or crisis of participants, recounted after the actual event and thus in a narrativized format. The Return section will explore how participants have managed and struggled to create meaning out of experiences, and how the community of SPSNs has helped to reintegrate their experiences into a shared world and helped individuals to find their transformative potential. I conclude this section by exploring some caveats to Campbell's model and issues around narrativization for consideration.

Context of the Hero's Journey

SPSNs are very similar to most other peer-support groups in that they are horizontal in structure, facilitators are considered "gatekeepers" but not authority, everyone should be considered equal and be given the same opportunities to share, everyone should avoid giving unrequested advice, and most importantly, everyone's stories should be seen as valid. The group meetings usually start with a minute of meditation or reflection, and then members can start sharing. There is a tea break which is very important to develop informal relationships with other members outside of the sharing ritual. Following this is a "free flow" conversation where everyone can jump in and discuss themes brought up previously. What makes the SPSN groups and community special for these participants is, firstly, the use of spiritual narratives, themes, and traditions to frame experiences, and secondly, the recognition or validation of these as meaningful rather than delusional.

Apart from the meaning-making practice within the SPSN community, participants often drew individually on many other types of spiritual practices that were also reported as helpful. Some were already interested in spiritual traditions and practices prior to their first crisis, but many saw these solidified by their experiences. OrangeTurtle, for example, was "always interested in spiritual stuff, the meaning of life, that sort of thing" and drew from a variety of traditions like Hinduism and Buddhism but also Pantheism and Wicca.

A few of them did convert to one religion, such as Christianity or Buddhism, but expressed that this was because it "resonated" with them more than other traditions, perhaps due to their upbringing or the people they met. Julian, for instance, explained that she converted to Christianity because she felt it offered her the "most effective tools" to access spirituality. OrangeTurtle also chose one specific path and church because it was "less overwhelming" than drawing on many traditions and made her feel more grounded.

Whilst some practices were considered too close to their experience or too "elating", others were qualified as "grounding". According to the International Spiritual Emergence Network website, "grounding" refers to being connected to one's body and "tips to achieve grounding" include eating healthy, being in nature, and avoiding intense spiritual practice. A few did mention they tried to avoid spiritual practices for a while after a crisis, like BillyCC: "After my third episode, part of my self-management plan... was I avoided all things spiritual". Julian found that meditating "didn't really make [her] safe or grounded" whereas "praying really works for [her]". Similarly, Diana stopped going to a shamanic women's circle, which was too intense for her and was "opening [her] up more". Instead, she has been practicing Zen Buddhism, which she describes as "a very grounding influence in [her] life". These practices played an important role in the way participants created their own idiosyncratic and embodied version of the Hero's Journey narrative.

The SPSN's groups offer a shared meaning-making practice that can go beyond words. For instance, simply being in the presence of others who have had similar experiences and giving as well as receiving validation from peers can help them to reintegrate experiences into the shared world. Julian expressed how experiences of ineffable "realness" can become palpable thanks to the interactions in the groups:

> Obviously proving the existence of God and souls is tricky but there is kind of a way to go okay, these experiences are also experienced by others, not just me... Being able to share that story with someone who had a similar experience or perhaps exactly the same experience, so getting validation in the world you know.

Julian highlights how interactions leading to validation and reassurance are key in the group settings; they can be shared through language but there is also a *knowing* or *feeling* that peers have had similar experiences, despite not finding the right words to describe them.

OrdinaryGeez also mentioned that, although the spiritual aspects of experiences are not always developed during sharing in a group setting, you know that these are important and valid for others because they attend. In fact, she felt like simply *knowing about* SPSNs and attending had contributed to make her third crisis more manageable:

> I think the group really helped; it's mostly given me a space, a community... There's lots of ways of dealing with this stuff, and people do have that thing in common of having religious or spiritual experiences, and being aware of it existing is already so reassuring, to know it's not crazy or weird.

The groups, as a community with their own narratives, space, and values, provide participants with enough to feel recognized and therefore not alone or alienated by their experiences.

The Departure and "opening up"

The Departure referred primarily to the onset of participants' first (or only) "crisis" marked by the beginning of participants' journey through the mental health system and institutions, as well as a visceral start to their spiritual or existential quest for meaning. Few participants saw their Departure as totally distinct from their everyday lives. They did often attribute a specific event to the onset of the first experience, like starting university or a job, falling in love, taking or trying new recreational drugs, undergoing a therapeutic treatment, or starting a new spiritual practice. Lucas[3] (2012, 157) mentioned very similar types of potential triggers in her work on spiritual emergency, which can often be "painful and difficult to cope with". Yet, it was generally perceived to be a combination of specific event(s) and a deeper, more progressive, opening of themselves to existential or spiritual questions about life, its meaning and purpose.

One of the participants Diana recounts the particular time in her life that preceded her first experience, evoking a multiplicity of factors leading to deep changes in her sense of self, as well as the beginning of an engagement with spirituality:

> I was [in Colombia] for 2 years, and then I realized the activism I was doing, that I had invested a lot of my sense of self in... wasn't working out, that these people needed more than a white English girl blogging about them, they needed proper help. That was a reality check. So that was my first breakdown, because it was a breakdown of worldview and dreams, and that was my first opening of a reality beyond my discursive mind... I guess there was something inside of me that deepened and opened, and I remember, I still have my journals. They go from just being like rants or comments on my day and becoming a lot about self-inquiry... So, I was having all these things, and started meditating, reading Eckhart Tolle. I

think that is quite important and I feel like that's why my breakdown is related to spirituality, because without having had those experiences it wouldn't have turned out the same.

Participants were not all like Diana, partaking in spiritual development prior to their Departure, but spiritual ideas and practices did often play a role in their lives as mentioned in the section above. Some did have departures within the Departure, as experiences were often multiple and triggers for onsets could vary each time. What was most homogeneously used by participants to describe their narratives of Departure was the metaphor of "opening up".

Wherever participants were in terms of their spirituality, all of them used the term of "opening up" when talking about the period prior to their first experience and/or when talking about specific events they interpreted as triggers. Diana talks about her breakdown of worldview as her first "opening of a reality beyond [her] discursive mind" and "something inside of [her] that deepened and opened" further. Diana's first time being sectioned took place a few months after her second ayahuasca ceremony, which, in hindsight, she sees as a more sudden "opening up" that was not controlled, facilitated, or guided adequately.

In a similar way, Jace, prior to his crisis, had his own breakdown of worldview when he started questioning theories of the mind, as a cognitive psychologist, and felt like there must be something more to consciousness than what science could prove. A few months after this, he took part in a psychotherapy training that really got him "out of rational thinking" and left him feeling "very opened up" shortly before he began having anomalous experiences. Liam was undergoing a stressful personal and professional period when an acupuncturist told him "to open up and open up" during a session that he interprets as having instigated his crisis. He initially felt intense positive energy, but it twisted and got overwhelmingly negative and debilitating.

This metaphor or idiom of "opening up" is the first meaningful turn in participants' narratives, illustrating first a progressive realization or change in perception of the world and self, and often more specific events. Compared to other terms like "breaking down", "journey", or "transformation," "opening up" is not a metaphor found in SPSN documentation or writing, and this shows that it is perhaps a deeper, more visceral, narrative translation of how participants felt. This first "opening up" is what propels them into the next phase of Initiation, from the known to the unknown world.

The Initiation and "psychosis"

The Initiation stage is the crux of the crisis, often comprising ambiguous sensory and symbolic contents in a dreamlike fashion. Many participants felt their experiences were not just spiritual or psychotic but both, overlapping or morphing into one another. Participants were generally able to describe in quite detailed manners these themes and contents due to their vividness, yet it remained difficult to explain these through shared linguistic or narrative frames.

For example, BillyCC remembers in detail her first crisis and section. She had just been training in Reiki and Distant Healing, and it took place after attempting to do a Distant Healing session for someone she met that night:

> My life flashed in front of me, time became linear, and that was really weird. Then was back in the room and had some sort of download from the universe. Once I got back to myself, I had this sensation of spreading out to all sentient being in the world, in the universe, and kept expanding and expanding and was such a beautiful, beautiful feeling… When I phoned my mum, she got me a cab to hers, the GP came and was very nice to me, but said to my mum I was completely psychotic, they got me to Casualty… I took medication and they put me in a room, and after 45 minutes I started having full on screaming in my ears, bad ghostly figures, and that was after the treatment. That was the first psychotic experience actually, the rest of it didn't feel psychotic.

BillyCC highlights both positive spiritual elements, and later, more traumatic negative elements of her initiation experience. She uses spiritual as well as bio-medical terms, an ambivalence that was shared and expressed by many others.

Some participants like Jace or Liam had one bounded experience a few years back. Others, like BillyCC, had several over the course of a few years and nothing since. A few like Julian had gone through more experiences and perhaps just come out of their latest one. For all participants, the first (or only) crisis was pivotal and represents an important "biographical disruption" (Bury 1982). Indeed, BillyCC adds: "When I think of something, my flowchart goes, 'Was that before or after my episode?' Because it changed everything, overnight".

SPSNs participants described elements of their experiences that could be considered out of the ordinary; some of them were very abstract whilst others more palpable, going from something such as "a warm feeling" to "speaking to angels in [their] living room". A lot of elements in the experiences seemed to belong both to the symbolic and palpable physical realms. It involved religious or spiritual symbolism, triggering certain thoughts and knowledge, but also physiological sensations and actions such as seeing, hearing, speaking, touching, and smelling.

The negative aspects were described by some of the following terms: "carrying all the guilt in the world", "feeling like a burden", "mad", "aggressive", "nasty part of [them] coming out", "fears", "traumas", "intense confusion", "grief", "screams", "ghosts", "dark figures", "frightening voices", "distressing thoughts", "paranoia", "being fallen", and "broken". These are mostly about external distressing figures or parts of themselves appearing as distressing, feeling attacked or chased.

The positive aspects were described by terms, such as: "feeling elated", "deep compassion", "bliss", "feeling connections to all sentient beings", "a sensation that everything is happening for a reason", "being special", "a sense of being god" or "Jesus" or "Buddha", "having a mission", "seeing/feeling a light", "warmth". These seem more about internal sensations and feelings, albeit extending to connections with others. The movement here is from the internal to the external, which might make individuals feel more in control.

OrdinaryGeez, for example, outlined how she almost finds pleasure in these ambivalent sensations:

> It's quite masochistic, you feel so alone but also it's also massively elating. For me [in] all the episodes, ... a large aspect is being paranoid and terrified and scared of your own imagination rallying up against you. But also extreme, intense peace, and they feel like they last a lifetime as well, so it balances out.

Others similarly expressed feeling at once bliss and horror, feeling like "God's channel at times and the Devil's punishment at others", making it difficult or impossible to disentangle the positive from negative aspects.

BillyCC's description of her first experience refers to the experience as both spiritual (at the beginning) and psychotic (at the end). A few, especially those who worked within the UKs NHS, also used both types of terminologies and narratives. OrangeTurtle for instance describes some of her experience in these terms:

> My main delusion at this point was, you know this idea of a collective unconscious, and of people being all connected, and thoughts being able to be shared in this unconscious and love network and spirits and ancestors, and like telepathy being real... I was having a great time but people started wondering if I was okay, and then they started appearing as demons, and then it escalated and I got sectioned.

OrangeTurtle talks about "spirits", "ancestors", and "telepathy" but introduces this as her main "delusion" at the time. Diana also talks about "visions" and "genuine expansion and insight" but also of "delusion and paranoia" and sees "it wasn't just enlightenment and wasn't just madness, it was a really crazy mixture of both". Many other participants used these lexical fields interchangeably, even though the narratives they employed to tell their stories were generally more in line with SPSNs than biomedical ones.

Like BillyCC, OrangeTurtle felt positively about the beginning of her experience, "having a great time", whilst frightening figures started appearing after close ones or hospital staff interfered. This highlights the weight that a narrative, as a frame or mold, can have on the physiological and psychological experience(s) of individuals. It can shape the experience; this can happen with family saying, "You've gone mad", and individuals' experiences becoming more akin to what they think "madness" might be like, but it can also work with spiritual frames such as the concept of "enlightenment" and experiences molding into one's idea of that.

Participants also often described feeling like their experiences felt "true" or "real" whilst medical practitioners tended to call these "delusions". Ann expressed a frustration when she said she knew her experience was "the truth" but "at the same time, [she] couldn't connect with it" once out of it, through shared explanatory frames. To recognize this complexity, participants often drew from several narratives, in fragmented ways. However, many found this frustrating; how can one get recognition that their experiences are true or real if they are so unique to them?

In a letter he wrote a few years back, David expressed this difficulty of reconciling the experiential domain with shared narratives: "I am constantly oscillating between [the experience's] utter uniqueness to me and a desperate need to communicate it". This encapsulates the difficulties participants had to, in other words, return from the unknown to the known world, and will lead us to further explore the role of the SPSNs and their meaning-making practices within it.

The Return and "transformation"

These sensory experiences, although ethereal in some ways, are intensely vivid for participants. The inability to communicate about them through shared frames, their ineffability, becomes a challenge for participants to engage in a process of Return to the known world. What is it about these groups that helps participants, if they are not always able to voice their experiences? In some ways, interactions within the SPSN community allow narratives to reframe experiences, to go beyond words, and to give the opportunity for individuals to transcend their own experiences or stories.

When I interviewed Julian, she had just come out of an episode and felt like this time the sensation of "realness" she had of spiritual aspects during her episode were still with her, better integrated in her shared reality, albeit, according to her, not in a debilitating way:

> It's taken a very, very long process, it's taken six more of those, very similar, to work through the stuff that comes out of me and which is usually quite suppressed and I can't access when not in the episode. As the years have gone on, I feel like the psychosis has become clearer. I always have an important mania. And this time, I kind of feel like the episode didn't end, I mean obviously I'm not manic anymore. But I can still see things clearing up, and am aware of connections to souls and God, but I'm functioning. It seems that after the crisis point, after having been medicated, it's not gone away like zhouu (hand gesture).

Julian's account emphasizes the extent to which the phase of Return can become a non-linear process, whereby experiences of the Initiation stage(s) must be reintegrated from the unknown to the known world. This can present some important and at times unrealistic challenges. Archetypal narratives like the Hero's Journey can never encompass fully these experiences, thus participants are left having to interpret and embody their own idiosyncratic narratives. Yet, these narratives do have transformative potential; they can firstly be exploited through sharing practices and interactions within the groups or outside. Most importantly the transformative potential also lies within the groups' structure, as peers can transcend their own selves and stories by helping others.

In the Initiation section, I wrote about how the narrative imposed on the experience, at the time, seems to have an impact on the lived experience in a range of ways. Whilst the lived experience of such a crisis cannot be forgotten, reframing, as Diana brings to light, "has the power to go back in time and change [the experience]". In hindsight, during a stage of Return, individuals can regain agency, and change their remembered experience, and even, future experiences. A few participants who had multiple experiences mentioned they could see how crises informed each other, how a narrative started taking shape from these experiences and shaped future experiences in turn. Julian told me she was able, thanks to her therapists, Alcoholic Anonymous groups, and the SPSNs, to look at the content of the psychosis and not "dismiss it as just illness". Analyzing parts of her episodes helped her to understand her past traumas, and her relationship to Christianity, in turn informing the next episodes, making them easier to integrate in normal life.

The breakdowns or crises can be transformed in hindsight by narratives, possibly transform future ones and individuals' selfhood by extension. This practice of reframing and meaning-making using narratives is deployed throughout the Return(s), within social interactions, with therapists, family, friends, and most importantly, within the SPSN groups.

In the last step of the journey according to Campbell (1949, 23), the individual "comes back… with the power to bestow boons on his fellow man". Many spoke about the benefits of realizing their experiences, and narratives used to make them meaningful, can be utilized to help other people as a "contribution", "mission", or "service and responsibility" that goes beyond themselves. Parsifal, for instance, said that helping others via peer-support helps him to "see [his] experience has value beyond [his] own life and beyond what it has done for [him]". He sees it as the "purpose" of the experience and "something that connects us to something universal". Concepts of "purpose" and "being connected to the universal" are spiritual themes, illustrating how helping others can be considered a spiritual practice in and of itself. PurpleTrousers similarly points out that helping others is intrinsically part of his healing process as well as his Buddhist beliefs: "My work with the SPSNs, some people say it's really altruistic, but as my Buddhist teacher would say you can't really help yourself without helping others, and you can't really help others without helping yourself".

Partaking in the groups as a practice in and of itself allows members to be healers simply by listening and offering validation to peers. Many recognized helping others was important for their own healing, by being experts by experience for the NHS like BillyCC and Diana, or OrangeTurtle with her work as psychologist and workshop facilitator. For some, it was an ambition prior to their experiences, but for many, it solidified after.

In both London and Oxford groups, the concept of the "wounded healer" came up when discussing the fact that many participants worked in mental health themselves. In medical anthropology, the term has been used to define "individuals who themselves have been healed from a serious disease [and] are chosen to become traditional healers" (Baer and Singer 2007, 106), and the disease is often later "divined as sent by the ancestors" (Reis 2000, 62).

When discussing this section of the research, OrangeTurtle remarked that the term "scarred healer" would be more suitable. Being a "wounded healer" implies the injury is still raw, vulnerable, and the pain still there. "Scarred" highlights a cellular transformation has taken place as the wound has healed. This discussion reflects criticisms of psychiatric understanding of psychotic disorders as chronic, instead re-appropriating the narrative to see these as transformative in a stage of Return. By becoming both "scarred" and "healers", participants Return through not only transcending themselves by helping others, but also transforming their selves or identities.

Caveats on Campbell's model: Unrealistic narratives

The primary drawback of using narratives, whether biomedical, spiritual, or the Hero's Journey, is the incapacity to encompass the complexity and ineffable realness of experiences. The idea of "transformation" was specifically criticized by some participants for overlooking the traumatic, negative elements of experiences. A few participants found that the darker aspects of their experiences would have to be overlooked in order to fit into this archetypal narrative, sometimes feeling like "escapism". OrangeTurtle expressed:

> The [transformation] narrative seems to be falling into this overly positive narrative. But actually, some of it feels like the pits of hell, and it's made to seem like it's all so spiritual and amazing, and actually no, there is also a lot of trauma.

Whilst it is beneficial to use empowering narratives, negating traumatic elements reproduces the essentialization of the biomedical narrative. This concurs with the main criticism of peer-support groups as replacing one label or discourse with another (Nguyen 2013). Hall and Sneyd (2019) discuss how biomedicine and spirituality both attempt to order disorder or explain human experiences, including the inexplicable. This attempt is always fragmented and incapable of encompassing the richness of human experience. Some participants were aware of this dynamic, such as Antares:

> [Psychiatry and spirituality] are both ways of framing things. They both tend quite strongly to have absolutist people who buy into that one way of looking at things and say this isn't just a way of looking at it, this is actually how things are.

Although lots of participants were convinced of the realness in their experiences, they often accepted there might be blurred boundaries between what felt "spiritual" or "psychotic", as was explored in the Initiation. I suggest that accepting a degree of uncertainty and flux in their interpretation of the transformation narrative might also be key in their Return. David emphasized how his practice of meaning-making has been multi-layered:

> I guess I constructed meaning out of my experiences a bit like the Frankenstein monster, out of any kind of scraps of philosophy, culture, religion,

literature, ... etc. that I found lying about. And I guess you could see it all as a postmodern hybridization, perhaps as a positive process of appropriating culture.

Participants' lived experience often did not fit one narrative or mold, thus they created their own hybrid narratives by drawing on a variety of sources. This hybridity was frustrating for some as it complicated their stories and made them less easy to reintegrate (Turner 1969) into the known world. Whilst the process of Return is complex and cannot be achieved fully through the use of narratives like the Hero's Journey, the SPSNs and being part of that community helped by practicing sharing, meaning-making, and helping others.

Discussion

The narrative of transformation participants employed, often inspired from the Hero's Journey, started homogenously with a period of departure or "opening up" to the world, themselves, and societal and existential questions. Similarly, Kirmayer (1993, 161) sees the transformative power of metaphors as a link between narrative and lived experience "through imaginative constructions and enactments that allow movement in sensory-affective quality space". The metaphor operates on the embodied as well as symbolic levels; participants are "opening up" their minds, bodies, and souls as they are propelled into the Initiation phase, from the known to the unknown world, where unique symbolic and sensory experiences await. The Initiation phase, a liminal experience or crisis, can be characterized by an individual "pass(ing) through a cultural realm that has few or none of the attributes of the past or coming state" (Turner 1969, 94–95), both disorientating and potentially insightful. Similar to a rite of passage, these experiences become meaningful because they are recognized, later, by peers in the group(s). The Return, or perhaps rather *becoming* returned, phase explores the process of reintegrating experiences into the shared "known" world. As experiences cannot fit perfectly into narratives as a mold, what helps some of them is firstly the acceptance of a form of Deleuzean *becoming* returned and an acceptance of hybrid narratives.

A transformation can be achieved through identification with a shared myth like the Hero's Journey, which will in turn transform "their experiential qualities and meaning" (Kirmayer 2006, 595). The biomedical narrative, which can be seen as labelling and institutionalizing, creates, in a similar albeit opposed process, what Luhrmann (2007, 146) qualifies of "chronic clienthood" or even "social defeat". Social defeat refers to how social alienation correlates with psychotic disorders, but also how a diagnosis contributes, cyclically, to chronic social defeat. By promoting a defeatist narrative, the biomedical one may reproduce negative and persistent psychotic experiences. Literature shows that socio-environmental factors do have an impact on the development and prognosis of diagnostics (Good et al. 2010; Luhrmann 2007, 2012, 2016a). This study shows how chronic clienthood and social defeat can potentially be countered by a change in socio-environmental factors like the reintegration into a community and a shared mythic narrative.

Furthermore, participants reported an overall increase in quality of life from taking part in these groups, notably because of reassurance and validation of spiritual experiences as "real". This corroborates with positive impacts of using spirituality in long-lasting hardships, such as illnesses (Roger and Hatala 2017; Moreira-Almeida et al. 2016). However, the negative aspects of using spiritual themes or narratives were different than some of the literature mentioned, namely that they can oversimplify or smooth out darker, negative parts of experiences.

The narrative of transformation and its metaphors take life in a specific social setting and, because of interactions with different agents, in a "brain-body-world entanglement" (Blackman 2012, 1). Going back to the Haidt and Durkheimian (2009, 8) conceptualization of the "sacred", a community can be seen as made out of "shared" emotions and experience (e.g., rites, practices, calendar, etc.) rather than "shared factual beliefs about the nature of god and the origin of the world". Thus, it is not the archetypal narratives in themselves that are beneficial, but rather the way these are embodied, shared, fragmented, or "broken" down (Kirmayer 2000) by the group. Recognizing the value of the group as a setting and community to share beyond words and to give and receive validation without needing a coherent narrative was helpful for these participants.

Moreover, participants found that what was most healing was to see their Return as a transcendental and transformative process of becoming "scarred healers". By extending the teleological purpose of their crises to helping others, they transcend their personal narratives, which implies a level of uncertainty or open-endedness. Their Deleuzean becoming does not require a resolution or endpoint and "accepts the indefinite as "lacking nothing" (Biehl and Locke 2010, 325). The teleological goal of transformation, paradoxically, remains open-ended to potentialities rather than frustrated or lacking something. A transformation also operates in terms of their selfhoods or identities, as they *become* both "scarred" and "healers". It underlines the tension between the chronicity of the crises as biographical disruption (Bury 1982) that has long-lasting impacts and the transformative aspect of the crises. The idea of a pure and linear Return is misleading as many will struggle with reintegrating experiences fully into their life but accepting hybridity and finding a community in which they can share these with are beneficial for participants' Return.

Implications for health care providers

The description of participants' experiences as not fitting neatly into either psychotic or spiritual categories may, firstly, lead health care providers to consider the complexity of patients' experiences, and secondly, allow spiritual themes to be discussed without systematically pathologizing them. Some psychologists in the UK, including one of my participants, advocate for a formulation approach (Johnstone 2017), referring to the use of narrativization to explore patients' experiences as a way to treat them and avoid diagnostic labels.

Narratives, words, and language used had important effects, whether during or after the crisis, on participants' experiences. Health care providers should be more aware of this and trained accordingly to use neutral language or terminology whenever possible to avoid diagnostic-related anxieties. If positive narratives cannot be deployed within mainstream health care, at the very least peer-groups and lay experts should be involved more importantly within institutions to provide optimistic experiential knowledge to patients. Since helping others with similar issues was perceived as transformative, health care providers and institutions could work on creating more opportunities to involve patients in peer-work or other activities, which could grant them a sense of purpose or mission.

Contributions and limitations

This research adds to the conversation about the need to replace or go beyond a narrative of "chronicity" or even of "recovery" for mental health problems. There is already a wide body of work demonstrating how a narrative of chronicity is not only inadequate to refer to psychotic disorders, but potentially damaging to individuals concerned (Good et al. 2010; Luhrmann 2007, 2012). The Recovery approach, widely adopted in the UK and the United States for over a decade now (Luhrmann 2016b), has arguably reinforced the system already in place rather than transmuting it, engaging in a "superficial redescription of existing treatment" (Luhrmann 2016b, 19). It can also be seen to reproduce a medicalizing narrative since the word "recovery" implies that there was an illness.

This research also reaffirms the usefulness and importance of lay expertise and peer-support, by highlighting the importance of *meaning* in crises. Whilst there is a danger in replacing one type of discourse with another more harmful one, these types of community-based activities can be deeply empowering and counter what Luhrmann (2007) calls "social defeat". Peer-support groups seem to particularly counter social defeat by giving a sense of mission or purpose to individuals, which transcends their own lives and paths. In addition, a focus on meaning and purpose as helping participants confirms the positive impacts a spiritual outlook on life can have (Roger and Hatala 2017).

I chose to explore narratives of experiences and use narrative theories to delve into participants' journeys. Narratives were the only way I could get access to these journeys as it would have been practically and ethically complicated to do participant observation of patients during their crisis, often on the wards. However, I do recognize the textuality is a limitation in this study, as I partly discuss experiences I qualify as "ineffable" and thus challenging to write about. A different methodological approach that would include the observation of the crisis unfolding, and perhaps the use of affect theories as a way to complement narrative ones would have helped to delve more deeply into the different stages of participants' journeys.

Whilst I did not aim for my sample to be representative of the clinical population in the UK, one demographical aspect (or lack thereof) stood out. My sample was comprised almost exclusively of white, British participants, whereas statistics in the UK show there is a significantly high prevalence of Black, Indigenous, and People of Color (BIPOC) on wards, notably males from

African and Caribbean backgrounds (Keating 2009; Kirkbride et al. 2008; Luhrmann 2007). There are many theories about this overrepresentation including that it is due to "social defeat" (Luhrmann 2007), meaning being underprivileged, under-represented, thus alienated or literally made submissive to the rest of society, like a young, Black, working-class man might experience in the UK. It led me to question whether this transformative narrative could be helpful for everyone or whether it might be catered to certain individuals who can educate themselves on alternative narratives and who have the time and space to reflect on the broader meanings of their crises. What narratives, if any, could counter "social defeat" and "chronic clienthood" of those on the wards? This also points towards the questions of whether all experiences can be seen as having the same transformative potential, and if not, what exactly makes one more "pathological" and another more "spiritual" or "transformative".

Conclusion

In this ethnographic research, I explored how members of the SPSNs' community and their peer-support groups utilize and embody certain narratives to make crises a source of transformation rather than a chronic life sentence. Some of the main findings demonstrate that narratives, like the Hero's Journey, are helpful to a certain degree because they allow people to find positivity and learning in their darkest experiences, but they often risk smoothing out the complexity and organic chaos of these. However, these narratives exist and can be shared through a meaning-making practice, attendance of the groups, validation of each other's experiences, reassurance, and community feeling. Finally, what most strongly sparked participants' transformative potential were the self-transcendent acts of helping others. These findings can be used to reflect more widely on psychotic disorders and patients diagnosed, how they are understood and treated by health care practitioners, and how they are perceived in society at large. More research should look at how positive narratives and community practices can be disseminated further than the SPSN groups.

Notes

1 The Recovery approach "identifies spirituality as a vital element in enabling people with severe mental health difficulties to rebuild a meaningful life" (Clarke 2008, 2).
2 Full list of pseudonyms: Ann, Jace, Liam, David, Dean, Purpletrousers, Antares, Thomas, Julian, Hermetica, BillyCC, Diana, Mike, Benjotécé, OliveMary, Katrina, Parsifal, Kirsty, OrangeTurtle, and OrdinaryGeez.
3 Catherine Lucas is one of the cofounders of the Spiritual Crisis Network.

References

Anthony, William A. 2000. "A Recovery-Oriented Service System: Setting Some System Level Standards." *Psychiatric Rehabilitation Journal* 24 (2): 159–168. doi:10.1037/h0095104

Baer, Hans, and Merrill Singer. 2007. *Introducing Medical Anthropology: A Discipline in Action.* Maryland: Alta Mira Press.

Bhati, Mahendra T. 2013. "Defining Psychosis: The Evolution of DSM-5 Schizophrenia Spectrum Disorders." *Current Psychiatry Reports* 15: 409. doi:10.1007/s11920-013-0409-9

Biehl, Joao, and Peter Locke. 2010. "Deleuze and the Anthropology of Becoming." *Current Anthropology* 51 (3). doi:10.1086/651466

Blackman, Lisa. 2012. *Immaterial Bodies: Affect, Embodiment, Mediation.* London: Sage Publications.

Bleuler, Eugen. 1978. *The Schizophrenic Disorders: Long-term Patient and Family Studies.* New Haven, CT: Yale University Press.

Borch-Jakobsen, Mikkel. 1992. *The Emotional Tie: Psychoanalysis, Mimesis and Affect.* Stanford: Stanford University Press.

Borges, Phil, and Kevin Tomlinson. 2017. *Crazywise.* Accessed May 5, 2019 from https://crazywisefilm.com/

Brett, Caroline, Charles Heriot-Maitland, Philip McGuire and Emmanuelle Peters. 2013. "Predictors of Distress Associated with Psychotic-Like Anomalous Experiences in Clinical and Non-Clinical Populations." *British Journal of Clinical Psychology* 53 (2): 213–227. doi:10.1111/bjc.12036

Bury, Michael. 1982. "Chronic Illness as Biographical Disruption." *Sociology of Health and Illness* 4 (2): 167–182. doi:10.1111/1467-9566.ep11339939

Butler, Udi M. 2009. "Notes on a Dialogical Anthropology." *Anthropology in Action, Journal for Applied Anthropology in Policy and Practice* 25 (3): 20–31. doi:10.3167/aia.2009.160303

Campbell, Denis. 2018. "Report Finds 'Serious Issues' With Use of Mental Health Act." *The Guardian.* Accessed July 31, 2019 from www.theguardian.com/society/2018/may/01/report-finds-serious-issues-with-use-of-mental-health-act

Campbell, Joseph. 1949. *The Hero with a Thousand Faces.* New York: Pantheon Books.

Cassaniti, Julia, and Tanya Luhrmann. 2011. "Encountering the Supernatural: A Phenomenological Account of Mind." *Religion and Society: Advances in Research* 2:37–53. doi:10.3167/arrs.2011.020103

Cassaniti, Julia, and Tanya Luhrmann. 2014. "The Cultural Kindling of Spiritual Experience." *Current Anthropology* 55(Supplement 10): 5000.

Clarke, Isabel. 2008. *Madness, Mystery and the Survival of God.* Alresford: O-Books.

Conrad, Peter. 1992. "Medicalisation and Social Control." *Annual Review of Sociology* 18: 209–232.

Estroff, Sue. 1989. "Self, Identity, and Subjective Experiences of Schizophrenia: In Search of the Subject." *Schizophrenia Bulletin* 15 (2): 189–196. doi:10.1093/schbul/15.2.189

Ezzy, Douglas. 2000. "Illness Narratives: Time, Hope and HIV." *Social Science and Medicine* 50: 605–617. doi:10.1016/s0277–9536(99)00306–00308

Foucault, Michel. 1965. *Madness and Civilization: A History of Insanity in the Age of Reason.* London: Tavistock.

Foucault, Michel. 1973. *The Birth of the Clinic: An Archeology of Medical Perception.* New York: Pantheon Books.

Good, Byron, Carla Marchira, Nida Ul Hasanat, Utami Sofiati and Subandi Muhana. 2010. "Is 'Chronicity' Inevitable for Psychotic Illness?: Studying Heterogeneity in the Course of Schizophrenia in Yogyakarta, Indonesia." In *Chronic Conditions, Fluid States: Chronicity and the Anthropology of Illness,* edited by Carolyn Smith-Morris and Lenore Manderson, 54–74. Ithaca: Rutgers University Press. doi:36019/9780813549736-005

Government of United Kingdom. 2018. *Modernising the Mental Health Act Increasing Choice, Reducing Compulsion. Final Report of the Independent Review of the Mental*

Health Act 1983. Accessed December 3, 2020 from https://assets.publishing.service. gov.uk/government/uploads/system/uploads/attachment_data/file/778897/Modernising_the_Mental_Health_Act_increasing_choice__reducing_compulsion.pdf

Green, Judith, and Nicki Thorogood. 2004. *Qualitative Research Methods*. London: Sage Publications.

Grof, Stanislov. 2000. *Psychology of The Future – Lessons from Modern Consciousness Research*. Albany: State University of New York Press.

Grof, Stanislov, and Christina Grof. 1989. *Spiritual Emergency: When Personal Transformation Becomes a Crisis*. New York: Penguin Putnam Inc.

Haidt, Jonathan, and Jesse Graham. 2009. "Planet of the Durkheimians, Where Community, Authority, and Sacredness are Foundations of Morality." In *Social and Psychological Bases of Ideology and System Justification*, edited by J. Jost, A. C. Kay and H. Thorisdottir, 371–401. New York: Oxford University Press.

Haidt, Jonathan. 2012. "Religion, Evolution, Science and Self-Transcendence." *Ted Talk*. Accessed on July 20, 2019 from www.ted.com/talks/jonathan_haidt_humanity_s_stairway_to_self_transcendence?language=en

Hall, Will, and Martha Sneyd. 2019. "Ayahuasca, Psychosis and Spiritual Awakening." *Mad in America*. Accessed on April 28, 2020 from www.madinamerica.com/2019/08/martha-sneyd-ayahuasca-psychosis-spiritual-awakening/

Heriot-Maintland, Charles, Matthew Knight and Emmanuelle Peters. 2011. "A Qualitative Comparison of Psychotic-like Phenomena in Clinical and Non-Clinical Populations." *British Journal of Clinical Psychology*. doi:10.1111/j.2044-8260.2011.02011.x

Huguelet, Philippe, Sylvia Mohr, Laurence Boras, Christiane Gillieron and Pierre-Yves Brandt. 2006. "Spirituality and Religious Practices Among Outpatients with Schizophrenia and Their Clinicians." *Psychiatric Services* 57 (3): 366–372. doi:10.1176/appi.ps.57.3.366

Illich, Ivan. 1975. "The Medicalization of Life." *Journal of Medical Ethics* 1 (2): 73–77. doi:10.1136/jme.1.2.90

International Mental Health Collaborating Network. 2020. "*Psychiatric Survivor Movement*" Accessed December 3, 2020 from https://imhcn.org/References/history-of-mental-health/psychiatric-survivors-movement/

Keating, Frank. 2009. "African and Caribbean Men and Mental health." *Ethnicity and Inequalities in Health and Social Care* 2 (2). doi:10.1108/17570980200900015

Johnstone, Lucy. 2017. "Psychological Formulation as an Alternative to Psychiatric Diagnosis." *Journal of Humanistic Psychology* 58 (1): 30–46. doi:10.1177/0022167817722230

Kirmayer, Laurence. 1993. "Healing and the Invention of Metaphor: The Effectiveness of Symbols Revisited." *Culture, Medicine and Psychiatry* 17: 161–195. doi:10.1007/BF01379325

Kirmayer, Laurence. 2000. "Broken Narratives: Clinical Encounters and the Poetics of Illness Experience." *Narrative and the Cultural Construction of Illness and Healing*, edited by C. Mattingly and L. Garro, 153–180. Berkeley, California: University of California Press.

Kirmayer, Laurence. 2006. "Towards a Medicine of the Imagination." *New Literary History* 37 (3): 583–601. doi:10.1353/nlh.2006.0046

Kirmayer, Laurence, and Norman Sartorius. 2007. "Cultural Models and Somatic Syndromes." *Psychosomatic Medicine* 69 (9): 832–840. doi:10.1097/PSY.0b013e31815b002c

Kirkbride, J.B, D. Barker, F. Cowden, R. Stamps, M. Yang, P.B. Jones and J.W. Coid. 2008. "Psychoses, Ethnicity and Socio-Economic Status." *The British Journal of Psychiatry* 193 (1): 18–24. doi:10.1192/bjp.bp.107.041566

Kleinman, Arthur. 1988. *Suffering, Healing and the Human Condition*. New York: Basic Books.
Kleres, Jochen. 2010. "Emotions and Narrative Analysis: A Methodological Approach." *Journal for the Theory of Social Behaviour* 41 (2): 182–202. doi:10.1111/j.1468-5914.2010.00451.x
Laing, Ronald D. 1967. *The Politics of Experience and the Bird of Paradise*. London: Penguin Books.
Laing, Ronald D. 1960. *The Divided Self: An Existential Study in Sanity and Madness*. London: Penguin Books.
Lucas, Catherine. 2011. *In Case of Spiritual Emergency: Moving Successfully Through Your Awakening*. Forres: Findhorn Press.
Luhrmann, Tanya. 2007. "Social Defeat and the Culture of Chronicity: Or, Why Schizophrenia Does So Well Over There and So Badly Here." *Culture, Medicine and Psychiatry* 31: 135–172. doi:10.1007/s11013-007-9049-z
Luhrmann, Tanya. 2011. "Hallucinations and Sensory Overrides." *Annual Review of Anthropology* 40: 71–85. doi:10.1146/annurev-anthro-081309-145819
Luhrmann, Tanya. 2012. "Beyond the Brain." *The Wilson Quarterly*. Accessed December 19, 2018 from http://archive.wilsonquarterly.com/essays/beyond-brain
Luhrmann, Tanya. 2016a. "Diversity within the Psychotic Continuum." *Schizophrenia Bulletin* 43 (1): 27–31. doi:10.1093/schbul/sbw137
Luhrmann, Tanya. 2016b. "Introduction." *Our Most Troubling Madness: Case Studies in Schizophrenia Across Cultures*, edited by T.M. Luhrmann and Jocelyn Marrow, 1–27. Oakland: University of California Press.
Moreira-Almeida, Alexander, Peter J. Verhagen, Bernard Janse van Rensburg, Avdesh Sharma, Christopher C.H. Cook. 2016. "WPA Position Statement on Spirituality and Religion in Psychiatry." *World Psychiatry* 15 (1): 87–88. doi:10.1002/wps.20304
Murray, Robin M., Diego Quattrone, Sridhar Natesan, Jim Van Os, Merete Nordentoft, Oliver Howes, Martha Di Forti and David Taylor. 2016. "Should Psychiatrists be More Cautious About the Long-Term Prophylactic Use of Antipsychotics?" *British Journal of Psychiatry* 209 (5): 361–365.
National Hearing Voices Network. 2020. "For People Who Hear Voice, See Visions, or Have Other Unusual Perceptions." Accessed December 3, 2020 from http://www.hearing-voices.org/
Nguyen, Vinh Kim. 2013. "Counselling Against HIV in Africa: A Genealogy of Confessional Technologies." *Culture, Health and Sexuality* 15: 440–452. doi:10.1080/13691058.2013.809146
Psychology Today. 2020. "*Transpersonal Therapy*." Accessed December 3, 2020. www.psychologytoday.com/intl/therapy-types/transpersonal-therapy
Polkinghorne, Donald E. 1988. *Narrative Knowing and the Human Sciences*. Albany: State University of New York Press.
Reis, Ria. 2000. "The 'Wounded Healer' as Ideology." *The Quest for Fruition Through Ngoma: Political Aspects of Healing in Southern Africa*, edited by R. van Dijk, R. Reis and M. Spierenburg. Oxford: Cambridge University Press.
Rethink Mental Illness. 2017. "*Mental Health Laws*." Accessed on December 3, 2020 from www.rethink.org/advice-and-information/rights-restrictions/mental-health-laws/mental-health-act-1983/
Roger, Kerstin Stieber, and Andrew R. Hatala. 2017. "Religion, Spirituality and Chronic Illness: A Scoping Review and Implications for Health Care Practitioners." *Journal of*

Religion and Spirituality in Social Work 37 (1): 24–44. doi:10.1080/15426432.2017.1386151

Spiritual Crisis Network UK. 2020. "*Spiritual Crisis, Often Called Spiritual Emergency, Awakening or Psycho-Spiritual Crisis, is a Turbulent Period of Psychological Opening and Transformation.*" Accessed December 3, 2020 from https://spiritualcrisisnetwork.uk/

Szasz, Tomas. 1972. "The Myth of Mental Illness." *American Psychologist* 15: 113–118. doi:10.1192/S0007125000178481

Tobert, Natalie. 2018. "Cultural U-Turns in Mental Well-Being: Acknowledging the Dilemma." *Journal of Humanistic Psychology* 1–10. doi:10.1177/0022167818762916

Turner, Victor. 1969. "Liminality and Communitas." In *The Ritual Process: Structure and Anti-Structure*, 94–113, 125–130. Chicago: Aldine Publishing.

Wetherell, Margaret. 2013. "Affect and Discourse - What's the Problem? From Affect as Excess to Affective/Discursive Practice." *Subjectivity* 6 (4): 349–368. doi:10.1057/sub.2013.13

World Health Organization [WHO]. 1973. "International Pilot Study of Schizophrenia and World Health Organization." *Report of the International Pilot Study of Schizophrenia.*

9 Prayer camps, healing, and the management of chronic mental illness in Ghana
A qualitative phenomenological inquiry

Francis Benyah

Introduction

In Ghana, mental illness is culturally and socially perceived as a chronic condition. Among the Akans[1] in particular, a popular saying or proverb such as *"ɔbɔdamfuɔ se ne dam kɔ a, na ɛnyɛ deɛ ɔde hunahuna mmɔfra"* literally means "if a lunatic says he or she has been cured of the lunacy, many a time traces of the lunacy that is capable of being used to frighten children persist." In other words, "if a person decides to desist from a well-formed habit, many a time, traces of the habit, at least enough to frighten, remain" (Amfo et al. 2018, 4). This proverb depicts the chronicity of mental illnesses in the minds of people, especially in the Akan communities of Ghana, and defines the extent to which these views are socially integrated. People are conscious of their dealings or relationships with individuals who have had a history or suffered from some form of mental illness in the past, for fear of rekindling their past negative disorders at the least provocation (Amfo et al. 2018). Cultural idioms such as this explain the sustained cycle and the production of mutually amplifying negative behaviors meted out to persons with mental illness, either in the present or the past. These negative attitudes towards the mentally ill in Ghana affect their everyday routines and functionality in terms of individually, socially, and economically.

This chapter investigates the use of spiritual and faith-based resources as coping mechanisms in dealing with the day-to-day dilemmas and uncertainties surrounding chronic mental illness in Ghana. The study is based on fieldwork conducted among persons with various forms of mental illness at two major prayer camps in Ghana. The chapter explores conceptions of mental illness and the strategies that are employed in their management and treatment. It also examines ways these approaches help in maintaining and sustaining hope amidst chronicity. In so doing, this chapter makes a significant contribution to the role and use of faith-based resources in aiding wellness for individuals with chronic mental illness conditions, especially those in the global south.

This chapter is divided into four sections. The first section reviews the meaning and understanding of mental illness in the Ghanaian or the West African context, and how or why religion, spirituality, and/or faith remain an important resource in this regard. The second section gives an account of the methodological processes

DOI: 10.4324/9781003043508-9

that were used in conducting the study. The third presents the results or findings from fieldwork, including 1) a descriptive account of participants' experiences in the use of faith-based resources in dealing with chronic mental illness, and 2) the role prayer camps play in this. The fourth section focuses on a discussion and conclusion by outlining implications for health care providers.

Ghana prayer camps

Prayer camps, as the name connotes, are religious and spiritual centers established in various locations across Ghana for purposes of prayer, healing, deliverance, Bible studies, and counselling. With the exception of a few that were established or founded by churches, prayer camps are mostly private, Christian religious groups that are usually managed by individuals with what are often referred to as "prophetic abilities" or "gifts".[2] Many of the leaders are self-professed religious charismatics who claim to have divine power or the "anointing of God" to heal and cure persons with conditions, such as infertility, cancer, and mental illness, through prayer and other non-medical means. In terms of worship style and praxis, prayer camps are more charismatic and Pentecostal in nature. The leaders promote beliefs in miracles, consultation with angels, and spiritual healing. The pneumatic ingredients, such as prophecies, visions, and tongues speaking are also evident in their practice of worship. In reality, prayer camps form "part of the greater complex of Pentecostal deliverance ministries that have evolved within the last two to three decades" (Heuser 2015, 280). As deliverance centers, prayer camps also serve as therapeutic centers and create important networks of care and support for the sick (Larbi 2001). The prophets or spiritual leaders of the camps mostly attempt to discover the supernatural causes of a problem and rid the person(s) from any demonic powers that are considered to be harmful to people's well-being. Healing rituals at the camps are often accompanied by periods of fasting and individual confinement (Larbi 2001).

Current literature and global discourses on the activities of prayer camps in Ghana and the healing of mental illnesses have highlighted some of the negative practices, abuse, and violations of human rights (Carey 2015; Edwards 2014). Arias et al. (2016, 13), for example, observe how "much of the previous literature has focused on the adverse practices conducted in the camps, including forced fasting, chaining, and caning," which they argue "have raised concerns regarding the viability of intersectoral partnerships." Claims to human rights abuses at the camps are also made in the report by Human Rights Watch (2012), a non-governmental organization (NGO) based in New York, and in the report by the United Nations Human Rights Council (2013); these are claims such as inadequate accommodations and forced religious practices (e.g., fasting). Global media have also described an overwhelmingly negative view of the camps by producing documentaries that seek to reveal and make evident some of the claims to abuse of persons with mental illness at the camps (BBC 2018; Carey 2015). Although current global political discourses on human rights cannot be disputed, the reality is also more nuanced and complex, as there are also positive experiences of individuals at the camps that are worth noting and deserve exploration, and which these previous reports often gloss over.

Not all prayer camps are engaged in abuses of human rights, and it would be unfair to generalize their activities into one whole. Previous studies and reports also miss an important component in the activities and operation of the camps, that is, the response the camps provide to beliefs that mental illness could be caused by demonic forces or antagonistic spiritual beings and require religious and spiritual means of remediation (Ae-Ngibise et al. 2010). State interventions, such as psychiatric hospitals, cannot adequately provide support for spiritual or existential issues raised by mental illness. Although previous literature does acknowledge negative attitudes, stigma, exclusion, and abuse of the rights of persons with mental illness in the Ghanaian society (Barke, Nyarko and Klecha 2011), the prayer camps are not fully appreciated for some of the individual and social benefits, primarily their role in providing community and support for those who are rejected from the wider society because of their mental illness. The prayer camps also need to be appreciated as a local response to growing mental health needs within a context of limited government funding and resources for psychiatric hospitals or homecare institutions (Ofori-Atta, Read and Lund 2010).

The camps that served as the focus of this study had between 20 to 40 residential facilities with one having a two-story building with rooms for visitors at a fee. Conditions relating to the standard of living have also been linked to human rights abuses as camps without the requisite infrastructure are sometimes found in the habit of keeping patients under unhealthy and dilapidated conditions with exposure to bad weather conditions (Arias et al. 2016; Edwards 2014; Human Rights Watch 2012). Rather, the situation reveals the material needs, lack of infrastructure, and the financial constraints under which these camps struggle to operate to help the problem of mental health in a limited resource setting with a population of about 30 million and only three main psychiatric hospitals, all concentrated in the southern part of the country. Civil society organizations, NGO workers, and international organizations such as Human Rights Watch, oftentimes overlook these functional aspects of the camps and can lack basic understanding of the structural and political issues within the local context in which they operate, including the role of culture, religion, and spirituality in the lives of the people.

Previous research on prayer camps in Ghana also mainly comes from Western disciplines such as clinical psychology (Ofori-Atta et al. 2010), anthropology (Read, Adiibokah and Nyame 2009; Read and Doku 2012), and secular human rights orientations and perspectives. These views can be understood to also underappreciate local cultural worlds and potential positive strengths of the prayer camps in Ghana. Western disciplines and global mental health efforts tend to focus on professional mental health interventions and therefore can marginalize local cultural or Indigenous forms of healing and community supports that can contribute to positive outcomes and recovery for those with chronic mental illness (Kirmayer and Swartz, 2013). To date, there are limited, or as of yet, no strengths-based studies on the positive activities of prayer camps in Ghana, and especially those from an emic religious studies perspective. This research seeks to

Healing and mental illness in Ghana

Healing and treatment practices offered at the prayer camps are embedded in local meaning systems, cultural symbols, and languages that resonate with the general Ghanaian population. A healing ritual at a prayer camp is generally viewed as having the ability to offer holistic cleansing and fostering personal transformation by invocations of God through Jesus Christ and the power of the Holy Spirit (Atiemo 2017). Local healing rituals also reassure or symbolize to the wider community that a person is no longer potentially dangerous because the vestiges of mental illness and associated evil powers have been destroyed or removed. As others have noted, "healing practices are embedded in local meaning systems that give them part of their social value and potential efficacy" (Kirmayer and Swartz 2013, 48).

Causal explanations for mental illness are often found in spiritual curses, the breaking of taboos, and offending a third party or a deity, among other examples (Kpobi and Swartz 2018). It is within this framework of non-material illness causation that mental illness primarily finds its interpretation and meaning in Ghana and other parts of Africa. As such, mental illness is not only explained, at times, in biological and physiological terms, but also, and perhaps more importantly, ingrained with supernatural undercurrents. This understanding of illness causation has also "continued into Pentecostal Christianity and the African Christian's understanding of illness is cast in the framework of the traditional interpretation" (Atiemo 2017, 267). In an African Pentecostal context, healing and health are recast in this traditional framework of understanding and the two (healing and health) are believed to be intimately "connected to social behavior, moral conduct, and spiritual forces" (Clarke 2014, 71; see also, Asamoah, Osafo and Agyapong 2014). Thus, Pentecostal explanations and theory of illness causation and healing reverberate with many "African, Asian cultures, and Latin American cultures that envision health as depending on the right relationships with the natural and spiritual worlds" (Brown 2011, 7; see also Hatala and Waldram 2016).

The dilemma between the two domains of potential causative factors, between the material and spiritual, determines and regulates how patients and family members negotiate their healing journeys in an attempt to find solutions to or in the management of a chronic condition, especially sicknesses in the realm of mental health that may defy methods of Western scientific treatment. In this sense, Read (2017, 172) observed that the practice of "trying out" medications from the hospital in the form of "pills or injections is as much part of the process of identifying a spiritual illness as consultations with healers or pastors" since "the success or failure of biomedicine is an important empirical marker of the cause and nature of illness."

After repeated forms of treatment have proved futile, including a visit to the psychiatric hospitals, patients and family members can resort to prayer camps to alleviate persistent suffering in the face of a chronic condition and its frequent fluctuations. The resort to prayer camps does not suggest a disbelief in biomedical science, but rather an additional resource to deal with the uncertainty of the nature and cause of the illness. Again, as Read (2017) observed, almost all the people she met during her fieldwork in Ghana had visited the psychiatric hospitals in search of a cure. This is not different from what I encountered at the prayer camps I visited in Ghana. What is at stake, however, is that the pluralistic nature of the belief systems fashions the "intracultural diversity and medical systems that are manipulated by patients according to the principles that go beyond traditional definitions of cultural specificity" (Jacobson-Widding and Westerlund 1989, 9).

Within this context, this chapter highlights both the individual and social role played by religious organizations facilitating prayer camps for the management of chronic mental illness in Ghana, and also explores how faith-based resources are harnessed in the search for wellness and wholeness. Although chronic illnesses have gained attention in health care globally (WHO 2005), far less attention has been placed on the role of religious institutions that can support this work. In fact, a decade and a half ago, Koenig (2009, 113) argued that "although the use of religion to help cope with stress is well established, less is known about how religious belief and activity are related to severe, persistent mental illness" and maybe other chronic health issues in general (Roger and Hatala 2017). In so doing, this is not an attempt to uncritically examine or romanticize the role of faith-based resources in the management of a chronic condition such as mental illness, but rather to uncover and outline the potential contribution, the local, cultural significance of the prayer camps, and such religious and/or faith-based resources that serve as an aspect of hope and wellness amidst uncertainty and chronicity.

Research methodology and methods

Design and positionality

This study is based on six months of fieldwork in Ghana. A qualitative phenomenological design was employed in an attempt to understand participants' own interpretation of their experiences of mental illness, its causal factors, and the various strategies adopted in remedying or managing its daily impacts. The design was useful in eliciting participants' narratives and lived experiences about self-care approaches used in the management of their conditions, how these approaches are related to the associated causes of mental illness, and specifically in exploring how religious and spiritual practices, both at the individual and community level, may support people in the management of chronic mental illnesses.

My own background as a Ghanaian with training in theology and religious studies gave me the necessary skills both conceptually and theoretically to examine the issues that underlie this study. My many years of visits to some of these prayer camps on personal pilgrimages were essential in providing an informed critique and analysis, as well as personal reflections from both emic and etic perspectives. In other words, the motivation to engage in a discussion such as this is influenced by my background knowledge of the camps and the role they offer in addressing an issue that has religious, public, and social significance.

Research setting and participants

Two major prayer camps were selected for the study, specifically in Cape Coast and Koforidua in the Central and Eastern regions of Ghana. The two camps were selected because they provide a good case example for the objectives and the central discussion made in this study. These camps have been in existence for over 60 and 25 years, respectively. Their long history and significant role and involvement in the management and the healing process of the mentally ill in Ghana were also influential.

The participants for this study were pastors, caregivers, and patients at the prayer camps. The patients were persons with a history of chronic mental health conditions who had started experiencing some level of wellness and were in a stable condition but were still living at the prayer camp. Reports from the caregivers and a psychiatric nurse who works at one of the camps indicated that some of the patients had previously visited the hospital and had been diagnosed with mental health conditions such as depression, schizophrenia, mania, and hallucinations. Some samples of medical reports on the patients are filed during registration at the prayer camp. The prayer camp, with the help of a nurse, also took the initiative of sending patients without any proper diagnosis to the hospital to obtain a formal medical diagnosis and in order to administer proper care and medication alongside supports offered at the camps. For the prayer camps, these medical reports were of much importance because they made evident the role of prayer and/or faith-based resources in helping deal with the problems of mental illness after repeated failed attempts from biomedical approaches.

Semi-structured interviews were conducted with 21 individuals involved with the camps, including four male pastors, six caregivers, five of whom were males and one female, and 11 individuals with a history of mental illness, which included seven males and four females. Their ages ranged from 26 to 65 years with a mean age of 38.5. For the pastors, the number of years they had practiced ranged from 15 to 35 years. The caregivers I interviewed had between 12 to 20 years' experience in taking care of the mentally ill at the camp. The caregivers had no formal training in psychology or psychiatry.

Participants with a history of mental health conditions had been previously diagnosed with severe forms of mental disorders including psychosis. Others had a history with drugs such as cocaine and cannabis. These participants had stayed at the camp for a period ranging from one to five years. Although the amount of time each participant was expected to remain at the camp was typically four months, explanation for their long duration of their stay indicates that they had been there as a result of the chronic or unstable condition of their mental illness. Some of them had had experiences of wellness and were discharged but later returned to the camp after relapse. Others had recovered but preferred staying at the camp because they felt safer and more "at home" with the care and support they received from the camp. Beyond the mental health concerns, other social and political factors, such as poverty, stigma, and discrimination, added to the reasons why some individuals preferred to stay at the camp.

Research process and procedure

The process to conduct interviews began first with a visit to the camps. My visit to each camp involved administrative procedures that included seeking research approval from camp leaders and clearance to conduct interviews. In the camps I visited, there were some levels of difficulty and resistance in getting verbal consent and approval from the camp leaders due to, according to them, the bad publicity they had received in previous times from some individuals who came to the camp with similar motives. They cited inappropriate reports, misinformation, or misrepresentation of their activities by some journalists in the media, and international bodies and human rights organizations as mentioned earlier. In consequence, they were suspicious of my true intentions. Eventually, after building relationships and trust over time and explaining the aims and objectives of the study, research permission was granted at two camps. In addition to ethical approval from the authorities of the prayer camps, ethics clearance for all aspects of this research was also granted through the Åbo Akademi University in Finland.

After approval from camp leaders, meetings were scheduled with caregivers in charge of the individuals at the camp. Prior to the meeting, I was taken on a "familiarization tour" at each of the camps, specifically in the sections where the mentally ill were kept. The tour brought into perspective a broader picture of the conditions of persons with chronic mental illness at the camp and further informed my discussion and interviews with the participants. Particularly, it helped in providing me with questions that were conceptually and theoretically relevant to the study. It also provided a basis in building rapport with those in charge of the camp residents and for subsequent recruitment for individual interviews of participants who were deemed to have "recovered" from their experience or are learning to manage well despite persistent challenge.

All interviews were conducted by the author. Languages used for the interview were English and Twi. The choice of language for a particular interviewee was dependent on the communication ability and fluency of the participant. However, in some cases, both languages were used interchangeably in a particular interview. The objectives of the study were first explained to the participants and verbal informed consent was obtained. Voluntary participation and withdrawal from the study at any time were assured. Participants were also assured of their confidentiality. All interviews were audio-recorded with permission and took place at the prayer camp. Time for each interview lasted approximately 60 minutes. Participants were asked about the story of their illness experience, their personal experience at the camp, and how the camp may have helped in the management of their illness.

Analysis

All interviews in both English and Twi were transcribed verbatim by the author. Interviews conducted in Twi were translated into English. In some instances, some of the words were translated back into Twi with the help of an independent linguist to ensure consistency and accuracy. Interpretative Phenomenological Analyzes (IPA) were used in analyzing the transcribed interviews (Smith et al. 2003). IPA afforded the researcher the opportunity to interpret and explain participants' own accounts of their experiences and the meaning they ascribed to them (Smith and Osborn 2003). The data were analyzed at two levels. The first level involved coding. Each transcript was coded two times to capture every detail of the conversation. The coding was done by the author. This enabled the researcher to systematically analyze the data and extract emerging patterns and ideas (Lindlof and Taylor 2017). At the second level, the transcribed interviews were analyzed manually using thematic analysis while following IPA. The thematic approach helped in classifying and presenting themes (patterns) that related to the data. The approach enabled the researcher to inductively extrapolate themes and preclude preconceived or anticipated themes.

The concept of healing (Appiah-Kubi 1981; Obeng 2004) and theories of chronicity (Estroff 1993) guided analysis as the study focused on the complexities of social and cultural understanding of illness and the role religion and spirituality played in negotiating personal identities in the face of persistent illness. A focus was placed on individual and group perceptions of mental illness and healing belief outcomes. Codes that shared relationships and addressed the main objectives of the study formed the basis of the identification or delineating of themes. Themes were further reviewed by the author and final results were generated into a systematic narrative with author's interpretations made with literature on chronicity, healing, and mental illness.

Results

There were four primary themes that emerged from the participants' accounts of dealing with personal fluctuations in the management of their chronic mental illness, and also caregivers' experiences in managing and offering care at the prayer camps, namely 1) perceived causes of mental illness, 2) the environment and sacred context of the prayer camp, 3) spiritual and physical resources in dealing with chronic mental illness, and 4) prayer camps and the management of stigma, discrimination, and exclusion.

Perceived causes of mental illness

Perceived cause(s) of mental illness largely contribute to a sense of uncertainty and dilemma in the attempt to find support for living a "normal" life. Throughout the study, participants expressed a belief in both the natural/physical and supernatural causes of mental illness, although the emphasis on the latter was more prominent (see also, Arias et al. 2016). As one camp leader expressed:

> We as black Africans, maybe the others don't believe, but when it even becomes difficult for them to bear, they rather end up turning to God for help. But for us, when you come here [prayer camp] to do something, then you have to believe that there is black power, there is African magic, witchcraft is there. You know those things? We the black people, there are curses too, envy is also there at the workplace. I will cause harm to you because I was there before you came. Why should you come for my position? We Africans too, sometimes the home you come from, no one does government work or go to school. If you try to go to school, they can make you go mad. If you try to get work from the public sector or get married, they can make you go mad. If you try to buy a car, buy designer shoes and dress, they will make go mad! This is there! For me, what I have seen with my eyes, no one can convince me that madness cannot be influenced or caused by evil forces. And if it is evil spirits that cause people to be mad, we also have to use the Spirit of God to drive the madness away.
>
> (prayer camp pastor 2)

Similarly, participants who were mentally ill and had recovered but were still staying at the camp also believed personally that their sickness was spiritually instigated. As one participant shared:

> My sickness was spiritual. If they had taken me to the asylum, then I don't believe I would have recovered. I was forever going to be in a state of illness because when they brought me here, no one gave me an injection or medicine. It was only prayer and the water they fetch from the cocoa farm (*cocoa ase nsuo*) and bathe me with that made me receive my healing. My hair and beard had developed dreadlocks…when I first came here, they took pictures of me. So, when I had my recovery, I realized that although the asylum is good, it doesn't help other people because if it is a spiritual attack like mine, there is no way the asylum can deal with it because you don't need those injections they give there. What you need is prayers!
>
> (participant 1)

Despite the Christian worldview that supernatural evil forces can be causes of mental illness like this above quote suggests, other views expressed by caregivers and patients indicate that physical causes of the sickness are not ruled out entirely:

> Indeed, the prayer camps help a lot…when you come to the prayer camp, we have our prophet there. The first welcome is to go and see him. He will pray for you and give you some directions (*akwankyere*). After three days, he will ask you to bring the person back and through that the healing takes place.

> Sometimes, he will also say God has done his part so take the person to the hospital for medical attention. When that is done then everything is balanced.
> (caregiver 3)

As outlined here, mental illness is believed to be primarily influenced or caused by supernatural evil spirits or forces. This notion of illness is reinforced by the theory of illness causation and the methods of healing. Yet, a mental illness is also considered to have both natural and supernatural causes. Obeng (2004) refers to this as a bipartite concept of illness denoting the ascription of illness to both the physical and the supernatural. With the physical, perceived pathogenic agents account for illness and sicknesses. In relation to the spiritual, a mental illness is believed to occur as a result of the breakdown of the social and moral code by an individual and/or offending a spirit or a deity in some way.[3] This may include ancestral spirits that pervade the local Pentecostal and Akan worldview, and/or a wrongdoing on the part of an individual or relative in the view of their ancestral spirits. Overall, most participants shared an assertion that malevolent spirits, such as those involved in witchcraft, or even a failure to perform a certain religious rite, are the primary causes of mental illness and disorder.

The environment and sacred context of the prayer camp

Since the participants and camp leaders attributed the cause of mental illness largely to supernatural agents, the prayer camp, as a religious space, was thus believed to provide the spiritual context and resources needed for recovery. Participants believed not only in the manifestation of a divine spiritual presence through prayers for faith healing, but that materials from the sacred ground of the camp were also endowed with a sacred quality and supernatural potency that manifested the presence of God for healing and restoration.

According to one of the pastors interviewed, the story surrounding the establishment of the camp made them believe that the camp was a special space demarcated by God through a vision revealed to the prophet and leader of the camp. As one leader shared: "In that vision, God gave him a complete picture of this place. It was a complete bush, far away from everywhere. But God gave him the picture of everything." According to the pastor, the prophet had a vision from God whilst he was fasting and praying at a prayer camp after he had gone through life crisis and failed attempts to live outside Ghana.

The leader's personal story of the prayer camp described a sacred place demarcated from its surroundings that holds religious significance and meaning, particularly with respect to the divine among those who patronize them (Thiessen and McAlpine 2013). The presence of church buildings and the observance of daily religious activities and social interactions facilitate both horizontal and vertical relationships between humans as well as between man and God or the spiritual world. In other words, one of the reasons that the prayer camp is regarded as a "sacred place" is because it is believed to be a meeting point between heaven and earth, a space between God and humanity.

The rechristening of a building, such as "the pool of Bethesda" for patients with severe forms of mental illness, draws their attention to the healing power of the divine (Kilde 2008). *Cocoa ase nsuo*, as mentioned by one respondent in the above quotations, literally means the water under the cocoa tree. This is a small river on the banks of one of the camps. According to one of the pastors interviewed, the prophet at one of the camps had a revelation from God to use the water for healing and other purposes as the Holy Spirit may direct. For mental illness and other diseases, it is understood that the *cocoa ase nsuo* aids wellness and recovery due to its associated sacramental value and therapeutic or ritualistic potential in effecting healing and transformation, something akin to a sensorial healing process (Hatala and Waldram 2016).

Apart from that, there is a general belief among patrons and visitors at the camp that the space around the cocoa tree makes people feel closer to nature while one mediates and prays to God. Interviews with participants revealed that individuals who go and pray at the space under the cocoa tree had encountered numerous miracles and breakthroughs in their lives and healing journeys. One can also argue that the spatial location, topography, and/or the geography of the prayer camp itself is therapeutic for visitors, patients, and worshippers. As many participants shared, the serene atmosphere, the low weather temperature as a result of the high plains, as well as the mountains and the natural environment has the tendency of reducing stress and anxiety, all common aspects of healing and wellness reported elsewhere (Hatala et al. 2020; Wood et al. 2017). It also helps one to cope with pain and this can contribute to one's health and wellness (Seymour 2016). These are a few of the potentially positive elements of the prayer camps that previous studies fail to appropriately acknowledge or highlight (Arias et al. 2016; Carey 2015; Edwards 2014).

Spiritual and physical resources in dealing with chronic mental illness

Patients also harness both spiritual and physical resources available at the prayer camp to find strength and build meaning amidst experiences of mental illness and chronicity. Such spiritual resources were described as healing rituals, exorcism or taking out of the evil spirits often associated with forms of witchcraft, "All-night" prayers, dawn prayer sessions, Bible studies, counselling services, and fasting. Fasting and prayers are a prerequisite for healing and everyone who is seeking any form of healing at the camps are encouraged to undergo a specific period of fasting, ranging from three to forty days, depending on the magnitude of one's illness and health condition. In Pentecostal and charismatic traditions as found in the prayer camps, fasting is a common practice. Some studies and other human rights reports suggest that fasting can be, at times, forced on the mentally ill at prayer camps in Ghana (Arias et al. 2016). Although there may be some select instances of this kind of abuse, this assertion or claim is not consistent across all the camps in Ghana. This current research, along with my own experience, suggests that the claim that fasting is being forced could be a misinterpretation on the part of non-Ghanaian observers who view these practices from secular orientations without understanding the religious milieu within which these activities take place. Many of the respondents I interviewed expressed positive indications about the role of fasting in their lives and how it has aided their recovery, mental health, and wellness. Additionally, in one of the prayer camps, a caregiver mentioned that individuals who are sick and are very weak are not allowed to go through fasting. For such individuals, their relatives who are willing and supportive to their wellness and healing process stay at the camp and fast on their behalf, if they desire. Indeed, in their observations of the practices at prayer camps in relation to fasting, Arias et al. (2016, 9) observed that "fasting was viewed as not necessary for all patients" and that "camps staff only encouraged patients without serious mental illnesses to fast, encouraging relatives or pastors to fast in the place of those unable to fast themselves." Regardless of these discussions, many participants in this study indicated a positive and rewarding experience in relation to their fasting, a finding other studies have noted as well (Cabo and Mattson 2019; Zhang et al. 2015).

Counselling services are also offered to everyone who reports to the camp with problems of mental illness and all other forms of ailments and problems. These services are handled by the prophet and, depending on the veracity of the issue, a referral is often made to a mental health specialist or the hospital for further assessment. In such cases, after meeting with specialists at the hospital, patients are then typically referred back to the camp to be further assisted with prayers, alongside the continued administration of Western medicine. In some cases where spiritual causal factors are ruled out, spiritual resources at the camp are still seen as helpful in terms of existential, social, and emotional support, and overall patient wellness.

There are also frequent Bible studies offered at the camp aimed at building and releasing the faith of patients for further support and healing. The "Word of God" in the Christian sense is used to motivate, to give hope and comfort for emotional and psychological needs, and to help people find positive interpretations of difficult experiences. As the participants and caregivers outlined, a number of Christian scriptures, such as Philippians 4:4, 7, 8, 13, and 19, are regularly used, read, and meditated on in dealing with anxiety and depression or other conditions at the camps. These spiritual resources are often described as being "therapeutic" in nature and provide some forms of meaning in relieving anxieties and emotional stress from chronic mental health conditions. For some of the patients, these acts also helped them get closer to God and pray more for "breakthroughs" in their healing and wellness journey. As one person reflected: "The Bible studies and all meetings are helpful. Sometimes you hear the stories of other people during church service and that gives you hope." For others, what they learned from the Word of God helped transform their lives and helped them recover from their chronic illness, habits, and behavior that contributed to their mental illnesses, including addiction and drug abuse:

> Essentially, it has been about the kind of advice and the spiritual activities we engage ourselves in at this place. My caregiver sometimes calls, sits me down and talks to me. He will ask me to sit beside him and he will give me

plenty of advice using the scriptures. He will ask me to compare myself to the other people. Then I will realize that the difference is now better as a result of me being at this place... I have been here before. But I went home and went back to my old ways, so I came back again. I have spent like one year now and I haven't gone back home again. I am here all the time.

(participant 8)

As outlined, the spiritual activities at the camp aided many individuals in their recovery from chronic habits, like smoking, drinking, or drugs, or provided a sense of deeper meaning underlying or sense of wellness within their chronic conditions.

In terms of physical resources, the prayer camps provide a conducive atmosphere by providing rooms or dormitories to house patients. By conducive atmosphere, I am referring to a provision of suitable environment devoid of any setbacks that will retrogress the recovery of patients but help cope with their situation. Yet, living conditions in terms of the provision of accommodation or housing may not be as perfect as one would imagine or wish to have at their homes. Most prayer camps in Ghana are financially limited and as a result are faced with the challenge of providing hostel facilities for their visitors. Nonetheless, there are camps (especially the ones used for the purpose of this study) that have managed at least to provide suitable forms of dormitories and hostel facilities for their visitors and patients. Thus, when considering diversity across the different prayer camps in Ghana, variation of living conditions does, of course, exist and should be acknowledged (Arias et al. 2016).

Although, patients are required to pay some amount of money for their daily subsistence, this is problematic for many who are not able to pay due to financial constraints. One caregiver expressed the following concerns:

To tell you the truth, here the patients only pay a little amount of money for their care and support. Most of the things are coming from papa [prophet and leader of the camp]. Because for some of them, they just bring the person here and they will not come back here again. We feed them both morning and evening. So, if we don't have anything with us, we just go to him and say old man [prophet] things are not going well too. Then he knows we are out of food items...We use some to also pay for the utility bills.

(caregiver 1)

He continued:

For the patients, some are willing to pay the monthly charge of 200 *cedis*. However, for most of them, their condition has been there for long [chronicity] and they have spent a lot of money searching for cure or solution at different places. By the time they come here, they have nothing to contribute to their upkeep and welfare while here. Everything now depends on us!

(caregiver 1)

The caregiver and the prophet's effort in providing some of the basic material facilities has greatly contributed in easing stress and frustrations usually encountered by people with chronic mental illness Ghana. In this way, too, the provision of shelter, care, love, and support fosters in patients a sense of community feeling that further supports their wellness and healing journeys. Sharing their experiences about such resources, some patients recounted: "My family don't bring me anything here but I eat and am okay. Gradually am becoming better. I feel like I'm home. For me, I even want to live here and not go anywhere again." As another person said: "The support we are receiving here is amazing. For me, it has helped to me forget about many things that were not helping my condition." And as another respondent also reflected about the relationships and community engendered at the camps:

> What is really important to me is that you have people here you can look up to. Our leader especially gives us some hope. We see others being prayed for getting their healing. It all helps us to have faith and pray more. It helps us to get more closer to God in anticipation.

Despite a lack of material resources that can exist, the shared experience and deep spiritual relationships of care and trust universally enhanced patients' connection with God, feelings of support, community connection, belonging, and wellness, as they are surrounded by others who share similar beliefs and faith in a supportive, positive, and uplifting environment.

Prayer camps and the management of stigma, discrimination, and exclusion

Social stigma, discrimination, and exclusion are often daily lived experiences encountered by persons with mental health problems (Mehta and Thornicroft 2013). In many ways, these forms of social suffering contribute significantly to, and worsen, the social plight of persons living with chronic mental health conditions in Ghana. As participants explained, prayer camps were aiding individuals with mental health conditions to cope with the problem of stigma, discrimination, and exclusion by creating a community of "brothers and sisters." Many caregivers and patients expressed how the prayer camp was offering social support and serving as a source of hope and restoration:

> You see, no one walks to the pharmacy shop and says I want to buy a drug or medicine that causes mental illness. What has happened to them can happen to any individual or person. We live together with them as brothers and sisters. That's why for many of them, after they have recovered, they don't want to go home…We don't discriminate against them.
>
> (caregiver 4)

The idea of living of "together with them as brothers and sisters" denotes the close knitted relationships that are built and exist between the caregivers and patients. At the camp, caregivers freely interact with patients. The caregivers and people living at the camp relate not as patient and client, but as friends and family. For some of the patients, these activities helped them to deal with anxieties, build their confidence level, regain control, and find meaning for their lives.

Interviews with participants also suggest that the problem of stigma, discrimination, and exclusion is largely encountered outside the camp, from the home, community, or even at the workplace. These experiences make life unbearable and sometimes worsen their mental illness. As one participant shared:

> You see, sometimes when they see you coming then they want to hide themselves. It was as if you are no longer a human being. It is very depressing. It worsens your case because you feel lonely and you begin to think about rejection and now maybe you feel like even committing suicide because no one wants you around him or her.

Another participant shared a similar view:

> As for mental illness like the one I went through, the problem here is the stigma. Both the family, society, friends, and love ones all think you are not useful any longer. I lost my relationship. I lost my job.
>
> (participant 9)

In many ways, individuals suffering from mental illness and other chronic conditions are, sometimes, rendered hopeless and marginalized by their families or communities due to the challenges associated with treatment and caregiving (Stanford and McAlister 2008). Moreover, mental health practitioners and family members who become exasperated with these challenges and the daily "homework" of care often give up in the health care and management of the sick person (Mattingly, Gron and Meinert 2011). Indeed, in some cases, I observed families and communities did not want to accept or associate with the person due to a sense of stigma:

> Some of them leave here, their families are not ready to receive them. Then they will return to the camp. Even when the person is showing signs of wellness, the community will be pointing fingers at him, "Oh, this man, he was insane." So, many people don't get closer to them. Then they have to return to where they will welcome him or her. Because you see, when the thing happened, he would sometimes break car windscreens, walk naked in his or her neighborhood and so forth. When you tell them the person is healed or better, some people don't really believe it. So, the person will come back and say that when I went home, I wasn't received. Then we would have to accept him or her back. That's the kind of problem we are in now.
>
> (caregiver 4)

Despite the obvious challenges that come with taking care of persons with chronic mental health conditions, the prayer camps offer an enabling, supportive environment and sacred community needed to help restore hope amidst persistent fluctuations of individuals' conditions. They are functioning as "informal health sectors" (Mattingly, Gron and Meinert 2011) with minimal or no support from appropriate health authorities or government agencies in Ghana. Reacting to this challenge, one of the leaders of the prayer camps said:

> That has been our biggest challenge but that is the essence of we being a Christian organization. You can't just throw them out there. Interestingly enough, there are also some who would not even like to go because they feel more comfortable here. We help them through different socialization processes as well.
>
> (prayer camp pastor 1)

In attesting to the support offered by the prayer camp in dealing with stigma and exclusion, a participant indicated:

> I feel very good staying here. I have been here for three years now. The people here live and relate with me as family. When I even go home, they still think I am mad, and people don't want to associate with me. Here too, no one will point fingers at you or something. My family members even hardly come here to visit me. But I am hoping and trusting God that everything will be fine. I owe the camp leader every gratitude. They have been very supportive and have shown concern and care to me and I now feel a sense of belongingness.
>
> (participant 10)

The situation at the camp is different from what pertains outside. At the camp, patients are treated with care and respect. They are made to feel loved and are given the necessary support and attention as part of a community. The demonstration of love frees up individual distress, anxieties, and disappointments that are often associated with chronic conditions and mental illness. It enhances an individual's relationship with others and God, and helps in the production of the religious and social capital needed for their recovery. In essence, the camps provide patients with meaning and a sense of personal value that counters segregation, discrimination, or fragmentation encountered in Ghanaian society outside the camp.

Discussion

The stories and experiences presented in this study highlight how the prayer camps in Ghana can help some individuals with chronic mental illness to better deal with their anxieties, recurrent or persistent behaviors, aspects of social stigma and discrimination, as well as the dilemma and uncertainties surrounding the beliefs, causes, and treatment of the chronic aspects of their mental illnesses. Although biological factors are not entirely disregarded, religious and spiritual beliefs associated with the illness are pervasive, and, as a result, faith-based approaches or spiritual resources are most often harnessed in mitigating and remedying illness experiences. These and many other interventions mentioned in this study are some of the positive ways the prayer camps are helping individuals with chronic mental conditions manage their situation through personal approaches, community-based strategies, and sacred aspects to the prayer camps, which can lead to improved mental wellness.

Issues of human rights abuses at the camps still need to be critically engaged with and discussed, yet these issues are not the case everywhere and in all prayer camps demonstrate, especially the ones used as the focus of this study. Similarly, Arias et al. (2016) also mentioned that some prayer camps "emphatically rejected" any form of corporal punishment or abuse. For instance, chaining is not universally applied and the attempt to generalize such claims only results in oversimplification of the activities of the camps. This study illustrates that not all prayer camps are engaged in human rights abuse and it would be unfair to generalize their activities into one whole as some studies seem to suggest. This would also lead the mental health and research communities to miss the positive and helpful role that the prayer camps do potentially offer for the lives of those suffering from chronic mental illness.

The idea of the camp as a sacred space for healing and deliverance provides an important context for the reconstruction of new identities. The camps remain, in a sense, nature sanctuaries were patients with no hope or sense of security in wider society find solace, cope with their illness, and bolster overall wellness (Seymour 2016). Individuals with a history of drug abuse report how fasting, prayers, and motivational messages from their caregivers had helped them to reflect on their lives, find meaning amidst challenge, and change from their old ways and self-defeating practices (Mustain and Helminiak 2015). This, significantly, points to the many ways in which the camps remain an important faith-based resource in helping individuals manage their chronic conditions. The religious and spiritual practices at the camp improve coping mechanisms and offer social support that fosters optimism and hope in the midst of crisis. Participants believe that staying at the camp helps in managing their fears, recurrent behaviors, and lifestyle that cause them to retrogress and take away any eventual promise of restoration. These findings are consistent with other studies that have shown that religion and spirituality play a crucial role in managing chronic conditions such as mental health (Garrett 2002; Gojer, Gopalakrishnan and Kuruvilla 2018; Koenig 2009; Park 2016). Koenig (2018, 164), for instance, has argued that most mental health patients mobilize religious beliefs and practices in managing stress to derive comfort, meaning, control, and social support. Others have also indicated how faith-based and/or spiritual practices are employed as coping mechanisms in ill-health situations to promote a general positive view of life (Hank and Schaan 2008).

Although scholars have been critical about the influence of evil forces and the role of or effectiveness of religion and spirituality in addressing the challenges of mental illness (Edwards 2014; Krause 2015), questions about whether or not illness could be influenced or caused by supernatural evil forces is not a very important one, in my view. Rather, a careful and thoughtful evaluation of people's theory of causation of illness helps in developing culturally and socially embedded approaches that have the tendency to provide holistic clinical measures to deal with ill health situations (Kirmayer and Swartz 2013). The important issue is that the belief in such forces exists, and this view is widely held in most African communities or societies, and even in a pervasive way in some Western countries or sub-groups (Stanford and McAlister 2008). The findings presented here point to a significant trust and confidence participants have in prayer camps in providing the needed interventions in managing and restoring hope and wellness amidst chronic uncertainties, especially in cases where scientific medicine is unable to offer help, or where families were unable to live with their loved ones any longer. The findings also show how people's causal explanations and beliefs of illness influence their decision-making behavior for treatment (Yendork et al. 2017, 2019).

There was a consensus among the participants interviewed about the ability of the prayer camps to provide meaningful relationships regarding care, networking, and social support. Patients at the camp often expressed the view that they felt loved, protected, and cared for, more so while at the camp than at home. Along with the housing and provision of basic material needs, this helps individuals deal with the management of their chronic condition and other related challenges associated with mental illness, such as counselling, medications, or treatment regimens. These findings show how the camps' caregivers understand the predicaments of the mentally ill, and the ways in which they function as forms of social mechanisms that are crucial in producing strength, building their confidence level, and taking them out of their destructive consequences as a result of their chronic conditions. The structural arrangements at the camp, whereby the caregivers freely interact and socialize with the patients, help in building the confidence of the patients and a safe and supportive environment for healing and wellness. They also ensure love and care, which are ingredients that are crucial in managing distress (Ammerman 2013; Turner 1969).

Conclusion: Toward intersectoral partnerships

The qualitative data presented in this study highlight the role played by faith-based resources in the management of chronic conditions in general and mental illness in particular. In a political and economic environment that is relatively starved of medical practitioners in the field of psychiatry and mental health care, treatment facilities, and appropriate funding (Ofori-Atta, Read and Lund 2010), prayer camps in Ghana have emerged as an alternative source of hope, care, and support. The prayer camps are situated as borderlands of mental health care in this context, holding individual, social, and religious significance (Mattingly, Gron and Meinert 2011). This study recommends the need for the government and state actors in the field of psychiatry and global mental health to develop policies and strategies in regulating the activities of prayer camps in the area of mental health care (Kirmayer and Swartz 2013). There is also a need for a sustained and integrative collaboration and/or intersectoral partnership between community health units and caregivers, healers or prophets serving at the prayer camps. In this vain, I agree with Arias et al. (2016) on the recommendation to assist prayer camps in providing interventions and intersectoral health care collaboration that will help improve the quality of life of patients at the camps. Specifically, the need for intersectoral partnerships, cooperation, open discussion, and engagement between medical staff and spiritual care workers that will help address some of the deleterious practices found in some prayer camps would be helpful in future work. Such collaborations or partnerships will likely ensure that training and proper care can enhance mutual understanding and respect among health care professionals, and thereby increase the support and wellness for mental illness patients and their families in Ghana.

Notes

1 The Akan is the largest ethnic group in Ghana, making up about 48% of the entire population. They include the Ashanti, Fanti, Bono, Ahanta, Adansi, Nzema, Akuapem, etc. (Meyerowitz 1958).
2 In Ghana, the founders or leaders of most of the established prayer camps are referred to as "prophets," both in and outside the camp. They are individuals believed to be endowed with the Holy Spirit, which allows them to see beyond the physical and thus communicate with the spiritual realm, diagnose, and bring solutions to people's problems through the intervention of the Holy Spirit. The name "prophet" holds religious and social significance in Ghana, due to the transcendental orientation of the people and also their assumed mediatory role.
3 A recent example in Ghana is the outbreak of COVID-19, where both traditional religious authorities and the church offered prayers and sacrifices to God to forgive the sins of the land and restore deliverance to the people.

References

Ae-Ngibise, Kenneth, Sara Cooper, Edward Adiibokah, Bright Akpalu, Crick Lund, Victor Doku. 2010. "'Whether You Like It or Not People With Mental Problems Are Going To Go To Them': A Qualitative Exploration Into the Widespread Use of Traditional and Faith Healers in the Provision of Mental Health Care in Ghana." *International Review of Psychiatry* 22: 558–567. doi:10.3109/09540261.2010.536149

Ammerman, Nancy. 2013. *Sacred Stories, Spiritual Tribes: Finding Religion in Everyday Life*. New York: Oxford University Press.

Amfo, Nana Aba Appiah, Ekua Essumanma Houphouet, Eugene K. Dordoye and Rachel Thompson. 2018. "'Insanity is From Home': The Expression of Mental Health Challenges in Akan." *International Journal of Language and Culture* 5 (1): 1–28. doi:10.1075/ijolc.16016.amf

Appiah-Kubi, Kofi. 1981. *Man Cures God Heals: Religion and Medical Practice among the Akan of Ghana*. New York: Friendship Press.

Arias, Daniel, Lauren Taylor, Angela Ofori-Atta and Elizabeth H. Bradly. 2016. "Prayer Camps and Biomedical Care in Ghana: Is Collaboration in Mental Health Care Possible?" *PLoS ONE* 11 (9): e0162305. doi:10.1371/journal.pone.0162305

Asamoah, Moses Kumi, Joseph Osafo and Isaac Agyapong. 2014. "The Role of Pentecostal Clergy in Mental Health-Care Delivery in Ghana." *Mental Health, Religion and Culture* 17 (6): 601–614. doi:10.1080/13674676.2013.871628

Atiemo, Abamfo Ofori. 2017. "In Need of a New Lens: An African Christian Scholar's Religious Critique of Western European Attitudes Toward Religion and Development in Africa." *Religion and Theology* 24: 250–273. doi:10.1163/15743012-02403005

Barke, Antonia, Seth Nyarko and Dorothee Klecha. 2011. "The Stigma of Mental Illness in Southern Ghana: Attitudes of the Urban Population and Patients' Views." *Social Psychiatry and Psychiatric Epidemiology* 46, 1191–1202. doi:10.1007/s00127-010-0290-3

BBC News. 2018. "Caged while Seeking Mental Health Help." Accessed February 12, 2019 from www.youtube.com/watch?v=p9Pl0MGu2YQ

Brown, Candy Gunther. 2011. "Introduction: Pentecostalism and the Globalisation of Illness and Healing." In *Global Pentecostal and Charismatic Healing*, edited by Candy Gunther Brown, 3–26. Oxford: Oxford University Press. doi:10.1093/acprof:oso/9780195393408.003.0001

Cabo, Rafeal de, and Mark P. Mattson. 2019. "Effects of Intermittent Fasting on Health, Aging, and Disease." *New England Journal of Medicine* 381: 2541–2551. doi:10.1056/NEJMra1905136

Carey, Benedict. 2015. "The Chains of Mental Illness in West Africa." *The New York Times*, October 11, 2015. Accessed May 20, 2021 from www.nytimes.com/2015/10/12/health/the-chains-of-mental-illness-in-west-africa.html?emc=edit_th_20151012&nl=todaysheadlines&nlid=59924205&_r=0\nhttp://www.nytimes.com/video/health/100000003764816/praying-for-a-cure.html

Clarke, Clifton. 2014. "Jesus in Theology and Experience of African Pentecostals." In *Pentecostal Theology in Africa*, edited by Clifton Clarke, 58–76. Eugene: Pickwick Publications.

Edwards, Jocelyn. 2014. "Ghana's Mental Health Patients Confined to Prayer Camps." *The Lancet* 383. doi:10.1016/S0140-6736(13)62717-8

Estroff, Sue. 1993. "Identity, Disability, and Schizophrenia: The Problem of Chronicity." In *Knowledge, Power and Practice: The Anthropological of Medicine and Everyday Life*, edited by Shirley Lindenbaum and Margaret Lock, 247–286. Berkeley: University of California Press.

Garrett, Catherine. 2002. "Spirituality and Healing in the Sociology of Chronic Illness." *Health Sociology Review* 11 (1): 61–69. doi:10.5172/hesr.2002.11.1-2.61

Gojer, Abigail, Rajesh Gopalakrishnan and Anju Kuruvilla. 2018. "Coping and Spirituality Among Caregivers of Patients with Schizophrenia: A Descriptive Study from South India." *International Journal of Culture and Mental Health* 11 (4): 362–372. doi:10.1080/17542863.2017.1391856

Hank, Karsten, and Barbara Schaan. 2008. "Cross-National Variations in the Correlation between Frequency of Prayer and Health among Older Europeans." *Research on Aging* 30 (1): 36–54. doi:10.1177/0164027507307923

Hatala, Andrew R., Chinyere Njeze, Darrien Morton, Tamara Pearl and Kelley Bird-Naytowhow. 2020. "Land and Nature as Sources of Health and Resilience among Indigenous Youth in an Urban Canadian Context: A Photovoice Exploration." *BMC Public Health* 20 (538): 1–14. doi:10.1186/s12889-020-08647-z

Hatala, Andrew R., and James B. Waldram. 2016. "The Role of Sensorial Processes in Q'eqchi' Maya Healing: A Case Study of Depression and Bereavement." *Transcultural Psychiatry* 53 (1): 60–80. doi:10.1177/1363461515599328

Heuser, Andreas. 2015. "Encoding Caesar's Realm – Variants of Spiritual Warfare Politics in Africa." In *Pentecostalism in Africa: Presence and Impact of Pneumatic Christianity in Postcolonial Societies*, edited by Martin Lindhardt, 270–290. Leiden: Brill. doi:10.1163/9789004281875_012

Human Rights Watch. 2012. "*Like a Death Sentence: Abuses against Persons with Mental Disabilities in Ghana.*" Accessed 2019 from www.hrw.org/report/2012/10/02/death-sentence/abuses-against-persons-mental-disabilities-ghana

Jacobson-Widding, Anita, and David Westerlund. 1989. *Culture, Experience and Pluralism: Essays on African Ideas of Illness and Healing.* Uppsala: Uppsala Studies in Cultural Anthropology.

Kirmayer, Laurence J., and Leslie Swartz. 2013. "Culture and Global Mental Health." In *Global Mental Health: Principles and Practice*, edited by V. Patel, H. Minas, A. Cohen and M.J. Prince, 41–62. Oxford: Oxford University Press.

Kilde, Jeanne Halgren. 2008. *Sacred Power, Sacred Space: An Introduction to Christian Architecture and Worship.* New York: Oxford University Press.

Koenig, Harold G. 2009. *Faith and Mental Health: Religious Resources for Healing.* Philadelphia and London: Templeton Foundation Press.

Koenig, Harold G. 2018. *Religion and Mental Health: Research and Clinical Applications.* London: Academic Press.

Kpobi, Lily, and Leslie Swartz. 2018. "Explanatory Models of Mental Disorders among Traditional and Faith Healers in Ghana." *International Journal of Culture and Mental Health* 11 (4): 605–615. doi:10.1080/17542863.2018.1468473

Krause, Neal. 2015. "Religious Doubt, Helping Others, and Psychological Well-being." *Journal of Religion and Health* 54 (2): 745–758.

Larbi, E. Kingsley. 2001. *Pentecostalism: The Eddies of Ghanaian Christianity.* Accra: Blessed Publications.

Lindlof, T. R. and B. C. Taylor. 2017. *Qualitative Communication Research Methods.* London: Sage Publications.

Mattingly, Cheryl, Lone Grøn and Lotte Meinert. 2011. "Chronic Homework in Emerging Borderlands of Healthcare." *Culture, Medicine, and Psychiatry* 35 (3): 347–375. doi:10.1007/s11013-011-9225-z

Mehta, Nisha, and Graham Thornicroft. 2013. "Stigma, Discrimination, and Promoting Human Rights." In *Global Mental Health: Principles and Practice*, edited by V. Patel, H. Minas, A. Cohen and M.J. Prince, 401–424. Oxford: Oxford University Press.

Meyerowitz, Eva L.R. 1958. *The Akan of Ghana: Their Ancient Beliefs.* London: Faber & Faber Limited.

Mustain, Joshua R., and Daniel Helminiak. 2015. "Understanding Spirituality in Recovery from Addiction: Reintegrating the Psyche to Release the Human Spirit." *Addiction Research and Theory* 23 (5): 364–371. doi:10.3109/16066359.2015.1011623

Obeng, Cecilia S. 2004. *Voices of Affliction: Aspects of Traditional Healing Practices and their Impact on Akan families in Ghana.* Cologne: Rudiger Koeppe Verlag.

Ofori-Atta, A., Ursula M.Read and C.A. Lund. 2010. "Situation Analysis of Mental Health Services and Legislation in Ghana: Challenges for Transformation." *African Journal of Psychiatry* 13: 99–108. doi:10.4314/ajpsy.v13i2.54353.

Park, Christine J. 2016. "Chronic Shame: A Perspective Integrating Religion and Spirituality." *Journal of Religion and Spirituality in Social Work: Social Thought* 35 (4): 354–376. doi:10.1080/15426432.2016.1227291

Read, Ursula M. 2017. "'Doctor Sickness' of 'Pastor Sickness'? Contested Domains of Healing Power in the Treatment of Mental Illness in Kintampo, Ghana" In *Spirit & Mind: Mental Health at the Intersection of Religion & Psychiatry*, edited by H. Basu, R. Littlewood and A. Steinforth, 167–188. Berlin: Lit Verlag.

Read, Ursula M., Edward Adiibokah and Soloman Nyame. 2009. "Local Suffering and the Global Discourse of Mental Health and Human Rights: An Ethnographic Study of

Responses to Mental Illness in Rural Ghana." *Global Health* 5: 13. doi:10.1186/1744-8603-5-13

Read, Ursual M., and V.C.K. Doku. 2012. "Mental Health Research in Ghana: A Literature Review." *Ghana Medical Journal* 46: 29–38.

Roger, Kerstin Stieber, and Andrew R. Hatala. 2017. "Religion, Spirituality and Chronic Illness: A Scoping Review and Implications for Health Care Practitioners." *Journal of Religion and Spirituality in Social Work* 37 (1): 24–44. doi:10.1080/15426432.2017.1386151

Seymour, Valentine. 2016. "The Human-Nature Relationship and its Impact on Health: A Critical Review." *Front Public Health* 4 (260): 1–12. doi:10.3389/fpubh.2016.00260

Smith, Jonathan A., Mike Osborn and Glynis M. Breakwell. 2003. "Interpretative Phenomenological Analysis." In *Qualitative Psychology: A Practical Guide to Research Methods*, edited by J. A. Smith, 51–80. London: Sage Publications.

Stanford, Matthew S., and Kandace R. McAlister. 2008. "Perceptions of Serious Mental Illness in the Local Church." *Journal of Religion, Disability and Health* 12 (2): 144–153. doi:10.1080/15228960802160654

Thiessen, Joel, and Bill McAlpine. 2013. "Sacred Space: Function and Mission from a Sociological and Theological Perspective." *International Journal for the Study of the Christian Church* 13 (2): 133–146. doi:10.1080/1474225X.2013.781911

Turner, Victor. 1969. *The Ritual Process: Structure and Anti-Structure*. Ithaca: Cornell University Press.

United Nations Human Rights Council. 2013. "Ghana's Criminal Justice and Mental Health Practices Needs Critical Attention to be More Humane." Accessed 2019 from www.ohchr.org/EN/NewsEvents/Pages/DisplayNews.aspx?NewsID=13990.23888591

Wood, Lisa, Paula Hooper, Sarah Foster and Fiona Bull. 2017. "Public Green Spaces and Positive Mental Health - Investigating the Relationship Between Access, Quantity, and Types of Parks and Mental Wellbeing." *Health Place* 48: 63–71.

World Health Organization [WHO]. 2005. *Preventing Chronic Diseases: A Vital Investment*. Geneva: World Health Organization.

Yendork, Joana Salifu, Gladys Beryl Brew, Elizabeth A. Sarfo and Lily Kpobi. 2019. "Mental Illness has Multiple Causes: Beliefs on Causes Mental Illness by Congregants of Selected Neo-Prophetic Churches in Ghana." *Mental Health, Religion and Culture* 21 (7): 647–666. doi:10.1080/13674676.2018.1511694

Yendork, Joana Salifu, Lily Kpobi and Elizabeth A. Sarfo. 2017. "'It's Only Madness that I Know': An Analysis of How Mental Illness is Conceptualized by Congregants of Selected Charismatic Churches in Ghana." *Mental Health, Religion and Culture* 19 (9): 984–999. doi:10.1080/13674676.2017.1285877

Zhang, Yifan, Changhong Liu, Yinghao Zhao, Xinggyi Zhang, Bingjin Li and Ranji Cui. 2015. "The Effects of Calorie Restriction in Depression and Potential Mechanisms." *Current Neuropharmacology* 13 (4): 536–542. doi:10.2174/1570159x13666150326003852

10 "God takes care of it"

Spiritual practices and mental wellness of people living with type 2 diabetes in Belize

Lindsay Allen, Lucia Ellis and Andrew R. Hatala

Introduction

This study originated from a multi-organisation collaboration[1] with the purpose of learning about how to prevent type 2 diabetes mellitus[2] from worsening in Belize. Diabetes is a major concern in Belize where the prevalence for adults (20 to 79 years of age) is 17.1% of the population, up from 9.8% in 2010 (World Data Atlas 2019). Belize ranks fifth poorest in the world and the poorest in amalgamated South and Central America for diabetes prevalence (WHR 2019). The proportional mortality attributable to diabetes has increased from 5.6% in 2001 to 11.95% of total deaths in 2019, and it is considered the leading cause of death in Belize alongside coronary heart disease (WHO 2016a; WHR 2019). There is high prevalence of the diabetes risk factors of being overweight (50.5%) and obese (20.6%) respectively (WHO 2016a). In a 2018 study of a random sample of Belizeans, 33.1% were found to be in a prediabetes range, while 8.5% of those were undiagnosed (Isabel 2018). Hospitalisation rates for diabetes-related complications such as heart attacks, strokes, renal failure, and amputations are also rising in Belize, a country considered among the "least developed" in Latin America (UNDP, n.d.).

There is an intricate latticework of intermingling ethnicities and cultures in Belize, with a population that self-identified in the 2010 Census as 53% Mestizo, 26% Afro-descendant Creole, 11% Indigenous Mayan (including three distinct groups, namely Yucatec, Mopan, and Q'eqchi'), 6% Garifuna, as well as Mennonite, Middle Eastern, Indian, and Asian. As such, the country is not only a notable place to advance prevention and intervention of diabetes (due to prevalence), but also to study the implications of chronic disease management in a context of cultural multiplicity (SIB 2013; OYE 2017). Living with chronic illness is challenging in any country, but chronicity takes on a specific meaning unique to Belize, as does wellness and resilience. An important pillar of resilience for people living with diabetes in Belize is found in spiritual or religious[3] attitudes and practices. Diabetes prevention, education, and treatment interventions that are designed to be culturally appropriate and take into account patient spirituality or religiosity in self-management strategies have been shown to positively affect health outcomes (George et al. 2013; Koenig 2014; Rivera-Hernandez 2016; Roger and Hatala 2017; Sridhar 2013; WHO 2018). This culturally sensitive care is not consistently

DOI: 10.4324/9781003043508-10

available in Belize, however, and it could represent an important overlooked resource for mental health support and promotion (Balboni et al. 2015; Koenig 2014, 2004).

We maintain that it is important to understand how patients' spirituality or religiosity affects compliance with care plans, health behaviours, coping with chronicity, mental health, wellness goals, social supports, physical functioning, and overall health in order to deliver care that best serves the people who utilise it. When health services are incongruent with the beliefs and cultural practices of the people they are meant to serve, patient uptake of care and adherence to care plans are negatively impacted (Anderson 2017; Waldram 2008), and this is often heightened in Indigenous contexts and cultures. With the Belize health system's efforts to curb the growing rates of diabetes and its complications, it is crucial to understand the perspectives of patients themselves regarding what works in diabetes care and self-management (Anderson 2017). In this chapter we will explore how the spiritual practices of people living with diabetes in Belize affect their commitment to self-management, their psychosocial health, and their mental wellness or their ability to transcend the difficulties of living with chronicity.

Chronicity and diabetes in Belize

Rates of diabetes (and other chronic illnesses) are swiftly rising around the world (Rivera-Hernandez 2016; WHO 2018). In their volume on chronicity and experiences of illness, Manderson and Smith-Morris (2010, 6) described causes of obesity and diabetes as "a result of economic transition: from agricultural subsistence to one of industrial wage labour…" and "the resulting decrease in physical activity and overconsumption of high-fat, nutritionally poor foods consistently and reliably produce poor metabolic health." These authors outlined the varying emergence of diabetes chronicity burdens across low-, middle-, and high-income countries, then state that populations are now affected worldwide regardless of "social boundaries of class or wealth" (Manderson and Smith-Morris 2010, 10). While its swelling prevalence is universal, diabetes is exacerbated by conditions of poverty, precarity, and structural violence; patients, for example, cannot take medications they cannot afford (Weaver and Mendenhall 2014).

A common feeling in Belize is that "everyone has diabetes" regardless of class, race, ethnicity, age, sex, or gender, though statistical evidence stratified across categories is scant (key informant, 2020). Literature specific to Belize agrees with the wider assertion that diabetes places a disproportional burden on Low-Middle Income Countries (LMICs), and within the country, there may be pockets of lower average incomes and higher diabetes prevalence (Dekker et al. 2017; WHO 2016b). A mixed-methods study by Dekker et al. (2017) found that the village of Elderidge, near Punta Gorda in southern Belize, had 79% of its population living below the poverty line and that diabetes was poorly controlled in 74% of patients. Physicians in this study were concerned regarding prescribing insulin for patients without refrigeration, with low levels of health literacy, and with limited education on disease process and self-management strategies (Dekker et al. 2017). The study also revealed a need for more wellness and lifestyle counselling for diabetes patients, including locally relevant nutrition advice; "We eat what we can afford," is how one participant framed the issue (Dekker et al. 2017, 8).

In 2014, Gulley and colleagues studied an occupational diabetes screening program at a major corporation in Belize and found that half of the employees had elevated glycaemic levels, most of the employees had previously been unaware. They cited economic constraints in purchasing diabetes-friendly food products (e.g., quality protein, complex carbohydrates, multigrain) as a major issue for employees (Gulley et al. 2014). Similarly, for the employees who did know they had diabetes, it was difficult to afford glucometers, testing strips, and oral medication, resulting in inadequate glycaemic control (Gulley et al. 2014). While this article shows potential in the areas of corporate social responsibility and worker productivity-driven research, and demonstrates a high, hidden prevalence, it also highlights the need to address the added burdens of mental wellness and the accessibility of nutritious food and medical supplies.

A university group from the United States carried out an education and screening program with the general public in Punta Gorda (Belize) and six of its surrounding villages in 2011 (Brown et al. 2013). Although less than 5% of participants reported experiencing diabetes symptoms, they found that 52.6% of participants had elevated blood glucose. Further, while Body Mass Index (BMI) is a globally accepted risk factor for diabetes, this data set showed no relationship, leading authors to question what kind of variation was underlying the difference that is manifesting in this part of Belize. Thus, while using patient BMI as a risk factor is tempting,[4] it is inadequate on its own, making blood glucose testing even more important; however, testing supplies are expensive and in short supply in Belize. Regardless of lacking prevalence data by income category, there are substantial economic factors to overcome in stretching T2DM prevention and treatment planning across Belize. As institutions are an important part of the interplay of forces exacerbating the condition, interdisciplinary cooperation is needed for solution-focused research and evidence-based development across silos; chronicity requires innovation of system planners.

Spirituality, mental wellness, and diabetes care

A 2018 systematic review found a positive relationship between patient spirituality or religiosity and improved management of T2DM (Darvyri et al. 2018). Spiritual practices, such as regular prayer, scripture reading, or communal worship, improved patient emotional adjustments to diagnosis, psychological endurance with chronic disease, mental health (including reduced depression and anxiety), glycaemic control, and quality of life (QoL) (Heidari et al. 2017; Darvyri et al. 2018). A structured review of articles from five continents between the years of 1970 to 2012 also found that practicing spirituality or religiosity is beneficial to diabetic patients' health, self-responsibility, self-management, mental health, coping strength, and social support systems (Permana 2018). In another literature review, religious practices, such as mosque and religious ceremonies attendance, religious support provided and received, and subjective religiosity were linked to improved mental wellness and lower psychological distress, as well as reducing alcohol, nicotine, and drugs use while improving physical exercise and diet (Heidari et al. 2017).

There is also literature particular to African American, Native American, Latino, Hmong, Adventist people (in the United States), and Indigenous Peoples (in Canada) with T2DM that describes a lack confidence in the medical system, and the need to shift into more holistic approaches with great importance placed on spirituality, mental wellness, and local cultural practices (Devlin et al. 2006; Jacklin et al. 2017; Koenig 2014). Spirituality is a central patient strength found in underserved communities in eastern United States (both urban and rural), and strengths-based care is essential to optimising outcomes (Aamar, Lamson and Smith 2015; Gupta and Anandarajah 2014). A study in Qom City, Iran, found significant positive correlations between religious practices and diabetes self-management, including regularly testing blood sugars, performing foot care, sticking to a specific diet, and not smoking (Heidari et al. 2017). Studies with Thai Muslim women, Thai Buddhist women, and Malaysians outlined similar findings (Lundberg and Thrakul 2013; Saidi, Milnes and Griffiths 2018). Other studies similarly show significant relationships between T2DM patients' spirituality or religiosity, reduced emotional and mental problems, and increased QoL scores (Yazla et al. 2017). Most evidence in these areas recommends embracing cultural, religious, and spiritual care, and collaborating with faith leaders for optimal health outcomes and support (Darvyri et al. 2018). Indeed, a faith-based intervention for Hispanic Catholic church-goers found improvements at 6, 9, and 12 months on glycated haemoglobin (HbA1C), waist circumference, QoL, mental health, and self-efficiency measurements (Wilmoth et al. 2019).

Studies on Muslim T2DM patients observing fasting during Ramadan provide further clinical management advice (e.g., pre-Ramadan assessment, Ramadan-specific education) (Lee et al. 2017). Knowing how Muslim patients tend to modify their pharmaceutical schedule around fasting, for example, helps providers to work more effectively with them (Al-Arouj et al. 2010; Lee et al. 2017). Fasting is not unique to Muslim observers. It is a common spiritual or religious practice in many of the world's faith and cultural traditions that requires understanding and a collaborative approach between health care providers, patients, and spiritual or religious leaders. A study in Ethiopia found Orthodox Christians, Protestants, and Muslims modifying timing and amount of dosages for diabetes around fasting rites (Habte et al. 2017). Taking insulin while fasting resulted in hypoglycaemic episodes that could be better managed with medical advice (Habte et al. 2017).

Diabetes is also exacerbated by psychological stress that adversely affects health behaviours such as exercise levels, dietary choices, and compliance to medication schedules (Hackett and Steptoe 2017). T2DM and depression are associated with poor glycaemic control and cardiovascular complications (Hackett and Steptoe 2017). Evidence has shown Eastern-based spiritual practices such as yoga and meditation reduce stress and depression (Ferguson, Willemsen and Castañeto 2010). Prayer has not been studied as much in this way, and there are concerns with studying spiritual or religious practices that must be considered, yet there are studies that suggest prayer has an alleviating effect on stress (Ferguson, Willemsen, and Castañeto 2010; Koenig 2008). For example, a mixed-methods study with Roman Catholic participants showed that an intervention of two private prayers per day and one two-hour group session per week for ten weeks decreased participants' overall self-reported stress (Ferguson, Willemsen and Castañeto 2010). Another quantitative study found prayer and encouraging self-talk to decrease stress levels in university students (Belding et al. 2010). Despite these studies, there is no wide consensus on which spiritual practices (e.g., yoga, meditation, prayer) affect T2DM-specific outcomes and in which ways.

Spirituality and T2DM in Belize

Belizeans draw on cultural or spiritual healing traditions for many diseases including T2DM. Indigenous Mayan healers, for example, have diabetes-specific prayers, rituals, and herbal medicines (Hatala, Waldram and Caal 2015). Garifuna healers conduct ceremonies with ancestral prayers calling on the help of the spirits of ancestors who may guide them to use specific medicinal plants and to embrace behavioural changes (Ellis 2010). Christianity is the most practiced religion in Belize in its many forms (e.g., Roman Catholic, Pentecostal, Seventh-Day Adventist, Anglican, Methodist, New Covenant, Mennonite, Indigenous-Christian, Garifuna-Christian), but there is little found in the literature about faith-based diabetes interventions (proven to work elsewhere) applied in this context. While we know that Belizeans practice a rich array of spiritual, religious, and faith-based practices, that cultural-spiritual healers provide care for their communities, and that faith-based missions mobilise international medical volunteers, it is not yet clear how to bridge health care and spiritual care efforts toward better outcomes for people living with T2DM in Belize.

While there is an abundance of literature on spirituality, religiosity, and faith-based practices positively affecting health and well-being, Roger and Hatala (2017) discuss the need for a more specific understanding of how medicine and health care can become responsive to the needs of patients from an increasing plurality of faiths. The purpose of examining spiritual and religious practices is to understand how they affect clinical practice (e.g., lifestyle counselling, behavioural changes, adherence to care plans, patient-provider relationships, the communication of diagnoses, etc.) for treatment to be efficacious. Certainly, providers are right to be concerned, as not all spiritual practices are easily compatible with medical protocols, and some even detract from them and their compliance. Authors found that diabetes patients seeking out spiritual healing in Ghana, Kuwait, and the United States, for example, would not consistency take their medications, which exacerbated complications (De-Graft Aikins 2005; Jeragh-Alhaddad et al. 2015; Koenig 2004).

In summary, more research at the interface of spirituality and chronicity is needed on T2DM in Belize to better understand: 1) prevalence trends across sociodemographic categories to identify key populations for prevention and education programs, 2) the role of corporate social responsibility in transformative research, 3) how to enhance self-management of material and medical resources for those living with chronic poverty, 4) which specific spiritual practices are being used and how they affect outcomes, 5) potential guidelines for health care providers regarding how to support their patients' spiritual resources for best results, and 6) how faith-based organisations can collaborate in health promotion efforts. This exploratory qualitative study was therefore a first step to address several of these gaps and provide direction for future research priorities and clinical practice.

Methodology

Research framework

This qualitative study used a Constructivist Grounded Theory (CGT) methodological design with an Interpretive Phenomenology (IP) approach. CGT allows for local people to inform and build the theory of what is happening in their lives with their collective lived experiences (Charmaz 2011). IP is interested in consciousness in day-to-day experiences (Hesse-Biber 2017). The questions of how people experience diabetes and spiritual or religious practice and make meaning of interactions are of particular interest for IP, requiring attention at the level of awareness, sensations, cognition, and interpretation (Hesse-Biber 2017). CGT and IP are often used together without the recognition that this is the case through *mudding, slurring,* or *blurring,* yet we are explicit about using both (Wimpenny and Gass 2000). While theoretical underpinnings differ at points during the research process, we found them complementary, and in practice, both rely on interviews as a main method of qualitative data generation.

Ethical considerations

The ongoing engagement with Belizean partners helped to ensure the spirit and intent of the study were aligned with community wellness and that no harm will come of it. The entire research process was explained to participants prior to consenting to the detail required by the University of Manitoba Ethics Review Board including purpose, scope, risks, benefits, compensation, declination, withdrawal, privacy, confidentiality, data usage, and storage. Participants were randomly assigned pseudonyms from a list of the most popular names in Belize and Central America. Data were kept on one password-encoded laptop in a locked office. The University of Manitoba Human Research Ethics Board approved the study (HS23313 [H2019:406]). Developments for a research ethics board in Belize are underway, and a Steering Committee guided the ethical processes for the Belizean side of the partnership.

Participants

The population of focus was decided by a local Steering Committee and involved adult Belizeans with T2DM who are not suffering from major complications (e.g., blindness, amputation, renal failure). Snowball sampling was used, starting with the local research coordinator, health care administrators, providers, and Belize Diabetes Association (BDA) offices. Our interviewee sample was 11 people (eight women, three men) between the ages of 48 and 89, including one person with partial blindness due to an occupational injury/wound healing complicated by diabetes. Participants were from four of the six districts of Belize, namely Toledo, Stann Creek, Cayo, and Belize City, representing people of Creole, Garifuna, and East Indian heritage. The sample was lacking Mayans, Mestizos, minorities, and people from the Corozal and Orange Walk districts, limited by the COVID-19 public health restrictions that arose.

Data generation

The primary qualitative method was interviewing, though site visits;[5] discussions with key informants, participatory observation, and field notes were also used. The interview questions were based on the Diabetes Quality of Life Questionnaire, although we modified it to include feedback from the Steering Committee and study participants; it was used as a conversation guide in semi-structured interviews (Hewitt 2007; Liamputtong 2007). All participants' first language was English, the national language of Belize, though varying in dialect. Interviews took place in February and March 2020.

Data analysis

Interview transcripts, corresponding memos, and field notes were coded using Dedoose software with one author taking the lead and other team members providing expert checking and inter-reader reliability for verification. Data were analysed line-by-line and paragraph-by-paragraph, attending to the underlying meanings of what is being said, portrayed, and assumed (Hesse-Biber 2017). Literal codes, focused codes, and analytic categories were used in a systematised order to analyse data for emerging themes through the CGT framework, keeping the human story central (Charmaz 2014). The trustworthiness of the analysis was ensured through: 1) discussion with Belizean stakeholders; 2) reflexivity and integrity as continuous practice; 3) asking how each part of the decision trail impact participants; 4) asking if the emerging theory and story makes sense in context; and 5) looking for the negative cases that disprove or alter emerging theories (Charmaz 2014; Hesse-Biber 2017).

Positionality

Religion and spirituality emerged as a major theme in this work. The authors come from a diversity of cultural and spiritual backgrounds, experiences, and influences, including Garifuna, Bahá'í, Buddhist, Christian, Jewish, and Indigenous ceremonies of North and South America. When we discuss religious beliefs and spiritual practices relayed to us by participants, it is for the purpose of informing the effect on their health and health care. We do our best to relay what was shared with us without having to agree/disagree, promote or dispute anyone's spiritual beliefs.

Results: Spiritual practices as diabetes care

Ten of the eleven participants in this study reported that they had a strong faith in God, ascribing many health and mental wellness benefits to this. The analysis of qualitative data from this study produced three main themes: 1) "All you need to do is do the right thing": Fasting and building determination, 2) "I don't stress about it": Spirituality lessening mental stress, and 3) "Once you pray, a lot of things get done easy": Prayer as a way of life. These themes focus on the manner in which spiritual practices (e.g., fasting, observing Lent, prayer, referring to sacred texts, meditation) help to build determination and commitment to healthy lifestyle choices for T2DM self-management, and provide relief for both inner tensions and external stressors that could otherwise exacerbate the condition. Our findings also highlight numerous types of prayers used to help with T2DM and chronicity (e.g., prayers for guidance on how to live, for protection from harm in surgery, for help meeting basic needs, for acceptance of one's condition, for surrendering to God's will, and of gratitude for each day of life) and that people most often engaged in spiritual practices daily at home, but did not necessarily attend formal religious events on a regular basis.

"All you need to do is do the right thing": Fasting and building determination

Central to diabetes self-management is eating a diet of fresh fruits and vegetables, proteins, and complex carbohydrates while avoiding addictive simple sugars (Ahmed, Guillem and Vandaele 2013; Franz and Evert 2012). Participants used spiritual fasting practices to strengthen their psychological determination to abstain from problematic foods that exacerbated diabetes symptoms. Inspired by his Garifuna spiritual outlook and practices, George, for example, controlled his blood glucose levels through daily fasting, eating only one small meal each day. Rather than dabble in moderating his consumption of desserts and sweet beverages, he abstained from sugar altogether and focused on eating fresh local produce. He disliked the trend he had seen of people with diabetes needing increasing anti-diabetic drug dosages without changing their lifestyle choices, an important consideration in a country where medications are not always available and/or affordable. As George explained: "We need to do more. We need to get to the root of the problem… I call for fasting, or intermittent faster. Because if you don't eat, your sugar won't go up. I could tell anybody that."

While fasting is not a prescribed activity or ritual of Garifunaduau, cleansing and purification are used in the Garifuna spiritual healing tradition. George was a proud Garifuna man who found personal power in fasting and exercise, having tried and abandoned numerous T2DM-related prescriptions he found ineffective and misaligned with his values. Practicing his spiritual regime positively reinforced his dedication to his health and to God while his faith reciprocated in strengthening his resolve; he experienced these elements coming together to improve his chronic condition and make life consistently more manageable without the use of pharmaceuticals.

Cynthia was also a Garifuna woman and a retired nurse. She went through months of "binge-eating" after she was diagnosed with T2DM, disbelieving of, and struggling with her shift in identity from being a health care provider to becoming a patient of the health care system with chronic disease. While she was in denial, her blood glucose levels were high and increasing. As Cynthia expressed:

> I was in denial. Because when I checked my sugar level, it will be 300, 400, but I don't care, I'm going to take my coke [Coca Cola], eat whatever I want. And it took me about six months to accept the condition I was in. I was in denial. I said, "No!" because maybe I had a lot of coke, maybe because I eat a lot of sweet things. I was in denial for almost six months before I accepted this; I am one of them [diabetic patients] now.

Cynthia came to accept her new limitations, in part, through perseverance, prayer, and faith in God, settling into a clear fortitude: "Having diabetes is a condition that you have to live with, and all you need to do, is do the right thing and have control." Cynthia considered her coming to acceptance of her condition an important part of being able to follow self-management guidelines, which she was now firm with herself about and committed to. Other participants shared this sentiment of strength and determination, and expressed an attitude of self-responsibility in balance with an acceptance of and surrender to God in an ultimate sense. Felisha, a Creole woman, also outlined:

> I hope that in the future, I live many more years and that diabetes don't bother me that much. I believe it's up to me to take care of myself. When God says it's time, I understand that part, but without that, just taking care of myself.

Study participants talked about God as someone or a force that helps them in their day-to-day lives with "heavy lifting" that may be too overwhelming to do on their own, and as a persuasive, consistent, and clear voice of health promotion and encouragement for self-care. As George explained: "For what to do, when to do, what not to do, I pray." While social support wavered in their lives from time to time (e.g., workout buddies dropping off, simple sugars at family gatherings, alcohol drinking expected at cultural celebrations), their sense of God's presence did not. In this way, comradery or social support extends for these individuals beyond the human realm to the spiritual worlds where God, or personified Creator, becomes their most reliable ally and consistent voice of support. Yvonne, a Creole woman, for instance captured this sentiment expressed by all participants when she shared that "What helps me stay motivated? Oh, everything! I'm a believer in God. He's the person who really keeps me going."

Some participants in this study also described specific religious observances that helped to solidify their own willpower and positive choices, such as Lent. Lent is a six-week Catholic observance of sacrifice or self-denial from an individually meaningful, often food-related, object of personal choice (people often give up sugar or red meat for Lent). When asked what the most challenging aspect of living with diabetes was, Yvonne again explained: "I think the carbs and the crave for sugar... This is Lent, it's the Lent season. And that is what I said I am going to give up for this, and if I survive, I know I'm good (laughing)." Yvonne credited observing Lent with fortifying her ability to overcome daily sugar cravings. This discipline and health promoting activity is difficult as sugar induces psychological processes of craving and reward that surpass neurobiological responses to many addictive drugs (Ahmed, Guillem, and Vandaele 2013). Observing Lent in this way, therefore, sets high self-expectations of willpower and positive self-choice, and these are reinforced through accountability to not only others in the spiritual community, but to God; faith in God helps one "rise to the occasion." Once this strength and ability is discovered and experienced through action in fasting and reflection on that action, the participants commented how this further strengthened faith in themselves-with-God while transforming old patterns of neurobiological responses and cravings.

For many of the participants, Lent also provided a powerful spiritual narrative and "hero" to emulate, namely the Christian biblical Easter story of the crucifixion, sacrifice, and resurrection of Jesus Christ. In Christianity, Jesus is interpreted as God personified and the highest expression of humanity. Participants shared how they drew strength from how Jesus endured being nailed to a cross while still emanating compassion towards his injurers, and through this story they understood their own personal and temporary renunciation or sacrifice (e.g., sugar) as relatively small. In this way, the Hero's Journey provides profound inspiration to overcome craving and addiction by creating, affirming, then cementing new and healthier neuropathways and habits of spiritual activity, choice, reward, and power.

Finally, gaining spiritual determination to abstain from cravings also applied to alcohol. Alcohol consists of simple sugars, and alcoholism is well known to exacerbate diabetes (Barcia et al. 2015; Kim and Kim 2012; Weaver and Mendenhall 2014). Maurice and Henry both quit previously significant amounts of partying and alcohol drinking when they were diagnosed with diabetes. Henry, an East Indian man, explained:

> Well, I grew up in a Catholic mission. Then I have turned over to a New Covenant Church... Yeah, it helps! Because before, man, I used to be out there drinking a beer, drinking all these things that don't agree with this diabetes thing... It's helped me a lot.

Living with diabetes can be more difficult, complicated, and fatal for those with a co-morbidity of alcoholism. Strong spiritual practices, such as prayer and fasting, coupled with accurate medical information, can facilitate with limiting alcohol and sugar consumption and with a determination to choose a different, more wellness-promoting, path in life.

"I don't stress about it": Spirituality lessening mental stress

Despite the seriousness of the topic, most participants smiled and laughed a lot throughout their interviews. Nine participants expressed that Bible readings, prayers, and meditations guided them to "not stress," that they were supported to maintain peaceful relationships with other people, and that their health and mental health benefitted accordingly. They described strategies like moving to the countryside, staying home more often, actively modifying their state of mind through meditation and prayer, not holding malice toward other people, emanating goodwill toward their community members, and asking God for what they need. In many cases, it was a matter of following their spiritual teachings regarding "dwelling within a trusting relationship with God" and "nurturing a positive outlook on life," such as those found in biblical texts, that were helpful at developing these positive mental attitudes and practices. When asked how she coped with the T2DM-related stress, Isabella, a Garifuna woman in her late eighties, outlined:

> I pray a lot. I refer to my Bible readings. I interact with my past students, my friends, and my family. They come to help me a lot. So far, I try to live a stress-free life, realising that I have lived a full life. I don't worry too much about other things that are not important. And I love people... I believe that as a Christian, as a child of God, I accept everyone. My mother used to say, "You don't do to others what we don't want them to do to you."

Yvonne similarly found mental stress-reducing reassurance and lifestyle guidance in sacred texts and prayer practice. As she expressed:

> The Bible tells you not to worry about anything... Make your concerns known to God. And because I used to, I worked for years, and I had a supervisor position, and it was very stressful, and I realise that stress makes you ill. When I read that, that is my foundation. You don't worry about anything. You tell him what you need, and he'll provide it. And he has. It has improved my mental health and my physical health of my body. It is a connection. And my health has improved because of that.

Reflective of these passages, when Felisha was also asked to say more about not holding malice, she explained her personal approach inspired by biblical passages, as well as her prayer and meditation practices:

> When having diabetes, you don't want to be frustrated. You don't want to be quarrelling with people. You don't want to get into any mess, you

know? So, if anybody want to quarrel with me, I don't pay them no mind. I just sit down there and let them talk, and when they get enough of talking, well, that's their thing. We are friends again. I don't hold malice and say, I am vexed with this one and I won't – No, no, no! That's the way how I live my life. And it's good for everybody who have diabetes. Don't wanna have nothing holding over their shoulder. Diabetes is enough… 'cause can't hold malice at people when you're sick too.

Making peace and setting boundaries on interpersonal drama in relationships was inspired by spiritual practices and teachings. Natalia, a working mother of three, semi-jokingly warned all her family members and colleagues that if they gave her stress or made drama, then they would kill her. Isabella evoked a spiritual sense of kinship with her fellow human beings as a way of life. She explained: "I try to be pleasant and welcoming to everybody. I love my children and try to instil into them that you have to be pleasant to everybody. To me that is the important part of life." Cynthia also said she had no stress except not being able to consistently afford what she needed. She and others described not stressing as a way of being in the world, and as a perennial rebuttal of negativity even in the face of poverty and chronic illness. Josefina, a busy Garifuna grandmother, similarly said: "I relax my mind and don't let nothing bother me." Meera, an East Indian woman, also shared: "I just don't worry about it because the more I worry about it, the worse it gets for me."

Overall, prayer, meditation, and referring to sacred texts helped participants to feel peaceful inwardly, as well as outwardly caring toward other people, affecting their relationships positively while mitigating their psychological stress to make for healthier, easier T2DM living.

"Once you pray, a lot of things get done easy": Prayer as a way of life

Participants in this research described various types of prayer that they draw on in their lives. As explored above, participants prayed for strength, determination, and commitment to healthy behaviours and overcoming addiction; they prayed for acceptance of their condition and the ability surrender to God's will; and they prayed for harmonious relations in their families, their communities, and peace within themselves. At the same time, they also talked about praying to stay mentally and spiritually strong even when they were feeling physically frail and facing poverty, which gave participants the "lift of God's presence," guiding their lives and making enduring chronicity easier.

Additionally, participants used prayer to feel closer with God and for returning to trust in times of turbulence. George had suffered four years of preventable medical complications and difficult experiences of the health care system that had left him partially blind and unsure which of his physicians (who were in disagreement) he could trust. He provided an example of the power of faith in enduring difficulties and of personal prayer for help in hard times:

> I believe in God, you know. I believe in God. I know that once you pray, a lot of things get done easy… I'm sure it helps. A lot, lot, lot. When your situation is not going forward, not getting there, that's when I pray.

Meera was experiencing health issues that were more pressing than her T2DM at the time of the interview. She decided not to think about or impose her will on the future, preferring to surrender to God. She used prayers like daily blessings to give thanks for each day of life. She provided an example of personal prayer for surrender to God's will and gratitude for life: "I live just one day at a time. Because then, there's no tomorrow. That's the way I see it. When you live to see another day, just say, Thank God."

Participants also shared how they prayed for protection of their health, including emergency surgeries in health care settings and daily preventative care practices at home. They often attributed good outcomes to the good will of God. Meera said:

> Recently, about a year now,… I get a surgery on like Tuesday, and Wednesday, I was home, praise God. Just like I didn't get a surgery. And I was worried because they say, I am a diabetic and could get hard to heal. But no.

Felisha described a similar experience:

> Two years ago, I got a hysterectomy… And thank God, I didn't catch not one infection. The eighth day after my surgery, I'm driving the car. The ninth day, I went to take out my stitches, I washed my clothes, I do everything. Without an infection, praise God, no infection.

Praying for health protection and asking that one's health needs be met not only crystallised patients' priorities within themselves, but it also multiplied feelings of gratitude when those needs were met and allowed for acceptance when difficulties arose. Similar to prayers of trust that God will provide, participants experienced feelings and thoughts of gratitude that replaced psychological stress and worry with a sense of peace and wellness. Prayers of gratitude for the blessings in life focused participants' thoughts away from wishing for another reality in which they do not have diabetes. When Meera was asked about her toughest daily challenges, she said: "I don't really find it hard… I personally thank God for it." Meera felt that complaining was not of any help to her, and that she had to sometimes fight for the state of her health and at other times, surrender. When Rosa, who was past the age of retirement, mentioned she was a (Methodist) minister, she was asked how her spiritual relationship might affect her health and/or her well-being. While she admitted that working her full-time job on top of her clergy work could tire her out, she shared an example of personal prayer for balance, health, trust, and in gratitude:

> I think that probably helps me to keep it in balance. I pray about it, pray for healing. Over all these years, all the time, it used to be, oh, 200 [blood glucose

levels], but it never affected my sight or anything. So, I said, probably God takes care of it. Praying and making sure that I meditate, and I watch it isn't getting any worse. Cause I hear about people talk about 400 and 500. Then their eyesight start going. But no, everything just kinda was normal, in order to live with it... (laughing) I don't have time to be sad. No, no, no! No time for sadness. Give thanks for everything! Every little thing.

From a different angle, Isabella practiced a synergy of Garifuna and Roman Catholic spiritual and religious traditions, sharing a unique insight into cultural variations on prayer practices. This included the spiritual work involved in divining the messages sent in dreams and calling on one's spiritual inheritance through ones' ancestors. She shared a little about the most sacred ceremony of honouring the ancestors by Garifuna family/community called the *Amalihani* (abbreviated to the *Mali*) which includes dance and prayers:

Well, you have the *Mali*. There is the belief. I personally admire our practices to invoke the help of the spirit of our ancestors. When we dream about the ancestors, and we talk with them as we are talking now. It is mainly in our dreams that we talk as Garifuna. It is a sad situation that the church condemns it and says it's paganism and what not. And this is what has caused a lot of people to look down on the culture, say negative things, and not want to accept themselves. And that is where we have gone wrong. That is it. But gradually now, the trend is changing because when our children go abroad to study, and they realise that has happened. They say, Well, this is me, I am Garifuna. I do not have to believe everything my ancestors' believed, but I can sift out and get the good out of it. Because from every good there is some bad, and from every bad there is some good (laughing and smiling).

Indigenous spiritualities, such as those of the Garifuna people, have survived many colonial oppressions, thus providing practitioners insight and fortitude in surviving types of social chronic adversity, including chronic disease. This spiritual philosophy and historical inheritance helped Garifuna people to survive, endure, be resilient, and thrive (Ellis 2010). It helped Garifuna participants, and similarly other Belizeans, to accept the aspects of diabetes that seem negative alongside those experienced as positive, in the sense that they are two sides of the same coin, or two parts of a whole, and this lessened emotional vicissitudes of living with diabetes, even the literal spikes and drops in blood sugar, which can feel dizzying, frightening, and weakening.

Discussion

This exploratory study identified that people living with T2DM in Belize use spiritual practices (e.g., prayer, fasting, meditation, rituals, reading sacred texts) that empower commitment to health-promoting behaviours. The study findings demonstrate that spiritual practices lessen the otherwise compounding psychological stresses of dealing with chronicity and can provide the strength and endurance needed to live each day, to live with peace, joy, and gratitude. Fasting, praying for acceptance of one's condition, and observing Lent, were examples of spiritual practices that helped build the discipline and determination needed for participants' diabetes self-management tasks. This included daily exercise and refraining from sugar and alcohol. Reading sacred texts, following spiritual teachings, engaging in prayer and meditation, all helped participants reduce the stress from their interpersonal relationships, their workloads, and their internal tensions. Numerous types of prayers were described by participants such as counting blessings, asking for protection, and listening for guidance. Ten of 11 participants engaged in spiritual practices at home each day but did not necessarily attend church or ritual on a regular basis. Overall, this study illustrates how spiritual practices are an important part of health and mental wellness for people living with chronic conditions such as diabetes and may represent an under researched resource, in Belize and elsewhere, for improving mental wellness outcomes.

Spirituality, mental wellness, and chronicity

A quantitative analysis between religiosity and self-management in older adults with diabetes in Mexico (Rivera-Hernandez 2016) found a positive association. This author illustrated that those involved in their church tend to exercise more, smoke less, and drink less alcohol. This also builds on a study that demonstrated similar results in a youth (aged 11 to 15) population in Canada where those with higher spiritual health scores engaged in less health risk-taking behaviour (e.g., less smoking, alcohol use, drug use, sexual intercourse); the study concluded that it is important to differentiate spirituality from religiosity, and that the former is a protective factor (Hatala et al. 2020).

While this and several other studies have "used church attendance as the main measure of religiosity" (Rivera-Hernandez 2016, 9), our study suggests many people find faith in God and spiritual practices important to managing diabetes, but do not necessarily attend church or religious events on a regular basis, instead relying on the day-to-day management of diabetes in homecare and "homework" (Mattingly, Gron, and Meinert 2011). By advancing the notion of "chronic homework" Mattingly, Gron, and Meinert (2011) drew our attention to the kind of cultural "work" that patients and families are expected to carry out in their home or "popular health sector" contexts in the day-to-day management of their chronic conditions. Such "low-tech" social technologies and day-to-day strategies, or "work of coping," these authors argue, have received minimal attention in the academic literature (Mattingly, Gron, and Meinert 2011), and we would add that a similar situation can be seen with spiritual or faith-based coping practices.

Through a movement toward promoting self-management, a substantial burden of chronicity "homework" is placed on patients involved in diabetes care (Roger and Hatala 2017; Mattingly, Gron and Meinert 2011). Self-management assumes patients can afford nutritious food, clean water, glucometers, testing strips, and to live in a peaceful place, with caregivers for the elderly, amputees, the visually impaired, or other people with complications; many people in Belize cannot afford these things, and rely on a patchwork of volunteer efforts, government, and private systems (key informants, 2020). While gender-based analysis is often missing in the T2DM studies, there are studies that note that such chronicity "homework" falls more often on the shoulders of women than of men (Arifin et al. 2020). According to Arifin et al. (2020), Indonesian women with diabetes, for example, have both more caregiving duties and greater stress than their male counterparts. These women manage their own diabetes without additional support, despite compounding stresses of paid work, housework, kin work, and chronicity homework, while men feel their diabetes does not contribute stress, because the women in their lives look after them (Arifin et al. 2020). Though most of our participants reported not experiencing much stress, those who did were working mothers, those who could not reliably afford what they needed, and those who had experienced negligence at the hands of the health care system.

Similarly, while spirituality and social support are often lumped together in the literature, this assumes people who attend a church, temple, or mosque benefit from the community and outreach of these communities (Darvyri et al. 2018; Permana 2018). Our study suggests that individual, at-home, spiritual practices pertaining to T2DM self-management merit more inquiry. A cross-sectional study on spirituality, social support, and diabetes in Peru defined "social support" as nurses counselling and collaboratively goal-setting with the patients, rather than the care one receives from one's spiritual community (Krederdt-Araujo et al. 2019). Authors found that when nurses provided spiritually intelligent social support services in their regular visits with diabetes patients, adherence levels to care plans increased (Krederdt-Araujo et al. 2019). Though health outcomes were not assessed subsequently, authors theorised that adherence to care plans would be expected to improve outcomes (Krederdt-Araujo et al. 2019). They concluded that this approach could improve clinical management by mobilising spirituality and social support to optimise patient self-care (Krederdt-Araujo et al. 2019). Our study confirms that these are worthy directions for health care providers and systems to pursue, not only in Belize but perhaps more generally as well.

Living with diabetes predisposes people to higher risk of psychological conditions like depression and excessive stress, both of which already disproportionately affect those living in poverty (Sam, Ghosh, and Richardson 2015; Weaver and Mendenhall 2014). Depression has been linked to long-term chronic diseases such as T2DM in studies in other countries (Darvyri et al. 2018; Heidari et al. 2017). Mental health issues carry substantial social stigma in some parts of Belize, and there is work to be done in addressing these issues. Key informants at the BDA suggest the need for screening all T2DM patients for depression and mental health issues. They have started practicing letting patients know that mental and emotional aspects are important aspects of health, offering links to supports and resources for the people that come through their doors. More efforts like this could help those living with T2DM in Belize through the difficulties of living with chronicity.

While depression and stress are typically more prevalent in people living with diabetes, the Belize situation may or may not agree with the literature. The small sample of people in our study consistently reported very little to no stress, but this cannot be generalised to the population at large. In a sample of impoverished youth living in Belize City, for example, different results could be anticipated. Stress and depression are possibly under-reported because of stigma, under-diagnosis, and/or low help-seeking behaviour. Alternatively, the pervasive feeling that was shared by participants (e.g., "I honestly have no stress," and "I don't get down," and "I don't let it bother me") could be indicative of the richness of the cultural and spiritual or religious practices in Belize. Participants laughed a lot, even when discussing the gravest consequences of having the disease, with remarkable capacity to find humour in dark circumstances and lightness in chronicity. Scheper-Hughes wrote about resilience as people "having a talent for life," the ways people adapt and endure not only chronic illness, but also difficult living conditions perpetuated under the forces constructed by macro-political economic movements (Vigh 2008, 18). Just as chronicity takes on meaning unique to Belize, so too does wellness and resilience. Spiritual practices greatly facilitate people with T2DM in Belize carrying on living with determination and commitment to health while rebuking stress and negativity in the face of chronic disease and poverty.

Our findings about health-enhancing spiritual practices can assist in improving both T2DM clinical management and self-management; this is in agreement with similar findings from countries such as Iran, Indonesia, Malaysia, Thailand, Sudan, Nigeria, Sweden, the United Kingdom, Australia, Canada, and the United States (Ahmed 2003; Arifin et al. 2020; Brown et al. 2013; Heidari et al. 2017; Jacklin et al. 2017; Lundberg and Thrakul 2013; Marshall and Archibald 2015; Permana 2018; Rubin, Walen and Ellis 1990; Saidi, Milnes and Griffiths 2018; Unantenne et al. 2013). Fasting, observing Lent and other rituals, prayer, meditation, and referring to sacred texts are some of the spiritual practices present in Belize that may represent an underutilised resource and source of wellness for people living with T2DM, chronicity, and the exacerbations of poverty. Health care providers (HCPs) and planners can therefore increase opportunities to support patient wellness and mental health by better understanding the local cultural resources and spiritual practices of patients, as well as through collaborating with spiritual or religious health practitioners and healers.

Implications for health care providers

Literature on the clinical management of diabetes for those who practice fasting outlines risks (e.g., hypoglycaemic events, malnutrition, etc.) and benefits (e.g., weight loss, reduced insulin intake, lower risk of heart attack and stroke, etc.) (Grajower and Horne 2019). There is also some literature on Ramadan-specific diabetes care (Al-Arouj et al. 2010; Lee et al. 2017). Our findings agree that it is important for HCPs to ask their patients about health-related spiritual or religious practices such as fasting, to advise patients on diabetes management implications of their spiritual fasting practices, and to work collaboratively with patients to develop appropriate care plans.

Similarly, HCPs can ask about spiritual practices such as prayer. Medical doctor and researcher Rossiter-Thornton (2002) described a non-denominational approach to addressing patient-centred needs that included a model called the Prayer Wheel. Our research findings suggest that this tool, or a similar tool adapted for the Belizean cultural context, would likely be: 1) welcome by patients, 2) facilitate patient-provider communication, 3) promote positive health behaviours, and ultimately 4) improve health outcomes. While physicians may be reluctant to address spirituality as a part of health care provision, there are important implications for clinical practice that can be addressed with a few short questions embedded into medical history interviews (George et al. 2013; Koenig 2004, 2014; Rossiter-Thornton 2002).

The literature calls for training HCPs on overall awareness of patient cultural and spiritual practices, on spiritual resource assessment, on positive associated factors, and on negative shifts to look out for (e.g., loss of faith in God with diagnosis, negative fatalism deterring self-help efforts) (Roger and Hatala 2017). Our findings agree with previous work suggesting that it can be beneficial for HCPs to routinely ask about patient spirituality in their medical history taking and improve adherence to care plans through being open to patient spiritual practices, referring patients to spiritual resources, and engaging with faith leaders (Heidari et al. 2017). Finally, our findings also suggest that individual HCPs in Belize can facilitate improved outcomes by sharing diabetes information with faith leaders and by becoming more knowledgeable about local spiritual practices, cultural activities, and resources, but that these efforts would further flourish with support from health care administrators.

Implications for health care system planners

Acknowledging and meeting the need for mental health services can be helpful in reducing social stigma, reducing depression and anxiety, and improving T2DM outcomes (Hackett and Steptoe 2017; Permana 2018; Weaver and Mendenhall 2014). Telling people matter-of-factly that mental health is an important part of health, that depression can be a part of diabetes but does not have to be, and that there is support available can be very helpful to overcome a cultural climate that was described by informants as: "We're a people who don't want to talk about our health, especially old people," and "If you say you have depression here, it casts you as an outsider, so, no people won't talk about themselves like that," and "Diabetes, like cancer, people are afraid to talk about it because they don't want people to know. If they talked about it, they could help it. But they give up hope." There were stories of a friend whispering confessions of having diabetes after years of hiding it and it being confused with HIV. It would be useful to get underneath these issues to help people share more about diabetes in a safe space, and there is a role for health system planners in this.

Day camp programs aimed at education for prediabetic youth in the United States have been successful at reducing prevalence and improving outcomes; physician organisers stress the importance of consistent messaging, defining the struggle against diabetes as a war against veracious sugar and sweet beverages (SSB) marketing campaigns (Stevens 2019). Stevens (2019) notes the challenges posed by the fact that eating right and exercising do not show youth immediately gratifying effects, while SSB consumption does. Our key informants discussed how the Belize economy has been transitioning toward more sedentary forms of employment, and that their population was increasingly consuming processed foods. Further, drinking SSB was often perceived as a symbol of higher social status, and that SSB companies often sponsor elementary schools that would be otherwise underfunded. SSB billboards can be seen in a central position in schoolyards promoting consumption to children, and providing permanent, influential messages. Still, evidence shows that something as small as a two-day diabetes camp filled with education and fun sports can make a significant difference in health outcomes while simultaneously mobilising communities (Stevens 2019). Supporting and evaluating educational day camps and prevention efforts in the context of Belize is an important area for future intervention and study.

Studies in marginalised communities in the United States have also shown success in faith-based intervention strategies with adults with T2DM from Pentecostal church groups (Marshall and Archibald 2015; Stevens 2019). Our study describes an underlying need for more T2DM prevention and education programming in Belize and suggests that intervention approaches such as collaborative educational sessions with combined health care and faith organisations would be beneficial in slowing the spread of diabetes in Belize. Our findings also suggest that bringing people together from the silos of health care and cultural-spiritual or religious traditions would also be beneficial in promoting interdisciplinary dialogue, understanding, problem-solving, innovation, research, and development initiatives with the shared purpose of improving care for people living with T2DM in Belize (see Figure 10.1 for more details).

Areas of future research

Participatory, transformative, and capacity-building research would be a useful area of study to increase research and development opportunities for aspiring researchers in Belize. Boosting local capacity may be especially important to communities such as the Indigenous Mayan where people are more comfortable working within their own worldview framework and speaking in their first languages with local interviewers. Interviews with local Community Health Workers (CHW), Allied Health professionals, herbal doctors, cultural-spiritual healers, and faith leaders could contribute much to the literature. It would be useful to understand more about culturally specific (e.g., Mayan, Mestizo, Garifuna, etc.) diabetes-related practices and beliefs and how they affect outcomes. Research on

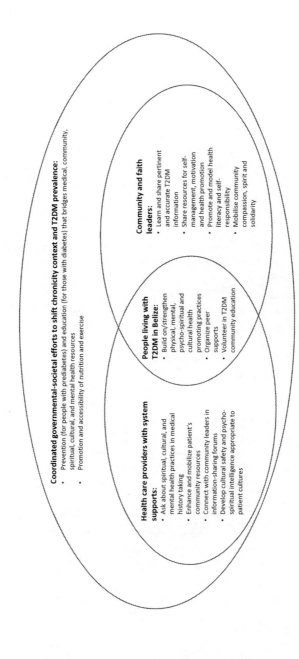

Figure 10.1 Recommendations for coordinated service provision between health care providers and community leaders.

prevalence differences across socio-demographic categories would be useful to identify priority populations for prevention and education programs. Research could also inform emerging guidelines for health care providers on how to address their patients' spirituality so as to move them toward the best health and mental health outcomes. Further research could also inform how the sectors of health and faith can exchange knowledge and collaborate in health promotion efforts.

Strengths and limitations

One strength of the study is that CGT provides in-depth knowledge within context, so it can readily inform location-specific health care policy decision-making, possibly leading to new understandings, new theories, or building on established theories (Charmaz 2014, 2011). It can generate ideas, policies, solutions, action, and theories from the grassroots level by digging into local realities; it is a good way to listen to the voices of people most impacted by issues, and it resists the importation of theories from elsewhere (Charmaz 2011; Creswell 2018; Hesse-Biber 2017).

A limitation of our study is that we did not have the opportunity to interview a representative sample, which would require more interviews with people from communities such as the Mayan, Mestizo, Mennonite, Chinese, migrant worker, other visible minority communities, as well as people from the Corozal and Orange Walk districts. Another limitation of the study is that it is not possible to analyse demographic differences across class, ethnicity, race, gender, age, geography, access to National Health Institute (NHI), or other describers due to the small sample size. Finally, we also acknowledge these findings did not focus on or demonstrate negative experiences with religion or spiritual practices and resistance with health care approaches to T2DM care.

Conclusion

The voices of the people of Belize are diverse, important, and insightful. This qualitative exploratory study allowed for some understandings to emerge where there had been a dearth of knowledge on spiritual attitudes and practices toward diabetes in Belize directly from people themselves. The main findings include that a central instrument of wellness in the face of chronicity is a rich and pervasive spiritual vision that guides people to healthier lifestyles, to find meaning, to psychological wellness, and to transcend daily suffering. Church attendance is not an adequate measure of spiritual practice in Belize because people frequently pray, meditate, and refer to spiritual texts at home as an important part of T2DM daily homework and self-management. There are important implications for HCPs, for policy and planning, and for research and development. In working toward becoming more hospitable to patients' spiritual understandings and experiences of chronic disease, the health care system has the potential to stop the silencing and marginalisation of those living in chronicity, of topics of spiritual health, and of the ways these forces coalesce. This, in turn, can lead to new innovations and collaborations for quality, integrative care.

Notes

1 In collaboration with local research coordinators, community health workers, the Belize Diabetes Association, the Ministry of Health Belize, the National Health Insurance Office, and the World Diabetes Foundation which all have representation on the project's Steering Committee, and in partnership with the University of Manitoba, Canada.
2 Type 2 diabetes mellitus accounts for the vast majority of diabetes in Belize and will be referred to interchangeably with the shorter terms "diabetes" or "T2DM" for the purposes of this paper.
3 Elaborating on the intricacies of definitions of the terms "spiritual" and "religious" are beyond the scope of this paper. "Spirituality" is used as a term inclusive of "religiosity." Similarly, "spiritual" is conceptualised as inclusive of "religious." For a more in-depth discussion, please refer to (Koenig 2008).
4 BMI is inexpensive to calculate and more "visible" than other risk factors.
5 Site visits included meetings at the offices of National Institute of Cultural Heritage, Ministry of Health, National Health Insurance office, Belize Diabetes Association (Punta Gorda, Dangriga, and Belize City locations), Punta Gorda Polyclinic, San Antonio Clinic, administration offices (Punta Gorda, Dangriga, Independence, and Belmopan), University of Belize, and in the community.

References

Aamar, Rola O., Angela L. Lamson and Doug Smith. 2015. "Qualitative Trends in Biopsychosocial-Spiritual Treatment for Underserved Patients with Type 2 Diabetes." *Contemporary Family Therapy* 37 (1): 33–44. doi:10.1007/s10591-015-9326-x

Ahmed, Awad Mohamed. 2003. "Cultural Aspects of Diabetes Mellitus in Sudan." *Practical Diabetes International* 20 (6): 226–229. doi:10.1002/pdi.508

Ahmed, Serge A., Karine Guillem and Youna Vandaele. 2013. "Sugar Addiction: Pushing the Drug-Sugar Analogy to the Limit." *Current Opinion in Clinical Nutrition and Metabolic Care* 16 (4): 434–439. doi:10.1097/MCO.0b013e328361c8b8

Al-Arouj, Monira, Samir Assaad-Khalil, John Buse, Ibtihal Fahdil, Mohamed Fahmy, Sherif Hafez, Mohamed Hassanein, et al.2010. "Recommendations for Management of Diabetes during Ramadan: Update 2010." *Diabetes Care* 33 (8): 1895–1902. doi:10.2337/dc10-0896

Anderson, Marcia. 2017. "*Indigenous Health Equity: Examining Racism as an Indigenous Social Determinant of Health.*" Indigenous Cultural Safety Collaborative Learning Series. Accessed March 21, 2020 from http://www.icscollaborative.com/webinars/indigenous-health-equity-examining-racism-as-an-indigenous-social-determinant-of-health

Arifin, Bustanul, Ari Probandari, Abdul Khairul Rizki Purba, Dyah Aryani Perwitasari, Catharina C.M. Schuiling-Veninga, JarirAtthobari, Paul F.M.Krabbe and Maarten J. Postma. 2020. "'Diabetes Is a Gift from God' a Qualitative Study Coping with Diabetes Distress by Indonesian Outpatients." *Quality of Life Research* 29 (1): 109–125. doi:10.1007/s11136-019-02299-2

Balboni, Michael J., Julia Bandini, Christine Mitchell, Zachary D. Epstein-Peterson, AdaAmobi, JonathanCahill, Andrea C.Enzinger, JohnPeteet and Tracy Balboni. 2015. "Religion, Spirituality, and the Hidden Curriculum: Medical Student and Faculty Reflections." *Journal of Pain and Symptom Management* 50 (4): 507–515. doi:10.1016/j.jpainsymman.2015.04.020

Barcia, Jorge M., Miguel Flores-Bellver, Maria Muriach, Javier Sancho-Pelluz, Daniel Lopez-Malo, Alba C. Urdaneta, Natalia Martinez-Gil, Sandra Atienzar-Aroca and Francisco J. Romero. 2015. "Matching Diabetes and Alcoholism: Oxidative Stress,

Inflammation, and Neurogenesis Are Commonly Involved." *Mediators of Inflammation* 2015. doi:10.1155/2015/624287

Belding, Jennifer N., Malcolm G. Howard, Anne M. McGuire, Amanda C. Schwartz and Janie H. Wilson. 2010. "Social Buffering by God: Prayer and Measures of Stress." *Journal of Religion and Health* 49 (2): 179–187. doi:10.1007/s10943-009-9256-8

Brown, Shelley M., Anna Monahan, Jena E. Daniels and Tracy R. Burton. 2013. "Type-2 Diabetes in Belize: A Cross-Sectional Study and Holistic Approach to Increasing Health Education." *Public Health Journal* 5 (3): 341–349.

Charmaz, Kathy. 2011. "Grounded Theory Methods in Social Justice Research." In *Handbook of Qualitative Research*, edited by Y. Lincoln and N.K. Denzin, 4th edition, 359–380. Thousand Oaks: Sage.

Charmaz, Kathy. 2014. *Constructing Grounded Theory*. London: Sage Publications.

Creswell, James W. 2018. *Qualitative Inquiry and Research Design: Choosing among Five Approaches*, 5th edition. Thousand Oaks: Sage.

Darvyri, Panagiota, Stavros Christodoulakis, Michael Galanakis, Adamantios G. Avgoustidis, Anastasia Thanopoulou and George P. Chrousos. 2018. "On the Role of Spirituality and Religiosity in Type 2 Diabetes Mellitus Management-A Systematic Review." *Psychology* 9 (4): 728–744. doi:10.4236/psych.2018.94046

De-Graft Aikins, Ama. 2005. "Healer Shopping in Africa: New Evidence from Rural-Urban Qualitative Study of Ghanaian Diabetes Experiences." *British Medical Journal* 331 (7519): 737–742. doi:10.1136/bmj.331.7519.737

Dekker, Annette M., Ashley E. Amick, Cecilia Scholcoff and Ashti Doobay-Persaud. 2017. "A Mixed-Methods Needs Assessment of Adult Diabetes Mellitus (Type II) and Hypertension Care in Toledo, Belize." *BMC Health Services Research* 17 (1): 1–11. doi:10.1186/s12913-017-2075-9

Devlin, Heather, Martha Roberts, Amy Okaya and Yer Moua Xiong. 2006. "Our Lives Were Healthier Before: Focus Groups With African American, American Indian, Hispanic/Latino, and Hmong People With Diabetes." *Health Promotion Practice* 7 (1): 47–55. doi:10.1177/1524839905275395

Ellis, Lucia. 2010. *Dimensions and Boundaries of Garifunaduau*. 3rd ed. Belmopan: African Advancement Association of Belize.

Ferguson, Jane K., Eleanor W. Willemsen and May Lynn V. Castañeto. 2010. "Centering Prayer as a Healing Response to Everyday Stress: A Psychological and Spiritual Process." *Pastoral Psychology* 59 (3): 305–329. doi:10.1007/s11089-009-0225-7

Franz, Marion J., and Alison Evert. 2012. *American Diabetes Association Guide to Nutrition Therapy for Diabetes*. 2nd ed. Alexandria: American Diabetes Association.

George, Linda K., Warren A. Kinghorn, Harold G. Koenig, Patricia Gammon and Dan G. Blazer. 2013. "Why Gerontologists Should Care about Empirical Research on Religion and Health: Transdisciplinary Perspectives." *Gerontologist* 53 (6): 898–906. doi:10.1093/geront/gnt002

Grajower, Martin M., and Benjamin D. Horne. 2019. "Clinical Management of Intermittent Fasting in Patients with Diabetes Mellitus." *Nutrients* 11 (4): 1–11. doi:10.3390/nu11040873

Gulley, Tauna, Dusta Boggs, Rebecca Mullins and Emily Brock. 2014. "Diabetes Screening in the Workplace." *Workplace Health and Safety* 62 (11): 444–446. doi:10.3928/21650799-20141014-01

Gupta, Priya S., and Gowri Anandarajah. 2014. "The Role of Spirituality in Diabetes Self-Management in an Urban, Underserved Population: A Qualitative Exploratory Study." *Rhode Island Medical Journal (2013)* 97 (3): 31–35.

Habte, Bruck M., Tedla Kebede, Teferi G. Fenta and Heather Boon. 2017. "Barriers and Facilitators to Adherence to Anti-Diabetic Medications: Ethiopian Patients' Perspectives." *African Journal of Primary Health Care and Family Medicine* 9 (1): 1–9. doi:10.4102/phcfm.v9i1.1411

Hackett, Ruth A., and Andrew Steptoe. 2017. "Type 2 Diabetes Mellitus and Psychological Stress-a Modifiable Risk Factor." *Nature Reviews Endocrinology* 13 (9): 547–560. doi:10.1038/nrendo.2017.64

Hatala, Andrew, Jonathan McGavock, Valerie Michaelson and William Pickett. 2020. "Low Risks for Spiritual Highs: Risk-Taking Behaviours and the Protective Benefits of Spiritual Health among Saskatchewan Adolescents." *Paediatrics and Child Health* 26 (2): e121–e128. doi:10.1093/pch/pxaa007

Hatala, Andrew R., James B. Waldram and Tomas Caal. 2015. "Narrative Structures of Maya Mental Disorders." *Culture, Medicine and Psychiatry* 39 (3): 449–486. doi:10.1007/s11013-015-9436-9

Heidari, Saeide, Mahboubeh Rezaei, Mahbobeh Sajadi, Neda Mirbagher Ajorpaz and Harold G. Koenig. 2017. "Religious Practices and Self-Care in Iranian Patients with Type 2 Diabetes." *Journal of Religion and Health* 56 (2): 683–696. doi:10.1007/s10943-016-0320-x

Hesse-Biber, Sharlene Nagy. 2017. *The Practice of Qualitative Research: Engaging Students in the Research Process.* 3rd ed. Thousand Oaks: Sage.

Hewitt, Jeanette. 2007. "Ethical Components of Researcher-Researched Relationships in Qualitative Interviewing." *Qualitative Health Research*, 17 (8): 1149–1159. doi:10.1177/0741713609334139

Isabel, Jeanne. 2018. "Examining the Incidence of Pre Diabetes in Belize." *American Society for Clinical Laboratory Science* 30 (4) doi:10.29074/ascls.118.000174

Jacklin, Kristen M., Rita I. Henderson, Michael E. Green, Leah M. Walker, Betty Calam and Lynden J. Crowshoe. 2017. "Health Care Experiences of Indigenous People Living with Type 2 Diabetes in Canada." *Canadian Medical Association Journal* 189 (3): 106–112. doi:10.1503/cmaj.161098

Jeragh-Alhaddad, Fatima B., Mohammad Waheedi, Nick D. Barber and Tina Penick Brock. 2015. "Barriers to Medication Taking among Kuwaiti Patients with Type 2 Diabetes: A Qualitative Study." *Patient Preference and Adherence* 9: 1491–1503. doi:10.2147/PPA.S86719

Kim, Soo Jeong, and Dai Jin Kim. 2012. "Alcoholism and Diabetes Mellitus." *Diabetes and Metabolism Journal* 36 (2): 108–115. doi:10.4093/dmj.2012.36.2.108

Koenig, Harold G. 2004. "Spirituality Religion, Spirituality, and Medicine: Research Findings and Implications for Clinical Practice." *Southern Medical Journal* 97 (12): 1194–1200. doi:10.1097/01.smj.0000146489.21837.ce

Koenig, Harold G. 2008. "Concerns about Measuring 'Spirituality' in Research." *Journal of Nervous and Mental Disease* 196 (5): 349–355. doi:10.1097/NMD.0b013e31816ff796

Koenig, Harold G. 2014. "The Spiritual Care Team: Enabling the Practice of Whole Person Medicine." *Religions* 5 (4): 1161–1174. doi:10.3390/rel5041161

Krederdt-Araujo, Sherin L., Karen A. Dominguez-Cancino, Reynelda Jiménez-Cordova, Mariella Y. Paz-Villanueva, Julio Mendigure Fernandez, Juan M. Leyva-Moral and Patrick A. Palmieri. 2019. "Spirituality, Social Support, and Diabetes: A Cross-Sectional Study of People Enrolled in a Nurse-Led Diabetes Management Program in Peru." *Hispanic Health Care International* 17 (4): 162–171. doi:10.1177/1540415319847493

Lee, Jun Yang, Chee Piau Wong, Christina San San Tan, Nazrila Hairizan Nasir and Shaun Wen Huey Lee. 2017. "Type 2 Diabetes Patient's Perspective on Ramadan

Fasting: A Qualitative Study." *BMJ Open Diabetes Research and Care* 5 (1): 1–6. doi:10.1136/bmjdrc-2016-000365

Liamputtong, Pranee C. 2007. *Researching the Vulnerable a Guide to Sensitive Research Methods*. London: Sage Publications.

Lundberg, Pranee C., and Supunnee Thrakul. 2013. "Religion and Self-Management of Thai Buddhist and Muslim Women with Type 2 Diabetes." *Journal of Clinical Nursing* 22 (13–14):1907–1916. doi:10.1111/jocn.12130

Manderson, Lenore, and Carolyn Smith-Morris. 2010. *Chronicity and the Experience of Illness*. New Jersey: Rutgers University Press.

Marshall, Jacqueline, and Cynthia Archibald. 2015. "The Influence of Spirituality on Health Behaviors in an Afro-Caribbean Population." *The ABNF Journal: Official Journal of the Association of Black Nursing Faculty in Higher Education, Inc* 26 (3): 57–62.

Mattingly, Cheryl, Lone Grøn and Lotte Meinert. 2011. "Chronic Homework in Emerging Borderlands of Healthcare." *Culture, Medicine, and Psychiatry* 35 (3): 347–375. doi:10.1007/s11013-011-9225-z

OYE. 2017. "Cultural Relations in Belize, The Creole Garinagu Conflict." *Belize: Open Your Eyes, Channel 5*. Belize. www.youtube.com/watch?v=y2IpFxUiNqM

Permana, Iman. 2018. "How Religosity and/or Spirituality Might Influence Self-Care in Diabetes Management: A Structured Review." *Bangladesh Journal of Medical Science* 17 (2): 185–193. doi:10.3329/bjms.v17i2.35869

Rivera-Hernandez, Maricruz. 2016. "Religiosity, Social Support and Care Associated with Health in Older Mexicans with Diabetes." *Journal of Religion and Health* 55 (4): 1394–1410. doi:10.1007/s10943-015-0105-7

Roger, Kerstin Stieber, and Andrew R. Hatala. 2017. "Religion, Spirituality and Chronic Illness: A Scoping Review and Implications for Health Care Practitioners." *Journal of Religion and Spirituality in Social Work* 37 (1): 24–44. doi:10.1080/15426432.2017.1386151

Rossiter-Thornton, John F. 2002. "Prayer in Your Practice." *Complementary Therapies in Nursing and Midwifery* 8 (1): 21–28. doi:10.1054/ctnm.2001.0594

Rubin, Richard, Susan R. Walen and Albert Ellis. 1990. "Living with Diabetes." *Journal of Rational-Emotive and Cognitive-Behavior Therapy* 8 (1): 21–39. doi:10.1007/BF01072092

Saidi, Sanisah, Linda Jane Milnes and Jane Griffiths. 2018. "Fatalism, Faith and Fear: A Case Study of Self - Care Practice among Adults with Type 2 Diabetes in Urban Malaysia." *Journal of Clinical Nursing* 27 (19–20): 3758–3767. doi:10.1111/jocn.14559

Sam, Johanna, Hasu Ghosh and Chris G. Richardson. 2015. "Examining the Relationship between Attachment Styles and Resilience Levels among Aboriginal Adolescents in Canada." *AlterNative: An International Journal of Indigenous Peoples* 11 (3): 240–255. doi:10.1177/117718011501100303

Statistical Institute of Belize [SIB]. 2013. *Statistical Institue of Belize, Belize Population and Housing Census; Country Report 2010*. Belmopan: Statistical Institute of Belize.

Sridhar, G. R. 2013. "Diabetes, Religion and Spirituality." *International Journal of Diabetes in Developing Countries* 33 (1): 5–7. doi:10.1007/s13410-012-0097-8

Stevens, Lancer. 2019. "*Land-Based Camps for Youth*." November 20, 2019. Diabetes Research Envisioned and Accomplished in Manitoba (DREAM): 8th Annual Diabetes Research Symposium: Lives of Youth with Type 2 Diabetes: Learning from the Land and the Lab. University of Manitoba, Winnipeg.

Unantenne, Nalika, Narelle Warren, Rachel Canaway and Lenore Manderson. 2013. "The Strength to Cope: Spirituality and Faith in Chronic Disease." *Journal of Religion and Health* 52 (4): 1147–1161. doi:10.1007/s10943-011-9554-9

United Nations Development Programme [UNDP]. n.d. "Human Development Reports - Belize." United Nations-Development Programme. www.bz.undp.org/

Vigh, Henrik. 2008. "Crisis and Chronicity: Anthropological Perspectives on Continuous Conflict and Decline." *Ethnos* 73 (1): 5–24. doi:10.1080/00141840801927509

Waldram, James B. 2008. *Aboriginal Healing in Canada: Studies in Therapeutic Meaning and Practice.* The Aboriginal Healing Foundation Research Series. Canada: Aboriginal Healing Foundation.

Weaver, Lesley Jo, and Emily Mendenhall. 2014. "Applying Syndemics and Chronicity: Interpretations from Studies of Poverty, Depression, and Diabetes." *Medical Anthropology: Cross Cultural Studies in Health and Illness* 33 (2): 92–108. doi:10.1080/01459740.2013.808637

World Health Organization [WHO]. 2016a. "Diabetes Profile by Country – Belize." World Health Organization. www.who.int/diabetes/country-profiles/blz_en.pdf?ua=1

World Health Organization [WHO]. 2016b. "Proportional Mortality (% of Total Deaths, All Ages)." World Health Organization. www.who.int/nmh/countries/blz_en.pdf?ua=1

World Health Organization [WHO]. 2018. "Country Cooperation Strategy – Belize." https://apps.who.int/iris/bitstream/handle/10665/136963/ccsbrief_blz_en.pdf?sequence=1&isAllowed=y

World Health Ranking [WHR]. 2019. "Belize: Diabetes Mellitus." World Health Ranking: World Life Expectancy. www.worldlifeexpectancy.com/belize-diabetes-mellitus

Wilmoth, Summer R., Leah Carrilo, Meixia Pan, Diana Chavarria, Bradley Wilhite, Deborah Parra-Medina and Meizi He. 2019. "Building a Healthy Temple: A Faith-Based Diabetes Self-Management Support Program." *Diabetes* 68 (Supplement): 690. doi:10.2337/db19-690-P

Wimpenny, Peter, and John Gass. 2000. "Interviewing in Phenomenology and Grounded Theory: Is There a Difference?" *Journal of Advanced Nursing* 31 (6): 1485–1492. doi:10.1046/j.1365-2648.2000.01431.x

World Data Atlas. 2019. "Belize BZ: Diabetes Prevalence: % of Population Aged 20–79." China Ethnic International Economic Cooperation (CEIC). www.ceicdata.com/en/belize/health-statistics/bz-diabetes-prevalence-of-population-aged-2079

Yazla, Ece, Mehmet Emrah Karadere, Ferit Kerim Küçükler, Çağatay Karşıdağ, Leman İnanç, Elif Kankoç, Melda Dönertaş and Emre Demir. 2017. "The Effect of Religious Belief and Forgiveness on Coping with Diabetes." *Journal of Religion and Health* 57 (3): 1010–1019. doi:10.1007/s10943-017-0504-z

11 Cultures of wellness and recovery

Exploring religion and chronicity in relation to severe mental illness

G. Eric Jarvis, Rob Whitley and Marie Nathalie LeBlanc

Introduction

Mental disorders cause immense suffering globally. Frequently, mental disorders begin during adolescence and in young adulthood, with symptoms and distress often lasting many years. For the more than 200 million people with severe mental disorders in the world (APA 2020; Bowie et al. 2010; GBD 2017; Solomon et al. 2000), this can mean significant symptoms and disability globally (Goldman, Gattozzi and Taube 1981). Traditionally, chronic suffering and dysfunction have been assumed for some psychiatric conditions, such as psychosis, mood disorders, and addictions, but in recent years the notion of recovery has been evolving, with significant input from mental health consumers (MentalHealth.gov 2019).

Conventional top-down clinical models of recovery created by mental health professionals, like psychologists and psychiatrists, tend to emphasize symptom reduction or elimination (Drake and Whitley 2014). In contrast, more bottom-up, consumer-driven notions of recovery tend to emphasize growth and transformation in areas such as employment, housing, social relationships, and community participation (Anthony 1993). Notions of recovery have also increasingly been enlarged to consider non-biomedical conceptions of illness and recovery, such as those associated with practices of spiritual and religious care or healing. These consumer-driven recovery models are often more flexible, allowing for adaptation to the unique needs and experiences of individuals with mental illness in their particular circumstances. This has led to a widespread consensus in the consumer advocacy movement that recovery is a deeply personal journey that is resistant to a "one-size-fits-all" definition and solution (Deegan 1996; Drake and Whitley 2014) and not circumscribed by biomedical conceptions of recovery and care alone.

Religion has various characteristic components, such as a structured belief system, prescribed rituals and practices, and typically an association with a group or community that shares the same beliefs and values (Koenig 2008). Religion also teaches and encourages various forms of spirituality, which may be loosely defined as an individual's relationship to a transcendent being or extra-human forces such as spirits, ancestors, and natural forces, concepts that are less dependent on group worship (Williams and Sternthal 2007). Religious variables have been neglected for decades in mental health research, despite the consistent finding that religious

DOI: 10.4324/9781003043508-11

beliefs and practices are usually associated with mental health and wellness on diverse measures (Koenig, King and Carson 2012). More specifically, religious participation and practice have been neglected aspects of personal recovery from severe or chronic mental illness. Yet, religious cultures, beliefs, and practices can offer powerful tools to assist patients and their families in times of illness and suffering. The re-evaluation of notions of chronicity and wellness, as some belief systems encourage, permit reinterpretation of the illness experience, reduce stigma, and foster recovery (Drake and Whitley 2014; Whitley 2012). Clinicians therefore need to better understand the religious and/or spiritual interpretations of illness, as well as the religious or spiritual resources that exist in the lives of their patients, and plan interventions accordingly. Neglecting to support, or even acknowledge, these resources may undermine the therapeutic relationship, or unwittingly may worsen suffering over the illness course.

In their compendium of mostly North American studies, *Handbook of Religion and Health, Second Edition*, Koenig et al. (2012) report that religion and spirituality are more often correlated with mental health than mental illness: depression (in 63% of the reported studies), suicide (75%), alcohol and drug use (86%), and delinquency (79%) are negatively correlated with religious measures while individual well-being (79%) and marital stability (87%) are positively correlated (Koenig et al. 2012). This implies that there is something protective, even helpful, about religious or spiritual belief, practice or values in the face of mental disorder and distress. Fallot (2001) also reported that most consumers, meaning those with mental disorders, found that religion and spirituality provided resources for recovery by providing helpful coping strategies (e.g., prayer, avoidance of substances, positive role models), social support and networking, and a sense of purpose and meaning to life experience, including mental illness. Important aspects of religious and spiritual dimensions of recovery in Fallot's work included a sense of self that could not be reduced to symptoms or diagnostic categories, potent roles for faith-based hope and persistence, the healing role of loving relationships (human and divine), and a search for existential self-improvement as part of the religious and recovery journeys. Ho et al. (2016) similarly found that clients and mental health professionals shared the belief that religion and spirituality are important in recovery from schizophrenia, but professionals tended to emphasize practical outcomes like support and symptom management, while patients emphasized experiential qualities like personal and emotional growth. Considering the different perspectives of clients and practitioners is an important, yet frequently neglected, aspect of recovery and positive outcomes.

Despite these findings, religious belief and practice do not always lead to health and fulfilment. For example, when surveying the general American public about religious beliefs and practices, some respondents prefer a non-religious life (Pew Research Centre as per Lipka 2016), while others may feel harmed by the very structures that buttress support and positive change in others. Religious suffering may manifest as excess guilt or unfulfilled self-expectations. A wide range of mental health concerns, for example, grandiosity and psychotic symptoms, may take on religious overtones that may be difficult to extinguish when religiously reinforced. When religious and spiritual beliefs, as interpreted by religious leaders, contradict psychiatric treatments, then Fallot (2007) states recovery may be compromised. Indeed, individuals with severe mental disorders, as well as those treating them, may have difficulty distinguishing between illness symptoms and religious imperatives or experiences (Fallot 2007). When an individual (from any cultural background or tradition) questions religious/spiritual beliefs and faith, a number of problems may emerge that can trigger distress and may complicate recovery from mental health problems. Indeed, 51% of studies find a positive correlation between religion and anxiety-related outcomes, while the relation between religion and psychosis, bipolar disorder, and personality disorders is more complex (Koenig et al. 2012).

Clearly, then, religion and spirituality are not always linked to mental health. Cognitive dissonance in this context refers to unsuccessfully reconciling the beliefs of one's religious upbringing with doubts or concerns about the existence of a loving God and may lead to intense suffering and distress (Zuckerman, Galen and Pasquale 2016). Loss of a worldview may also ensue as religious beliefs are abandoned, and the individual loses purpose and meaning in life (Heiner 1992; Zukerman et al. 2016). Loneliness and isolation may accompany a decision to abandon traditional beliefs since friends and family no longer share the same worldview (Heiner 1992; Williams and Sternthal 2007). Abandoning religious beliefs and practices may lead to conflict with family and friends, or at least attempts on their part to bring the individual around to their former religious views (Zuckerman at al. 2016). Further losses may include reduced access to social networks at churches, synagogues, mosques, or temples, with consequent loss of social capital and opportunity. Some atheists or the non-religious may face discrimination from the wider society due to mistrust of those with doubts about God and religion (Heiner 1992; Lipka 2016). In this regard, Ross (1990) identified a horseshoe-shaped, curvilinear relationship between distress and religious belief, with the highest levels of distress occurring in those with weak, but not absent, religious conviction. Similarly, Rosmarin, Krumrei and Andersson (2009) found that affiliation (Christian, Jewish, etc.) was a poor predictor of distress, but mistrust in God among members of religious communities was associated with distress. Subjects endorsing statements like "God ignores me," "God is not in total control," and "I don't need God" or "God treats me unfairly" scored high on mistrust of God. This implies that in situations where religion is the perceived cause of problems, recovery from mental illness may become uncertain.

This chapter will review and critique the literature on chronicity in Severe Mental Illness (SMI) given its neglect as a subject of study and the common assumption by mainstream mental health practitioners that severe mental illnesses, like schizophrenia and bipolar disorder, are unremitting. This chapter also will challenge conventional attitudes by reinterpreting notions of recovery in the context of religious and spiritual practice and faith. Specifically, religious and spiritual case material from the Cultural Consultation Service (CCS) and First Episode Psychosis Program (FEPP) in Montreal, Canada, will be summarized and assessed thematically with respect to chronicity and recovery from severe mental illness. Lastly, a clinical framework for fostering recovery in religious or spiritual contexts of SMI will be offered.

Religious cultures of recovery in the face of adversity

Faith traditions typically provide their adherents with foundational stories that teach and inspire hope in the face of adversity. The widely known Jewish exodus from slavery, as recounted in Exodus chapters 1–15 of the Jewish and Christian Bible, is an example of a story, some would say myth, that provides a pattern of liberation from suffering despite modern critical readings that complicate the discussion (Kirk-Duggan 2012). Binz (1993) suggests that such a powerful narrative of gaining freedom from oppression under the watchful eye of a loving God provides tools for individuals of all ages to overcome personal challenges and move forward toward a more hopeful position.

Many other examples exist. Martin Luther's questioning of the religious paradigm of his time came at a high personal cost. Judd (2016) chronicles that Luther experienced significant depression, anxiety, and obsessive-compulsive behavior, which only resolved through a reliance on the Grace of God. By letting go of despair and putting his trust in a higher power, Luther became a prominent Christian reformer, and his success in the face of significant adversity has inspired Protestant Christians around the world.

The Latter-Day Saints' recovery from religious persecution in the mid-nineteenth century was accomplished in part by what Arrington and Bitton (1992) call the mythic potency of the new religion, or its capacity to give meaning and purpose to sacred stories and events. Embedded in this mythically potent narrative are such elements as the search for true and authoritative religion, ancient ties to Old Testament prophecies and practices, modern revelation including new scriptures like the Book of Mormon, a restoration of the ancient Church of Christ, and eschatological claims that include the founding of a new Zion by the Latter-Day Saints and the gathering of scattered Israel. All of these mythic elements gave impetus and strength of will to early converts (called "pioneers") to overcome successive expulsions and to establish a Latter-Day Saint society in the Western United States, an achievement that has inspired later generations.

As a last example, the impact of the Hajj pilgrimage to Mecca on individual well-being has been well documented (Alnabulsi et al. 2018). The Hajj, which is a lengthy and expensive journey, and thus a ritualized form of adversity in its own right, represents a foundational story of faith for its participants with ample opportunity for self-change. Alnabulsi et al. (2018) surveyed pilgrims in Mecca and found that the Hajj strengthens Muslim identity while at the same time increasing tolerance for non-Muslims. The authors cited the famous example of Malcolm X who reported being changed by the unity among Muslims from all backgrounds and races that he experienced in Mecca. Variables significantly associated with positive attitudes to non-Muslims included perceived cooperation and unity among Hajj participants and having a positive Hajj experience. These examples of religious traditions and cultural practices demonstrate ways in which a spiritual orientation and foundational stories may contribute to successfully triumphing over adversity, of which recovery from mental illness is just one kind.

Recovery and the chronicity of Severe Mental Illness

Severe Mental Illness (SMI) is an umbrella term referring to schizophrenia spectrum disorders, schizoaffective disorder, bipolar disorder, and major depression, which share characteristics regarding symptom severity, functional impairment, and treatment trajectories (Bartels 2004; Becker and Drake 2003). Historically, mainstream psychiatry has typically considered SMI to be chronic, persistent, deteriorating, and incapacitating over the whole life-course. For most patients, this means a grim and nihilistic prognosis, reflected in a mental health system founded on an intensely paternalistic and pessimistic ethos (Anthony 1993; Deegan 1988, 1996). This has been reflected in historic and contemporary psychiatric practices for people with SMI, which often involves lengthy and involuntary institutionalization, prescription of high-dose medication with significant side effects, supervised and regulated housing, and sheltered "therapeutic" activities. For example, patients are sometimes encouraged to participate in meaningless activities such as making raffia mats or wicker baskets (hence the derogatory term "basket case" for people with mental illness), while being discouraged from engaging in everyday, normative, meaning-making activities such as tertiary education, meaningful employment, independent housing, and creating a family.

Indeed, psychiatry tends to extend its authority to envelop all these aspects of patients' lives, generally curtailing attempts at independence, and instead taking an approach dominated by a "shield and protect" philosophy (Drake and Whitley 2014).

This historic approach, arising from paternalistic perspectives that equate people with mental illness with children and a related desire to protect them from unjust criminal conviction (see Zukowski 2018), stands in stark contrast to other areas of medicine, where such medical overreach has been rarely seen, and patient autonomy and choice still are considered sacrosanct. In other words, psychiatric rehabilitation was more or less unknown for most of the 20th century, until the recent international paradigm shift toward the notion of recovery, which has been embraced by governments and jurisdictions across the world (Mental Health Commission of Canada 2009; MentalHealth.gov 2019). Recovery principles stand in stark contrast to paternalistic and pessimistic notions of SMI chronicity, as can be seen in the broad definitions offered by the Mental Health Commission of Canada (2009, 28):

> Recovery involves a process of growth and transformation as the person moves beyond the acute distress often associated with a mental health problem or illness and develops newfound strengths and ways of being.

This definition overlaps with another influential (and broad) definition of recovery that has been the driving force behind such "recovery-work" in the United States. This comes from a statement by the U.S. Department of Health and Human Services Substance Abuse and Mental Health Services Administration (2004, 1):

Mental health recovery is a journey of healing and transformation enabling a person with a mental health problem to live a meaningful life in a community of his or her choice while striving to achieve his or her full potential.

Neither of these definitions explicitly highlight symptom remission as a key facet of recovery, moving the definition away from traditional clinical priorities. Instead, they focus on hopeful, positive, and optimistic processes (as much as outcomes), and concepts such as "growth," "healing," and "transformation." These definitions indicate that the recovery paradigm is more holistic and person-centered than other paradigms that emphasize "continuing care," "coping," or "medication stabilization" (Berwick 2009; Mezzich 2007).

The recovery paradigm has roots in three separate literatures that emerged in the 1990s and have continued to offer strong evidence against notions of chronicity and in favor of a more hopeful vision of recovery. These are 1) numerous overlapping psychiatric epidemiological studies indicating that SMI is frequently episodic or transient, including WHO studies indicating better outcome for schizophrenia in poor as opposed to wealthy societies (Hopper, Harrison and Wanderling 2007; Jablensky et al. 1992; Leff et al. 1992), 2) an amassed corpus of research from the new field of psychiatric rehabilitation indicating that psychosocial interventions can foster core aspects of recovery for people with SMI, and 3) the writings and outreach activity of people with SMI in the "consumer-survivor" movement, detailing their lived experience of recovery in poignant, accessible, and engaging books, articles, and videos.

Numerous epidemiological studies (and meta-analyses), mainly from Europe and the United States since the end of the 19th century, indicate that between 30% and 50% of people with SMI receiving standard psychiatric treatments show full or substantial remission of symptoms five to ten years after first onset (Harding et al. 1987; Harding and Zahniser 1994; Hegarty et al. 1994). Davidson and Roe (2007) call this process of symptom remission "recovery *from* mental illness", thereby representing the traditional clinical approach to recovery. This research shows that clinical recovery is possible, even for the most severe SMIs, thus challenging the prevalent clinical and popular belief that SMI is a chronic and incapacitating disease afflicting the life-course, and leaving the person unable to partake in normative activities (Mueser and McGurk 2004).

Research from the field of psychiatric rehabilitation also suggests that even those with SMI who remain symptomatic can participate in valued activities and social roles, for example paid employment, education, or independent living, as long as they are given the right services and supports (Becker and Drake 2003; Davidson 2003; Whitley, Harris and Drake 2008). This has led to the development of a panoply of effective evidence-based interventions for people with SMI, such as supported employment or supported housing, that enable people to live an independent and more meaningful life. Davidson and Roe (2007) call this "recovery *in* mental illness." This vision of recovery is based on the wider rehabilitation model used for physical health issues such as injuries or accidents, where high-quality and effectively implemented interventions can significantly improve independence, functioning, and quality of life, even in the presence of ongoing symptoms. Thus, rehabilitation science has offered the hope that recovery can occur despite the presence of SMI.

Perhaps most importantly, new perspectives have emerged from the consumer movement describing their own first-person experience of recovery through books, articles, videos, media appearances, and other outreach activities. These include poignant autobiographical memoirs detailing lived experience, often portraying the suffering and distress caused by SMI, as well as the journey of recovery and strategies of resilience. Popular autobiographies include *The Center Cannot Hold* by Elyn Saks (2007), outlining recovery from schizophrenia, and Matt Haig's *Reasons to Stay Alive* (2015), describing recovery from depression. These works offer hope and inspiration by illuminating the realities of recovery from SMI. Pat Deegan (1996, 1997) has written first-person accounts of recovery in articles published in psychiatric journals in an attempt to educate clinicians and transform dominant psychiatric narratives. In these contexts, recovery often involves highly personal factors, such as reconnecting with family, making a meaningful contribution to the local community, or rediscovering religious or spiritual connections and thereby moving the focus away from clinical or functional aspects to more existential and social concerns, and reinforcing that SMIs are not always chronic, deteriorating, or incapacitating conditions.

Reinterpretation of recovery in religious context

The first-person narratives giving voice to a consumer movement indicate that people with SMI often face a paucity of uplifting and life-affirming experiences, especially in the aftermath of an acute illness episode. One factor that can potentially mitigate the oftentimes distressing outcomes of SMI is involvement in religious and spiritual pathways, communities, and practices. A religious or spiritual pathway in this context refers to adopting a certain lifestyle and focus over the life course (Lee, Pearce and Schorpp 2017), or it may refer to a more formal choice to follow a sacred vocation, as in choosing full-time commitment within a religious structure like the Catholic Church (Gaunt 2018).

Many first-person narratives mention the important role of spirituality and religion in fostering recovery and helping to fill the existential void arising from SMI (Drake and Whitley 2014). This is also consistent with several qualitative research studies (Ho et al. 2016; Laudet et al. 2006; Starnino 2016), indicating that people with SMI (and indeed dual diagnosis), frequently seek and obtain hope and solace in God (sometimes defined as a supreme being, a higher power, or the divine) and/or through involvement in a religious pathway. Despite the diversity of groups under study in this area (Ho et al. 2016; Nicholls 2002, Laudet, Morgen and White 2006), religion and spirituality were deemed of importance by participants and linked to recovery in most cases. This can involve solitary private activities, such as prayer in the home and consultation of scripture, and/or communal public activities such as belonging to a community of believers or volunteering at a place of worship (Whitley 2012).

In a qualitative study of African American Protestant Christian religious believers with SMI, Whitley (2012) found that participants attributed progress in their recovery to private and public religious activities, including a personal relationship with God and meaningful involvement in local churches. Interestingly, participants frequently deployed theological concepts such as faith, hope, forgiveness, and redemption to place their recovery in a spiritual context. For example, these notions were used to frame new beginnings and the importance of ongoing transformation of the self. Such concepts could be seen as analogous to hopeful principles of recovery that emphasize growth and progress in the journey of life and that were inconsistent with perceptions of chronicity.

In other words, commonly held theological beliefs overlap considerably with commonly held recovery principles, with both emphasizing a positive and gradual transformative experience in the face of hardship and distress. Along these lines, Whitley and Drake (2010, 1248) aptly developed the term "existential recovery" defined as "having a sense of hope, empowerment, agency, and spiritual well-being...which includes factors such as religion, spirituality, meaning and values." For some people, existential recovery is an essential aspect of recovery, promoted by spiritual activity and religious participation.

Further evidence suggests that this form of recovery can be especially important for ethno-racial groups with high religiosity, including African Americans and Caribbean immigrants (Whitley et al. 2006, 2012). Indeed, some research indicates that African Americans may turn to religion and its institutions due to alienation and estrangement from the official mental health system (Neighbors, Musick and Williams 1998). Moreover, the language and conceptual universe of religions may resonate more with some minority communities, such as African Americans and Muslim immigrants, to name two examples, than the language and conceptual universe of psychiatry and allied professions (Ibrahim and Whitley in press 2020), an insight that may prove to be useful for clinicians as they work with patients, and that suggests limitations of the frameworks employed by mental health professionals.

Indeed, there is still an ambivalent relationship between religion and psychiatry, meaning that the incorporation of religiosity and religious resources into clinical care is still sub-optimal (Ibrahim and Whitley in press 2020). This may deter service utilization and weaken the therapeutic alliance in religious patients but can improve as service providers adopt a religiously and culturally informed way of implementing their clincial work. Lack of religious competence in psychiatry is concerning, given that religiously oriented worldviews overlap considerably with recovery-oriented worldviews: both tend to be positive, hopeful, and transformative, meaning that they are by definition inconsistent with nihilistic beliefs about chronicity.

Study: A typology of religious and spiritual representations in psychiatric consultation

Research context

In order to challenge conventional attitudes of recovery from SMI and to better understand the role and context of religious – spiritual practice and faith in this process, case material from the Cultural Consultation Service (CCS) in Montreal, Canada, was summarized and assessed thematically. The CCS at McGill University has received almost 1000 referrals since 1999 to assess issues of culture, religion and spirituality, ethnicity, and migration. The CCS uses linguistic interpreters and culture brokers to conduct in depth cultural consultations of migrants and refugees, with extensive clinical, ethnographic, cultural, religious and spiritual information about patients. While the cases discussed in this chapter come from the CCS, where patients are almost entirely of immigrant or refugee origin, the articulation between religiosity and mental illness may be of clinical importance in patients of any background. While it may take on different meanings and roles, European and North American cultures also have traditions in which these concepts are intertwined, as evidenced by pilgrimage sites devoted to healing at Saint Joseph's Oratory in Montreal and Lourdes in southern France.

Methodology

For this project, investigators (GEJ, MNL) gathered CCS data from 2015 to thematically assess religious and spiritual representations (through everyday practice, words, stories, emotions, and values) in patients referred to the CCS to 1) suggest categories of representations in this population, 2) highlight how representations may inform psychiatric evaluation and treatment, and 3) offer reflections on how such representations may influence the recovery of individuals and families from the effects of SMI. The Ethics Review Board of the Jewish General Hospital approved the project.

A trained research assistant collected data from CCS charts from 2015, including relevant sociodemographic and clinical information for each patient and descriptive and thematic material related to religious and spiritual representations drawn from CCS reports of clinical interviews. Specifically, the study focused on gathering information on religious and spiritual items, such as religious affiliation of patients and their family members, religious practice, involvement of religious/spiritual leaders in the evaluation, the relation of religion and spirituality to the presenting problem, and religious and spiritual interventions that may have been part of the cultural consultation. Thematic analysis of the relation of religion and spirituality to the presenting problem proceeded according to Braun and Clarke (2006), which included searching and reviewing the data, defining and naming themes, developing an initial list of themes, and producing a preliminary report. This procedure produced 41 patient histories for analysis from 2015 CCS data. The case vignettes described have been changed to obscure key identifying details of the patients to preserve anonymity.

Study results

Of the 41 patients in 2015, most were single female, immigrants to Canada, with a mean age of 34 years (see Table 11.1). Ethnicity and mother tongue were

Table 11.1 Characteristics of cases (n=41)

Item	Result
Mean age	34 years
Female	26 (63%)
Single, never married	22 (54%)
Immigrant	35 (85%)
Ethnicity & mother tongue	Hyper-diverse (no dominant category)
Interpreter used	17 (41%)
Culture broker used	8 (20%)
Social worker referral	19 (46%)
Religious affiliation • Christian • Muslim • Hindu • Buddhist • Other • Not religious • Not documented	 15 (37%) 7 (17%) 4 (10%) 2 (5%) 3 (7%) 6 (15%) 4 (9%)
Formal religious participation	18 (44%)
Religion or spirituality related to the presenting problem	25 (61%)
Religious or Spiritual intervention(s) recommended	17 (41%)

hyper-diverse, meaning that there was no dominant group in the sample. The cases in this study were interviewed by psychiatrists, either a white male, white female, or South Asian female. Patients most often came from countries in the Middle East (8/41) and spoke Arabic (7/41), but were of Christian affiliation (15/41). While 18/41 of the subjects endorsed formal religious participation, religion or spirituality related to the presenting problem in a slight majority (25/41). Examples will be reviewed in the Case Material section below. The source of the case material was the Cultural Consultation report in which the evaluating psychiatrist records information directly from the patient and includes summary statements from the cultural formulation, a kind of culturally informed assessment. The CCS recommended religious or spiritual interventions, in combination with standard psychiatric treatments like medication, for 17/41 patients (see Table 11.1).

Religious and spiritual interventions included encouraging patients to attend religious services, accessing sacred texts, performing private religious rituals in the home, and inviting religious leaders to discuss problems and potential solutions, including healing practices. Thematic analysis identified four principal themes, namely, 1) religion or spirituality as *cure* of the presenting problem in which the patient strives to *overcome* the problem, 2) religion or spirituality as *comfort or support* in which the patient comes to *accept* the problem, 3) religion or spirituality as perceived *cause, idiom, and interpretation* of the presenting

Cultures of wellness and recovery 231

Table 11.2 Religious or spiritual representations of the presenting clinical problem (n=38)

Category	Number	Relation to recovery
Cure of problem	4 (10%)	Potentially positive
Comfort/support	11 (29%)	Potentially positive
Cause of problem	9 (24%)	Complex
Predicament	14 (37%)	Potentially negative

problem in which the patient attributes an underlying reason to *explain* the problem, and 4) religion or spirituality as *predicament* in which the patient *hesitates* or is unable to resolve the problem. Some patient narratives organized around a single theme, whereas others had more than one. Religion and spirituality as cure, comfort or support, in which the patient overcomes or accepts the problem, suggested a potentially positive role in recovery from mental disorder; whereas religion and spirituality as cause or predicament, in which the patient attributes underlying reasons (potentially positive but often negative) and hesitates or is unable to resolve the problem, indicated more complex relationships between religion and recovery (see Table 11.2). Religious and spiritual cause in the context of these cases refered to a clinical narrative in which the patient implies or directly attributes religion or spirituality as the explanation of the problem, whereas religion and spirituality as predicament, in which the patient was unable to resolve the problem due to ambivalence or guilt about aspects of religious belief or practice, did not identify a root cause of the problem per se but rather described a religious or spiritual dilemma that may make a situation more confusing or complex, or may contribute to distress without expressly causing it.

The remaining sections provide case vignettes, examples of the four themes from patient histories, and quotations and will discuss the interpretation of the themes by drawing upon examples from the 2015 dataset as well as relevant material from other clinical settings such as FEPP. Importantly, the findings from the examples relate to well-known dimensions of the cultures and societies of the study cases and thus are not idiosyncratic findings; rather they situate themselves well when considering the roles of religious and spiritual beliefs and practices in recovery.

Theme 1: Cure (Overcome)

A single man in his mid-twenties, who is originally from West Africa and a devout Muslim, was referred by a psychologist to assess whether or not he needs medication and to confirm a diagnosis of Post-Traumatic Stress Disorder (PTSD) and Major Depressive Disorder in the context of the deaths of family members and threats to his life by hostile extended family. Symptoms include headache attributed to "thinking too much," stomach pains, grief for his lost family, poor sleep fatigue, poor concentration and memory, lack of motivation, tearfulness, sad mood, guilty feelings, irritability, avoidance of others, and the sense that his life is no longer worth living. While still in West Africa, he looked for someone to help him (*féticheur* in French):

> He then visited an elder, or traditional healer, who gave him something that made him vomit and he brought up two frogs that were alive and breathing – the patient was convinced that they were sent to him by his uncle – he slowly improved but has never fully recovered and is afraid that the frogs may have returned as the elder warned.
>
> (case 2015–32)

Healers (animist, Christian, and Muslim) are commonly approached for help in West African societies, especially for ailments that can not be rapidly cured in biomedical contexts, such as persistent headaches, stomach aches, and mental disorders. This individual expressed his hope that he could return to the healer to follow up with the treatment he had received and hopefully have a complete cure. To sufferers from diverse cultural backgrounds, religion and spirituality as cure may represent the hope that mental illness and the suffering it entails are not what mental health professionals say (i.e., chronic and persisting) and that a spiritual intervention, if properly implemented, has the potential to entirely remove the affliction. In what is often a clash of belief systems, the patient hopes that reliance on faith and religious or spiritual cures will ultimately show that the psychiatrist is wrong, and that the religious intervention will vindicate the patient's religious worldview by affecting a resolution.

The history of a 36-year-old woman was also illustrative of this religious "cure" typology. She had been feeling observed for several months in her apartment, especially by her sister, who she thought was tapping her telephone lines. At its most intense, the woman could feel the energy coursing through the telephone lines. When she became aggressive toward her sister because of the perceived meddling in her life, the sister called the police, and they brought her to the hospital. The inpatient team treated her for two months with antipsychotic medication with minimal benefit. Given the slow pace of recovery, and consonant with her beliefs as a devout Christian, the patient asked for "a spiritual Baptist healing" as the only way to overcome her suffering. The inpatient team was worried that acquiescing to her demands would expose her to unproven, expensive, or even harmful therapies while taking her away from standard psychiatric care. The CCS consultant negotiated a compromise: a leader of the woman's religious community would attend a meeting to discuss the spiritual healing and what it would entail. The patient would need to travel to a city five hours away to receive the intervention. She would need to stop all medications. The whole process would take several days and would consist of prayer and exhortation. The woman signed herself out from the hospital to undergo the religious healing. When symptoms persisted following the healing, she eventually made her way back to the hospital for ongoing treatment. Even though the hoped-for cure did not take place, the gesture by the team of letting her try the religious or spiritual healing improved the therapeutic alliance, and she was eventually ready to be discharged to her home on friendly terms with her hospital team despite differences in conceptual understanding about the illness. Recovery in this patient's case was assisted by the religious or spiritual intervention even though the results were less than anticipated. Hence, patients that believe in a religious or spiritual cure for their problem generally hope that they can overcome their suffering through to an adherence intervention consistent with their worldview.

Theme 2: Comfort/support (Accept)

Unlike religion as cure, religion or spirituality as comfort and support implies a greater willingness on the patient's part to accept that there is a problem, or at least acknowledge that there is a degree of suffering that may not be easily resolved but that can still be mitigated by an appeal to religious beliefs, practices, and lifestyle. A woman with depression, who spoke only Hindi, was referred by Child Protection Services to assess her withdrawn behavior toward family and to rule out psychotic disorder. She was isolating in her home, withdrew from most activities, was worried about being threatened by "black magic" (the patient's term), excessively washed herself and dishes, and feared contamination, with impaired overall function and reliance on her sister to provide for most basic needs:

> It is after her Dad and infant died she really starts to get depressed, these were terribly sad events, she says, "Those who die must go to paradise," so they sang hymns and prayers, there was much weeping, for the dead baby, they poured milk on his tombstone.
>
> (case 2015–38)

The woman recalled this information as she related events leading to her depressed state and invoked a belief in life after death as a comforting idea that buffered against the devastating loss of father and child in the same month. The rituals of singing hymns, prayers, and pouring milk, mingled with weeping, were shared activities conducted in religious and community context, with powerful comforting and supportive functions.

When a young man in his early twenties began to seek the monastic life, at first his family was deeply concerned. He was admitted to the hospital, but the same thoughts persisted. He became more religious than his family and began to frequent marginal figures in his community. Eventually, he disappeared to a monastery in the country of origin of his parents but did not tell anyone where he had gone. The abbot of the monastery called the parents to explain that their son was not entirely well and needed to return home. Back in Canada, the patient continued taking antipsychotic medication for the next year. Although explicit psychotic symptoms and behaviors had disappeared, the heightened religiosity did not. After months of careful planning, and with the blessing of his parents, he moved to another monastery while taking low dose antipsychotic. He found the simple, austere lifestyle of the monks pleasing and stabilizing; they provided a structure and a tolerant environment that comforted and supported the patient despite ongoing symptoms and promoted a lasting recovery.

Sometimes, religious environments do more than provide a structure. When a woman in her late twenties was threatened with deportation, members of her cloistered community sought the help of the CCS. The woman had joined a conservative Catholic order several years before from another country. Her symptoms of psychosis were well known to the community and consisted of chronic auditory hallucinations of a benign nature. Remarkably, the leader of the order had asked the patient to record what the voices were telling her, and he would review the writings and offer interpretations of what they might portend. The woman was given daily tasks in the kitchen and a prescribed religious routine under the supervision of her superiors. This tolerant micro-society gave the patient purpose, status, and meaning to her symptoms, and functioned simultaneously as an employment program complete with coaches and instructors. She was able to function happily in this way with low-dose antipsychotic medication. The main role of the CCS was to attest to this situation and to write a letter of support for her to remain in Canada as a productive member of the religious order. In this case, non-interference from the government and mental health services was the best prescription for health and recovery for an individual that found comfort and support from a religious community, and a context for symptoms that could have worsened in other settings. Hence, patients that experience religious and spiritual comfort or support in the face of their problems generally can move toward an acceptance of their difficulties through belief in a higher power and the support of fellow believers.

Theme 3: Cause (Explain)

Not everyone derives direct benefit from religious or spiritual beliefs and practices. For some, religion or spirituality may be the perceived cause of problems or may contribute to predicaments that may be difficult to resolve. An 11-year-old girl born in Canada to parents from West Africa was referred by her social worker to evaluate the severity of anxiety symptoms and the presence of attention deficit/hyperactivity disorder. She isolated herself socially, and had nightmares and many fears and avoidance behaviors, with hypervigilance and learning problems:

> The child experiences fear associated with witchcraft, she believes her grandmother to have been the victim of witchcraft which caused her death, the parents share her beliefs, and mother stopped sending the patient to school out of fear that her daughter will be a victim of witchcraft.
> (case 2015–20)

In West Africa, there is a well-known phenomenon of schoolgirls falling into trances in school (see Masquelier 2018; Smith 2001). There may be a link between this young girl's experience in Canada and the occurrence of similar behaviors in the country of origin. Hence, a religious or spiritual cause of a sociocultural predicament creates distress in a family and problems in how they interface with the wider society, which in turn could contribute to a possible mental illness or disorder, or at least staying home from school. Another possibility would be that such externalizing behaviors fall short of disorder and represent, rather, an "idiom of distress" in which the symptoms perform a semiotic function as protest against social injustice or suffering, a protest that could never be stated directly due to the disempowered status of the sufferer (Boddy 1989; Nichter 1981, 2010). The direct effect of social conflict on the bodies of these schoolgirls, as manifested by trance states, may represent a sociosomatic expression of distress as discussed by Kleinman and Becker (1998). Idioms and sociosomatic expressions of distress may derive from cultural themes, and hence may have a causal relationship to the individual's distress even though the sufferer may not be aware of what is taking place and may not explicitly make the causal link themselves.

The social aspects of religious and spiritual belief and practice, while often a benefit to participants, may also cause distress and exacerbate underlying disorder. When a man in his late forties was referred to the CCS for assessment of schizophrenia, it quickly became clear that the reported paranoid symptoms were more apparent than real. He belonged to a religious minority that advocated endogamy of its members, but the patient had fallen in love with a non-member and wanted to marry her. His behavior had come under disapproval from the leadership of the community, and he had been formally disciplined (shunned). These developments had created intense distress for the patient, who had experienced a sincere conversion to the denomination many years earlier. Unfortunately, under these circumstances he had lost trust, and his suspiciousness had been judged to be an exacerbation of schizophrenia for which the patient already had been treated successfully and was stable. The only way to resolve this dilemma was for the patient to meet with community leaders to explain his situation and petition for readmission to full status. The CCS offered to moderate and negotiate such a meeting, but the patient preferred to resolve the situation on his own and was lost to follow up. In this case, the religious structures governing discipline for contravention of norms was the direct cause of distress in a patient with a chronic mental disorder.

Sometimes, the negative aspects of religious communities are malignant, such as when a charismatic leader abuses vulnerable members of the group. A young woman, referred to the CCS to evaluate a history of childhood sexual abuse, had been raised in a religious cult by her parents and offered to the leader for his sexual gratification. Years later, she extricated herself from the movement and sought psychotherapy to work through her ordeal. Her enduring symptoms of PTSD were a direct consequence of childhood trauma situated in a religious context.

In other cases, individuals or families may endorse religious or spiritual causes of mental disorder and distress. Patients from religious backgrounds may assume spiritual origins of psychotic symptoms, such as spiritual attack, spirit possession, *jinn*, a curse, or a spell as the mechanism of distress. When spiritual interventions do not produce the hoped-for results, patients are often left with a spiritual cause but with few religious or spiritual options to resolve the ir suffering. Problems of this nature may undermine recovery by delaying access to mental health services, while simultaneously casting doubt on religious belief systems.

Overall, patients often use religious or spiritual explanatory models to understand their problems. While these attributions theoretically could be positive, in practice they often assume a negative tone, such that patients and their families may blame someone or something for their suffering. Sometimes the patient may not be aware of a causal link between religious and spiritual representations and their problem, so the clinician suggests possible causes and explanations in the case formulation.

Theme 4: Predicament (Hesitate or unable)

Religious beliefs or ideas may not be the attributed specific cause of mental health problems but may instead be just one part of a web of cultural, social, family, and personal experiences that may be difficult to unravel, thereby contributing to a religious or spiritual dilemma or predicament. A 44-year-old single man with chronic schizophrenia, a Sunni Muslim from the Middle East, was referred by his psychiatrist to evaluate family discord. The father was insisting that his son will experience an improvement of his symptoms if he lives according to the Five Pillars of Islam (Sunni), namely, *Shahadah* (declaration of faith), *Salat* (prayers), *Zakat* (charitable donation), *Sawm* (fasting), and *Hajj* (pilgrimage to Mecca). The patient has never had complete remission of psychotic symptoms for more than 20 years, with frequent command hallucinations that dominate his thoughts and actions:

> I cannot live the Five Pillars of Islam, How can I? I cannot fast because of diabetes. I cannot give to the poor because I have no money. I cannot do the Hajj because I cannot travel. I can't even pray because of the voices.
> (case 2015–31)

In *Roqya* clinics, which are Islamic healing centers, a standard claim among some Muslims is that mental illness results from the actions of *jinn* (spirits) and prescribed religious norms (the Five Pillars of Islam) are the best medicine against these malevolent entities (LeBlanc and Koenig in press 2020; LeBlanc in press 2020). The predicament for the man in this vignette was that he could not take the steps his father requested due to crippling symptoms of mental illness. Consequently, the CCS arranged a meeting with a Muslim scholar (Imam) to negotiate a compromise between father and son and to mitigate the patient's religious predicament. Mother had already agreed to accept her son as Allah had created him. With the support of the Imam, the CCS recommended that the father adopt a patient attitude with respect to his son's progress. Instead of giving to the poor (a formal obligation in Islam), the CCS recommended that the patient help the poor through volunteer work, but only when he is ready. The Imam offered to meet with father to help him gradually accept God's will in the case of his son.

A 20-year-old man left his homeland with his family of origin due to war. He studied hard while a refugee in a second country and was admitted to a high-ranking university. During his studies, he read material about the origins of the universe that challenged his conservative Christian faith. Try as he might, he could not reconcile what he was reading with the Bible or the religion of his youth. Gradually, he completely lost faith and no longer believed in God. When he mustered the courage to tell his family of his struggles, they were not sympathetic but exhorted him to redouble his efforts to live the faith. When this did not work, a series of deeply offensive arguments ensued, causing him to leave the family home to live on his own. He persisted with his newfound beliefs despite intense loneliness and financial hardship. His family actively continued to berate him because he had abandoned God and religion and had brought dishonor to them. He found hope when admitted to a graduate program in the field of his choice. The psychiatrist did not assign the patient a depression diagnosis, but rather highlighted that his distress represented a religious predicament with cognitive dissonance and family turmoil. The young man preferred not to discuss the situation with his family because the issues were sensitive, so he elected to avoid his family altogether and stabilized gradually over the course of time as he became more involved in his studies.

Other religious or spiritual predicaments may be less individually focused and may derive from couple dynamics. A 31-year-old man was referred to the CCS to evaluate treatment resistant depression and to see if sociocultural factors may be at play since all other interventions had not helped. He had experienced a sincere conversion to a new religion more than a decade before. When he called home for his family to find him a potential bride, they promised that they would find someone who would be open to his new faith. The couple was happily married until their two children were born. At that time, the patient's wife entrenched herself in the religion of her youth and wanted her children to be raised the same way. The patient had hoped that his family would follow his newfound faith. The disagreement became intractable to the point that his wife generously offered a divorce so that her husband would be free to find someone more religiously compatible. Her only condition was that she would keep the children so that they would be raised according to her religious convictions. This proposal precipitated a severe depressive disorder in the patient, who loved his wife, did not want a divorce, and most certainly did not want to give up his children to start a new family. Predicaments such as these overlap with religion and spirituality as cause but represent a network of problems that contribute to distress and undermine recovery. Family and social predicaments are complicated and require sensitive evaluation and carefully negotiated terms to resolve. Hence, patients may experience religious and spiritual representations as a predicament and may, therefore, hesitate or be unable to resolve the problem due to complicated family and personal matters that incapacitate decision making and disable productive problem-solving.

A clinical framework for fostering recovery in religious and spiritual context

For a variety of reasons, some mental health practitioners may not routinely focus on the religious or spiritual aspects of their patients' lives: time pressure, practice frameworks that discourage the open expression of religious and spiritual topics, and a lack of familiarity evaluating cultural clinical material all may undermine religiously competent assessment (Jarvis 2014, 2017). The qualitative study of CCS referrals outlined in this chapter found that religion and spirituality had a direct bearing on the presenting problem of most of the patients referred for assessment. Given that the CCS is a specialty service that almost exclusively sees immigrants and refugees, the same findings may not hold for other settings. Nonetheless, it is important to note that many CCS patients reported formal religious and spiritual participation, such as attending services regularly, taking part in prayers, or reading sacred texts, implying that religious or spiritual practices and participation may be more common in some clinical populations than expected. The same may hold true for religious and spiritual issues framing the problems that patients disclose to their evaluating psychiatrist, psychologist, family doctor, social worker, nurse, or other clinicians. To not broach matters of religion and spirituality in mental health evaluations risks completely missing what is most at stake for some patients and their families. Hence, part of culturally competent care must of necessity include time and attention given to religion and spirituality, not just in immigrants and refugees, but in patients from all backgrounds (Whitley and Jarvis 2015).

Tools exist to assist clinicians in their efforts to understand their patients from cultural and religious perspectives. The Outline for Cultural Formulation (OCF) in the DSM-5 guides general inquiry into the patient's cultural life, touching on the cultural identity of the individual, cultural conceptualizations of distress, cultural features of vulnerability and resilience, and cultural features of the clinician-patient relationship (APA 2013a). The problem with the OCF is that it lacks specific guidance about how to elicit the needed information. To remedy this problem, the Cultural Formulation Interview (CFI) was developed and added to the DSM-5 (Jarvis et al. 2020a). The CFI is a 16-item semi-structured interview that offers questions for each of the OCF categories (APA 2013a). The CFI is brief, should be conducted at the beginning of the clinical evaluation, is applicable to any clinical setting, and builds rapport between clinicians and patients. The CFI offers an informant version for interviewing families (APA 2013b) in addition to supplementary modules that allow for greater depth of questioning on key cultural topics (APA 2013c). Supplementary Module 5 of the CFI considers spirituality, religion, and moral traditions directly. The module consists of 16 additional questions having to do with religious and spiritual identity, their role in the life of the individual, their relationship to the presenting problem, and related stresses or conflicts. After one or two practice runs, clinicians from any discipline should feel empowered to conduct deeper investigations into the religious and spiritual life of their patients.

Another cross-cultural tool is the cultural consultation model, which has been developed and implemented by the CCS at McGill University in Montreal, Canada. The CCS was founded in 1999 to provide culturally appropriate psychiatric evaluation to diverse patients referred by family doctors, psychiatrists, and other hospital and community clinicians (Kirmayer et al. 2003). The CCS employs the OCF to flexibly modify the standard psychiatric evaluation according to the needs of patients and their families. The CCS uses linguistic interpreters and culture brokers to bridge the gap between the patient's culture of origin and the professional culture of psychiatry (Kirmayer et al. 2015). The CCS model has been adapted for use in other countries (Jarvis et al. 2020b), has been rated favorably by culture brokers and referring clinicians (Kirmayer et al. 2008), and contributes to resolving diagnostic dilemmas in the patients it has evaluated (Adeponle et al. 2012, 2015).

The themes and examples reported by the CCS religious representations study suggest a tentative framework that may inform religious and spiritual pathways to recovery. When clinicians use cultural tools to evaluate their patients, they will discover that religious or spiritual identity is crucial to some people, that religious and spiritual representations are central to the problems that some individuals are facing, and that clinicians will better understand how to modify the usual interventions to allow room for religious or spiritual applications, when appropriate. For the patients that hope to overcome their suffering by finding a religious or spiritual cure, practitioners need to establish a culturally safe space to discuss the various options and what the patient's preferences may be (Williams 1999). In this way, the clinician will be in a position to guide the patient toward helpful rather than potentially harmful practices, meet with family members and religious leaders to evaluate the kinds of religious interventions that could produce the hoped-for cure, and encourage tolerance for, rather than abandonment of, standard mental health treatments, such as psychoeducation and medication. Similarly, for the patients that come to accept their suffering through comforting religious and spiritual beliefs, or through reliance on the emotional support offered by fellow believers, the clinician should assess these personal and community resources and seek to reinforce those that enhance resilience. This will involve discussing doubts and new challenges while seeking to adapt the implementation of religious and spiritual resources according to changing circumstances. With the patient's permission, this may involve meetings with members of the family or religious community to assess the quality of the ongoing support and to determine if the patient's symptoms are becoming burdensome or overwhelming. In some cases, clinicians may need to employ linguistic interpreters and culture brokers to clarify the clinical picture. In these ways, religiously-oriented patients may negotiate a personalized recovery, augmented by appropriate religious or spiritual interventions, in which biomedical approaches are not coercively applied but become one aspect of holistic, person-centered care.

As already noted in the CCS study cases, religious and spiritual representations may not always alleviate suffering but, instead, may contribute to distress. Clinicians need to take careful note of these kinds of complaints so that they may be in a position to assist. When patients invoke a religious or spiritual cause of their distress, they may expect a cure to be possible if they can only find the right kind of healer to perform the proper intervention. The clinician, however, needs to carefully evaluate proffered explanations of suffering because, in many cases, the patient will blame someone or something for their ill fortune, with negative consequences for mental health and social networks, especially when standard mental health treatments and religious and spiritual interventions have failed or are taking longer than expected. In these cases, clinicians must patiently evaluate, then gently challenge, causal explanations in a respectful, non-judgmental manner. In this way, clinicians may humbly (Tervalon and Murray-García 1998) guide the patient toward a re-evaluation of causes and explanations of the religious or spiritual aspect of their suffering, restoring damaged connections to family and community in the process to the degree that the patient is willing. As already noted, in some cases, clinicians should seek the help of interpreters and culture brokers to assist in this process. In a similar way, patients that are facing a religious or spiritual predicament that is causing or exacerbating their suffering may be unsure how to proceed and therefore may hesitate to take steps to resolve the dilemma. This hesitation may not be related to mental disorder, but instead may reflect the complexity of family or community relations regarding faith in God, the proper way to conduct one's life according to religious and spiritual standards, and the guilt that may come from not fulfilling religious role expectations, such as getting married and having children by a certain age. There may not be an obvious resolution to these cultural, religious, and spiritual predicaments, but the attentive clinician will take appropriate time to understand the problems before suggesting psychosocial or medical treatments. In these particularly delicate situations, and with the patient's consent, the clinician may invite a religious leader to a discussion with the patient and the family to review options, reinforce education about the patient's SMI, and propose a tentative way forward. In this way, religious causes and predicaments that are undermining recovery may receive due attention, while respecting their sensitive and complex nature.

Conclusion: Untying the Gordian knot of severe mental illness, recovery, and religious practice

In this chapter, the focus has been on exploring the plurality of recovery experiences from and in mental illness, with a specific focus on the role of religious and spiritual traditions, beliefs, and practices. Religions include foundational stories that inform belief systems, which provide inspiration and behavioral models to adherents as they face and seek to overcome adversity. Biomedical and psychiatric notions of recovery from mental illness are not sufficient to grasp the complexity of recovery experiences. In this chapter, we suggest that in some contexts, recovery concepts must make room for religious and spiritual interpretations of the pathways to wellness for the patients and families that are confronted with severe mental illness.

Through the presentation and analysis of cases from the CCS, the chapter has also suggested a typology of religious representations in psychiatric consultation, consisting of *religion or spirituality as cure*, as *comfort or support*, as *a cause of mental disorder*, and as *a source of complexity and predicament* in relation to mental illness. These themes offer a tentative framework to reflect upon the improvised approaches that individuals and families may deploy to untie the Gordian knot of severe mental illness, recovery, and religious belief or practice. This chapter concludes by elaborating on a clinical framework for fostering recovery as implemented by the CCS in Montreal, Canada. The CCS focuses on holistic, person-centered evaluation of patients with SMI that seeks to embed standard biomedical interventions within a broader cultural framework (Kirmayer et al. 2014) so that spirit, mind, and body receive the care that each deserves.

On a final note, the interplay between chronic SMI, recovery, and religious or spiritual beliefs and practices may appear to be a hopelessly complicated one, and there will most certainly be challenges going forward. If clinicians and researchers alike can take a step back to remember what is really at stake – personal, grounded, and individually tailored roads to recovery – and if real attention can be paid to these processes, then perhaps the Gordian knot will unravel to become more apparent than real. Recovery from and within mental illness will be about what is most meaningful to individuals in family, community, and spiritual contexts. And that will make all the difference in understanding lived experiences of severe mental disorder and negotiated pathways to hope and meaning.

References

Adeponle, Ademola B., Brett D. Thombs, Damielle Groleau, Eric Jarvis and Laurence J. Kirmayer. 2012. "Using the Cultural Formulation to Resolve Uncertainty in Diagnoses of Psychosis Among Ethnoculturally Diverse Patients." *Psychiatric Services* 63 (2): 147–153. doi:10.1176/appi.ps.201100280

Adeponle, Ademola B., Danielle Groleau and Laurence J. Kirmayer. 2015. "Clinician Reasoning in the Use of Cultural Formulation to Resolve Uncertainty in the Diagnosis of Psychosis." *Culture, Medicine, and Psychiatry* 39 (1): 16–42. doi:10.1007/s11013-014-9408-5

Alnabulsi, Hani, John Drury, Vivian L. Vignoles and Sander Oogink. 2018. "Understanding the Impact of the Hajj: Explaining Experiences of Self-Change at a Religious Mass Gathering." *European Journal of Social Psychology* 50: 292–308. https://doi.org/10.1002/ejsp.2623

American Psychiatric Association [APA]. 2013a. *Diagnostic and Statistical Manual of Mental Disorders*, 5th Edition. Arlington: American Psychiatric Association.

American Psychiatric Association [APA]. 2013b. "*Cultural Formulation Interview (CFI) - Informant Version.*" Arlington: American Psychiatric Association.

American Psychiatric Association [APA]. 2013c. "*Supplementary Modules to the Core Cultural Formulation Interview (CFI).*" Arlington: American Psychiatric Association.

American Psychiatric Association [APA]. 2020. "*What is Schizophrenia?*" Arlington: American Psychiatric Association. Accessed on May 15, 2010 from www.psychiatry.org/patients-families/schizophrenia/what-is-schizophrenia

Anthony, William A. 1993. "Recovering from Mental Illness: The Guiding Vision of the Mental Health Service System in the 1990s." *Psychosocial Rehabilitation Journal* 16 (4), 11–23.

Arrington, Leonard J., and Davis Bitton. 1992. *The Mormon Experience*. Urbana and Chicago: University of Illinois Press.

Bartels, Stephen J. 2004. "Caring for the Whole Person: Integrated Health Care for Older Adults with Severe Mental Illness and Medical Comorbidity." *Journal of the American Geriatrics Society* 52: s249–s257. doi:10.1111/j.1532-5415.2004.52601.x

Becker, Deborah, and Robert Drake. 2003. *A Working Life for People with Severe Mental Illness*. New York: Oxford University Press.

Berwick, Donald M. 2009. "What 'Patient-Centered' Should Mean: Confessions of an Extremist." *Health Affairs* 28 (Supplement 1): w555–w565.

Binz, Stephen. 1993. *The God of Freedom and Life: A Commentary on the Book of Exodus*. Collegeville: Liturgical.

Boddy, Janice. 1989. *Wombs and Alien Spirits: Women, Men, and the Zar Cult in Northern Sudan*. Madison: University of Wisconsin Press.

Bowie, Christopher R., Colin Depp, John A. McGrath, Paula Wolyniec, Brent T. Mausbach, Mary H. Thornquist, James Luke, Thomas L. Patterson, Phillip D. Harvey and Ann E. Pulver. 2010. "Prediction of Real-World Functional Disability in Chronic Mental Disorders: A Comparison of Schizophrenia and Bipolar Disorder." *American Journal of Psychiatry* 167: 1116–1124. doi:10.1176/appi.ajp.2010.09101406

Braun, Virginia, and Victoria Clarke. 2006. "Using Thematic Analysis in Psychology." *Qualitative Research in Psychology* 3: 77–10. doi:10.1191/1478088706qp063oa

Davidson, Larry. 2003. *Living Outside Mental Illness: Qualitative Studies of Recovery in Schizophrenia*. New York: New York University Press.

Davidson, Larry, and David Roe. 2007. "Recovery from and Recovery in Mental Illness: One Strategy for Lessening the Confusion Plaguing Recovery." *Journal of Mental Health* 16 (4): 459–470. https://doi.org/10.1080/09638230701482394

Deegan, P.E. 1988. "Recovery: The Lived Experience of Rehabilitation." *Psychosocial Rehabilitation Journal* 11 (4): 11–19. https://www.nami.org/getattachment/Extranet/Education,-Training-and-Outreach-Programs/Signature-Classes/NAMI-Homefront/HF-Additional-Resources/HF15AR6LivedExpRehab.pdf

Deegan, P.E. 1996. "Recovery as a Journey of the Heart." *Psychiatric Rehabilitation Journal* 19 (3): 91–97.

Deegan, P.E. 1997. "Recovery and Empowerment for People with Psychiatric Disabilities." *Social Work and Health Care* 25 (3): 11–24. doi:10.1300/J010v25n03_02

Drake, Robert, and Rob Whitley. 2014. "Recovery and Severe Mental Illness: Description and Analysis." *The Canadian Journal of Psychiatry* 59 (5): 236–242. doi:10.1177/070674371405900502

Fallot, Roger D. 2001. "Spirituality and Religion in Psychiatric Rehabilitation and Recovery From Mental Illness." *International Review of Psychiatry* 13: 110–116. doi:10.1186/s12888-016-0796-7

Fallot, Roger D. 2007. "Spirituality and Religion in Recovery: Some Current Issues." *Psychiatric Rehabilitation Journal* 30 (4): 261–270. doi:10.2975/30.4.2007.261.270

Gaunt, Thomas P. 2018. *Pathways to Religious Life*. New York: Oxford University Press.

Global Disease Burden [GBD]. 2017. "Disease and Injury Incidence and Prevalence Collaborators. Global, Regional, and National Incidence, Prevalence, and Years Lived with Disability for 354 Diseases and Injuries for 195 Countries and Territories, 1990–

2017: A Systematic Analysis for the Global Burden of Disease Study 2017." *Lancet* 392: 1789–1858. doi:10.1016/S0140-6736(18)32279-7

Goldman, H.H., A.A. Gattozzi, and C.A. Taube. 1981. "Defining and Counting the Chronically Mentally Ill." *Psychiatric Services* 32 (1): 21–27. doi:10.1176/ps.32.1.21

Haig, Matt. 2015. *Reasons to Stay Alive*. Edinburgh: Canongate Books.

Harding, Courtenay M., and James Zahniser. 1994. "Empirical Correction of Seven Myths about Schizophrenia with Implications for Treatment." *Acta Psychiatrica Scandinavica* 90 (Supplement 384): 140–146. doi:10.1111/j.1600-0447.1994.tb05903.x

Harding, Courtenay M., George W. Brooks, Takamaru Ashikagu, John S. Strauss and Alan Breier. 1987. "The Vermont Longitudinal Study of Persons with Severe Mental Illness, II: Long-term Outcome of Subjects who Retrospectively met DSM-III Criteria for Schizophrenia." *American Journal of Psychiatry* 144 (6): 727–735. doi:10.1176/ajp.144.6.727

Hegarty, J.D., R.J. Baldessarini, M. Tohen, C. Waternaux and G. Oepen. 1994. "One Hundred Years of Schizophrenia: A Meta-Analysis of the Outcome Literature." *American Journal of Psychiatry* 151 (10): 1409–1416. doi:10.1176/ajp.151.10.1409

Heiner, Robert. 1992. "Evangelical Heathens: The Deviant Status of Freethinkers in Southland." *Deviant Behavior* 13 (1): 1–20. https://doi.org/10.1080/01639625.1992.9967895

Ho, Rainbow Tin Hung, Caitlin Kar Pui Chan, Phyllis Hau Yan, Ping Ho Wong, Cecilia Lai Wan Chan, Pamela Pui Yu Leung and Eric Yu Hai Chen. 2016. "Understandings of Spirituality and Its Role in Illness Recovery in Persons with Schizophrenia and Mental-Health Professionals: A Qualitative Study." *BMC Psychiatry* 16 (1): 86. doi:10.1186/s12888-016-0796-7

Hopper, Kim, Glynn Harrison and Joseph Wanderling. 2007. "An Overview of Course and Outcome in ISoS." In *Recovery from Schizophrenia: An International Perspective; A Report from the WHO Collaborative Project, The International Study of Schizophrenia*, 23–38. New York: Oxford University Press.

Ibrahim, Ahmed, and Rob Whitley. (In press 2020). "Religion and Mental Health: A Narrative Review with a Focus on Muslims in English-Speaking Countries." *British Journal of Psychiatry Bulletin*, 1–5. doi:10.1192/bjb.2020.34

Jablensky, Assen, Norman Sartorius, G. Ernberg, M. Anker, A. Korten, J.E. Cooper, et al.1992. "Schizophrenia: Manifestations, Incidence, and Course in Different Cultures. A World Health Organization Ten-Country Study." *Psychological Medicine Monograph Supplement* 20, 1–97. doi:10.1017/s0264180100000904

Jarvis, G. Eric. "Cultural Consultation in General Hospital Psychiatry." 2014. In *Cultural Consultation: Encountering the Other in Mental Health Care*, edited Laurence J. Kirmayer, C. Rousseau and J. Guzder, 293–314. Thousand Oaks: Springer.

Jarvis, G. Eric, Stephanie Larchanche, Rachid Bennegadi, Micol Ascoli, Kamaldeep S. Bhui and Laurence J. Kirmayer. 2020. Cultural Consultation in Context: A Comparison of the Framing of Identity During Intake at Services in Montreal, London, and Paris." *Culture, Medicine, and Psychiatry*. doi:10.1007/s11013-019-09666-1

Jarvis, G. Eric, Laurence J. Kirmayer, Ana Gomez-Carillo, Neal A. Aggarwal and Roberto Lewis-Fernandez. 2020. "Update on the Cultural Formulation Interview." *Focus* 18 (1): 40–46. https://doi.org/10.1176/appi.focus.20190037

Judd, Daniel K. 2016. "Clinical and Pastoral Implications of the Ministry of Martin Luther and the Protestant Reformation." *Open Theology* 2: 324–337. https://doi.org/10.1515/opth-2016-0027

Kirk-Duggan, Cheryl A. 2012. "How Liberating is the Exodus and for Whom? Deconstructing Exodus Motifs in Scripture, Literature, and Life." In *Exodus and*

Deuteronomy, edited by Athalya Brenner and Gale A. Yee, 3–28. Minneapolis: Augsburg Fortress Publishers.

Kirmayer, Laurence J., Danielle Groleau, Jaswant Guzder, Caminee Blake and G. Eric Jarvis. 2003. "Cultural Consultation: A Model of Mental Health Services for Multicultural Societies." *Canadian Journal of Psychiatry* 48: 145–153. doi:10.1177/070674370304800302

Kirmayer, Laurence J., Brett Thombs, Thomas Jurcik, G. Eric Jarvis and Jaswant Guzder. 2008. "Use of an Expanded Version of the DSM-IV Outline for Cultural Formulation on a Cultural Consultation Service." *Psychiatric Services* 59 (6): 683–686. doi:10.1176/ps.2008.59.6.683

Kirmayer, Laurence J., G. Eric Jarvis and Jaswant Guzder. 2014. "The Process of Cultural Consultation." In *Cultural Consultation: Encountering the Other in Mental Health Care*, edited by L.J. Kirmayer, C. Rousseau and J. Guzder, 47–70. New York: Springer.

Kirmayer, Laurence J., C. Rousseau, G. Eric Jarvis and Jawswant Guzder. 2015. "The Cultural Context of Clinical Assessment." In *Psychiatry*, 4th ed., edited by A. Tasman, J. Kay, J. A. Lieberman, M.B. First and M. Riba. New York: John Wiley and Sons.

Kleinman, Arthur, and Anne E. Becker. 1998. "Sociosomatics: The Contributions of Anthropology to Psychosomatic Medicine." *Psychosomatic Medicine* 60, 389–393. doi:10.1097/00006842-199807000-00001

Koenig, Harold G. 2008. *Medicine, Religion, and Health: Where Science and Spirituality Meet*. West Conshohocken: Templeton Foundation Press.

Koenig, Harold G., Dana E.King and Carson Benner. 2012. *Handbook of Religion and Health*, 2nd ed. New York: Oxford University Press.

Laudet, Alexandre B., Keith Morgen and William L. White. 2006. "The Role of Social Supports, Spirituality, Religiousness, Life Meaning and Affiliation with 12-Steps Fellowships in Quality of Life Satisfaction Among Individuals in Recovery from Alcohol and Drug Problems." *Alcohol Treat Q* 24 (1–2):33–73.

LeBlanc, M.N. (in press 2020). "The Institutionalization of Spiritual Healing in West Africa: The Emergence of Roqya Clinics in Ivory Coast." In *New Spiritualties and the Culture of Well-Being*, edited by Géraldine Mossière. New York: Springer.

LeBlanc, M.N. and B. Koenig. (in press 2020). *Faith, Healing and Development: The Spiritualization of Public Health in Côte d'Ivoire*. London: Routledge.

Lee, Bo Hyeong Jane, Lisa D. Pearce and Kristen M. Schorpp. 2017. "Religious Pathways from Adolescence to Adulthood." *Journal for the Scientific Study of Religion* 56 (3): 678–689. https://doi.org/10.1111/jssr.12367

Leff, J., N. Sartorius, A. Jablensky, A. Korten and G. Ernberg. 1992. "The International Pilot Study of Schizophrenia: Five-Year Follow-up Findings." *Psychological Medicine* 22 (1): 131–145. doi:10.1017/s0033291700032797

Lipka, Michael. 2016. "10 Facts about Atheists." Washington, DC: Pew Research Center. Accessed November 16, 2017 from www.pewresearch.org/fact-tank/2016/06/01/10-facts-about-atheists/

Masquelier, A. 2018. "Schooling, Spirit Possession, and the 'Modern Girl'in Niger." In *Femmes d'Afrique et Emancipation: Entre Normes Sociales Contraignantes et Nouveaux Possibles*, edited by Muriel Gomez-Perez, 177–196. Paris: Karthala.

Mental Health Commission of Canada. 2009. "*Toward Recovery and Well-being.*" Ottawa: Mental Health Commission of Canada. Accessed July 28, 2020 from www.mentalhealthcommission.ca/sites/default/files/FNIM_Toward_Recovery_and_Well_Being_ENG_0_1.pdf

MentalHealth.gov. 2019. "Recovery Is Possible." Accessed May 15, 2020 from www.mentalhealth.gov/basics/recovery-possible
Mezzich, J.E. 2007. "Psychiatry for the Person: Articulating Medicine's Science and Humanism." *World Psychiatry* 6 (2): 65–67.
Mueser, Kim T., and Susan R.McGurk. 2004. "Schizophrenia." *Lancet* 363 (9426): 2063–2072. doi:10.1016/S0140-6736(04)16458-1
Neighbors, H.W., M.A. Musick and D.R. Williams. 1998. The African American Minister as a Source of Help for Serious Personal Crises: Bridge or Barrier to Mental Health Care? *Health Education and Behavior* 25 (6): 759–777. doi:10.1177/109019819802500606
Nicholls, Vicky. 2002. *Taken Seriously: The Somerset Spirituality Project*. London: The Mental Health Foundation.
Nichter, Mark. 1981. "Idioms of Distress: Alternatives in the Expression of Psychological Distress: A Case Study from South India." *Cultural Medical Psychiatry* 4: 379–408. doi:10.1007/BF00054782
Nichter, Mark. 2010. "Idioms of Distress Revisited." *Cultural Medical Psychiatry* 34: 401–416. doi:10.1007/s11013-010-9179-6
Rosmarin, D.H., E.J. Krumrei and Gerhard Andersson. 2009. "Religion as a Predictor of Psychological Distress in Two Religious Communities." *Cognitive Behaviour Therapy* 38 (1): 54–64. https://doi.org/10.1080/16506070802477222
Ross, Catherine E. 1990. "Religion and Psychological Distress." *Journal for the Scientific Study of Religion* 29 (2): 236–245. doi:10.2307/1387431
Saks, Elyn R. 2007. *The Center Cannot Hold: My Journey Through Madness*. London: Hachette.
Smith, James H. 2001. "Of Spirit Possession and Structural Adjustment Programs: Government Downsizing, Education and Their Enchantments in Neoliberal Kenya." *Journal of Religion in Africa* 31 (4): 427–456. doi:10.2307/1581468
Solomon, David A., Martin B. Keller, Andrew C. Leon, Timothy I. Mueller, Phillip W. Lavori, M. Tracie Shea, William Coryell, Meredith Warshaw, Carolyn Turvey, Jack D. Maser and Jean Endicott. 2000. "Multiple Recurrences of Major Depressive Disorder." *American Journal of Psychiatry* 157: 229–233. doi:10.1176/appi.ajp.157.2.229
Starnino, Vincent R. 2016. "Conceptualizing Spirituality and Religion for Mental Health Practice: Perspectives of Consumers with Serious Mental Illness." *Families in Society: The Journal of Contemporary Social Services* 97 (4): 295–304. doi:10.1606/1044-3894.2016.97.36
Tervalon, Melanie, and Jann Murray-García. 1998. "Cultural Humility Versus Cultural Competence: A Critical Distinction in Defining Physician Training Outcomes in Multicultural Education." *Journal of Health Care for the Poor and Underserved*, 9 (2): 117–125. doi:10.1353/hpu.2010.0233
United States Department of Health and Human Services and Substance Abuse and Mental Health Services Administration. 2004. *National Consensus Statement on Mental Health Recovery*. Rockville, MD: U.S. Department of Health and Human Services.
Whitley, Rob, Laurence J. Kirmayer and Danielle Groleau. 2006. "Understanding Immigrants' Reluctance to Use Mental Health Services: A Qualitative Study from Montreal." *The Canadian Journal of Psychiatry* 51 (4): 205–209. doi:10.1177/070674370605100401
Whitley, Rob, Maxine Harris and Robert E. Drake. 2008. "Safety and Security in Small-Scale Recovery Housing for People with Severe Mental Illness: An Inner-City Case Study." *Psychiatric Services* 59: 165–169. doi:10.1176/ps.2008.59.2.165

Whitley, Rob, and Robert E. Drake. 2010. "Recovery: A Dimensional Approach." *Psychiatric Services* 61 (12): 1248–1250. doi:10.1176/ps.2010.61.12.1248

Whitley, Rob. 2012. "'Thank You God': Religion and Recovery from Dual Diagnosis among Low-Income African Americans." *Transcultural Psychiatry* 49 (1): 87–104. doi:10.1177/1363461511425099

Whitley, Rob, and G. Eric Jarvis. 2015. "Religious Understanding as Cultural Competence: Issues for Clinicians." *Psychiatric Times: Diversity and Cultural Competence Special Report* 32 (6). Accessed May 20, 2021 from https://www.psychiatrictimes.com/view/religious-understanding-cultural-competence-issues-clinicians

Williams, David R. and Michelle J. Sternthal. 2007. "Spirituality, Religion and Health: Evidence and Research Directions." *Medical Journal of Australia* 186: S47–S50. doi:10.5694/j.1326-5377.2007.tb01040.x

Williams, Robyn. 1999. "Cultural Safety – What does it mean for our work practice?" *Australian and New Zealand Journal of Public Health* 23: 213–214. https://doi.org/10.1111/j.1467-842X.1999.tb01240.x

Zuckerman, Phil, Luke W. Galen and Frank L. Pasquale. 2016. *The Nonreligious: Understanding Secular People and Societies.* New York: Oxford University Press.

Zukowski, Lea A. 2018. "To Shield and Protect: The Competence to Stand Trial Doctrine in New Mexico." *New Mexico Law Review* 48: 96–123. https://digitalrepository.unm.edu/nmlr/vol48/iss1/3

12 Global mental wellness and spiritual geographies of care
Concluding remarks

Andrew R. Hatala and Kerstin Roger

Introduction

Ten years ago, Manderson and Smith-Morris (2010) changed the landscape of how we understand chronic illness by situating the theory of chronicity in cultural contexts and heightening our sensitivity to the impact of structural factors shaping disease patterns, their management, and outcomes. While much has changed around the world over the last decade, what has remained consistent is the severity of the burden that chronic conditions place on those living with them and the systems of support tasked with their care. On most global indices, the rates of chronic conditions, mental illness, non-communicable diseases (NCDs), and disability have been stable for many years or are on the rise, often advancing across diverse regions, cultures, and pervading socioeconomic classes (Hajat and Stein 2018). Initiated in the 1990s, the Global Burden of Disease (GBD) study represented a scientific collaboration of 500 researchers that quantified the comparative magnitude of health loss due to disease and injury worldwide. Gathering data from across the globe in 1990, 2005, 2010, and 2019, the GBD studies have produced nearly one billion health estimates for 187 countries (GBD 2019; Murray et al. 2013). This research brings into full relief the global health burden of various chronic conditions and mental illnesses, highlighting a global health crisis of chronicity.[1] Similarly, the World Health Organization (WHO) estimated that by 2030, the proportion of total global deaths due to diverse chronic conditions was expected to be 70 percent and the global burden of disease compared to 56 percent in 2010 (WHO 2007). Other researchers have noted that three in five global deaths are now attributed to four chronic conditions, namely, cardiovascular disease, cancer, chronic lung diseases, and diabetes (Wang et al. 2016). Mental and behavioral disorders, in particular, are also now recognized as among the leading causes of chronicity and global disability with an estimated 22.2 percent of all years lived with disability attributable to these disorders, and mood disorders (including major depression, bipolar disorder, and dysthymia), anxiety, alcohol and drug abuse, and schizophrenia among the top twenty (Pike et al. 2013). On other accounts, mental, neurological, and substance-use (MNS) disorders constitute 13 percent of the global burden of disease, surpassing both cardiovascular disease and cancer (Collins, Patel and Joestl 2011). Not without its challenges, the increasing

DOI: 10.4324/9781003043508-12

burden of chronic conditions and mental illness continues to make diverse systems of prevention, management, and care a global priority.

To address these growing health concerns, the fields of public and global mental health deal with illness conditions at the population, state, and global level. The need for a public and global approach to protect and promote health and mental health, as well as to reduce the burden of chronic conditions and mental disorders, is increasingly recognized (Das and Rao 2012; Jakovljevic et al. 2019; Patel and Prince 2010; Wahlbeck 2015). In particular, researchers and practitioners working within the well-known framework of Global Mental Health (GMH) have focused on lessoning the burden of mental illness across the world by advancing screening, diagnosis, and care; they are developing, implementing, and evaluating evidence-based practices that can be scaled-up, increasing affordability and access for effective community-based services and interventions, strengthening mental health training of local personnel and laypersons, and promoting, at a more cultural and political level, the value of mental health in societies around the world (Patel et al. 2008; Patel 2014). Today, efforts in GMH often address the growing mental illness inequities between low-income and high-income countries, as well as marginalized or structurally oppressed populations within wealthy nations (e.g., Indigenous peoples, refugees, urban poor) (see Lancet Global Mental Health Group series of articles published between 2007 and 2011; Patel et al. 2008; Prince et al. 2007). Taken together, global health promotion and GMH represent complex endeavors assisting people to protect, improve, and promote their mental health at individual, national, and global levels (Kirmayer and Gold 2012; Patel 2014; Patel et al. 2011).

Despite the efforts to build a solid scientific foundation for global health promotion and GMH, the priorities and frameworks employed to date have been largely informed by mental health professionals and their institutional partners located in wealthy Western countries (Kirmayer and Pedersen 2014). Such approaches tend to reflect the dominant interests of Western knowledge, biomedicine, and psychiatry, and may therefore give insufficient attention to locally defined priorities, worldviews, and cultural perspectives (Mills 2014), including, we would add, an appreciation of spiritual, religious, or faith-based practices and their role in care management. As Kirmayer and Pedersen (2014) observed, there continues to be tension about the application of a public or GMH approach, grounded mainly in biomedicine and current evidence-based psychiatric practices, and transcultural psychiatry that is a more socially and culturally informed community-based approach that emphasizes the social determinants of mental health and the imperatives of listening to local priorities, strengthening community resources, and developing endogenous solutions (Bemme and D'Souza 2014; Saraceno and Dua 2009; Saraceno et al. 2007). A key concern here, then, is that by addressing global rates of chronic illness and mental disorder through universalizing and Western-centric therapeutic frames that are not necessarily locally relevant and culturally consonant can have potential unintended negative consequences, including inappropriate rates of overdiagnoses and intervention, pharmaceuticalization of mental health and social suffering, displacement of local knowledge and expertise, increased stigma, or poorer health outcomes overall (Dumit 2012; Ecks

2005; Good 1994; Good et al. 2010; Kirmayer and Pedersen 2014; Kleinman 2005; Mills 2014). Indeed, just as GMH tends to emphasize professional mental health interventions exported from biomedically informed positivist or materialistic epistemological frameworks, it also tends to marginalize local grassroots or Indigenous forms of knowledge and care, which include healing, spiritual, or religious worldviews applied for hundreds of years, and accepted forms of social or community integration that can potentially contribute to positive outcomes, wellness, and recovery (Alarcon-Guzman and Castillo-Martell 2020; Hatala, Waldram and Caal 2015; Kirmayer and Swartz 2013; Mills 2014; Sax 2014).[2]

As this diverse collection of chapters from around the globe attests, a notable portion of the local priorities, community resources, and endogenous solutions to support mental wellness amidst chronicity are found within spiritual, religious, or faith-based strategies. Thus, although global public health and GMH have done much to address current inequities and rising global rates of chronicity and mental disorder on the one hand (Patel 2014; Patel et al. 2011; Patel et al. 2008; Patel and Prince 2010; Wang et al. 2016), and social scientists, cultural psychiatrists, and health researchers have contributed considerably to our understanding of the lived experiences of chronicity and mental illness through interpretive efforts on the other (Good et al. 2010; Manderson and Smith Morris 2010, Mattingly, Gron and Meinert 2011; Sangaramoorthy 2018), important critical questions still remain about how people draw on spiritual, religious, or faith-based resources to manage various chronic conditions, how such spiritual or religious supports help their day-to-day vicissitude, and how such processes also form part of a network of informal care that augments public or institutional services offered through formalized community, biomedical, or psychiatric health care systems.

The chapters in this collection offer a depth of insight into these issues and point to important areas of future work and research. A prominent theme of this collection of chapters is that health and mental health service providers in public institutions or organizations can support, learn from, and utilize a diverse array of spiritual, religious, or faith-based resources that patients prioritize or effectively position in their own daily work of care management. A broad empirical thrust of these chapters, therefore, is to argue that as individual, social, and institutional systems of care, biomedically informed psychiatric and Western trained health care practitioners (psychiatry, psychology, social work, etc.) on the one hand, and religion, spiritual, and faith-based community practitioners (chaplains, healers, etc.) on the other, should be allies in the promotion of mental health and wellness, both for individuals, and also on a broader scale, for a global approach to care. Together, these diverse practitioners have a vital opportunity to jointly shape a future of individual, community, and global care strategies and wellness interventions. By expanding on a global mental health approach on the one hand, and cultural psychiatry on the other, we refer to this framework as *Global Mental Wellness*, a collaborative and interdisciplinary agenda that demands a better understanding of core concepts such as spirituality, religion, and faith, their role in supporting mental wellness amidst chronicity, their potentials for harms and increased forms of distress, as well as an appreciation of their cultural interconnectedness and respective limits. Moreover, this framework also implies that researchers and practitioners adopt a biopsychosocial-spiritual perspective of wellness in their care that is beyond a typical biomedical vision of health and illness underlying chronic conditions, global health promotion, and mental illness (Hatala 2013; Manderscheid et al. 2010), and at the same time, legitimize the inclusion of a spiritual domain in epidemiologic discourse on the global determinants of chronicity, mental health, wellness, and healing (Jakovljevic et al. 2019; Levin 2003).

In this concluding chapter, we highlight major themes that emerged across the diverse chapters, drawing attention to particular aspects of care and mental wellness involving both individual strategies and community approaches. We also draw attention to future questions and areas of research the authors point to that we find promising. By and large, the authors in this collection do not reproduce narratives of globalization and change documented over the years. Nor is their intent to dwell on images of suffering, passivity, and stigma that can be prevalent in discourses of chronicity, social suffering, precarity, or global illness, especially those concerning individuals and communities suffering from mental illness in impoverished nations (Desjarlias et al. 1995). Rather, the goal was to explore—through over 300 in-depth interviews analyzed in the different chapters with individuals living in chronicity and those offering care, as well as extensive ethnographic observations from nine diverse global contexts including, Brazil, Belize, Canada, France, Ghana, Germany, Netherlands, Somaliland, United Kingdom—how various religious, spiritual, and faith-based practices and worldviews can augment mental wellness amidst chronicity. This is not to ignore or excuse the ways in which religion and spirituality can and have had negative impacts on individuals and communities. Knowing and respecting this reality, however, this collection and these authors focus on a positive or strengths-based approach, providing different forms of evidence about how religious, spiritual, and faith-based practices and worldviews support peoples' daily living. In so doing, we frame our concluding remarks around the promotion of Global Mental Wellness within the contexts of chronicity and what we develop as the spiritual geographies of care. We conclude that by building greater understandings of and working relationships across epistemic divides of biomedically informed health care providers and religious, spiritual, or faith-based practitioners—and ultimately between science and spirituality more generally—the potentials for individual and public harms and distress related to religious or spiritual practices and worldviews can be mitigated and the global burden of chronicity and mental illness can be met in a more sustainable manner, appropriately aligned with and accessing local priorities, community resources, and endogenous solutions that may already be present and active in various communities around the globe.

Mental wellness and the spiritual determinants of chronicity

The word "chronicity" stems from Latin "chronicus" relating to time and from the Greek "khronikos" or "khronos," meaning of time. It designates the "condition of being chronic," and typically refers to an illness condition that is "prolonged or slow to heal" or social suffering and distress that "continues over an extended period of time" (Sangaramoorthy 2018; Vigh 2008). Sue Estroff (1993, 250), in her life course research with schizophrenia patients, defined chronicity as "the persistence in time of limitations and suffering and to the resulting disabilities as they are socially and culturally defined and lived." In so doing, Estroff argued that conditions of time, development, social relations, and broader contextual or cultural factors driving health care structures and supports together give rise to or inhibit meaning-making processes during lived experiences of chronicity.

In positioning chronic illness and social distress in the context of globalization and global health, social scientists have since argued the need to interrogate how perspectives of chronicity are often reflective of the particular cultural and historical traditions of Western biomedicine, and the interpersonal and structural power relations within its many global manifestations (Good 1995; Manderson and Smith-Morris 2010). As part of this critique, critical health researchers have underscored how essential it is to problematize "chronicity" as a construct, highlighting the need to relate chronic health issues to social inequity and injustice (Lock 2001; Manderson and Smith-Morris 2010; Miles 2010). "Chronic" here is typically viewed as the persistence of symptoms over the course of a disease or social struggle for which there is no immediate remediation. Medical anthropologists have since challenged such biomedically informed discourses of chronicity, calling for a shift from conceptions of illness as temporally bound toward an understanding of the fluidity and flexibility of illness and social conditions over the life course (Manderson and Smith-Morris 2010; Sangaramoorthy 2018). Researchers have also highlighted the various processes of disruption, transition, and transformation that constitute chronic experiences (e.g., HIV, poverty, war, psychosis, diabetes, and even global pandemics) and how continuous day-to-day management poses significant medical, economic, and psycho-social challenges, and especially for those in resource-limited settings (Farmer 2004; Lund et al. 2010; McGrath et al. 2014; Russell and Seeley 2010; Watkins-Hayes, Pittman-Gay and Beaman 2012; Vigh 2008). In medical contexts, researchers have also troubled long-standing dichotomous relations between "chronic" and "acute" by exploring how a variety of everyday life conditions (e.g., sleep, trauma, birth, aging, and addiction) and forms of social suffering are increasingly medicalized, highlighting the many domains of life that are gradually viewed through a "chronic" lens and thereby requiring constant medical or pharmaceutical intervention (Dumit 2012; Goodman et al. 2013; Manderson and Smith-Morris 2010; van der Lee et al. 2007). These critiques emphasize the various frameworks through which chronicity can be viewed and the difficulties or potential dangers of universally applying, and also prioritizing, biomedically informed, Western-centric categories and therapeutic frames given the many ways that societies and cultures shape persistent experiences of distress and illness, as well as the ways in which people seek relief, wellness, and care (Ecks 2005; Fassin 2012; Good et al. 2010; Miles 2010).

What emerged across the chapters in this collection was that through spiritual, religious, and faith-based worldviews and practices, chronic conditions of various kinds—whether intermittent psychosis, oppressive forces of colonization and social marginalization, attacks of spirit possession, or other forms of persistent mental duress—were often externalized from individual-level suffering, symptoms, or diagnostic categories (Jarvis et al. Ch. 11; Moratz Ch. 4; Morton et al. Ch. 7). This externalizing is, in part, what fostered the construction of meaning, purpose, and "recovery" despite enduring forms of social and individual suffering. Chronic illness in this context is reimagined as outside the person, not as part of the core spiritual self (McGregor and McKinley Ch. 3). It, the illness or unjust social affliction, can then be changed, transformed, or engaged, while the core self is unharmed. Although such forms of chronicity can emerge from a spiritual worldview and conception of reality (e.g., spirit possession), the individual sufferer was not always bound by an "illness identity" of some kind and concomitant stigma that may occur in a more individualized or secularized context (Becker 1998; Charmaz 1991; Estroff 1993; Hatala, Waldram and Crossley 2013).

Moving one step further, while some chapters detailed the self, illness, or personalized social distress, some focused more on the value of relationships in the context of spiritual communities. Indeed, a specific theme that emerged from the chapters was how chronicity was oftentimes negotiated within relational contexts and was indeed a relational process. In other words, if the context or processes surrounding the chronicity are transformed or given a new meaning, then often this in itself was an important factor ameliorating its potential harms. In this way, spiritual, religious, and faith-based practices fostered "cultures of recovery" that, as they reinterpreted chronicity as temporary intrusions to a stable core self, emphasized wellness as a deeply personal journey involving growth and transformation, flexibility and adaptation to particular contexts and circumstances (Jarvis et al. Ch. 11). This recovery "journey" also involved movements across and within what we refer to as spiritual geographies toward wellness and a more positive view of the future (Remy-Fischler Ch. 8). Healing, recovery, and transformation amidst chronicity, then, was as much about a spiritual worldview as it was about a relationship between aspects of the self, and others, and the self with the external world—a person in context moving forward in helpful or healing-oriented relationships, and especially those of a spiritual nature. Thus, the chapters in this collection push us to consider more deeply what could be called the *spiritual determinants of chronicity*; that is, the various forces that impact the psychological, phenomenological, and moral experiences of time and struggle, and how specific spiritual, religious, or faith-based practices help to shape and reshape those experiences in wellness affirming ways. Whether through nourishing exchanges during Catholic pilgrimage to Lourdes' holy shrines in France (Goldingay et al. Ch. 6), the aesthetics of care in Brazilian spiritual surgeries (Kurz Ch. 5), sacred prayer and dance of honoring the ancestors by Garifuna Indigenous families in Belize (Allen et al. Ch. 10), or becoming good ancestors through subtle forms of ceremony-making among urban Indigenous youth in Canada (Morton et al. Ch. 7), these practices shifted contexts of relationships towards a hoped-for future, thereby transforming a challenging past or present into an imagined landscape of possibility.

Along these lines, the chapters in this collection also exemplify how the nature of chronicity can vary based on the creation and recreation of complex networks or communities of care. While there is evidence that people with chronic conditions and mental illness can face stigmatization and social exclusion in various ways (Mehta and Thornicroft 2013), there is also some indication that people whose behavior is not threatening or disruptive may be better integrated in smaller communities and cultural contexts where unusual experiences are not necessarily labeled as shameful and discriminated against, but may be given positive meaning and moral value (Goldingay et al. Ch. 6; Benyah Ch. 9). Moreover, as research has shown, the course and outcome of various chronic conditions, and especially forms of severe mental disorders, may depend not solely on access to services, medication, skills, and the availability of professional care, but also on the reactions to individual persons in a holistic way, to the tone and manner of care provided, and to the support provided by family members and the immediate social network of community resources (Adeponle, Whitley, and Kirmayer 2012; Campbell and Burgess 2012; Good et al. 2010; Myers 2010). As such, there is growing evidence that connected communities with programs designed to promote social inclusion, spiritual networks, and empathy have the potential to make an important contribution to mental wellness (Alarcon-Guzman and Castillo-Martell 2020; Jakovljevic et al. 2019). Indeed, as the chapters in this collection describe, connections with communities fostered by spiritual worldviews and ethos, in particular, disrupted and re-interpreted experiences of isolation, sequestration, stigmatization, or how the ill or precariously suffering are often set apart spatially from mainstream populations. What these chapters outline is how spiritual, religious, and faith-based practices can embrace and draw people together under a common empathic framework or vision of sacred reality, and this context and form of relationality fundamentally changes the experience and process of chronicity. A key component of a Global Mental Wellness agenda, therefore, must also include inquiry about how communities grounded within and inclusive of spiritual aspects of reality can challenge the stigmatization or social exclusion so often afflicting those with mental illness and other forms of chronicity globally, and how such spiritual networks of care can shift our common perceptions of chronicity and stigma in both form and process.

Spiritual geographies of care

For many individuals around the world, living amidst chronicity and the pursuit of mental wellness extends beyond a local material and social world of existence. The daily concerns of chronicity often include movement across and within the *spiritual geographies of care*, the internal and external worlds that provide coping resources, cultural contexts of care, communities engendering a sense of belonging and purpose, and moral frameworks for interpretation during experiences of persistent hardship, crisis, and struggle. This idea of geography is appealing in part because it can be used both literally and metaphorically; it can refer to a kind of figurative internal psychological or existential terrain as well as to the physical features of land, community, and sacred places on the earth. Indeed, as the different chapters outline, the transformation of and movement across spiritual geographies is at once psychological, with respect to an inner journey of self-interpretation or meaning-making amidst challenging experiences that find direction and guidance from spiritual insights, connections, and realities; phenomenological or embodied, insofar as the mode of dwelling in and inhabiting a world is transformed or reimagined by conducting spiritual activities, engaging with sacred communities, and benefitting from those relationships; and moral insofar as such activities resist and challenge dominant normalizing discourses of identity oftentimes carried within a global health agenda and its universalizing Western-centric therapeutic frames, and thereby invite innovative alternatives for wellness amidst social suffering and chronicity. In this way, the idea of geography is also appealing because it signifies spaces and places of resistance to universalizing expansions of medicalization in general, and a pharmaceuticalization of mental health and social suffering in particular; it remains a site of challenge to encroaching secular biomedical worldviews and notions of moral normalization. These spiritual geographies of care, insofar as they exist at all, resist, in various ways, the globalizing powers of a Western-centric rationality that can, at times, ethically impel action on populations and subjectivities overtly, as well as ideologies, epistemologies, and ontologies perhaps more covertly (Good 1994). It is here that "global health is also about competing truths and competing ethics" (Fassin 2012, 107).

Within these contested geographies, the chapters in this collection also allude to a spiritual or religious modernity (Moratz Ch. 4), that is, the bringing of a contemporary capacity for spiritual engagement with a physical habitation in particular spaces and places, times across history and into the present. Spiritual geographies therefore also encompass external notions of land and nature in that they can respond to colonial histories of stolen land and at the same time inform transformative healing from cultivating sacred relationships with or repossession of the land (McGregor and McKinley Ch. 3; Morton et al. Ch. 7). Similarly, they are reflective of deepening reconnections with a sense of being "grounded" on the soil as part of a pilgrimage where one is moving towards or within a symbolic place like Lourdes, France (Goldingay et al. Ch. 6), or accessing the peaceful and calming environments surrounding prayer camps in Ghana, Western Africa (Benyah Ch. 9). From these external geographies, and how they shape and inform the experiences of care, wellness, and chronicity, spirituality is not simply the individualized practices performed in the day-to-day phenomenal world; it is also fundamentally about an embodied world, a place and space, practices which require physical manifestation and holding ground, and a worldview where supernatural and other-than-human interactions and relationships are a normal and expected aspect of existence.

Appreciating spiritual geographies of care demands a deeper understanding of spirituality, how it relates to related concepts of religion and faith (Freitas et al. Ch. 2), and how it cultivates determinants of chronicity and wellness, those both potentially supportive and harmful. As the chapters in this collection outline, spirituality can be understood as a quality of human beings who are concerned or preoccupied with higher meaning or purpose in life rather than solely with affairs of the material world (Jarvis et al. Ch. 11; Benyah Ch. 9). In this way, spirituality is a dimension of human experience related to the sacred or a transcendent reality widely defined. Spirituality also relates to the inner essence of the self or human nature, and the sense of harmonious interconnectedness with self, others, the world, nature, and the spiritual aspects of reality (Freitas et al. Ch. 2; McGregor and McKinley Ch. 3). At the individual level, transformation, vitality, meaningfulness, and connectedness each are essential elements of a spiritual experience (Remy-Fischler Ch. 8). Indeed, a form of connectedness or belonging emerged as a core aspect of spirituality outlined by many of the chapters, seen as a feeling of union or harmony with another being or place, engaging in meaningful practices that center or align the outside and the internal worlds, and for some, this includes relationships with a living prophet, dead or imagined persons, a cultural, ethnic, or political group, nature and land, or the universe (Allen et al. Ch. 10; Kurz Ch. 5; Morton et al. Ch. 7). Despite differences in perspective or terminology, the chapters reflect similar spiritual perspectives in current literature (Canda and Furman 2009; Fisher 2011; Ho and Ho 2007; Hungelmann et al. 1996), especially the capacity to be conscious of oneself, to achieve peacefulness and growth despite illness-induced limitations, and to have a relationship with other-than-human persons that can support and relate to humans in diverse ways (Jarvis et al. Ch. 11). Thus, we found the term spiritual geographies of care useful insofar as it helps us consider both the internal and external "places" where practices that promote connections, transcendence, meaning-making processes occur, and especially the vicissitudes or movements across different spaces of meaning, growth, flexibility, recovery, and trust. Whether in a remote Pentecostal prayer camp in Ghana (Benyah Ch. 9), during spiritual support groups in the United Kingdom (Remy-Fischler Ch. 8), Qur'anic healing from spirit possession in Somaliland's *cilaaj* clinics (Moratz Ch. 4), or in one's rural Belizean home during private moments of fasting and prayer (Allen et al. Ch. 10), care and wellness are felt and known in diverse ways by traversing these spiritual geographies.

Connected with spirituality, religion is arguably one of the most distinctive human phenomena that has been and continues to be a source of individual and community growth, strength, social solidarity, and resilience, as well as a source of personal strain, terrorism, and interreligious conflict (Abu-Raiya 2013; Csordas 2009). As the chapters in this collection highlight, religion can depict a particular institutionalized or personal system of beliefs and practices (worship) related to the divine (Moratz Ch. 4), as well as provide particular patterns of practice for people to follow and draw strength from (Jarvis et al. Ch. 11). These practices concern the existence, nature, and worship of God or spirits, and divine involvement in the universe and human life, as well as concerns with the next world or a life after death (Kurz Ch. 5). Religious pathways can be complex and dynamic processes in which people are in search of whatever they hold significant, including faith, family, community, or the sacred itself (Freitas et al. Ch. 2). As other chapters also explore, religious figures and educators can provide great stories or prescriptive meta-narratives about how people should and could live in the context of prolonged suffering (Allen et al. Ch. 10; Remy-Fischler Ch. 8).[3]

As an aspect of both religious traditions and spirituality, faith was another common theme in the chapters, outlined as confidence or trust in relationships with others, with certain practices, and a spiritual realm of other-than-human persons (Allen et al. Ch. 10). Faith-based practices, then, can involve those activities motivated by such convictions and conscious knowledge of one's spiritual nature and reality. Faith can also be healing by connecting individuals to like-minded groups that can offer tangible and emotional support and encouragement (Remy-Fischler Ch. 8). Faith can also support wellness by engendering soothing emotions that buffer or mitigate the harmful effects of stress (Kurz Ch. 5). In this way, faith can support wellness outcomes by establishing an interpretive framework, a mode of thinking and explanatory narrative that affirms one's innate sense-making ability, better accommodating individuals to their challenging life experiences and place in the world (Morton et al. Ch. 7). Research also now suggests that such feelings and interpretations elicited by positive faith-based thoughts, beliefs, and experiences, personal or communal, may promote neurobiological resilience by directly modulating various neurological and epigenetic parameters indicative of pathophysiology (Russo et al. 2012).

Similarly, hope is also a familiar and important topic in anthropological discussions of chronicity and wellness (Mattingly, Gron and Meinert 2011). Although previous research has explored the way that living with chronic conditions can create significant life disruptions and even despair (Becker 1997), the chapters here also highlight the ways in which hope is a process harnessed and opened by spiritual and religious connections, communities, and relationships (Allen et al. Ch. 10). Important, too, is that hope is fundamentally about the future, about projecting one's faith into a future time where struggle and hardship may be mitigated, or where one's actions are seen in the context of future generations and sacred relatives or ancestors (Morton et al. Ch. 7). As people produce future hoped-for scenarios of action by anticipating and predicting the near and distant future through a social and spiritual imaginary, they locate themselves in the world in relation to other actors, both material and spiritual, and seek to grasp a sphere of existence previously unexperienced yet nonetheless moved towards in anticipation. Action and environment here are in constant dialogue (Vigh 2008), yet the self is not just in relation to context or environment of a social or material making, but a spiritual realm with other-than-human persons in deep relationship with and witnesses to human suffering and striving (McGregor and McKinley Ch. 3). In this way, one of the key roles of spirituality, religious, and faith-based striving in chronicity is about carving out futures, centered on notions of hope and wellness, that people reach for and inhabit in various ways.

The fact that those drawing on religious, spiritual, or faith-based forms of support and care have been frequently associated with higher degrees of wellness and quality of life, optimism, and happiness when compared to people who do not draw on such resources is widely supported in current scientific literature (de

Bernardin et al. 2017; Roger and Hatala 2017; Peres et al. 2018). Likewise, religiousness and spirituality can also help people deal with stressful situations and emotions, like fear, anguish, sadness, and anger, because they tend to develop internal cognitive mechanisms that help people reframe experienced adversities in new ways (Hatala, Desjardins and Bombay 2016; Pargament, Feuille and Burdzy 2011). As spirituality and religiousness are components of people's psychological wellness, there is even evidence showing an association between low levels of spiritual and religious beliefs or practices with increased mental illness or impairment (Weber, Lomax and Pargament 2017) and greater risk-taking behaviors (Hatala et al. 2020). Since research has identified spirituality as a key resource amidst chronic conditions in health care contexts (Ai et al. 2010; Büssing and Koenig, 2010; Craig et al. 2006), it is important, in both the private and public sectors, to identify how to better utilize these evidence-based resources, and how doing so involves an expanded notion of wellness and "recovery" amidst chronicity (Jarvis et al. Ch. 11). In this context, the idea that people living with chronic conditions can experience wellness, and furthermore, that spirituality and faith-based practices may be supports towards wellness, may problematize and challenge the increasing medicalization of a so-called "popular health sector" of home-based care (Mattingly, Gron and Meinert 2011).

Although this collection and these authors focus on a strengths-based approach, it is furthermore important to highlight that the chapters in this collection do outline various moments when religion and spirituality can become a source of conflict and tension (Jarvis et al. Ch. 11), or when relationships with other-than-human persons are a cause for worry and struggle (Moratz Ch. 4). It is crucial to appreciate, therefore, that the practice of religion and spirituality can harness deeply negative aspects of oppression, harms, and abuses, underlining intolerance and stigma rather than the positives ideals such as compassion, justice, and love (see Morton et al. Ch. 7 for examples in the contexts of settler colonialism). As such, at the individual level these potential negative impacts for some need to be acknowledged by care providers and practitioners. Working with individuals may require that practitioners have knowledge of historic harms, systemic abuses, or well-known infractions caused within religious groups, or by specific spiritual practices, so that they can better support individuals on their wellness journeys. Religious, spiritual, and faith-based worldviews and practices, in this sense, may indicate their own contexts of struggle, challenge, and additional duress, and should therefore also be explored as part of the spiritual determinants of chronicity. More broadly at global levels, one must also recognize that these potential harms and variations of experience are partly shaped by geopolitical, cultural, and macro psychosocial contexts (Zimmer et al. 2018). Accordingly, another key element of a Global Mental Wellness agenda and important area of future research involves a better understanding of how spiritual geographies of care can be both a source of hope and strength, dealing with mental wellness but also working through harms possibly produced by religious or spiritual affiliations, as well as a source of tension or added stress when those harms appear to be unresolvable, and especially how these dynamics might compound or impact other modes of care and help-seeking and vary based on place and space.

Towards a collaborative Global Mental Wellness agenda

The chapters in this collection indicate that, despite notable tensions and potential harms, diverse contemporary forms of global spiritual and religious consciousness continue to permeate humankind. According to a comprehensive demographic study of more than 230 countries and territories conducted by the Pew Research Center's Forum on Religion and Public Life (2020), it is estimated that in 2020 there were 6.6 billion religiously affiliated adults and children around the globe, representing 84 percent of the world population of 7.8 billion.[4] These numbers are expected to grow in future years. Notwithstanding an outmoded secularization theory that assumed religious or spiritual worldviews and practices would gradually disappear and be replaced by a scientific rationality in a modern world (Habermas 2008), religious and spiritual worldviews and practices have maintained, reformulated, and re-envisioned relations between the sacred and mundane, spirit and matter, within everyday individual and social life. As Csordas (2009, 91) similarly notes in relation to what he called "global geographies of the spirit" in Catholic Charismatic Renewal, "contrary impulses toward universal culture and cultural fragmentation have both become imbued with an aura of enchantment" and that:

> At the least, such phenomena are of interest because they constitute the religious dimension of a global social system; at the most they portend that religious consciousness will be seen to be a defining feature of contemporary global consciousness.

If religious, spiritual, and faith-based practices remain a significant force in the lives of many people on the planet, then humanity—and particularly the scientifically informed biomedical community endeavoring to alleviate the health burdens of a global crisis in chronicity—must in some way come to terms with the roles and spaces such practices occupy in the modern world.

We thus conclude that the future solutions to the rising health problems of chronicity and a global burden of mental health disability will involve, to some extent, a Global Mental Wellness agenda that is grounded within a contemporary "religious consciousness" (Csordas 2009) or "post-secular modernity" (Habermas 2008). This vision embraces the spiritual nature of humanity, our interactions with aspects of spiritual reality, and values the knowledge, connections, and relationships that emerge from these worldviews as important resources for care and mental wellness. At its core, this agenda will involve learning about strengthening relationships between spiritual, religious, and faith-based care providers on the one hand, and biomedically informed health care practitioners variously defined on the other—a practical harmony between science and spirituality. The one can and should not ignore the other, given that both, in different ways and spheres of influence, endeavor to improve chronic and poor mental health in various ways. If this collection does anything useful, we hope it can help stimulate and advance a necessary conversation amongst stakeholders across the mental health and wellness expertise divide to take steps towards collaboration between the silos of care. As most of the chapters in this collection illustrate, both have much to offer each other. To mitigate the growing burden of global mental illness and chronicity, therefore, we argue it is time to take a more nuanced look at the ongoing role of religion and spirituality in the modern world and to explore their potentially constructive contribution to global health and wellness. These are not arguments in favor of one existing religious or spiritual system over another. On the contrary, it is a position where we move beyond sectarianism or cultural fragmentation in our understanding of such worldviews and practices. The health sciences and religion or spirituality should (and can) have the same goal of promoting individual, public and global mental wellness for those who practice in a faith-based way, predicated on a positive and optimistic view of human nature, deepened awareness of body-mind-spirit interactions and relationships, and a spiritual domain and worldview (Jakovljevic et al. 2019; Levin 2003).

Moving towards a practical science-spirituality harmony as envisioned here is no easy task, yet it is essential if meaningful intersectoral collaborations across epistemic domains are to be advanced in respectful ways. At one level, this will involve a certain reformulation of terms and concepts. In a pragmatic and simplified way, both science and religion or spirituality, at their best, can be viewed as complementary systems of knowledge and practice concerned with the betterment of humanity (Arbab 2018). Science here is largely concerned with an exploration and application of material truths, whereas religion or spirituality are largely concerned with the exploration and application of non-material (or spiritual) truths. Importantly, then, science and religion or spirituality conceived in this way significantly overlap: both are largely concerned with service towards and the betterment of the human condition; both can involve the exercise of rational thought, imagination, and intuition, as well as skeptical thinking; both rely on disciplined and systematic observations in the pursuit of knowledge and its generation; and both require virtues, such as curiosity, honesty, integrity, and cooperation. As well, we see parallels in that both share a recognition of the fallibility of human knowledge, which invites humility and openness; both are, to a great extent, social enterprises pursued by communities of people that need to develop shared vocabularies and complex forms of social interaction and organization; and both must contend with a variety of individual, social, and political forces that can distort or pervert their expression (Arbab 2018; Smith 2019). For these reasons, it is important to avoid false dichotomies between science and religion or spirituality; rather, it may be fruitful for the kind of collaboration we envision that they are understood as evolving, complimentary, and overlapping systems of knowledge and practice that require ongoing efforts and "normative discourses" to ensure their practices and tangible applications are aligned with ideal principals (Karlberg 2020).

This notion of "normative discourses" that regulate practice and application requires deeper consideration when approaching a sought-after harmony between science and spirituality. While such discourses can bring about a useful standardization for practice and ensure ideal principles are adhered to, they can also lead to harmful stigmatization and oppression of large groups of people and knowledge systems. In the history of science, universalizing normative discourses began with rational and empirical standards and have since expanded to include ethical standards of practice along with institutional mechanisms needed to enforce them and train future scientists under their ideals (Oreskes 2019). The gross ethical failures of previous scientific research—such as the infamous Tuskegee study or eugenics programs to take but two examples—propelled the widespread establishment of standard institutional ethical review boards and peer review processes for the protection of human rights and personal safety (Oreskes 2019). Although such practices are considered normative today, these ethical failures of the past indicate that normative standards evolve over time as communities of practitioners engage together in discourse and practice about the scientific enterprise as a whole (Arbab 2018). While such training, sociocultural processes, and standards are far from perfect and ethical violations can still occur, some form of public accountability and acceptability is increasingly regarded as essential to the "proper" practices of science today (Karlberg 2020).

Perhaps, then, we can also consider how diverse religious, spiritual, or faith-based practices could be subject to parallel forms of public accountability and acceptability, both locally and globally. This kind of heightened public discourse could be an important step to ensure that the harmful abuses and human rights violations that have occurred in the name of religion or spirituality are seen as distinct from an envisioned science-spirituality harmony. Indeed, as Karlberg (2020, 73) has observed regarding the role of religion in modern society:

> Transcending conflict and violence committed in the name of religion has become a global imperative. Even though this will not be easy, the stakes have become too high to ignore this. But this will require a deep rethinking of the concept of religion and its normative dimensions, along with a corresponding change in the way we invoke the term "religion."

Thus, just as scientific practice has clearly become an object of growing public scrutiny in recent years, and critical assessments of practice are regular themes in contemporary public discourse (Oreskes 2019), so too, we argue, could religious and spiritual practices that aim to support the wellness of diverse groups of people around the world also be held to a parallel set of common principles, those based on, for example, a peaceful coexistence or the promotion of wellness or social justice (Karlberg 2020). The advancement of discourses about accountability and acceptability of spiritual, religious, or faith-based practices—in ways that would adhere to local priorities and knowledge while also seeking broader common principles and connections—would likely help to refine and define what is meant by these core terms in relation to chronicity and wellness, delimit terrorism, violence, oppression, and other forms of abuse as valid forms of religious or spiritual practice, and clarify for skeptical health practitioners and global human rights advocates what is meant by the sought after science-spirituality harmony underlying a Global Mental Wellness framework.

The chapters in this collection highlight that much work is needed if we are to take seriously and advance these aims, at the individual, community, and more structural or global levels. In a review of the relationship between schizophrenia and religion, for example, Mohr and Huguelet (2004) reported that patients' concerns about their psychiatrists' views of their spiritual or religious beliefs kept them from discussing religion or spirituality with their psychiatrists. Similar findings were also reported by Ho et al. (2016) and Osokpo and Riegel (2019). This tension is not an uncommon story, especially in global contexts of Indigenous health and healing (Allen et al. 2020). Largely related to observed dichotomies between or tensions among spiritual, religious, and scientific domains, this situation reveals that there can be a lack of discussion, understanding, and consensus between patients and various health or mental health professionals regarding spirituality and religious matters, a theme also stressed by the authors of this collection from multiple perspectives.[5]

By accepting that there is a vital spiritual component to personhood, at least in the worldview of many individuals, health practitioners may be better equipped to mobilize the salutogenic spiritual resources that can, in many ways, facilitate wellness alongside, or in addition to, a biomedically informed approach to care. At the individual level, therefore, clinical history-taking ought to include an assessment of a patient's religious and spiritual history and current cultural practices (Allen et al. Ch. 10; Jarvis et al. Ch. 11). Inventories and assessment tools exist in growing number for use by primary care physicians, psychiatrists, and mental health providers, with healthy patients and both medically and psychiatrically ill patients, and for assessment of normative practices and beliefs and experiences, religious, or spiritual problems, and a history of spiritual interventions, such as faith healing (Levin 2003). Biomedically informed mental health professionals can also make timely referrals, where appropriate, to professionals trained in pastoral counseling or psychology, as well as Indigenous or spiritual healers variously defined, and examples of these informal or formal partnerships in Canada and elsewhere seem promising (Allen et al. 2020). Pursuit of these partnerships can ensure that growing concerns for and acceptance of cultural sensitivity and safety in clinical encounters and patient care is expanded to include spiritually sensitive and safe care as well (Jarvis et al. Ch. 11). Although some steps have advanced in recent years towards appreciating the religious and spiritual forces shaping individual lives and wellness outcomes (Büssing and Koenig, 2010; Habermas 2008), there is still much work to do in building trust and respect required for integration across epistemic worldviews, cultures of healing, and diverse systems of care.

From another vantage point, with an estimated shortfall of over one million mental health specialists in Low Middle Income Countries (LMICs) (Kakuma et al. 2011), there is also a need to look for local resources, models of community integration, and partnerships across diverse sectors of expertise to bridge a growing global care gap for chronic conditions and mental illness. Consequently, it is essential that global health practitioners learn to increase the number and variety of skilled workers prepared to address diverse health care needs, and that this increased human capacity be deployed in integrated community-care settings, especially beyond the stand-alone mental health hospital (Kakuma et al. 2011). Multiple demonstrations validate these kinds of innovative collaborative strategies, involving task-sharing as both cost-effective and feasible (Patel et al 2007; Patel 2014). The WHO Mental Health Gap Action Programme, for instance, has articulated a prioritized set of conditions and promotes capacity building by enhancing the training of non-specialized care providers in integrated community settings (Patel et al. 2007). As part of their grand challenges in global mental health, Collins, Patel and Joestl (2011) similarly argued for advances in areas around community wellness and collaboration: 1) to support community environments that promote physical and mental well-being throughout life; 2) to provide effective and affordable community-based care and rehabilitation; and 3) to develop sustainable models to train and increase the number of culturally and ethnically diverse lay and specialist providers to deliver a variety of care services. Research also underscores that the need to scale up health care resources within countries cannot be a singular strategy, nor may it be the most effective alone (Alvarado et al. 2013; Kakuma et al. 2011).

As this collection suggests, such appeals for community integration and intersectoral partnerships must involve a more serious consideration of the resources that spiritual, religious, or faith-based practitioners and communities can offer. Part of this needs to be an acknowledgement that biomedical or mental health practitioners are not the only ones with experience, expertise, and capacity to care for people with mental illness and various kinds of chronicity. Part of this, too, needs to be an appreciation of the knowledge, capacity, and evidence-based endogenous solutions such diverse spiritual or faith-based practitioners can hold and utilize in their own ways (Allen et al. 2020). Whether Indigenous Elders working to build and restore connections to the land and a spiritual identity (McGregor and McKinley Ch. 3), spiritual chaplains serving as counselors in a hospital or hospice setting (Freitas et al. Ch. 2), Spiritual Peer-Support Networks that support meaning-making transformations within diverse contexts of mental health care (Remy-Fischler Ch. 8), or spiritual healers of various kinds supporting patients in rural areas as well as urban centers (Benyah Ch. 9; Kurz Ch. 5), such practitioners and the communities they represent signify, we argue, an important hidden resource that can help address the global care gaps for mental illness and chronicity, and thereby increase global opportunities for enhanced wellness across multiple domains. Indeed, as others have also noted, finding "windows of compatibility" to enhance collaboration between formal mental health services and traditional Indigenous healers, for example, may offer a complementary pathway toward more locally accessible resources for community-based care (Hatala 2008; Hatala and Waldram 2016; Ndetei et al. 2008; Waldram and Hatala 2015). A Global Mental Wellness framework, therefore, must consider alternative models and innovative social or community strategies of care beyond those typically informed primarily by a biomedical, Western-centric framework in order to close a growing global care gap in these areas.

As Kleinman and Hall-Clifford (2010, 251) also observed, "chronicity makes it unavoidable that professional and family caregivers move to the center of our understanding of health care" and that "this will require a cultural revolution in global health planning and program development." We agree with these authors that in the global context of chronicity a "new agenda for global health" is required, one that "reimagines the role of health services and the role of communities of care" (251). Yet, we contend that this "new agenda" must move beyond the social and material conditions of biomedical care, Western knowledge systems and expertise, questions of access and distribution, or public health interventions. Rather, these conversations around a "new agenda" must begin to push into and embrace the spiritual, religious, and faith-based resources that people access and traverse alongside family caregivers and various community professionals to provide care and support their mental wellness outcomes amidst chronicity. Moreover, even the shift in recognizing the "largely unexplored" realm of the "popular health sector" mentioned by Mattingly, Gron, and Meinert (2011)—where treatment and care of sickness take place in families, among friends and neighbors in homes and communities—does not adequately acknowledge the spiritual geographies traversed during the day-to-day management of chronicity. Thus, although rightly critical of globalization and modernity, universalizing and Western-centric therapeutic frames, capital flows and enterprise, medicalization, pharmaceuticalization of mental health and social suffering, bio-power and expert control of the body and health care (Dumit 2012; Ecks 2005; Good 1994; Good 1995; Inhorn and Wentzell 2012; Manderson and Smith-Morris 2010; Mills 2014; Susser 2009), medical anthropologists and critical social scientists have done little to interrogate the spiritual determinants of chronicity, that is, the vital relationships with spirits, ceremony, other-than-human persons, the nexus of care within sacred communities, spiritual connections with the land and a sacred identity, prayer, fasting and diverse spiritual practices, among other aspects, that various individuals draw on to augment care and mental wellness. Thus, the "new agenda" that Kleinman and Hall-Clifford (2010) called for us to consider could build on the Global Mental Wellness framework traced out here, and indeed we hope this diverse collection of chapters can serve as an initial theoretical and empirical point of departure for others to pursue.

In conclusion, based on the chapters and recommendations outlined in this collection, we envision certain structural arrangements regarding collaborative systems of care that are: 1) *based* on a model of wellness and recovery that involves a mind-body-spirit balance across diverse cultural contexts of care; 2) *designed* through engagement with affected individuals, their families, and their communities, as well as with the relevant faith-based, religious, or spiritual care practitioners; 3) *governed* in a culturally appropriate, sensitive, and safe way integrating local traditions, healers, knowledge keepers, and through the customs of people by which they are offered; 4) *offered* by collaborative teams of medical professionals, faith-based healers, or spiritual and religious communities of care seeking to balance evidence-based practice with a science-spirituality harmony; and 5) *accessible* to all people and their families founded on models of spiritually informed community-based care. Taken together, this collection offers a critical discussion of and outlines some strategies for future research, intervention, and clinical practice, based on a "post-secular" worldview that is multisectoral, cross-cultural, transdisciplinary, and balanced across insights from science and spirituality (Habermas 2008). This will, we hope, in part provide the basis for a Global Mental Wellness agenda that is more inclusive, participatory, and responsive to local spiritual, religious, and faith-based practices, worldviews, strengths, resources, and realities that have great potential to enhance mental wellness and care for those struggling with various forms of chronicity around the globe.

Notes

1 The Global Burden of Diseases, Injuries, and Risk Factors Study (GBD) 2019 provides a rules-based synthesis of the available evidence on levels and trends in health outcomes, a diverse set of risk factors, and health system responses. GBD 2019 covered 204 countries and territories, as well as first administrative-level disaggregations for 22 countries, from 1990 to 2019.
2 There are also the additional critical reflections Fassin (2012) offers regarding a global health agenda, particularly that the notions of both "global" and "health" are not so clearly defined or understood. As Fassin argued, "the globalization of health must therefore be thought of as a heterogeneous and contested historical phenomena…" (p. 99) and that "this unique combination of expansion and normalization, of failures and resistances, of abandonments and rumors, suggest that globalization is definitely not the monolithic homogenizing process many have denounced, but rather a melange of uniformity and distinctions, of power and innovations" (p. 108).
3 Although of course religion generally remains a significant aspect of many people's lives around the world and those struggling with various forms of chronic conditions, we employ the overarching notion of spiritual geographies of care here due to the ways in which this concept can envelope both religious and spiritual experiences, but refer also to the different landscapes in which such practices can and do happen. This term can signify a diverse set of internal and external resources people can draw on to support their care trajectories and coping needs, involve a spiritual nature to humanity, and a transcendent realm including but also beyond the material world.
4 This number is also expected to be an underrepresentation as it does not fully account for a large population of people who feel that are "spiritual but not religious."
5 This is not to ignore the fact that, at an individual level, many biomedically trained health care providers may also be spiritual or religious themselves. There is a difference between a biomedical system (what we often call "scientific" here) as it functions and shapes how health practitioners operate, and that of the belief systems (i.e., spirituality and religions) of health practitioners themselves. Although we are drawing attention to more systemic and cultural aspects of this conversation here, a potential tension between care providers system of beliefs and worldviews and how this relates to those being cared for is another important area to examine in more detail.

References

Abu-Raiya, Hisham. 2013. "On the Links between Religion, Mental Health and Inter-Religious Conflict: A Brief Summary of Empirical Research." *Israel Journal of Psychiatry and Related Sciences* 50 (2):130–139.

Adeponle, Ademola B., Rob Whitley and Laurence J. Kirmayer. 2012. "Cultural Contexts and Constructions of Recovery." In *Recovery of People with Mental Illness: Philosophical and Related Perspectives*, edited by A. Rudnick, 109–132. New York, NY: Oxford University Press.

Ai, Amy, Bruce Rollman and Candyce Berger. 2010. "Comorbid Mental Health Symptoms and Heart Diseases: Can Health Care and Mental Health Care Professionals Collaboratively Improve the Assessment and Management?" *Health and Social Work* 35 (1): 27–38. doi:10.1093/hsw/35.1.27

Alarcon-Guzman, R. and H. Castillo-Martell. 2020. "The Role of Community Mental Health in a New Architecture of World Psychiatry and Global Mental Health." *Salud Mental* 43 (5): 235–240. doi:10.17711/SM.0185-3325.2020.032

Allen, Lindsay, Andrew R. Hatala, Sabina Ijaz, Dave Courchene, Burma Bushie. 2020. "Indigenous-led Health Care Partnerships in Canada." *Canadian Medical Association Journal* 192 (9): E208–E216. doi:10.1503/cmaj.190728

Alvarado, Ruben, Alberto Minoletti, Elie Valencia, Graciela Rojas and Ezra Susser. 2013. "The Need for New Models of Care for People with Severe Mental Illness in Low- and Middle- Income Countries." In *Improving Mental Health Care: The Global Challenge*, edited by Graham Thornicroft, Mirella Ruggeri and David Goldberg, 78–95. Chichester: John Wiley & Sons.

Arbab, Farzam. 2018. "An Inquiry into the Harmony of Science and Religion." In *Religion and Public Discourse in an Age of Transition: Reflections on Bahá'í Thought and Practice*, edited by Geoffrey Cameron and Benjamin Schewel, 131–162. Waterloo, ON: Wilfrid Laurier University Press.

Becker, Gaylene. 1997. *Disrupted Lives: How People Create Meaning in a Chaotic World*. Berkeley: University of California Press.

Bemme, Doerte, and Nicole A. D'Souza. 2014. "Global Mental Health and its Discontents: An inquiry into the Making of Global and Local Scale." *Transcultural Psychiatry* 51 (6): 850–874.

Büssing, Arndt, and Harold G. Koenig. 2010. "Spiritual Needs of Patients with Chronic Diseases." *Religions* 1 (1): 18–27. doi:10.3390/rel1010018

Canda, Edward R., and Leola D. Furman. 2009. *Spiritual Diversity in Social Work Practice: The Heart of Helping*. New York: Oxford University Press.

Campbell, Catherine, and Rochelle Burgess. 2012. "The Role of Communities in Advancing the Goals of the Movement for Global Mental Health." *Transcultural Psychiatry* 49 (3–4):379–395. doi:10.1177/1363461512454643

Charmaz, Kathy. 1991. *Good Days, Bad Days: The Self in Chronic Illness and Time*. New Jersey: Rutgers University Press.

Collins, Pamela, Vikram Patel, Sarah Joestlet al.2011. "Grand Challenges in Global Mental Health." *Nature* 475, 27–30. doi:10.1038/475027a

Craig, Carol, Clarann Weinert, Joni Walton and Barbara Derwinski-Robinson. 2006. "Spirituality, Chronic Illness, and Rural Life." *Journal of Holistic Nursing* 24 (1): 27–35. doi:10.1177/0898010105282526

Csordas, Thomas J. 2009. "Global Religion and the Renchantment of the World: The Case of the Catholic Charismatic Renewal." In *Transnational Transcendence: Assays on Religion and Globalization* edited by Thomas J. Csordas. Berkeley: University of California Press.

Das, Anindya, and Mohan Rao. 2012. "Universal Mental Health: Re-Evaluating the Call for Global Mental Health." *Critical Public Health* 22 (4): 383–389. doi:10.1080/09581596.2012.700393 de Bernardin, Gonçalves, Juliane Piasseschi, Giancarlo Lucchetti, Paulo Rossi Menezes, Homero Vallada and Gianni Virgili. 2017. "Complementary Religious and Spiritual Interventions in Physical Health and Quality of Life: A Systematic Review of Randomized Controlled Clinical Trials." *PloS One* 12: e0186539. doi:10.1371/journal.pone.0186539.

Desjarlias, Robert, Leon Eisenberg, Byron Good, and Arthur Kleinman. 1995. *World Mental Health: Problems and Priorities in Low Income Countries.* Oxford: Oxford University Press.

Dumit, Joeseph. 2012. *Drugs for Life: How Pharmaceutical Companies Define Our Health.* Durham, NC: Duke University Press.

Ecks, Stefan. (2005) "Pharmaceutical Citizenship: Antidepressant Marketing and the Promise of Demarginalization in India." *Anthropology & Medicine* 12 (3), 239–254, doi:10.1080/13648470500291360

Estroff, Sue. 1993. "Identity, Disability, and Schizophrenia: The Problem of Chronicity." In *Knowledge, Power and Practice: The Anthropological of Medicine and Everyday Life*, edited by Shirley Lindenbaum and Margaret Lock, 247–286. Berkeley: University of California Press.

Fassin, Didier. 2012. "That Obscure Object of Global Health." In *Medical Anthropology at the Intersections: Histories, activisms, and futures*, edited by Marcia Inhorn and Emily A. Wentzell, 95–116. Durham, NC: Duke University Press.

Farmer, Paul. 2004. "An Anthropology of Structural Violence." *Current Anthropology* 45: 305–326.

Fisher, John. 2011. "The Four Domains Model: Connecting Spirituality, Health and Well-Being." *Religions* 2 (1): 17–28. doi:10.3390/rel2010017

Good, Byron J. 1994. *Medicine, Rationality, and Experience: An Anthropological Perspective.* Cambridge, MA: Cambridge Press.

Good, Byron, Carla Marchira, Nida Ul Hasanat, Utami Sofiati and Subandi Muhana. 2010. "Is 'Chronicity' Inevitable for Psychotic Illness? Studying Heterogeneity in the Course of Schizophrenia in Yogyakarta, Indonesia." In *Chronic Conditions, Fluid States: Chronicity and the Anthropology of Illness*, edited by Carolyn Smith-Morris and Lenore Manderson, 54–74. Ithaca: Rutgers University Press. doi:36019/9780813549736-005.

Good, Mary-Jo Delvecchio. 1995. "Cultural studies of biomedicine: an agenda for research," *Social Science and Medicine* 41 (4): 461–473. https://doi.org/10.1016/0277-9536(95)00008-U

Goodman, Richard A., Samuel F. Posner, Elbert S. Huang, Anand K. Parekh and Howard K. Koh. 2013. "Defining and Measuring Chronic Conditions: Imperatives for Research, Policy, Program, and Practice." *Preventing Chronic Disease* 10: E66. doi:10.5888/pcd10.120239

Global Burden of Disease [GBD]. 2019. "Disease and Injuries Collaborators Global Burden of 369 Diseases and Injuries in 204 Countries and Territories, 1990–2019: A Systematic Analysis for the Global Burden of Disease Study 2019." *Lancet* 396: 1204–1222. doi:10.1016/S0140–6736(20)30925–30929

Habermas, Jurgen. 2008. "Notes on Post-Secular Society." *New Perspectives Quarterly* 25 (4): 17–29. doi:10.1111/j.1540-5842.2008.01017.x

Hajat, Cother, and Emma Stein. 2018. "The Global Burden of Multiple Chronic Conditions: A Narrative Review." *Preventative Medicine Reports* 12: 284–293. doi:10.1016/j.pmedr.2018.10.008

Hatala, Andrew R. 2008. "Spirituality and Aboriginal Mental Health." *Advances in Mind-Body Medicine* 23 (1): 6–12.

Hatala, Andrew R. 2013. "Towards a Biopsychosocial-Spiritual approach in Health Psychology: Exploring Theoretical Orientations and Future Directions." *Journal of Spirituality in Mental Health* 15 (4): 256–276. doi:10.1080/19349637.2013.776448

Hatala, Andrew R., Michelle Desjardins and Amy Bombay. 2016. "Reframing Narratives of Aboriginal Health Disparity: Exploring Cree Elder Resilience and Well-being in Contexts of 'Historical Trauma'." *Qualitative Health Research* 26 (14): 1911–1927. doi:10.1177/1049732315609569

Hatala, Andrew R., Jonathan McGavock, Valerie Michaelson and William Pickett. 2020. "Low Risks for Spiritual Highs: Risk-taking Behaviors and the Protective Benefits of Spiritual Health among Saskatchewan Adolescents." *Paediatrics and Child Health*, pxaa007, doi:10.1093/pch/pxaa007

Hatala, Andrew R., and James B. Waldram. 2016. "The Role of Sensorial Processes in Q'eqchi' Maya Healing: A Case Study of Depression and Bereavement." *Transcultural Psychiatry* 53 (1): 60–80. doi:10.1177/1363461515599328

Hatala, Andrew R., James B. Waldram and Thomas Caal. 2015. "Narrative Structures of Maya Mental Disorders." *Culture, Medicine and Psychiatry* 39: 449–486. doi:10.1007/s11013-015-9436-9

Hatala, Andrew R., James B. Waldram and Margaret Crossley. 2013. "Doing Resilience with 'Half a Brain': Navigating Moral Sensibilities 35 Years after Hemispherectomy." *Culture, Medicine and Psychiatry* 37 (1): 148–178. doi:10.1007/s11013-012-9294-7

Ho, David Y.F., and Rainbow Tin Hung Ho. 2007. "Measuring Spirituality and Spiritual Emptiness: Toward Ecumenicity and Transcultural Applicability." *Review of General Psychology* 11 (1): 62–74. doi:10.1037/1089-2680.11.1.62

Ho, Rainbow Tin Hung, Caitlin Kar Pui Chan, Phyllis Hau Yan, Ping Ho Wong, Cecilia Lai Wan Chan, Pamela Pui Yu Leung and Eric Yu Hai Chen. 2016. "Understandings of Spirituality and Its Role in Illness Recovery in Persons with Schizophrenia and Mental-Health Professionals: A Qualitative Study." *BMC Psychiatry* 16 (1): 86. doi:10.1186/s12888–12016–0796–0797

Hungelmann, JoAnn, Eileen Kenkel-Rossi, Loretta Klassen and Ruth Stollenwerk. 1996. "Focus on Spiritual Well-Being: Harmonious Interconnectedness of Mind-Body-Spirit - Use of the JAREL Spiritual Well-Being Scale." *Geriatric Nursing* 17 (6): 262–266. doi:0.1016/ s0197–4572(96)80238–80232

Inhorn, Marcia, and Emily A. Wentzell. (Eds.) 2012. *Medical Anthropology at the Intersections: Histories, activisms, and futures.* Durham, NC: Duke University Press.

Jakovljevic, Miro, Asim Kurjak, Ana Jerkovic, Aziz Hasanovic and Mijo Nikic. 2019. "Spirituality, Religiosity, and Nationalism from the Perspective of Public and Global Mental Health." *Psychiatria Danubina* 31 (4): 382–391. doi:10.24869/psyd.2019.382

Karlberg, Michael. 2020. *Constructing Social Reality: An Inquiry into the Normative Foundations of Social Change.* Ottawa, ON: Associations of Bahá'i Studies Press.

Kakuma, Ritsuko, Harry Minas, Nadja van Ginneken, Mario R. Dal Poz, Keshav Desiraju, et al.2011. "Human Resources for Mental Health Care: Current Situation and Strategies for Action." *Lancet* 378: 5–11. doi:10.1016/S0140-6736(11)61093-3

Kirmayer, Laurence J., and I. Gold, 2012. "Re-Socializing Psychiatry: Critical Neuroscience and the Limits of Reductionism." In *Critical Neuroscience: A Handbook of the Social and Cultural Contexts of Neuroscience* edited by S. Choudhury and J. Slaby. Oxford: Blackwell.

Kirmayer, Laurence, and Duncan Pedersen, 2014. "Toward a New Architecture for Global Mental Health." *Transcultural Psychiatry* 51 (6): 759–776. doi:10.1177/1363461514557202

Kirmayer, Laurence J., and Leslie Swartz. 2013. "Culture and Global Mental Health." In *Global Mental Health: Principles and Practice*, edited by V. Patel, H. Minas, A. Cohen and M.J. Prince, 41–62. Oxford: Oxford University Press.

Kleinman, Arthur. 2005. *Culture and Psychiatric Diagnosis and Treatment: What are the Necessary Therapeutic Skills?* Utrecht: Trimbos-Instituut.

Kleinman, Arthur, and Rachel Hall-Clifford. 2010. "Afterword: Chronicity - Time, Space, and Culture". In *Chronic Conditions, Fluid States: Chronicity and the Anthropology of Illness*, edited by Lenore Manderson and Carolyn Smith-Morris, 247–251. New Brunswick, NJ: Rutgers University Press.

Levin, J. 2003. "Spiritual Determinants of Heath and Healing: An Epidemiologic Perspective on Salutogenic Mechanisms." *Alternative Therapies in Health and Medicine* 9 (6): 48–57.

Lock, Margaret. 2001. *Twice Dead: Organ Transplants and the Reinvention of Death*. Berkeley: University of California Press.

Lund, Crick, Alison Breen, Alan J. Flisher, Ritsuko Kakumab, Joanne Corrigall and John A. Joska, et al.2010. "Poverty and Common Mental Disorders in Low- and Middle- Income Countries: A Systematic Review." *Social Science and Medicine* 71 (3): 517–528. doi:10.1016/j.socscimed.2010.04.027

Manderscheid, Ron, Carol Ryff, Elsie Freeman, Lela McKnight-Eily, Satvinder Dhingra and Tara Strine. 2010. "Evolving Definitions of Mental Health and Wellness" *Preventing Chronic Disease* 7 (1): 2–6.

Manderson, Lenore, and Carolyn Smith-Morris. 2010. "Chronicity and the Experience of Illness." In *Chronic Conditions, Fluid States: Chronicity and the Anthropology of Illness*, edited by Lenore Manderson and Carolyn Smith-Morris, 1–18. New Brunswick, NJ: Rutgers University Press.

Mattingly, Cheryl, Lone Gron and Lotte Meinert. 2011. "Chronic Homework in Emerging Borderlands of Healthcare." *Culture, Medicine and Psychiatry* 35 (3): 347–375. doi:10.1007/s11013-011-9225-z

McGrath, Janet W., Margaret S. Winchester, David Kaawa-Mafigiri, Eddy Walakira, Florence Namutiibwa, Judith Birungi, et al.2014. "Challenging the Paradigm: Anthropological Perspectives on HIV as a Chronic Disease." *Medical Anthropology* 33 (4): 303–317. doi:10.1080/01459740.2014.892483

Mehta, Nisha, and Graham Thornicroft. 2013. "Stigma, Discrimination, and Promoting Human Rights." In *Global Mental Health: Principles and Practice*, edited by V. Patel, H. Minas, A. Cohen and M.J. Prince, 401–424. Oxford: Oxford University Press.

Miles, Ann. 2010. "Ecuadorian Women's Narratives of Lupus, Suffering, and Vulnerability." In *Chronic Conditions, Fluid States: Chronicity and the Anthropology of Illness* edited by Lenore Manderson and Carolyn Smith-Morris, 113–130. New Brunswick, NJ: Rutgers University Press.

Mills, China. 2014. *Decolonizing Global Mental Health: The Psychiatrization of the Majority World*. London: Routledge.

Mohr, Sylvia, and Phillip Huguelet. 2004. "The Relationship Between Schizophrenia and Religion and its Implications for Care." *Swiss Medical Weekly* 134 (25–26):369–376.

Murray, Christopher J., Theo Vos, Rafael Lozano, Mohsen Naghavi, Abraham D. Flaxman, et al.2013. "Disability-Adjusted Life Years (DALYs) for 291 Diseases and Injuries in 21 Regions, 1990–2010: A Systematic Analysis for the Global Burden of Disease Study 2010." *Lancet* 380: 2197–2223. doi:10.1016/S0140-6736(12)61689-4

Myers, Neely L. 2010. "Culture, Stress and Recovery from Schizophrenia: Lessons from the Field for Global Mental Health." *Culture, Medicine and Psychiatry* 34 (3): 500–528. doi:10.1007/s11013-010-9186-7

Ndetei, D., L.I. Khasakhala, J. Kingori, A. Oginga and S. Raja. 2008. "The Complementary Role of Traditional and Faith Healers and Potential Liaisons with Western-Style Mental Health Services in Kenya." *Africa Mental Foundations* 22. http://www.africamentalhealthfoundation.org/reports.html#.Ug1XbWTF0kc

Oreskes, Naomi. 2019. *Why Trust Science?* New Jersey: Princeton University Press.

Osokpo, Onome, and Barbara Riegel. 2019. "Cultural Factors Influencing Self-Care by Persons with Cardiovascular Disease: An Integrative Review." *International Journal of Nursing Studies* 103383. doi:10.1016/j.ijnurstu.2019.06.014

Pargament, Kenneth, Margaret Feuille and Donna Burdzy. 2011. "The Brief RCOPE: Current Psychometric Status of a Short Measure of Religious Coping." *Religions* 2: 51–76. doi:10.3390/rel2010051

Patel, Vikram, Ricardo Araya, Sudipto Chatterjee, Dan Chisol, Alex Cohen, et al.2007. "Treatment and Prevention of Mental Disorders in Low-Income and Middle-Income Countries." *Lancet* 370: 991–1005. doi:10.1016/S0140-6736(07)61240-9

Patel, Vikram. 2014. "Why Mental Health Matters to Global Health." *Transcultural Psychiatry* 51 (6): 777–789. doi:10.1177/1363461514524473

Patel, Vikram, Niall Boyce, Pamela Y. Collins, Shekhar Saxena and Richard Horton. 2011. "A Renewed Agenda for Global Mental Health." *Lancet* 378 (9801): 1441–1442. doi:10.1016/S0140-6736(11)61385–61388

Patel, Vikram, Preston Garrison, Jair de Jesus Mari, Harry Minas, Martin Prince and Shekhar Saxena. 2008. "The Lancet's Series on Global Mental Health: 1 Year On." *Lancet* 372 (9646): 1354–1357. doi:10.1016/S0140-6736(08)61556-1

Patel, Vikram, and Martin Prince. 2010. "Global Mental Health: A New Global Health Field Comes of Age." *Journal of the American Medical Association* 303 (19): 1976–1977. doi:10.1001/jama.2010.616

Peres, Mario F.P., Helder H. Kamei, Patricia R. Tobo and Giancarlos Lucchetti. 2018. "Mechanisms Behind Religiosity and Spirituality's Effect on Mental Health, Quality of Life and Well-Being." *Journal of Religion and Health* 57 (5): 1842–1855. doi:10.1007/s10943-017-0400-6

Pew Research Center's Forum on Religion and Public Life. 2012. *PEW-Templeton Global Religious Future Project*. Accessed on May 20, 2021 from http://www.pewforum.org/global-religious-landscape.aspx

Pike, Kathleen, Ezra Susser, Sandro Galea and Harold Pincus. 2013. "Towards a Healthier 2020: Advancing Mental Health as a Global Health Priority." *Public Health Reviews* 35 (1): 1–25. doi:10.1007/BF03391692

Prince, Martin, Vikram Patel, Shekhar Saxena, Mario Maj, Joanna Maselko, et al.2007. "No Health Without Mental Health." *Lancet* 370: 859–877. doi:10.1016/S0140–6736(07)61238–0

Roger, Kerstin, and Andrew R. Hatala. 2017. "Religion, Spirituality and Chronic Illness: A Scoping Review and Implications for Health Care Practitioners." *Journal of Religion and Spirituality in Social Work: Social Thought* 37 (1): 24–44. doi:10.1080/15426432.2017.1386151

Russell, Steven, and Janet Seeley. 2010. "The Transition to Living with HIV as a Chronic Condition in Rural Uganda: Working to Create Order and Control When on Antiretroviral Therapy." *Social Science and Medicine* 70 (3): 375–382. doi:10.1016/j.socscimed.2009.10.039

Russo, Scott J., James W. Murrough, Ming-Hu Han, Dennis S. Charney and Eric J. Nestler. 2012. "Neurobiology of Resilience." *Nature Neuroscience* 15: 1475–1484. doi:10.1038/nn.3234

Sangaramoorthy, Thurka. 2018. "Chronicity, Crisis, and the 'End of AIDS.'" *Global Public Health* 13 (8): 982–996. doi:10.1080/17441692.2018.1423701

Saraceno, Benedetto, and Tarrun Dua. 2009. "Global Mental Health: The Role of Psychiatry." *European Archives of Psychiatry and Clinical Neuroscience* 259 (2): S109–117. doi:10.1007/s00406-009-0059-4

Saraceno, Beneddetto, Mark van Ommeren, Rajaie Batniji, Alex Cohen, Oye Gureje, John Mahoney, et al.2007. "Barriers to Improvement of Mental Health Services in Low-Income and Middle-Income Countries." *Lancet* 370 (9593): 1164–1174. doi:10.1016/S0140-6736(07)61263-X

Sax, William. 2014. "Ritual Healing and Mental Health in India." *Transcultural Psychiatry* 51 (6): 829–849. doi:10.1177/1363461514524472

Smith, Todd. 2019. "Science and Religion in Dynamic Interplay." *Journal of Bahá'í Studies* 29 (4): 11–49.

Susser, Ida. 2009. *AIDS, Sex, and Culture: Global Politics and Survival in Southern Africa*. Malden, MA: Wiley-Blackwell.

van der Lee, Johanna, Lidwine B. Mokkink, Martha A. Grootenhuis, Hugo S. Heymans and Martin Offringa. 2007. "Definitions and Measurement of Chronic Health Conditions in Childhood: A Systematic Review." *Journal of the American Medical Association* 297 (24): 2741–2751. doi:10.1001/jama.297.24.2741

Vigh, Henrik. 2008. "Crisis and Chronicity: Anthropological Perspectives on Continuous Conflict and Decline." *Ethnos* 73 (1): 5–24. doi:10.1080/00141840801927509

Wahlbeck, Kristian. 2015. "Public Mental Health: The Time is Ripe for Translation of Evidence into Practice." *World Psychiatry* 14: 36–42. doi:10.1002/wps.20178

Waldram, James B., and Andrew R. Hatala. 2015. "Latent and Manifest Empiricism in Q'eqchi' Maya Healing: A Case Study of HIV/AIDS." *Social Science and Medicine* 126: 9–16. doi:10.1016/j.socscimed.2014.12.003

Wang, H., M. Naghavi, C. Allen, et al.2016. "Global, Regional, and National Life Expectancy, All-Cause Mortality, and Cause-Specific Mortality for 249 Causes of Death, 1980–2015: A Systematic Analysis for the Global Burden of Disease Study 2015." *Lancet* 388 (10053): 1459–1544. doi:10.1016/S0140-6736(16)31012-31011

Watkins-Hayes, Celeste, Lisa Pittman-Gay and Jean Beaman. 2012. "'Dying From' to 'Living With': Framing Institutions and the Coping Processes of African American Women Living with HIV/AIDS." *Social Science and Medicine* 74 (12): 2028–2036. doi:10.1016/j.socscimed.2012.02.001

Weber, Samuel R., James W. Lomax and Kenneth I. Pargament. 2017. "Healthcare Engagement as a Potential Source of Psychological Distress among People without Religious Beliefs: A Systematic Review." *Healthcare (Basel, Switzerland)* 5 (2): 19. doi:10.3390/healthcare5020019

World Health Organization [WHO]. 2007. *Projections of Mortality and Burden of Disease to 2030*. Geneva: World Health Organization.

Zimmer, Zachary, Florencia Rojo, Mary Beth Ofstedal, Chi-Tsun Chiu, Yasuhiko Saito and Carol Jagger. 2019. "Religiosity and Health: A Global Comparative Study." *SSM – Population Health* 7 (April): 100322–100006. doi:10.1016/j.ssmph.2018.11.006

Index

Note: Figures are indexed in *italic* page numbers and tables in **bold** page numbers.

aadizookaan 45–7
abuses 59, 174–5, 183, 189, 257, 260
activation-synthesis hypothesis 51
aesthetics 11, 76–7, 79–81, 83, 85, 87, 89, 91–2, 132, 138; of care 81, 90–2, 252; of healing 80–1
Afro-Brazilian concepts 82
Afro-Brazilian religious 21
alcoholism 204
Allen, Lindsay 13
altruism 109–11, 118
ancestors 82, 161, 199, 208, 221, 252, 256
Anishinaabek 10, 37–8, 41, 43–4, 48, 53–4; communities 37, 43, 53; culture 40, 45, 50, 52; Indigenous perspectives 37, 40, 44, 53; knowledge 40, 46, 54; knowledge holders 10; language 37, 41; social relationships 50; strategies 40; teachers 124; territories 10; traditions 51; understanding of mental wellness 43; values 37, 39, 41–3, 45, 47, 49, 51, 53; wellness 48; youths 48, 141
anthropologists 40, 48, 57, 65, 77, 79, 81, 251, 263
antipsychotic medication 232–4
anxiety 13, 18, 20, 28, 51, 59, 67, 87, 183–4, 187–8, 197; diagnostic-related 167; outcomes 223; symptoms 234
anxiety disorders 154
ASH *see* activation-synthesis hypothesis
asylums 181

BDA *see* Belize Diabetes Association
Bear Walking (practice) 48, 52
beliefs 13, 20, 27–8, 37, 39, 48–9, 64–6, 72–3, 102, 150, 174–5, 190, 221–3, 232–4, 255–6; allopathic 100; Buddhist 163; cultural 104; modern 71; newfound 237; nihilistic 228; popular 226; religious/spiritual 236; shared 32; traditional 223
Belize 13, 196–7, 199–201, 209–16, 250, 252; districts of 201; economy 213; health systems 196; partners 200
Belize City 201, 211, 216
Belize Diabetes Association 201, 210, 216
Belizeans 195, 199, 208, 212; adult 200; ranking fifth poorest in the world 195; stakeholders 201
beneficiaries 21–2, 24, 30
Benyah, Francis 12
Berens, William 46, 52
Bernard, Claude 17
bimaadiziwin 37–41, 44–7, 50–1, 53
biomedical 7, 10, 13–14, 38, 40, 76, 151–2, 160–1, 164–5, 177–8, 221, 239–41, 249–51, 258, 261–4; dualities 7; reductionism 126; research 40; treatment 76
biomedical care 13, 263
BIPOC *see* Black, Indigenous, and People of Color
Bird-Naytowhow, Kelley 12
Black, Indigenous, and People of Color 167
Blackfoot lands 130
Bliatout, Bruce T. 49
BMI *see* Body Mass Index
Bobiwash, Alan 124
body 46, 48, 50, 52–3, 58, 83–5, 88–90, 100–1, 103, 138, 140, 165, 167; aesthetics and spirituality of 132, 138; biological 82; energetic 76, 83, 92; growing 12, 149; parts 77, 87–8; patients 66, 88; physical 46; spiritual 87

Body Mass Index 197, 216
Braga, Ana Maria 76
brain 10, 38–9, 51, 90
Brazil 11, 17, 20–2, 32, 78–84, 90–2, 250; and 92% of the population declare themselves followers of some religion 21; eleven thousand deaths are attributed to psychiatric causes per year 19; health care 22, 77–8, 92; and the Spiritist movement in urban environments of 11
Brazilian 21, 84, 92, 252; institutions 31; Kardecism 76–92; psychologists 30; society 79; Spiritism 11, 77–8, 81–2, 90
Brenner, Suzanne 61, 72
Brown, George W. 38
Buddhism 87, 157
Burao 10, 62–5, 67–71; population of 57, 68; society 63; Somalis in 70

camp leaders 179, 181–2, 188
Campbell, Denis 148, 151, 156, 163–4, 253
Campbell's Hero's Journey 151, *156*
camps 174–5, 178–9, 181–91; *see also* prayer camps
Canada 37, 40, 42–3, 50–1, 124–8, 130, 209, 211, 233–5, 239, 241, 250, 252
Canadian Research Initiative in Substance Misuse 41
cancers 4, 50, 87, 107, 115, 174, 212, 247
capacity 18, 142, 211, 224, 255, 262; local problem-solving 80; professional 132
capital, high cultural 154
CAPS *see* Centros de Atenção Psicossocia
care 4–7, 14, 17, 31–3, 77–83, 92, 100–3, 107–9, 111–15, 117–18, 135–6, 179–80, 185–8, 190, 195–6, 203, 247–51, 253–9, 261–4; aesthetics of 81, 90–2, 252; charitable 78; clinical 228; continuing 226; family 5, 84; fraternal 84; free day 85; gap 79, 82, 92, 261–2; geography of 247–264; holistic 31; home-based 257; humanized 21; integrative 215; interdisciplinary 31; intimate 118; management 248–9; medical 106; mental 19; nourishing 112, 114; personal 115, 239; plans 196, 199, 210, 212; politics of 76–7, 79–81, 83, 85, 87, 89, 91–2; practices 7, 207; professional 32, 253; religious 22, 221; services 22, 262; spiritual 14, 19, 22, 31, 114, 198, 250, 253–5, 257, 264; trauma-informed 149
care providers 250, 257; faith-based 258; non-specialized 262; trained health 264

caregivers 40, 133, 136–7, 178–82, 184–7, 189–91, 210, 263
Catholics 21, 23, 102, 107, 113, 117, 134, 199, 208; beliefs 113; Irish families 154; pilgrimage to Lourdes 252
CBKT *see* community-based knowledge translation
CBPR *see* community based participatory research
CCS *see* Cultural Consultation Service
CEB *see* Centro Espírita Barsanulfo
Centre for Addictions and Mental Health, Toronto 40
Centro Espírita Barsanulfo 85, 89
Centros de Atenção Psicossocia 21–3, 27, 31–2, 84
ceremonies 39, 44, 46, 50, 67, 133–4, 136, 138–9, 141, 263; *ayahuasca* 159; Garifuna healers conducting 199; healing 66; Indigenous 201; personal 134; religious 197; *saar* 61–2, 65, 67; sacred 208; spiritual 127; street pipe 141; traditional spirit 67
CFI *see* Cultural Formulation Interviews
CGT *see* Constructivist Grounded Theory
chaplaincy 22, 31–2; mental health 22; professional 22; services 32
chaplains 9–10, 17, 19, 22–33, 249; male 23; professional 22, 31; and psychologists 22, 24–6, 28, 30, 32–3; spiritual 262
characteristics of cases **230**
charitable donations 236; *see also* donations
charity 82–6, 92
Charmaz, Kathy 7, 131–2, 200–1, 215, 252
Child Protection Services 233
children 46–7, 52, 57, 63, 66, 136, 142, 205–6, 208, 213, 233, 237; frightening 173; healthy 58; raising 59
Christ, Jesus 86, 160, 176, 204
Christian 19, 63–4, 82, 115, 117, 133, 201, 205, 223, 230, 232; dogma and personal belief 111; faith 32, 237; religion 32; worldview 181
Christianity 1, 48, 126–7, 139, 154, 157, 163, 199, 204
chronic conditions 2–7, 40, 43, 46, 89, 91–2, 100–2, 107–8, 176–7, 185, 187–90, 209, 247–51, 253, 256–7; and clienthood 148, 165, 168; diverse 2, 247; increasing 6; managing 189
Chronic Conditions and Fluid States 5
chronic diseases 5, 100–1, 197, 203, 208, 211, 215

Index 273

chronic health problems 11, 101, 177–8, 184, 186–7, 251
"chronic homework" 5, 209
chronic illness 1–2, 4, 7, 9, 11, 13, 58, 73, 76, 80, 82, 195–6, 247–8, 251–2; distributing 125; mental 9–10, 37–43, 45, 50, 53, 73, 173–5, 177, 179–81, 183, 185–9; unique 58
chronicity 1, 3–5, 7–9, 11–14, 17–18, 81, 100–3, 107–9, 111–13, 128, 173, 180, 195–7, 209–11, 215, 223, 247, 249–54, 256–60, 262–4; criteria 18; and deficits 150; defined 251; enduring 206; global rates of 14, 249; narrative of 152, 167; notions of 13, 222, 226, 228; perpetual 71; reinterpreted 252; and research 6; social 132; spiritual determinants of 250, 252, 257, 263; theory 5, 12, 125, 247; time of 108, 112
church attendance 209, 215
Church of Christ 224
church services 184
churches 25, 27, 29, 103, 109, 133–4, 174, 182, 208–10, 223–4, 227–8
CHW *see* Community Health Workers
cilaaj 70
civilizations 16, 60–1
classes 50, 53, 78, 80, 85, 196; differences across 215; disadvantaged 79; of female students 63; socioeconomic 247
clients 1–2, 4, 9, 11, 25–32, 82, 187, 222, 228–9; characteristics 23; deconstructing 28; experiences of 28; struggling to sustain strategies and language to help service providers 9
clinical practices 199–200, 212, 264
clinicians 14, 85, 222, 227–8, 238–41
clinics 6, 91–2, 148, 152; *cilaaj* 58, 61–2, 67–8; healing 62; Koranic 61; Roqya 236; Somaliland 255
collaboration 13–14, 112, 114, 191, 215–16, 259, 262; collegiate 113; integrative 190; intersectoral health care 191, 259; multi-organisation 195; ongoing 10; scientific 247; sympathetic 114
collection 2, 4–5, 7–9, 14, 249–51, 253–4, 257–9, 261–4; current 6; highlight 255, 261; new 1; outline 254; transdisciplinary 2
colonial 12, 49, 63, 80, 125–9, 132, 135, 139–42, 208, 254; settlers 135; borders 63; chronicities 140; history 254; interference 49; oppression 208
colonialism 12, 140, 142

colonization 3, 10, 38, 48–9, 54, 124, 141, 252
communities 2–4, 6–10, 38, 42–3, 47–50, 107–9, 113–15, 117–18, 127, 129–30, 138–9, 155, 157–8, 165–6, 186–8, 213–16, 226–7, 249–50, 253–6, 259–63; cloistered 234; connected 253; diverse 14; ethical 118; faith-based 2; formalized 249; global 1; health workers 213, 216; international 63; isolated 141; leaders 214, 235; local 227; loving 118; minority 215, 228; new 6, 117; pilgrimage 107; religious 21, 78, 223, 232, 234–5, 239, 263; remote 125; resources 14, 214, 239, 248–50, 253; sacred 188, 254, 263; social 79; spiritual 204, 210, 252; temporary 104; transient 113; transnational Sunni Muslim ummah 61; underserved 198; well-functioning 108–9, 117; wellness 200, 262
community-based 12, 128, 131; care 262, 264; knowledge translation 10, 42, 44–5; participants 44; research 12, 128–31
conditions 2–4, 18, 100–1, 174–5, 177, 179, 184–6, 188, 196–7, 202–3, 206, 209; acute 100–1; chronic mental 189; connected 49; degenerative 5; dilapidated 175; distressing 132; incapacitating 227; long-term 106; medical 125; neurological 18; psychological 210; social 39, 251; stable 178; stress-inducing 125; unstable 178
conflict 21, 59–60, 70, 223, 238, 257; interpersonal 70; interreligious 255; intrapersonal 5; scientific-religious 21; social 235; unresolved 58
connections 20, 22–3, 44–5, 47–9, 126–8, 134–5, 138, 160, 162, 253–6, 258, 260, 262–3; human-nature 128; Indigenous Peoples 128, 135; intimate 12; kinship 47; positive social 44; religious 256; restoring damaged 240, 262; sentient 127; severing 126; spiritual 49, 135, 263; strong 87
Constructivist Grounded Theory 200, 215
conversations 45, 84, 89, 129, 131, 142, 167, 180, 258, 263–4; charged 6; cross-cultural 37; cultural revival 52; free flow 156; informal 66, 71; ongoing 37
countries 19–22, 32–3, 195–6, 202, 210–11, 230, 233–5, 237, 239, 258, 262, 264; developing 4; high-income 196, 248; neighboring 82; Western 190, 248
Creator 134, 138, 203; *see also* God

Cree people 130, 133
Creole woman 203
crises 5, 12, 14, 107, 148, 151–3, 156–60, 162–3, 165–8, 189, 253; first 157, 160; global 258; participants 152
CRISM *see* Canadian Research Initiative in Substance Misuse
crucifixion 204
cultural 3, 5–7, 13–14, 16–17, 37–9, 48, 57–61, 80–2, 125–8, 130–3, 137–41, 175–7, 195–6, 198–9, 211–14, 228–30, 235–41, 247–9, 251, 257–64; assumptions 101; backgrounds 44, 223, 232; fragmentation 258–9; pride 138; sensitivities 64, 261
Cultural Consultation Service 13, 223, 229–30, 232, 234–9, 241; charts 229; data for assessment of schizophrenia 229, 235; and FEPP in Montreal 229; investigators 229; model 239; patients 238; referrals 238; reports 229; study cases 239
Cultural Formulation Interviews 238
cultural practices 61, 139–40, 196, 224; current 261; local 198; maintained 127
culture brokers 229–30, 239–40
cultures 8, 39, 43–4, 47–9, 61–3, 124, 128, 133–4, 149, 151, 195–6, 229, 231; appropriating 165; in Belize 195; patient's 239; popular 101; professional 239; religious 13, 222; residual 117–18; separate 140; universal 258; of wellness and recovery 221–40
cures 9, 11, 48–9, 69, 71, 76, 100–1, 103–4, 112, 114, 230–3, 239–41; acute 100; complete 232; inexplicable 100, 103; miraculous 11, 100–2, 104–5; spiritual 232–3, 239; unexplained 100, 103

data 23, 132, 197, 229; analysis 81, 132, 201; coding software 155; collection 42, 131, 247; collection procedures for CBPR Project 2014–15 and CBPR Project 2017–18 131; ethnographic 57, 65, 71, 155; interpretation 81; qualitative 190, 200–2; unpublished 57–8, 65–6, 68–71
de Freitas, Marta Helena 9–10
deaths 13, 19, 52, 90, 195, 231, 233–4, 255; in Belize 195; biological 83; total from diabetes 195
Dedoose software 132, 201
Deegan, Pat 221, 225, 227
delusions 91, 149, 161

demographic features 131, 155, 167, 215
depression 18, 20, 25, 38–41, 46, 49–50, 178, 198, 210–12, 222, 225, 227, 233; awareness 43; chronic 38, 49; diagnosis 237; experiencing significant 224; reducing 13, 197, 212; resistant 237
devil 16, 161; *see also* witchcraft
diabetes 4, 50, 195–9, 201–16, 236, 247, 251; in Belize 195–6, 213, 215–16; care 13, 196–7, 202, 209, 211; and chronicity in Belize 196; management of 209; patients 13, 197, 199, 210; predisposing people to higher risk of psychological conditions 210; prevalence 195–6; prevention 195; rates of 196; risk factors 195; self-management 198, 202, 209; symptoms 197, 202; Type 2 (mellitus) 13, 195, 216
diagnosis 4, 8, 13, 18, 39, 69, 87, 101, 191, 197, 199; disease-oriented 8; dual 227; formal medical 178; spiritual 89
Diagnostic and Statistical Manual of Mental Disorders 18, 39, 149, 238
diagnostic categories 12, 101, 148, 222, 252
Dieppe, Paul 11
diet 198, 202
dimensions 8, 20, 24, 231, 255; diverse 126; multiple 53, 77; normative 260; physical 20; religious 258; spirit-filled 72; ultimate 20
disabilities 3, 8, 18, 109, 221, 247, 251
discourses 3–5, 8, 10, 61, 67, 72–3, 79, 85, 149–51, 164, 167, 259–60; authorized 103; civilizing 141; contemporary public 260; cultural 7; current global political 174; dominant normalizing 254; epidemiologic 250; informed 251; medical 71, 80; normative 259–60; psychological 32; religious 21; scientific 90; social media 66; technical 30; theological 16
discrimination 79, 179–80, 186–8, 223; associated 8; respective 24
diseases 11, 16, 18, 49–50, 79, 84, 101, 105, 163, 247, 251; acute 100; cardiovascular 247; chronic lung 247; chronic mental health 13, 16; incapacitating 226; infectious 5, 100; non-communicable 101, 247
disorders 8, 13, 17, 27, 51, 73, 126, 182, 221, 235, 247; acute 100; behavioral 247; chronic 101; depressive 237; eating 18; emotional 25; hyperactivity 234; negative 173; personality 223; psychic 26–7; relational 17; schizoaffective 225; severe 241

distress 4, 6, 13, 79, 114, 221–3, 227–8, 231, 235, 237–9, 249–51; acute 225; chronic personal 79; emotional 87, 107; idioms of 59–60, 72, 91, 235; individual 4, 188; individual's 235; intense 235; managing 190; mental 59, 151; and mental disorder 6, 222, 235; personal 90; psychological 19, 198
diversity 3, 12, 49, 149, 185, 201, 227; cultural 32; intracultural 177; measures of 13, 222
divine 115–16, 118, 182–3, 222, 227, 255; involvement 255; origins 16; powers 174
divorce 237
doctors 11, 21, 23, 65, 77, 107, 111–12; herbal 213; medical 84–5, 87, 212; resident 103; sucking 46; using traditional medicines 46
doctrines 20, 27, 82, 126, 134; formal 20; religious 133
domain 19–20, 31–2, 106–8, 111, 116, 148, 176, 251; biological 17; epistemic 259; experiential 162; interpersonal 3; multiple 262; scientific 261
donations 87
dreams 37, 45–6, 48, 51–3, 133, 136, 158, 208; important 52; recurring 136; understanding 51
drugs 25, 29, 148, 178, 185–6; addictive 204; recreational 158; use of 198, 209, 222
DSM *see* Diagnostic and Statistical Manual of Mental Disorders
East Africa 58, 60
East Indian heritage 201, 204, 206
eating disorders 18
economics 78, 81, 110; benefits 138; challenges 76; dependence 62; inequality 111
economy 111–12
education 13, 42, 83, 195, 197–8, 213–14, 226, 240; formal 64; limited 196; programs 199, 213, 215; tertiary 225
egoism 86; *see also* vanity
Eisenstadt, S.N. 61, 72
Elders 45, 47, 129, 131, 133–4, 232, 263; Indigenous 262; responsibility of 45
Ellis, Lucia 13
Emerging Proud Network 12, 151, 153
emotions 10, 12, 17, 47–8, 51, 59, 229, 257; engendering soothing 256; hurt 71; negative 51; positive 51; shared 166
employment 213, 221, 225–6; programs 234; supported 226

empowerment 228
endogenous solutions 14, 249–50; developing 248; evidence-based 262
energies 87–8; discharging 88; donating 87–8; local 90; negative 47; spiritual 136
environment 18, 81–2, 85–6, 90–2, 109, 125, 180, 182, 185, 188, 256; agricultural 81; contemporary 18; cultural 90; economic 190; harsh 59; natural 49, 132, 135, 139, 183; religious 234; sensory 91; socio-political 79; supportive 113, 190, 262; tolerant 234; urban 11, 134
epidemiological studies 150, 226
episodes 38, 152–3, 157, 160–3; acute illness 227; hypoglycaemic 198; singular psychotic 148
epistemologies 254
equality 108–11, 113, 115–18
Estroff, Sue 5, 152, 180, 151–2
ethics 43, 105, 130, 154, 179; approval 64; board 154; clearance 179; committee 63, 105; competing 254
ethnicities 195
ethnographic 11–12, 81, 148, 229; field research 11; modes 105; observations 250; research challenges 72
etiology 5
Europe 1, 16, 127, 226; 19th-century 82; history 148; religious philosophies 128, 139
evaluation 42, 44, 189, 229; clinical 238; person-centered 241; psychiatric 229, 239; sensitive 237
Evangelicals 21, 23
evangelizing missions 83, 127
events 47, 51, 62, 67, 127, 134, 141, 152–6, 158–9, 224, 233; hallucination-like 149; hypoglycaemic 211; recurring 137; sad 233; singular 125; social 112
evolution 8, 18, 39, 86
existential 25, 158, 184, 227; issues 29, 175; meaning 19; self-improvement 222; terrain 253
exorcism 68, 183
experiences, noetic 105–6
experiential knowledge 63, 155, 167
experiential qualities 165, 222
exploration 3–4, 73, 175, 259; ethnographic 57; sensitive 104

facilitators 155–6
faith 1–3, 25–6, 104, 107–8, 113, 116, 184, 186, 188, 203–4, 206, 223–4, 228, 236–7,

254–6; groups 7; healing 182, 261; leaders 198, 212–14; lost 237; organisations 213; traditions 224
faith-based 6, 173–4, 259; missions 199; organisations 200; practices 1, 3–4, 6–8, 199, 248, 250, 252–3, 256–8, 260, 264; resources 7, 173, 177–8, 190, 249, 263
Fallot, Roger D. 222
families 4–6, 9, 21–2, 46, 133, 135–6, 138, 161, 186–8, 190–1, 205–6, 222–3, 232–3, 235–41, 263; adopted 133; and caregivers 263; complicated 237; extended 231; hostile 231; interviewing 238; members of 24, 58, 176, 187–8, 206, 229, 231, 239, 253; new 237; observed 187; and social predicaments 237
Farmer, Paul 79
Fassin, Didier 264n2
fasting 45, 47, 134–5, 174, 182–4, 189, 198, 202, 204, 208–9, 211–12; and building determination 202; ceremonies 50; daily 202; forced 174; observing 198; periods of 174, 183; rites 198; spiritual 202, 212
female students 63
FEPP see First Episode Psychosis Program
fieldwork 59, 80, 105, 107, 173–4, 177; activities 153; ethnographic 10, 62; experiences 82
First Episode Psychosis Program 13, 223, 229
First Nations 43, 48, 50, 127, 142; non-status 142; populations 50, 130; status 142
First Nations University of Canada 130
focus groups 11, 105
food 59, 77, 137, 202; local 106; nutritious 197, 210; poor 196; processed 213
Foucauldian perspectives 16, 72
Foucault, Michel 148
fragmentation 84, 127, 161, 164, 166; cultural 258–9; encountered in Ghanaian society outside the camp 188; overspecialization 84
framework 4, 14, 44, 103, 113, 150, 153, 176, 239, 241, 248–51; analytic 60; of chronicity 3, 125, 128; clinical 223, 238, 241; conceptual 102; cultural 241; deprivation 59; environmental repossession 126; epistemological 249; medical 104; mental 25; methodological 105, 130; moral 253; political 80; traditional 176
Franco, Divaldo Ferreira 83
friendships 110, 114, 132
Fukuyama, Francis 60–1

Garifuna 195, 201–2, 208, 213, 252
GBD see Global Burden of Disease
gender inequality 59
geographies 113, 124–6, 133, 140–2, 183, 215, 253–4; contested 254; external 9, 254; locating 132; personal 133; urban Indigenous 125
geography 122, 124, 183, 215, 253–4
geography of care 247–64 see also spiritual
Gesler, Wil 108
Ghana 12–13, 173–8, 182–3, 185–6, 188, 190–1, 199, 250, 254–5; Akan communities of 173; eastern regions of 178; healing and mental illness in 176; management of chronic mental illness in 173, 175, 177, 179, 181, 183, 185, 187, 189; population 176; prayer camps 174; society 175, 188
Ghanaians 173, 177
"gift economy" 110–12
Global Burden of Disease 221, 247, 264
global health 8, 20, 247, 251, 254, 259; crisis 247; planning 263; practitioners 261; programming 5; promotion 248, 250
global health agenda 254, 263–4
global media 174, 227; see also media
global mental health 14, 175, 190, 248–9, 262
global mental wellness 8, 14, 247, 249–51, 253, 255, 257–64
globalization 250–1, 263–4
GMH see global mental health
God 28–9, 116, 161–2, 182–3, 186, 191n3, 202, 204–6, 208–9, 212, 223–4, 227–8, 237, 240
Goldingay, Sarah 11
"good ancestors" 2, 124–5, 129, 132, 135, 137–40, 142
greenspace 141
groups 20, 24, 27–8, 105–10, 112, 151–5, 157–8, 162–3, 165–6, 168, 221, 227; diverse 260; dominant 230; ethno-racial 228; heterogeneous 142; large 103, 259; like-minded 256; local 155; marginalized 228; political 255; sessions 28–9, 199; small 67, 103; university 197; worship 221
guilt 71, 83, 89, 150, 160, 231, 240
Gulley, Tauna 197

Hajj 224, 236
hallucinations 16, 27, 32, 149, 178
Handbook of Religion and Health 222
Hatala, Andrew 12–14, 130

Index 277

HCPs *see* health care providers
healers 58, 62, 64, 70, 81, 87, 136–7, 163–4, 166, 176, 232; cultural-spiritual 199, 213; faith-based 263; religious 10, 68; spiritual 87, 91, 261–2; traditional 163, 232; wounded 163
healing 2–3, 11–12, 50–1, 64–5, 68–70, 80–1, 83–5, 92, 100–2, 104–6, 108–9, 114–15, 118, 124–5, 137–9, 173–6, 180–4, 189–90, 226, 249–50; aesthetics of 80–1; clinics 62; cooperation 11, 82, 84, 92; experiences 11, 76, 92, 103–4; faith 182, 261; Indigenous 80, 261; journeys 107, 124–5, 127–9, 131–3, 135, 137, 139–42, 176, 183, 186, 226; non-miraculous 104; performance of 92; personal 11; physical 2, 71; power 70, 183; practices 11, 46, 52, 61–2, 65, 67, 72, 77, 80, 82, 131; prayers 63; processes 69–70, 102, 106, 108, 149, 163, 178, 183–4; Qur'anic 10, 58, 62, 255; religious 66, 71, 232; rituals 79, 174, 176, 183; Spiritist 77, 83, 89, 92; spiritual 76, 81–2, 84–5, 89, 174, 199, 232–3; techniques 69; traditional 61, 67; transformational 79, 89; transformative 254
health 2–4, 6–7, 23–5, 37, 51, 84–5, 126, 131–2, 176, 196–7, 202–5, 207, 209–12, 215–16, 222, 248–50, 264; behaviours 196, 198, 212; chronic 101, 114; cultural 214; global public 249; holistic 51; poor metabolic 196; practitioners 13, 142, 261, 264; professionals 11, 21–3, 82, 261; promotion 42, 126, 203, 214; psychosocial 196; relations between religiosity, spirituality and mental 21, 25–8; research 51, 126, 130, 249, 251; services 130, 196, 262–3; spiritual 8, 23, 27, 29–30, 37, 106, 150, 215; systems 21, 213, 228, 264; urban 141
health care 22, 42, 49, 81–2, 84, 92, 177, 187, 199, 202, 263; administrators 201, 212; approaches 215; Brazilian 22, 77–8, 92; context of mental 6, 10, 31, 257; distribution 82; diverse 261; humanized 22; infrastructure 84; mainstream 167; mental 22; modern 4; official 81; policy 215; practitioners 6, 14, 113, 168, 258; professionals 11, 21–3, 82, 112–13, 191, 261; providers 166, 174, 211, 215; Spiritist 82–3, 89; systems 4, 203, 206, 210, 215
health care providers 13, 166–7, 174, 198, 200, 203, 210–12, *214*, 215; and community leaders *214*; and institutions 167; potential guidelines for 200; and systems 210
health outcomes 42, 195, 210, 212–13, 248, 264; negative mental 10; optimal 198
health problems 100–1, 107, 258; age-related 101; significant 4
holism 48–9, 104
Holy Spirit 176, 183, 191
home communities 142
homelands 127, 130, 138–9, 141, 237; ancestral 125, 128; articulating 125; reclaiming 126
"homework" 187, 209–10
hospitals 2–3, 22–3, 42–3, 48, 87, 91–2, 176, 178, 182, 184, 232–3, 239; modern 114; psychiatric 84, 175–7; public 84
human nature 37, 129, 255, 259
human rights 174–5, 189, 260
humanities 2, 4, 11, 82, 104–5, 109, 182, 204, 258–9, 264
humility 43, 45, 47, 72, 259
Huntington, Samuel 60–1
Hyde, Lewis 110
hymns 118, 233

ideologies 61, 254
ideals 78, 257, 260
identity 18, 43–4, 72, 134–5, 141, 152, 164, 166, 203; cultural 238; individualistic 5; personal 180; spiritual 132, 238–9, 262
illness 2–3, 5–14, 17, 37, 46, 48–9, 58–9, 70, 84–5, 166–7, 176–7, 179–83, 188–90, 221–2, 250–2; causes of 176, 182, 190; conditions 54, 173, 248, 250; experiences 5, 76, 91, 152, 179, 189, 196, 222; global 250; persisting 5, 126, 180; somatic 82; spiritual 48, 176; symptoms 223; times of 13, 222
"illness narratives" (of patients) 77, 79, 91
immigrants 228–30, 238
Indian Residential Schools 50, 127, 132
Indigenous 43, 80, 124–5, 128, 131, 133, 139–40, 142, 261; and Afro-Brazilian concepts 82; communities 10, 38, 42, 46, 126–7; cultures 139; determinants of health and resilience 126; futures 125, 140–1; healing 80, 261; identities and bodies 140; languages 133; Mayan 195, 199, 213; methodologies 131; nations in Canada 124; and non-Indigenous researchers 129; perspectives 12, 125; populations 38; spiritualities 127, 208;

teachings 133; and Western paradigms 40, 129; young people in Canada 128
Indigenous Peoples 53, 126–7, 130, 198, 248; in Canada 125–6; rights of 139
Indigenous youth 12, 126, 129–31, 134, 140–2; in Canada 126, 130; and local organizations 130; urban-dwelling 133
informants 63–4, 66–7, 107, 212
initiation 156, 159, 164; experience 160; phase 165; section 156, 162; stage 159, 162
institutions 2, 9, 20–3, 79, 81, 84, 105, 124, 148, 158, 167; homecare 175; military 22–3; official health care 91; religious 21, 79, 154, 177
interdisciplinary care 31
Interpretative Phenomenological Analysis 180
Interpretive Phenomenology 200
interventions 10, 20, 100–1, 129, 189–91, 195, 199, 232, 237, 239, 248; faith-based diabetes 198–9; land-based 142; public health 263; religious 232, 239
interviewees 23–5, 31, 58–9, 64–6, 69–70, 179; female 58, 69–70; male 57–8, 65–6, 68–9, 71; sample 201
interviews 10–11, 23–6, 30–1, 64, 105, 107, 129, 131, 153–5, 179–80, 200–1, 205, 207, 213, 215; clinical 229; individual 179; local 213; transcripts 65, 155, 180, 201
IP *see* Interpretive Phenomenology
IPA *see* Interpretative Phenomenological Analyzes
IRS *see* Indian Residential Schools
Islam 1, 61, 67–8, 72, 236
Islamic healing centers 68, 236
Islamic lifestyle practices 69
Islamic literature 69
Islamic modernity 57, 61, 68, 72
Islamic religious cures 57, 66
Islamic societies 68

Jarvis, G. Eric 13
Jesus Christ 86, 160, 176, 204
jinn 57–8, 63, 65–6, 68–71, 235–6; evil 57; hurting the 69; independent 70; language 65; person 70; possession 67, 71; spirits 57, 63, 66–7, 71
Jung, Carl 151

Kardecist Spiritism 80, 82
Kirmayer, Laurence J. 39, 90
KK *see* Knowledge Keeper
Kleinman, Arthur 4, 39, 49, 77, 152, 263

knowledge 12, 38, 40–2, 45–6, 48, 63, 65–6, 68–9, 81, 83, 86, 104, 106, 129–32, 257–60; conscious 256; experiential 63, 155, 167; human 259; ontological 10; system 40–1; translation 10, 40, 42
Knowledge Keeper 45, 263; *see also* Elders
Koranic clinics 61
KT *see* knowledge translation
Kurz, Helmar 11
Lancet Global Mental Health Group 248
land 1, 3, 37, 41, 45–6, 49–51, 53, 124–42, 191, 254–5, 262–3; dispossession 12; management of 107; and nature 12, 128, 134–6, 138, 141, 254; operationalizing 141; sacredness of 124–5, 140–1; settlement 125; stolen 254; urban 126, 128–9, 137, 140–2
landscapes 8, 31, 115–17, 124, 132–3, 247, 264; diverse geographic 7; imaginative 117, 252; important tonal 2; remote 124; therapeutic 102, 116; urban 125, 128–9, 138–9
languages 9, 38, 41, 101, 109, 111, 113, 151, 157, 176, 179, 228; Indigenous 133; metaphorical 41; national 201; neutral 167; psychological 24
leaders 40, 174, 182, 185–6, 188, 191, 232, 234–5; camp 179, 181–2, 188; community 124, 214, 235; faith 198, 212–14; group 109; religious 21, 29, 31–2, 198, 223, 230, 239–40; spiritual 174
LeBlanc, Marie Nathalie 13
Lewis, I.M. 58–60, 62–3, 67
life 8–9, 28–9, 44–5, 49, 115–16, 134–7, 139–40, 157–8, 166–8, 202–3, 205–7, 226–8, 231–3, 251, 255; cultural 238; daily 32, 202, 207; experience of 17, 222, 227, 256; good 37–9, 41, 46, 48, 78, 107, 137; healthy 27; holistic 54; home 110; human 5, 21, 255; meaning in 106; monastic 233; non-religious 222; quotidian 116; religious 6, 103, 238; situations 51, 59, 90; social 78, 258; spiritual 37, 39, 46, 48, 53; stages of 46–7; stress-free 205
life-cycles 137–9
lifestyle 18, 189, 227, 233; austere 234; choices 202; counselling 197, 199; guidance 205
literature 1, 4, 12–13, 20, 22, 58, 60, 62, 66–7, 165–6, 174–5, 196, 198–9, 210–11, 213; academic 5, 209; current 1, 174, 255; faith-based health 6; reviews 20, 197; scientific 256

Index   279

LMICs *see* Low-Middle Income Countries
loss 39, 50, 53, 67, 107, 109, 137, 212, 223, 233; deep persistent 136; family 139; feeling 51; historical 137; vision 87; weight 211
Lourdes 11, 100–9, 111–18, 229, 254; Catholic pilgrimage to holy shrines in France 252; ethos underpinned by the beneficial practices of deep-listening and well-intentioned care 114; experience of 110; power of the miracle of 104; rituals 105; structures 110
love 47, 51, 83–4, 100–1, 103, 105, 107–9, 111–13, 115, 117–18, 135–6, 186–7, 190; frustrated 59; network 161; rejected 59; unconditional 136
Low-Middle Income Countries 196, 261
Luhrmann, Tanya 149, 165
Luiz, André 83
Luiz, Emmanuel 83
Luther, Martin 224

malades 106, 108–12
management 5, 13, 18, 173, 176–80, 187, 190, 209–10, 247–8, 251, 263; care 248–9; of chronic conditions 2–3, 190; clinical 210–11; disease 13; improved 197; of stigma 180, 186
Manderson, Lenore 4–5, 8–9, 125, 196, 247, 249, 251, 263
Marian Catholic pilgrimage site, Lourdes 11, 100, 102
Marília, São Paulo/Brazil 80–1, 84–5
Mattingly, Cheryl 4–6, 141, 187–8, 190, 209, 256–7, 263
Mauritius 73
McGregor, Leslie 10
McKenzie, Marcia 125, 132, 140
meaning units 24, 28, 30
meat 62, 68, 76
Mecca 224, 236
media 174, 179, 227; mainstream 92; productions 65, 77; public 81; social 6, 66
medical 2–5, 7–8, 10–11, 13–14, 16–19, 79–80, 82–5, 91–2, 100–1, 103–4, 106–8, 111–12, 114–15, 148–9, 163–5, 177–8, 197–9, 239–41, 249–51, 261–4; anthropologist 40, 251, 263; anthropology 2, 5, 149, 154, 163; complications 206; diagnostic terms 8; ethics 111; professionals 71, 84–5, 263; science 4, 42, 100, 103, 114; treatment 27–8, 83, 92, 148, 240; volunteers 106, 199

Medical Bureau (shrine) 100, 102–4, 107, 112–13
medicalization 7, 149, 254, 257, 263
"medication stabilization" 226
medications 79, 176, 190, 196, 199, 202, 232; antipsychotic 232–4; heavy 79; high-dose 225; oral 197; regular 76; schedules 198
medicine 46–8, 68, 71, 100–1, 103–4, 111, 113–14, 117, 124, 181, 186; acute 100; chronic 100; cosmopolitan 89–90, 92; herbal 69–70, 199; modern 100; pharmaceutical 69; sacred 131, 134, 136; scientific 190; Western 48–9, 101, 107, 184
meditation 28, 118, 156, 198–9, 202, 205–6, 208–9, 211
mediums 11, 81–2, 85, 87–9
mental disorders 6, 13, 16–20, 27, 31–2, 38–9, 148–9, 221–2, 231–2, 235, 240–1, 248–9; *see also* mental health
mental health 7–8, 12–14, 16–23, 25, 26, 27, 28, 29–32, 40–1, 50–1, 126, 128, 150–1, 175–6, 189, 196–8, 205, 211–12, 222–3, 248–50; activism 154; care 10, 16, 18–19, 22–3, 28, 30–1, 33, 190, 262; challenges 155, 262; chronic problems 13; conditions 178, 186; consumers 221; crisis 154; difficulties 168; disability 258; disorders 107; emerging "crisis" in 151; evaluations 238; improved 13; institutions 31; interventions 126, 141, 175, 249; issues 8, 82, 101, 210; long-term 10; outcomes 215; pharmaceuticalization of 248, 254, 263; policies 10; poor 8, 258; practices 30–1, 214; practitioners 187, 223, 238, 262; pre-existing 6; problems 100–1, 107, 148, 167, 186, 223, 225–6, 236; professionals 21, 31, 221–2, 228, 232, 248, 261; providers 261; psychologists 25; research 13, 42, 67, 221; resources 214; service providers 249; services 9–10, 17, 21–2, 32, 154, 212, 234; specialists 184, 261; systems 158, 225; training 248; treatments 239–40; and wellness 20, 41, 128, 222, 249
Mental Health Act 1983 148
Mental Health Commission of Canada 225
Mental Health Gap Action Programme 262
mental hygiene 83
mental illness 2–3, 9–10, 12–14, 37–8, 62, 71, 173–8, 180–4, 186–90, 221–9, 235–6, 240–1, 247–50, 253, 261–2; chronic

9–10, 37–43, 45, 50, 53, 73, 173–5, 177, 179–81, 183, 185–9; explanation of 12; global 259; increased 257; management of chronic 173, 177; negative 40; persistent 177; recovery in 226; social aetiology of 38
mental wellness 1–9, 13–14, 37–8, 41, 43–4, 46–8, 54, 124–5, 128–30, 132, 134–5, 141–2, 195–9, 201–3, 209, 249–50, 253, 257–8, 263–4; displaces a deficit model of health 7; interventions 139; outcomes 263; programming 39; promoting 139
mental wellness workshops 43–4
Métis 130–2, 142, 142n1, 142
migrant workforce 125
mind 1, 4, 10, 12, 48, 51, 53, 130, 134, 159, 165, 205–6; body and soul 102; discursive 158–9; people's 53; positive 134
miracles 100, 102–4, 112, 118, 174, 183
miyo-wîcêhetowin (Cree concept) 124–5, 128–9, 132, 134, 138–9, 142
modernity 57, 60–1, 65, 72–3, 92, 263; Islamic 57, 61, 68, 72; post-secular 258; religious 57, 254; secular 58; Somali 62, 68, 72; vision of 66, 72; Western patterns of 61
Moratz, Aaron 10–11
Morton, Darrien 12, 130
movement 9, 61, 114, 134, 160, 165, 209, 235, 252–5; consumer 227; cultural 126–7, 141; service-user 148
MS *see* multiple sclerosis
MU *see* meaning units
multiple sclerosis 4, 88, 101
music 86–7, 90–1
Muslims 63, 72, 81, 198, 224, 230, 232, 236

narratives 11–12, 51, 81, 108, 115, 150–5, 158–9, 161–8, 177, 250; alternative 168; archetypal 162, 166; of experiences 12, 167; hybrid 165; idiosyncratic 162; personal 66, 166; psychiatric 109, 227; service provider 1; shared 162; spiritual 155, 157
National Health Institute 215
National Health Insurance Office 216
National Health Service 154, 163
National Hearing Voices Network 149, 151
National Wellness Institute 8
natural laws 129, 139

nature 11–13, 44–5, 48–9, 53, 127–9, 134–6, 138–41, 174, 176–7, 183–4, 253–5; benign 234; complex 240; extraordinary 103; human 37, 129, 255, 259; and land 12, 128, 134–6, 138, 141, 254; pluralistic 177; psychological 31; sanctuaries 189; spiritual 47, 252, 256, 258, 264
NCDs *see* non-communicable diseases
negative life-cycles 137–9
negative relations between religiosity and spirituality and mental health 28
neuroscience 51
nexus 80, 102, 108, 118–19, 263; of beneficial factors **119**; of beneficial factors that enable the healing process 102; of beneficial factors that facilitate nourishing exchanges 118; of performativity and sensory perception 80
NGO *see* non-governmental organization
NHI *see* National Health Institute
NHS *see* National Health Service
Nichter, Mark 59, 72, 80, 91, 235
nishnaabemwin 37, 41
noetic experiences 105–6
non-clinical groups 12, 149
non-communicable diseases 101, 247
non-governmental organization 174–5
non-Indigenous researchers 129
non-Indigenous youths 126
normalization 254, 264
nourishing exchanges (concept) 100, 102, 104, 106, 108–10, 112–18, 252
nutrition 85, 197, 214
Nwora, Emmanuel Ifeka 9

OBI *see* Ontario Brain Institute
OCF *see* Outline for Cultural Formulation
OMV *see* Order of Malta Volunteers
Ontario Brain Institute 40, 43
ontologies 10, 48, 106, 140–1, 149, 254
Order of Malta Volunteers 107, 109
organizations 12–13, 22, 129–31, 133, 149, 153, 175, 177, 179, 249; faith-based 13; partnering 131; religious 22, 177; social 78, 80, 91; youth-serving 129
outcomes 8, 10, 195, 198–200, 207, 209–10, 212–13, 215, 222–3, 226–7, 247–9, 261, 263–4; anxiety-related 223; distressing 227; healing belief 180
Outline for Cultural Formulation 238–9

Palagini, Laura 51
palliative care 114
parents 46, 52, 58, 129–30, 133, 136, 233–5

Parkinson's disease 4, 105, 112
partnerships 43, 47, 191, 200, 216, 261; formal 261; intersectoral 174, 190–1, 262; ongoing research 132
pastors 134, 176, 178, 182–4
patients 4–6, 13–14, 21–2, 69, 77, 79, 81–2, 84–92, 111, 117, 166–8, 175–8, 183–91, 196, 198–200, 209–12, 222, 225, 228–41, 261–2; attributes of 231; care of 113, 261; chronic 78, 81, 91; diabetic 13, 197, 199, 203, 210; healthy 261; histories of 13, 229, 231; mental illness 189, 191; preferences of 239; psychotic 150; religious 228; schizophrenic 73; spirituality 195, 197, 212; spirituality of 195, 197, 212; symptoms 40, 239
PD *see* Parkinson's disease
peace 63, 65, 88, 108, 161, 206–7, 209, 255
peer-support groups 12, 149–50, 153, 155–6, 163–4, 167–8, 260
peers 30, 40, 152, 157–8, 162–3, 165, 214
Pentecostal church groups 213
perspectives 19–20, 32–3, 39–40, 43, 45, 47, 49, 53–4, 62, 78–80, 82, 84, 86, 150–2, 175–6; biomedical 38; biopsychosocial-spiritual 250; cultural 248; diachronic 57, 60; disparate 6; epistemological 131; multidisciplinary 33; paternalistic 225; phenomenological 23, 32; psychological 24; religious 175, 238; spiritual 13, 255
phenomena 12, 21, 24, 60, 72, 104, 111, 148, 234, 258; cultural 60; historical 264
physicians 111, 196, 206, 212, 261
pilgrimages 102, 106, 109–10, 112–14, 116, 141, 236, 254; annual 107; groups 106–7, 112–13, 115–16; personal 177; practices of 101, 114; season 103; sites 229; studies 102, 106, 111
pilgrims 11, 100–7, 109–10, 112, 114–17; assisted 109; individual 103; "malades/assisted" 106; in Mecca 224; returning home 109–10, 113; sick 107–8
places of worship 25, 227; *see also* churches
politics 63, 77–8, 80, 91–2, 124; of healthcare 11, 91; local 81; official 92
population 42, 48, 57, 62, 64, 191, 195–6, 200, 209, 211, 213, 248, 254; aging 101; clinical 167, 238; estimated 12; large 264; mainstream 253; non-clinical 150; oppressed 248; priority 215
positive relations between religiosity and spirituality and mental health 26
possession 11, 57–60, 62, 64–5, 67–9, 71–2, 79; bodily experience of 63–4, 67; cults 59, 67; experiences 59, 72; healing spirit 66; interpreting 60; *jinn* 67, 71; Lewis's interpretation of spirit 59; people experiencing 59; recurring chronic 58, 62; women experiencing 63
Post-Traumatic Stress Disorder 38, 50–1, 231, 235
poverty 79, 90, 126, 179, 196, 206, 210–11, 251; chronic 200; insistent 4; persistent 125; and wealth 8
power 46, 60, 63, 68, 70, 73, 104, 109–11, 124, 129, 163, 204, 206; black 181; demonic 174; divine 174; evil 176; and healing 70, 183; higher 224, 227, 234; inversion 109; personal 202; transformative 165
practitioners 3, 14, 222, 239, 248–50, 257, 260, 262
prayer camps 173–91, 254; in Ghana 13, 173–6, 183, 185, 188, 190; pastors 181, 188; Pentecostal 174, 255
Prayer Wheel (model) 212
prayers 25–6, 28, 84, 86–8, 90, 115–16, 118, 134, 136, 174, 181–4, 198–9, 202–9, 211–12, 232–3; "all-night" 183; ancestral 199; of gratitude 207; healing 63; personal 206–7; private 199; regular 13, 197; sacred 252; thanksgiving 87
prediabetes 195, 214
priorities 44, 207, 248; academic 43; community's 43; cultural 14; local 248–50, 260
problems 17–18, 25, 49, 51, 77, 79, 91–2, 110–11, 114, 174–5, 184, 186–7, 223, 230–1, 233–40; causes of 231, 234; chronic 100; clinical 229–31, 238; epistemological 17, 81; global 3; interpersonal 83; interpretive 60; learning 234; mental 150, 198; people's 191; relational 237; social 54; solving 47, 213; visualizing 88
process 8, 10, 22, 41, 43–6, 68–9, 102, 104, 116, 118, 132–3, 151, 225–6, 240–1, 251–3; biochemical 90; consultation 69; dynamic 255; economic 112; educational 84; ethical 200; functional 129; linear 110; methodological 173; non-linear 162; opposed 165; psychological 204; reconstructional 84; relational 252; socialization 188; sociocultural 260; transcription 64; transformative 140, 166

professional practices 22–5, 30–1
professionals 2–4, 9, 17–18, 20–3, 29–33, 153, 222, 261; health care 11, 21–3, 82, 112–13, 191, 261; medical 71, 84–5, 263; mental health 21, 31, 221–2, 228, 232, 248, 261
programs 40, 47, 49, 141, 253; community-based suicide prevention 40; cultural 44, 61; day camp 213; graduate 237; school-based mental wellness 40
prophets 174, 181–5, 191
psychiatric 12, 16–19, 78, 81, 84, 150–1, 154, 221, 225–9, 232, 239–41, 248–9; health care systems 232, 249; hospitals 84, 175–7; rehabilitation 225–6; survivor movement 151; systems 154; treatments 223, 226, 230
psychiatrists 21, 31, 148, 153–4, 221, 230, 232, 236–7, 239, 261; cultural 249; evaluating 238
psychiatry 20, 39, 148, 164, 178, 190, 225, 228, 239, 248–9
psychological stress 198, 206–7
psychological treatment 28
psychologists 9–10, 17, 19, 21–32, 85, 163, 166, 221, 231, 238; and chaplains 22, 24–6, 28, 30, 32–3; cognitive 159; and other health professionals 22, 31; Western-trained 17
psychology 16, 31, 51, 151, 178, 249, 261; clinical 175; contemporary Western 20; cultural 140; popularized transpersonal 151; students 21
psychosis 5, 13, 87, 148–9, 152–3, 159, 162–3, 178, 221, 223, 251–2
psychotic 149, 151, 159–61, 164, 166; deliriums 26; disorders 20, 148–54, 164–5, 167–8, 233; episodes 12, 148; experiences 150, 160, 165; patients 150; symptoms 27, 222, 233, 235–6
PTSD see Post-Traumatic Stress Disorder
public hospitals 84
Punta Gorda (Belize) 196–7, 216

QoL see quality of life
qualitative health research 154
qualities, experiential 165, 222
quality of life 10, 13, 150, 166, 191, 197–8, 201, 227, 256
Qur'an 57–8, 62, 65–70, 72
Qur'anic 10, 58, 61–2, 66–7, 69, 255; healers 61–2, 66–7, 69; healing 10, 58, 62, 255; readings 68; teachings 66; verses 69

Rahtz, Emmylou 11
recovery 2–4, 7, 10, 14, 167, 181–5, 188, 221–9, 231–41, 249, 252, 255, 257; approaches to 151, 167–8; clinical 226; cultures of 13, 252; definition of 225; existential 228; experiences 240; from mental illness 226; models 221; movements 149–50; notions of 221, 226, 228, 240; personalized 222, 239; religious cultures of 224
recuperation 25–6
refugees 229, 237–8, 248
relations 17–18, 20–3, 25–8, 30–2, 38, 40, 42, 46–8, 53, 138, 140, 182, 184, 221, 256; good 50, 125; harmonious 206; human-nature 125, 141–2; re-envisioned 258; significant 78; social 77, 251
relationships 9–10, 16, 39–46, 48–53, 102, 129, 131, 136, 154–6, 186–7, 206, 252, 254–9, 261, 263; ambivalent 228; animated 134; causal 111, 235; clinician-patient 238; close 186; and the community 186; complex 231; conjugal 59; curvilinear 223; good 125, 129, 135, 137, 139; healing-oriented 252; holistic 10; human-to-human 71; importance of 39, 49, 54; individuals 188, 221; negative 135; patient-provider 199; peaceful 205; personal 228; postcolonial 80; sacred 6, 124, 254; social 50, 91, 221; spiritual 186, 207; therapeutic 14, 222; trusting 139, 205; unhealthy 136; value of 43, 252; working 14, 250
religion 1–3, 6–8, 19–21, 27–8, 31–2, 72, 103–4, 113, 134, 139, 221–3, 227–8, 230–1, 233, 237–8, 240–1, 249, 254–5, 258–61, 264; Afro-Brazilian 80; authoritative 224; in Belize 199; Christian 32; dualistic utopian 127; new 224, 237; practiced 199; radical 27; and recovery 231; and schizophrenia 261; and spirituality 1–3, 8, 189, 222–3, 227, 229–32, 234, 237–8, 250, 257, 259, 264; Western 127
religiosity 10, 17, 19–23, 25, 26, 27, 28, 29–32, 195–9, 209, 216, 228–9; experienced 30; handling 29; heightened 228, 233; impact on chronic physical and mental problems 150; personal 23; public 68; and spirituality 10, 16, 19–27, 30–2, 150; subjective 198
religious 1, 25, 227, 229–30, 235–6; anthropologists 79; beliefs 13, 27, 177, 189, 201, 222–3, 227, 231, 233, 257, 261;

case material 13; citizens 142; competence 228; consciousness 258; convictions 237; correctness 67; cults 235; delirium 27–8; denominations 21, 23, 32; diversity 32; experiences 16, 20, 27, 63; groups 21, 25, 174, 257; institutional arrangements 133; minority 235; observances 204; participation 222, 228, 230; persecution 224; practices 13, 29, 58, 63, 150, 174, 197–200, 211–12, 229, 240; proselytism 27–8; rituals 11, 230; and spiritual interventions 230; worldviews 63, 72, 232, 249
Remy-Fischler, Raphaëlle 12
research 5–6, 10–11, 21–2, 24, 30–1, 40–3, 50–1, 60–1, 63–4, 71–2, 128–30, 150–2, 154–5, 167–8, 175, 213, 215, 226, 249–51, 256–7; academic 41; anthropological 155; break-and-enter 42; capacity-building 213; community-based participatory 12, 128, 131; empirical 1, 8; ethics board 200; ethnographic 63, 168; findings 2, 108, 212; funders 44; methodology 177; methods 11, 23; objectives 104; participants 1–2, 60; planned 112; population 58; process 179, 200; projects 23, 42–3, 85, 129; psychological 106; qualitative 131; questions 62, 152–3; recent 17, 30; relationship-based 10, 42–3, 45; scientific 84, 260; solution-focused 197; teams 42–4, 104, 129, 132; transformative 199
resources 48, 50, 79, 83, 175, 177, 182, 186, 210, 212, 222, 262, 264; cultural 211; faith-based 189; personal 28; physical 180, 183, 185; religious 14, 228; spiritual 13, 183–4, 189, 200, 212, 222, 239, 261; underutilised 211
responsibilities 18, 21, 30, 41–3, 45–7, 49–51, 53, 59, 71, 78, 138–9; ancestral 142; collective 62; corporate social 197, 199; individual 82; moral 129, 138, 140; shared 41, 139; spiritual 137
risks 17, 53, 58, 125–6, 200, 210–11
rituals 62, 127, 199, 202, 208–9, 211, 233; healing 79, 174, 176, 183; historic 19; Lourdes 105; prescribed 221; religious 11, 230
Roger, Kerstin 14
Roman Catholics 102, 113, 199, 208; *see also* Catholics
Roqya Clinics 236
Rosenlicht, Nicholas 51
Royal College of Physicians 111
Royal College of Psychiatrists 148
Ruas, Evelyn Figueira Lima 9

saar ceremonies 61–2, 65, 67
sacred places 118, 133, 182, 254
sacrifice 62, 69, 191, 204
safety 115–16, 118, 132, 214, 260–1
schizophrenia 5, 18, 148–50, 178, 222–3, 226–7, 235, 247; chronic 236; patients 251; and religion 261; spectrum disorders 225
science 38, 103–4, 148, 159, 250, 258–60, 264; biomedical 177; evidence-based 42; medical 4, 42, 100, 103, 114; rehabilitation 227; social 2, 104, 110; Western 40, 51
self-care 3, 78, 81, 92, 108, 115–17, 203; approaches to 177; optimising patient 210
self-management 9, 196–7, 199, 202, 209, 211, 214–15
services 2, 7, 19, 21–2, 24–5, 31, 33, 111, 130, 253, 259; alternative 154; chaplain's 22; community-based 248; counselling 183–4; customer 18–19, 25, 32; institutional 249; medical 18; psychiatric 12; religious 230; supportive 21
settler-colonial chronicities 125, 129, 132, 139, 141; life-cycles perpetuating 132; pervading 135; youth enduring 126
settler-colonialism 12, 140, 142
settler-colonization 125–8, 140
Shaking Tent (practice) 48, 52
sheikh 68–70
sickness 46, 176, 181–2, 263; *see also* illness
Sioux Lookout Indian Zone Hospital 48, 50
social defeat 165, 167–8
social media 6, 66
Social Science and Medicine 5
social stigma 186, 188, 210, 212
social support 186, 189–90, 203, 210, 222; networks 32, 41; systems 197
social technologies 5, 209
software 132, 155, 201; data coding 155; Dedoose 132, 201
Somali 57–8, 63–4, 66–8, 70–2; modernity 62, 68, 72; research population 59; society 59, 67; spirit possession in modernization theory 65
Somaliland 10, 57, 61–3, 65–72, 250; *cilaaj* clinics 255; society 11
spirit possession 11, 58–69, 71–3, 235, 252, 255; attacks of 57, 66, 252; chronic 10,

62, 73; Somali experiences of 59, 61, 63, 65, 67, 69, 71; study of 58, 62
Spiritism 76–7, 81–3, 85, 92; Brazilian 11, 77–8, 81, 90; and health care in Brazil 82; Kardecist 80, 82
Spiritist 76, 80, 84–5, 91; concepts 82; doctrine 82, 84–6; healing 77, 83, 89, 92; health care 82–3, 89; institutions 80, 82; knowledge 81; practices 80, 85, 87; procedures 92; therapy 81, 92
spirits 9–11, 39, 46–54, 57–8, 60–8, 77, 82–3, 85, 87, 89, 127–9, 136–7, 161, 199–200, 258; ancestral 182; appeasing 57; benevolent 88; damaged 51; enlightened 86; evil 57–8, 181, 183; existence of 57; human 82; immortal 82; invisible 63, 72; malevolent 71, 182; strong 87; troublesome 71
spiritual 31, 49, 100, 208, 229, 256, 261; attacks 181, 235; attitudes 215; Beings 37, 45–6, 49–50, 127, 129, 175; beliefs 5, 128, 188, 202, 222–3, 231, 234–5, 239, 241; causes 231, 235–6, 239; crisis 12, 148, 151–2; determinants 250, 252, 257, 263; development 84, 89, 159; dimensions 20, 29, 222; elements 118, 160; encounters 128–9, 132–5, 139–42; experiences 23–4, 27–8, 32, 85, 102, 106, 151, 158, 166, 255, 264; fasting 202, 212; geographies 14, 247, 252, 254–5, 263; interventions 127, 229–30, 232–3, 235, 239–40, 261; issues 87, 89, 107, 238; life 37, 39, 46, 48, 53; practices 1, 3, 6, 11, 13, 135–6, 157, 189, 196–7, 199–202, 206, 208–12, 215, 238, 260; progress 82–3, 89; representations 229, 237, 239; self 39, 45–7, 50–3, 252; support groups 255
Spiritual Crisis Network 12, 150–1, 153, 168
spiritual healing 76, 81–2, 84–5, 89, 174, 199, 232–3; in Brazilian Kardecism 76; far-distance 76; practices 80; traditions 199, 202
Spiritual Peer-Support Networks 12, 151–3, 156, 158, 161–3, 165
spirituality 1–11, 13, 16–17, 19–25, 26, 27, 28, 29–32, 127–8, 132, 140–1, 149–51, 157–9, 196–9, 209–10, 221–3, 227–33, 237–8, 249–50, 254–61; and health 37, 103; holistic 106; Indigenous youth 126, 128, 141; legitimizing Indigenous 127; mobilising 210; patient 195, 197, 212; relationships to 154, 156; and religion 1–3, 8, 189, 222–3, 227, 229–32, 234, 237–8, 250, 257, 259, 264; and religiosity 10, 16, 19–27, 30–2, 150; traditional 128; and wellbeing 155; of youth 125–6, 128, 140–1
SPSNs *see* Spiritual Peer-Support Networks
stigma 3, 6, 8, 14, 17, 175, 179–80, 186–8, 250, 253, 257; concomitant 252; increased 248; management of 180, 186; social 186, 188, 210, 212
stigmatization 149, 253, 259
strategies 2, 5, 8–9, 20, 59–60, 127, 133, 173, 177, 205, 209; Anishinaabek 40; collaborative 262; community-based 189; faith-based 213, 249; global care 249; individual 250; professionalized 14
Strauss, Anselm 5
stress 18, 20, 38, 40, 50, 63, 65, 85–6, 89, 198–9, 202, 205–6, 209–11, 256–7; chronic 50; compounding psychological 209–10; emotional 184; excessive 50, 210; levels 199; managing 189; mental 202, 205; ongoing social 38; reducing 183
stressors 40–1, 48, 50; cumulative 46; external 202; ongoing 38; positive 40
stretchers 86–8, 116
students 21, 63, 130, 199, 205; female 63; psychology 21
substance misuse 38, 41, 44, 50
suicides 20, 40, 50, 53, 126, 222
support 25, 62–3, 86, 88–91, 105–6, 174–5, 179–80, 184–6, 188, 190–1, 212, 222, 230–1, 233–4, 249, 255–6, 262–4; emotional 184, 239, 256; experienced 86; healing 118; Indigenous 54; loving 113; mutual 87; ongoing 239; patient wellness 211; religious 198; remote 113; wellness outcomes 256

Tanner, Adrian 40, 48, 57, 65, 77, 79, 81, 251, 263
teachings 10, 40, 45, 50, 129, 133, 135–6, 206
teams 21, 42–4, 87–8, 233; inpatient 232; members 104, 132, 201; transdisciplinary 104
teamwork 17, 33
therapists 81, 163
therapy 18, 80, 85, 89–90
tourists 103, 106
traditions 32, 57, 60–1, 72, 79, 92, 106, 113, 157, 223, 229; Anishinaabek 51;

charismatic 183; cultural 198; epistemological 45; historical 251; local 263; moral 238; oral 37, 127, 137; religious 208, 213, 224, 256; spiritual 157, 240
transformations 2–3, 7, 9, 91–2, 151, 153, 159, 162, 164–6, 168, 225–6, 251–2, 254–5; cellular 164; hybrid 128; identity 128, 138; narrative of 151–2, 166; ongoing 228; participants 165; personal 82, 176; positive 12; symbolical 91
traumas 9, 50, 53, 136–7, 139, 160, 163–4, 251
TRC *see* Truth and Reconciliation Commission
trust 28, 41–4, 77, 155, 179, 186, 206–7, 224, 255–6; building of 261; lost 235; personal 63; significant 190
Truth and Reconciliation Commission 50, 126–7
Tuck, Eve 125, 132, 140

United Nations Human Rights Council 174
university students 21, 63, 130, 199, 205; *see also* students
urban centers 126, 141, 262
urban dwellers 142

Valentine, J. Randolph 41
values 39, 43–4, 107–8, 111, 124–5, 127, 132, 163, 166, 221–2, 228–9, 248, 252; ancestral 134; core 129; moral 129, 253; personal 188; religious 21; sacramental 183; social 176; spiritual 127, 129, 133
vanity 86, 191
visions 61, 72, 103, 161, 174, 182, 226, 253, 258; core transcendental 61; cultural 61; pervasive spiritual 65, 215
volunteers 103, 106–8, 110–12, 114–16, 214; female 108; male 108; medical 106, 199

Warber, Sara 11
Weber, Max 60, 72, 257
wellness 1–9, 11–14, 20, 37–8, 40–1, 47–9, 102, 104–5, 124–6, 128–9, 140–1, 177–8, 183–7, 189–91, 221–3, 239–41, 249–52, 254–7, 259–61; aiding 173; community's 53; defining 7; determinant shaping 126; embodied 140; enhanced 262; experience of 7, 257; goals 196; identity transformations 137, 142; interventions 125, 128, 140, 249; mental 1–5, 7–9, 13–14, 37–8, 41, 43–4, 46, 48, 54, 124–5, 128–30, 132, 134–5, 141–2, 195–9, 209, 249–50, 253, 257–8, 263–4; psychological 215, 257; sources of 128, 137, 211; spiritual 104
West Africa 231–2, 234
Western medicine 48–9, 101, 107, 184
Whitley, Rob 13
WHO *see* World Health Organization
witchcraft 16, 161
workers 22, 70, 197; migrant 215; skilled 261; social 21, 23, 234, 238
workshops 40, 43–6, 52–3; co-developed 40; evaluations 44; facilitators 52, 163; mental wellness 43–4
World Diabetes Foundation 216
World Health Organization 18, 20, 87, 150, 177, 195–6, 247
worship 25, 109, 113, 174, 227, 255

youth 40, 43–4, 46–7, 49–50, 61, 65, 125, 128–39, 142, 209, 213, 237; collaborators 129; impoverished 211; informed 135; narratives 128–9, 140; participation 130, 132; prediabetic 213; spirituality 125–6, 128, 140–1; wellness 132, 140

Zen Buddhism 157